by the same author

Tin Soldiers on Jerusalem Beach

KIBBUTZ
MAKOM

KIBBUTZ MAKOM

MAKOM

Report from an

Israeli Kibbutz

by Amia Lieblich

Pantheon Books

NEW YORK

LIBRARY OF CONGRESS CATALOGING IN PUBLICATION DATA

Lieblich, Amia, 1939–
Kibbutz Makom: report from an Israeli kibbutz.

(Pantheon village series)
1. Kibbutzim—Case studies. I. Title.
II. Series.
HX742.2.A3L53   307.7   81–47204
ISBN 0–394–50724–X   AACR2

Manufactured in the United States of America
FIRST EDITION

*. . . A breeze blowing from the West brings back
my years of happiness, when I was marching on,
pale, yet with eyes burning,
along the roads of my brave homeland.
. . . I look at my hands, sun-scorched,
fingernails hardened. And I would not trade
this world of yours, never,
not for the best of all possible worlds.*

—NATAN ZACH
Translated from the Hebrew by Gideon E. Schwarz

Contents

Part 4 / Makom—Where To?

307

Introduction

Makom

Makom is the pseudonym given to the kibbutz that is the subject of this book. This book is an attempt to present Makom from the perspective of its current and former members. This study, not intended as a precise or objective history, presents in the introduction only minimal facts and descriptive characteristics of the kibbutz. The more complete picture of Makom is left to emerge from the stories of its residents.

Makom sits on the southern slopes of Galilee and faces Mount Gilboa in the fertile Valley of Yizrael, which cuts across the northern part of Israel from east to west. It was founded in 1928 by a group of seventeen young Israelis from Tel Aviv; later, these settlers were followed by others —more Israelis as well as young Jewish pioneers from other countries. In 1931, the young kibbutz joined the Kibbutz Hameuchad Movement, and in 1934, after several moves and a continuous struggle for land, Makom settled into its permanent quarters.

Makom's history can be roughly subdivided into four periods, which are described in detail in the members' accounts. Phase one includes the consolidation of the founding group and its first struggles in the establishment of a kibbutz. A difficult time of both physical and social crisis and hardship, this period is often viewed with nostalgia and admiration today.

The settlement of the kibbutz in its permanent location in 1934, and its early attempts at a livelihood, characterize Makom's second phase. A continuous assimilation of new immigrants from various countries, as well as the active participation of Makom's members in the struggle for free *aliya** and an independent state, distinguish this time. The end of the second period and the beginning of the third are marked by the establishment of the State of Israel in 1948. For the kibbutz, the third period also focuses on the political division that took place in 1952, the defection of about two hundred members to Adama** and the transfer to Makom of a roughly equivalent number of kibbutzniks from Molad.** Most significantly, this time signals the onset of gradual economic growth, which prevails to this day.

The fourth period, beginning around 1960 with the realization of

---

*Literally, "ascent"; an immigration, especially the wave of immigration to Israel.

**Adama and Molad are fictitious names, as is the name of Ginat (see p. 31) and all the personal names used in the book.

economic independence, brings us to the present day. Economic issues, the increasing size of the community and its attempt to assimilate its own second and third generations are the contemporary concerns of the kibbutz.

With a population of about 650 adult members—400 children and 150 temporary residents, such as volunteers, Ulpan* students and *garin*** members—Makom is one of the largest kibbutzim in Israel. Makom's main sources of income come from the production of agricultural machinery and food canning. Further economic gain is derived from the kibbutz's agricultural crops: wheat, cotton, olives, citrus fruit, beef, fish, and honey.

Makom offers common education. The kibbutz has a comprehensive school consisting of twelve grades, each class having its own living unit. From the age of six weeks, all kibbutz children are raised in the children's homes and taken care of by a *metapelet*. † Each afternoon, they visit with their parents, then spend the rest of their time in children's company. In addition to studying, participating in social activities and working, the kibbutz children sleep and take most of their meals together. Parents and children do maintain, however, a very close relationship, which is manifested in different ways.

The kibbutz society is a direct democracy. Committees cover all aspects of life, and all the committees (with the exception of the Social Committee) are responsible to the elected secretariat. The entire adult community may take part in the decision-making process through the assembly, which meets every Saturday night.

The Study

As the idea of writing an oral history of a kibbutz developed, I searched for a kibbutz that would suit the purposes of my writing. Suitable meant a kibbutz willing to cooperate and whose members would talk candidly to a stranger holding a tape recorder, a community willing to assume the risks involved in self-exposure. Furthermore, as an Israeli, instilled from childhood with my country's admiration for the kibbutz system, I hoped to become closely acquainted with a successful kibbutz, in which human weakness would be marginal to, rather than the focus of, its story. Obviously, such a community would also be less defensive about revealing its shortcomings.

*An intensive Hebrew course, usually pursued in a live-in arrangement, such as in a kibbutz.

**Literally, "kernel"; a group of people brought together for the purpose of settlement.

†Nursemaid in charge of a group of children in the kibbutz system.

The pitfalls of generalizing about the kibbutz movement from the study of a single kibbutz concerned me. While I promised to avoid generalizations, I searched at the same time for a "moderate" kibbutz—one which would not be extremist in its ideological position. I preferred a kibbutz belonging either to the Ichud* or Meuchad** movements, both of which are in the mainstream, rather than to the more left-oriented Kibbutz Ha'artzi† or to the religious kibbutz movements. Finally, there were my more specific requirements to consider: I wished to study a kibbutz with at least two generations of adults, the founders and their offspring; a large variety of occupations; and a heterogeneous population.

I discovered Makom through meeting one of its members (Chana, see p. 86) in a human-relations workshop. One evening, I questioned her about my idea for the study. She reacted with interest and tempered encouragement, mingled with a touch of suspicion: What was I trying to find out? As we continued to discuss the project, I learned that Makom was deeply interested in its own history, and that it was embarking on a year-long celebration of its fiftieth anniversary; the time and place seemed right for the study I had in mind. As Chana promised to talk with the appropriate kibbutz authorities about my idea, I felt optimistic about my chances; I had not been flatly refused, and in Chana I sensed the confidence which I considered essential for my work. Chana was not the whole kibbutz, however, and I was eager to meet other kibbutzniks to obtain their reactions.

Following this, I sent a written proposal to Makom. Several weeks later I was invited to present myself and my intended project at a meeting in the kibbutz.

On a spring day in May 1978, I made my first trip to Makom. The meeting took place in the room* of Chana and her husband, Zvi. I found the "room" astonishing: The living room was packed with antique furniture, magnificently carved chairs, a sofa, and a table, all of which barely fitted into the tiny space. Modern pictures, mostly drawings, decorated the walls. Later I found out that the furniture had been brought from Europe by Zvi's mother (see Zvi I, p. 74) and that the pictures were drawn by an artist who lived in the kibbutz.

Several people sat in the room; coffee was served. My primary impression was of a group of animated, middle-aged friends. The atmosphere was relaxed, and, although the group was testing me, this test

---

*Kibbutz movement, founded in 1951, that broke from the kibbutz Hamechud; closely aligned with Mapai.

**Center kibbutz movement that tended left after the division from the Icud.

†Left-wing kibbutz movement, closely aligned with Mapam.

*In Makom, "room" is the term used for the members' private living quarters. This anachronistic term is used even for the present-day apartments, which consist of a living room, a bedroom, a bathroom and a kitchen.

was largely concealed by their casual conversation.

Chana introduced me to the group. They were the members of the secretariat and Yehuda, the man in charge of the archives of the kibbutz. I presented my goal—to record an oral history of Makom. I talked about the exposure involved and proposed using pseudonyms for the kibbutz and its members. As we all tacitly understood, this would conceal the identity of the kibbutz and its members from the broad public, but not from themselves.

From the participants' reactions, I understood that anonymity was not an issue of utmost importance. "Our own criticism of the kibbutz is very harsh and widely discussed among us," they implied. "So what else could be a threat to reveal?" Moreover, some members said that there was nothing to be ashamed of in Makom; my project would probably develop a positive picture of the kibbutz and there was no reason not to expose it to the world's eyes and to give the community, its founders, and its members due credit.

A different perspective was articulated by Yehuda, who explained that he had a wealth of material accumulated in the kibbutz archives, of which he took particular pride, and that indeed it was time for somebody to construct the history of Makom from these documents. He preferred the "real" history, based on this material rather than on the subjective "distorted" accounts I would obtain through interviews. Evidently, he was looking for a historian with whom he could share his deep concern for the preservation of the kibbutz's past and was somewhat disappointed at my project, which would not be a "truthful history."

The youngest person attending the meeting, the cashier of the kibbutz, raised some appropriate questions: What was my own attitude towards the kibbutz—what was my background and my possible bias? How would I select the people to be interviewed to ensure that they were representative of the kibbutz? What would I ask the participants? Would I generalize about the Israeli kibbutz or make a single case study of Makom?

I agreed that all these were very important issues which any investigator must try to clarify as he outlines his study. I told the group more about myself and my plan for the project. I had never been a kibbutz member, but I had belonged to a youth movement, which was kibbutz oriented, and had spent several summers in work camps in kibbutzim. I agreed that generalizing about the greater institution from the study of one kibbutz was unjustified. The problems of the selection of participants and the contents of the interviews were to become, indeed, the central problems of the study.

As the conversation continued, the participants expressed their apprehension, which focused on two points: concern that they might inadvertently contribute to a project which would be "bad press" for the kibbutz; and, even more, apprehension of seeing themselves as presented in the stories of other kibbutz members. I sensed that those present, all central members of the community, felt detached from the rank and file, and were not sure what attitudes I might uncover while interviewing some of the kibbutz's more peripheral members.

When these anxieties were expressed and discussed, a decision was made to begin with a pilot study. I proposed to visit the kibbutz for a while and become acquainted with it, speaking informally to as many people as possible and conducting about ten interviews with people of various ages, occupations, and standing in the kibbutz. I would then write several stories based on these interviews and submit them to the kibbutz at large. Following this pilot stage, both the kibbutz and I would be able to make a final decision concerning the whole project. We all agreed upon this.

As I was about to leave, I heard Chana remind Yehuda to prepare a short speech for the next day. The veterans of the kibbutz were invited to the President's house; this invitation was one of the first and most exciting events of the Jubilee year. I tried to grasp the meaning of fifty years in the history of a community or in the life of an individual; I tried to envision the Valley as it was fifty years ago, when the first steps towards its settlement and cultivation had just started, and I felt a growing desire to find out about the people, the place, their story.

This initiated a series of visits to Makom, in the course of which one hundred interviews were conducted and recorded; many more informal conversations and observations contributed to my growing understanding of, and fascination with, the kibbutz.

The selection of interviewees was an ongoing process. The first twelve names were suggested by the liaison committee appointed to follow my project. Our aim was to include individuals representative of the different subgroups in the kibbutz, from old to young, central to marginal, veteran to newcomer. In the following stage, after the approval of the project, I took the main initiative in the selection process. Four women, with whom I became friendly, were my advisers in the selection. Each of them suggested people whom they considered representative of the diversity of personalities and backgrounds at Makom. My foremost concern was to locate the people who were critical of the community and belonged to its "opposition" as well as people whose voices were usually silent. Of my four advisers, two were first-generation members, and two kibbutz-born. One considered herself to be on the periphery of the community and another saw herself as "opposition." The initial list of names seemed, therefore, to lead towards a rather heterogeneous and, hopefully, representative sample. Once the interviews themselves were started, additional names were suggested by those I interviewed, and often incorporated into my list. Whereas, at the beginning, people were often reluctant to be interviewed, as the project got under way, several people asked to meet me and offered their own accounts for the book. I did not reject any of these approaches. The process of finding other interesting people continued; gradually the stories became more repetitious, and a total picture of the kibbutz began to emerge from the individual stories.

There were, of course, people whom I wanted to meet, who refused to be interviewed. Their refusals were usually explained on the basis of time constraints or shyness. Occasionally, people declined participation because they were opposed to my study. One such refusal was that of a prominent member of Makom, who said that all previous books about kibbutzim had presented the kibbutz in a biased, unfair, or superficial manner, so he was unwilling to participate in what would inevitably result in another, similar study. Another time, I was refused because I was not a kibbutznik myself; therefore, my attempt to understand the kibbutz was deemed as doomed to failure. The total number of refusals was about twenty out of the 120 people I approached in Makom.

The secretariat of the kibbutz was helpful in conducting the interviews. I was given a private room in the kibbutz while I visited. One of the technical secretaries, Vered, arranged the schedule of the interviews according to my list of names. She also contacted the participants for me. Additional help was provided by the editor of the local newsletter, who often published notes about my work and its progress, thus creating an atmosphere of cooperation and support for my study.

In addition to the hundred interviews conducted in Makom, twenty former members of the kibbutz were located and interviewed. Eight were members of Adama who had left Makom during the 1952 political division, and twelve were former members now living in Jerusalem after leaving the kibbutz individually.

Scenes from Makom

The experience of getting to know Makom proved immensely exciting for me. As I made frequent visits throughout the summer and fall of 1978 and the winter and spring of 1979, I witnessed the change of weather and seasons in the fields and gardens of the kibbutz, and in the faces of these hardworking people. Besides the accumulation of the recorded interviews, many images and impressions formed in my mind.

It is a clear, cool day in Jerusalem. At 6:00 A.M., I am waiting for the bus to Makom. In my mind I see the already familiar route. Only the changing weather paints the slopes in varying shades of brown/yellow/green.

The route from Jerusalem to Makom, in the Valley of Yizrael, travels east through the Judean Desert, down to the Dead Sea, then north via the Jordan Rift. By car, it takes thirty minutes to descend from Jerusalem, 900 meters above sea level, to the Dead Sea, which is more than 350 meters below sea level—the lowest spot on earth. The transition from the busy city, with its crowded streets, green parks, and sound of church bells, to the still, brown-white mountainous desert is abrupt. The road turns to the north and passes through Jericho, with its fragrant citrus groves, winter palaces, and archaeological excavations. Out of this oasis town, the route continues north and parallels the Jordan River, visible from time to time from the curving road. The road runs over white, dusty, soft marl and is separated from the river itself by a high barbed-wire fence, which serves as the boundary between Israel and the Kingdom of Jordan. To the west of the road, on the eastern slopes of the Samarian Mountains, one passes a mélange of scattered army camps and new Israeli settlements. After another hour of driving, one arrives at Beit Shean, the crossroads to Tiberias to the north and the Valley of Yizrael to the west.

On this October morning in 1978, the line for the bus is, as usual, comprised of soldiers—young boys and girls in khaki uniforms who have free return tickets to their camps. The only paying passengers are two Norwegian volunteers on their way to a northern kibbutz, and myself. The driver seems to know everybody and the destination of each soldier. As the bus leaves the station, nearly all of the soldiers doze off immediately. The soldier next to me places his rifle between us, and, like his colleagues, drowses, his head bumping my shoulder to the rhythm of the bus's movement.

The sun is rising over the Moab mountains in front of us, and in Jericho it is already unbearably hot. We stop at an Arab coffee shop for fresh orange juice. One by one, the soldiers get off the bus at their respective army camps, miraculously waking as they approach their destinations. The bus overheats and we stop again. Clearly I am going to miss my connection in Beit Shean.

Beit Shean, formerly an Arab town, is now an immigrant's town with the accompanying social problems. Within a radius of about fifty kilometers, however, the idea of the kibbutz was born, implemented, developed, and brought to its present, modern form. The Valley of Yizrael, of which Beit Shean constitutes the eastern corner, is, in a sense, the cradle of modern Israel, the ideal that Israel would like to project.

Beit Shean, for me, is a run-down bus station, where a clerk sells tickets but refuses to give out information. In the small restaurant, truck and bus drivers take breaks, sipping cold drinks, and several kibbutzniks wait for connections. One tells me that the bus to Makom indeed left ten minutes ago. There are no cabs in Beit Shean, I am told at the restaurant, but another bus will leave for Afula, the central town of the Valley, in a short while. I decide to take this bus although I will have to walk two kilometers to Makom.

The occupants of the Valley bus are in sharp contrast to the travelers from Jerusalem. This bus is completely "civilian," crowded at this late-morning hour with housewives, shopping bags, and children. The Valley is all green-brown patches of cultivated fields. The road passes many kibbutzim, their red roofs and meticulously attended lawns visible from the bus.

I alight alone at the junction and begin my walk, on a different road, to Makom. My new road is rather narrow, fast trucks overtake the heavy agricultural machines, and there is no sidewalk for pedestrians. The noon sun blazes. I enjoy the view of the cotton fields to my left, the Gilboa Mountains to my right, and try to ignore the heavy weight of my knapsack and tape recorder.

Suddenly, a van stops and a suntanned driver, in blue fatigues, smiles and offers me a ride. He is an elderly man with a kind face. Helping me put my pack behind the seat, he says, "Well, we're both going to be on time for lunch. I bet you're hungry."

"Lunch where?" I ask.

"At home, in Makom, of course. Don't you think I recognize a daughter of Makom coming home?"

I smile quietly, grateful for his mistake. I am surprised to discover how flattered I feel when mistaken for a daughter of this kibbutz.

Late afternoon in Makom. A light breeze cools the kibbutz after the heat of the day. Young parents stroll with babies on the white paths. Children run to their grandparents' rooms for treats. Two ladies, one carrying an aluminum container with a warm meal, are engaged in an animated conversation near the sickroom. A group of neighbors, all rather elderly, sit on the lawn. The men are talking about today's archaeological findings in a dig that the local school children are conducting. A white-haired woman waters the plants around her house. A scooter passes and is frowned upon by those sitting on the grass. A farmer in blue work clothes, returning late from the fields, heavily mounts the steps to his second-floor apartment. A group of teen-agers, passing noisily, greets the elderly group on the lawn. Two blond volunteers in shorts and heavy boots walk towards their dorm, speaking English. As the sun sets, many watch it calmly.

Early morning. I awaken in a hard, narrow bed to the sound of birds singing in the huge trees. From farther away, I hear the sounds of hens and cows, and some dogs barking. An airplane is spraying the fields, back and forth, around the kibbutz. People are walking hurriedly on the paths. At 6:00 A.M., everybody seems to be wide awake and busy.

From the outside, the apartments of each separate area in the kibbutz look alike; but, within, each room reflects the personalities of its occupants. The apartments of older, long-time kibbutzniks are tiny and extremely modest. They are situated, by and large, in two-story buildings. A dining table is often the focal point of these living rooms. A TV set in the corner; an air conditioner under the window. Many books and paintings of local artists decorate the walls. A corner of toys for visiting grandchildren. Plants, flowers, and fruit bowls are placed among newspapers, picture albums, records, and musical instruments. Some rooms have long rows of Yiddish, English, or German literature, brought from "back home." Some display great-grandparents' china, and many have different souvenirs from trips or wars, and photographs of deceased family members.

The younger members generally live farther out in the periphery, in the newer neighborhoods on the hills. Their apartments are spacious and furnished in contemporary styles; their kitchens are well equipped and adjoin the large living areas. Ceramic dishes, wooden chairs, and cotton curtains are often handmade by the inhabitants. Some gardens have displays of rare flowers and cacti; some have rocks and archaeological objects. Small plastic swimming pools, swings, and tree houses indicate the presence of children.

The children's homes are in the center of the kibbutz, surrounded on all sides by adult homes and, farther out, factories and agricultural buildings. The children's territory is marked by many large, original toys: abandoned and repainted cars, trucks, tractors, and even an airplane; sand boxes and activity areas; small animal sheds and bird coops. Bicycles and tricycles lie momentarily forgotten; dogs wander freely through the multicolored fences. The children wear used, sometimes shabby, clothes. In the heat of the summer, many run about barefoot and display healthy, tanned bodies. All give the air of being extremely well tended.

Every foot of land within the residential area of the kibbutz is cultivated. Even at the dry peak of summer, there is an abundance of flowers, green trees, and beautiful lawns. Always, at least one gardener is in sight. The paths are meticulously clean. The golden-brown hills and the blue sky seem a divine frame for this careful, human creation.

The dining room is a huge, airy hall. A glass wall opens onto a sun-flooded veranda, which faces the Gilboa Mountains. The three other walls are pleasantly decorated by the schoolchildren's artwork. At the entrance, a bulletin board announces various classes, meetings, and trips. People sit in twos and threes, scattered about the room. A single person walks with his tray, finds a group of acquaintances, and joins them. Ulpan students and volunteers sit crowded together. High-school students occupy some tables to the right. There is a continuous hum of voices, constant movement. This is an obvious gathering place—people come here to find somebody, relay a message, arrange a meeting. News is shared, gossip is passed with the salt. At some tables, however, more important decisions are being made. At others, usually where older members sit, one can overhear echoes of last night's Talmud lesson, or a discussion of a new book in the library. Once, as I was having lunch with Amos, the social secretary, I counted within twenty minutes, six people who approached him with various messages or requests. He, too, did not seem to swallow a single bite without remembering something, excusing himself repeatedly, and rushing towards a member.

"You didn't eat anything," I said, as Amos stood to leave.

"That's plenty for me. Usually you won't even find me in the dining hall. There's just not enough time."

Friday night in the dining hall. The room has been transformed. White tablecloths, fresh flowers, and carafes of red wine on the tables. All join for a short Shabbat ceremony and a seated meal. The women are wearing full-length dresses; the men, white shirts. At many tables, grandparents, parents, and children sit together. A holiday atmosphere dominates in spite of the inevitable noise of babies crying, parents scolding, and pots and pans clattering in the kitchen. I look around at the faces. Will I distinguish the workers from the clerks, the farmers from the teachers, the drivers, cooks, administrators? Their faces are tanned and lined. In their Shabbat clothes, they all look both alike and different, as all people do. Justly so, since they are all members of a theoretically equal society.

During the week, people are busy working. Nevertheless, numerous people walk unhurriedly on the paths, as if on vacation. They stop, completely at their leisure, to talk with toddlers taken for walks by their *metapelets.* I visit the various "branches": the factories, kitchen, laundry. I take a drive in the fields, all named after members who fell in the wars. I meet several members whom I already know quite well, and wonder at the incongruity between their personalities, talents, and the kinds of jobs they perform daily. A woman who wrote educational programs for the whole country sits in the laundry room folding shirts, pants, and towels throughout the day. A member who knows the whole history of early Zionism by heart peels vegetables in the kitchen, enthusiastically, as if it were a holy mission. A man who teaches at the kibbutz teachers' college, sits, twice a week, on the line in the food factory, sorting olives. While he performs this monotonous work, he listens to classical music through earphones, his head nodding to the rhythm of the melody. Physical work is a value practiced in the kibbutz.

In the evening, lights are turned on along the paths, and the dining hall, at the center of the kibbutz, is brightly illuminated. Parents walk their children back to the children's homes to put them to bed. Most people rest in their rooms, watching TV. Some attend various meetings and study groups.

A Talmudic study group gathers in the library. Twelve people, young and old, sit at the table and listen to the teacher. Though it is late and someone dozes off, most participate actively in the discussion.

In the gymnasium the girls' basketball team is in training. The coach's instructions can be heard far away in the quiet night.

In the clubhouse, tea and cookies are served for people who prefer to mingle rather than stay in their rooms. Tonight, there is a discussion on the future of the assembly meeting, a central kibbutz institution which seems to be on the decline. About fifty members attend—the "serious" people of the community and the members of the secretariat. Promptly at 11:00 P.M., a summary is presented by the chairman. There is a policy of closing all meetings at 11:00, to allow for enough sleep before the following day's work.

It is almost midnight when I return, exhausted, to my room. The night is tranquil under the starry sky. The silhouette of the Gilboa in the moonlight seems close enough to touch. The smells of the fields and the cattle carry in the wind. A frog is calling, the owls awaken, and the crickets are singing. The homes are dark and the streetlamps attract a multitude of insects. In the children's homes, the night watchwoman knits warm hats for soldiers. A child cries in his sleep. Outside, I meet a young mother rushing to her child, a coat over her nightgown.

"My child was nervous today, and he often wakes up about this time. I'm going to see if he still has a blanket over him."

"Good night," I say.

"Good night, sleep well, and don't push yourself so much."

Everybody seems to worry that I might overwork myself.

Gradually I become a familiar face in this large community. Many members begin to inquire about my progress. There is a growing curiosity on their part: What am I finding in the search? How are they perceived by an outsider? More importantly, can any of the information I have gathered help the administration in solving the social problems of the kibbutz? And finally, do I have a strong sense of the third generation's identity? What are they really like? What do they want? Furthermore, would I be willing to give a complete copy of my transcriptions to the archives of the kibbutz?

As people become better acquainted with me, they often ask me to give an informal professional opinion on various matters. What would I say, as a psychologist, about. . . . Would I help somebody decide on his major at the university? Could I advise Efrat on her school project on early suicides? (See p. 298.)

Jokingly, but perhaps not completely so, members frequently invite me to bring my family to the kibbutz and join them for good.

A spring evening marks my last working visit to Makom. After my last two interviews, I am scheduled to present my preliminary summary at the club. About forty people arrive, most of them members whom I interviewed during the past year. They are anxious to hear my impressions about their home and society: Are we indeed mediocre today? Aren't we better than most other citizens of the country? Do you see in what direction we are heading?

I cannot read into the future. Indeed, at this point, I can hardly even paint a cohesive picture of the past and present. Hesitantly, I present my account, images here and there, impressions, dilemmas. I am aware that I must finish my report by 11:00 P.M. At the end, Amos arises, smiling.

"We want to thank you for the important social work you did for our community. It was very helpful of you to let a hundred members talk their hearts away. . . . Just sympathetic listening is sometimes sufficient therapy."

I am surprised and deeply moved.

As for me . . . the year in which I studied Makom was very dry. Such a heavy drought had not hit the area for years. Crops were lost, the water supply was down, and all the agricultural businesses suffered. As the winter months drew on, people became alarmed. On cloudy days, the sky was scrutinized hopefully. The warm weather and the lack of rain were constant topics of conversation. I caught their mood and watched for clouds.

This fall, the showers started very early and unexpectedly. At home in Jerusalem, I awakened from my sleep to the din of thunderstorms. The rain continues throughout the night.

I was surprised to find myself reacting like a farmer. "How wonderful. Rain at last. Water for Makom."

Indeed, studying Makom and writing about it has deeply affected me. I started my study with a mildly positive attitude toward the kibbutz. As an Israeli woman, educated here, I was proud of the kibbutz as one of the best Israeli creations. Moreover, as an active member of a youth movement in my teens, I was infused with the kibbutz idealism and the message to "actualize the values" by joining a kibbutz myself. In spite of the fact that my life has led me elsewhere, that I preferred privacy to living in a collective, that I put my individual wish to study above the demands of the youth movement, a belief in the kibbutz as a highly valuable way of life has always remained part of my personal outlook. Even without knowing it intimately, I have always seen the kibbutz as part of "beautiful Israel." This, I assume, has been the prevalent attitude toward the kibbutz in Israel.

As a result of my frequent visits to Makom and my numerous conversations with its members, I felt that my initial attitude was reinforced. I was impressed by the place and its inhabitants, the quality of life and the ongoing attempt to live by ideals. Often, when criticizing their own creation, I felt that the members were too harsh toward themselves, more severe than an outside judge might be. Moreover, I have frequently felt that their self-criticism is constructive and is used to improve the situation, to correct their mistakes. I appreciated this awareness, the ability to face failures bravely as well as to take pride in success.

Yet, I have also learned a great deal more about the problems and conflicts confronting a large kibbutz at the end of the 1970s, and I discovered that, like all other ideas, the idea of the kibbutz has been shaped and reformed by time and reality. It is an idea realized by human beings, with their strengths and weaknesses, their immense dedication *and* their incessant fluctuations vis-à-vis the initial conception. Although seventy years old, the kibbutz as a life-style has not stabilized yet.

I emerged from my endeavor with the same positive attitude I started with, but with an added dimension of knowledge and wishes for a worthy future.

The Book

Following my field work in Makom, Adama, and Jerusalem, I transcribed all interviews in Hebrew. Of these, sixty-one were selected for publication in the book. An attempt was made to offer the broadest perspective on the history of the kibbutz and its present state by including as many viewpoints as possible. The published set of stories includes men and women of different ages, backgrounds, and occupations.

In organizing my interviews into a book, the main distinction I made was between those concentrating on the kibbutz's past and those interviews primarily describing its present. The early history of the kibbutz is presented in the first section of the book, which is organized around three themes: the establishment of the kibbutz, the absorption of new members in the mandate days, and the organization of a security system. Makom's members were instrumental in the struggle for the establishment of the Israeli state, in early military organizations, and in illegal immigration activities; this first section sheds light on the important role the kibbutz played in the history of Israel.

The next distinct period in Makom's development centers on the division within the kibbutz movement and in the individual kibbutzim. The division in Makom is closely intertwined with the histories of two other kibbutzim, Molad and Adama; the local version of this event is presented in the second part of the book from the perspective of people who joined, left, or remained in Makom during the crisis.

Each of the historical sections closes with a family's personal account of this time period. These family portraits are used to recapitulate some of the ideas and points discussed earlier in the section, offering a more cohesive approach to the interactions between personalities and their time frame.

The third part of the book covers the present situation of the kibbutz. Its first chapter focuses on six members who hold central positions in the public sphere of Makom. These six reports portray the various roles and responsibilities which have evolved in order to maintain the communal organization; they also depict some of the organizational problems which challenge the kibbutz today. Individual services available to kibbutz members, such as socialized programs for the sick, elderly, newcomers, and others in need, are described in the second chapter. Personal accounts by several recipients of these services help provide ways to evaluate the efforts of the kibbutz as a welfare state.

The kibbutz is a relatively structured framework which determines many aspects of the lives of its members. The following two chapters present stories of individuals who have struggled against the collective and have consistently refused to conform to its demands. The first of these chapters portrays four people who found, within the milieu of the kibbutz, ways to establish themselves as nonconforming members, accepted individualists. With the growing liberalism of the kibbutz, one may expect to find a greater number of members belonging to this category. However, many of those who rebelled against the pressure of collective society ultimately left the kibbutz altogether. Some examples of those who left the kibbutz, people who did not find fulfillment within the community, are presented in the next chapter.

The last section of the book relates the stories of several young members of Makom, some second- and some third-generation kibbutzniks. And so, the story of Makom, from its beginnings in the accounts of its older members to the present moment as described by its youth, is complete. An attempt to understand the younger members, particularly those who were born and raised in Makom, may serve as an indication of the future of the kibbutz.

My primary interest was, however, not clearly defined "subjects," but individuals, the people themselves, their needs, wants, hopes, and thoughts. In order to allow the personalities themselves to predominate, I did not dissect the interviews so that they would "fit" chapter headings. Each interview covers many subjects, and is not restricted to the topic indicated by the chapter heading. I did, of course, edit the interviews. Each interview lasted for one or two hours, and, therefore, had to be reduced for both interest and considerations of space.

As may be expected in a transcribed oral history, the reader will find that some episodes or evaluations tended to recur during the course of interviewing, as if belonging to the common myth, the implicit truth, of kibbutz life. On the other hand, inconsistencies in, and even contradictions of, the history of the kibbutz and its present situation also occurred frequently in the interviewing process. Whether due to faults of memory or to different perceptions of the same facts, we will never know.

Acknowledgments

This book is dedicated to my friends in Makom, and to Makom's ex-members in Adama and Jerusalem, whose names have been changed to protect their anonymity. Without their openness and tireless cooperation this book could never have been.

The idea of this book was conceived by André Schiffrin, to whom I am especially grateful. In our meeting in Jerusalem he presented me with the challenge of recording an oral history of a kibbutz. This started a slow process of growing fascination and involvement on my side, and a gradual inclusion of many friends, so-called subjects or informants, assistants, typists, and editors who participated in different facets of this endeavor.

My friend, Dan Bar-On of Revivim, a kibbutz in southern Israel, provided me with the necessary perspective of another social scientist and kibbutz member. He encouraged me to conduct the study, introduced me to Makom, and supported me during my many moments of self-doubt along the way. Tamar Landau and Dafna Tuval have patiently coped with endless hours of taped interviews and meticulously performed their transcriptions.

As in my former book, Meir Perlow, now a graduate student in psychology, was of immense assistance in bringing the characters of this book to life in English, which naturally is not the original language of the interviews. Furthermore, his dedicated judgment was invaluable in the painful selection of people and themes to be omitted from the original manuscript, and in the organization of the vast amount of material into meaningful categories.

The most difficult editorial task of this book was to cut it into printable size yet preserve the picture of Makom in its richness and totality. The final stage of this process was carried out by Philip Pochoda of Pantheon Books, who demonstrated great respect for the original manuscript and performed the operation with expertise and care.

This is where I would like to thank the generous and helpful participation of more than fifty people who gave me the privilege of talking to them yet whose stories were not included in the final version of this report. Although their stories were fascinating and revealing, their perspectives were covered by other people of similar background. To these individuals, my apologies.

The Hebrew University of Jerusalem, and the Department of Psychology in particular, have provided me with a fertile environment in which to conduct my research and to write the book. Partial support for the study was granted by the Research Fund of the Faculty of Social Sciences and the Human Development Center. Constant assistance was provided by the two secretaries of the Department of Psychology, Miriam Bajayo and Rachela Shaked. My colleagues were tolerant of my frequent absence from the office during the field work, and have been interested, encouraging, and supportive throughout this long process. In particular, Dr. Anat Ninio and Dr. Yoram Bilu maintained unwavering curiosity about my progress, and this interest refueled my energy time and time again.

Finally, it is my family who made it all possible. Israel, my husband, was extremely cooperative. Yuval and Maty, still young, have shown mature independence, and Eliav, who was born just as I completed the field work, was my closest companion in the long process of writing it all up. To all these individuals my profound gratitude.

Amia Lieblich
Jerusalem
Spring 1980

Part 1

THE
EARLY
PAST

The
Beginning

YEHUDA *(age 69)*

Of the seventeen people who founded the kibbutz, Yehuda is the only member living in Makom today. He is, therefore, an institution of sorts. Appropriately enough, Yehuda is in charge of the Archives, which are largely his own creation.

Our conversation takes place in the Archives—a wooden hut behind the secretariat offices. It is well organized, with three tiny rooms and a vast accumulation of material. Our half-day-long appointment starts with a detailed explanation of the Archives, its aims, uses, and system of organization—all defined and developed by Yehuda who has no previous experience or education in this area. Yehuda points out that his Archives are different from most, for besides saving material for future historical documentation, they also contain reference material used for such practical purposes as organizing holiday celebrations, teaching various classroom subjects, and, of course, writing obituaries and memorial booklets for the deceased. He stresses the fact that the Archives continually serve the community, not merely historical needs.

Now sixty-nine, Yehuda devotes his full working day (due to his age, about five hours) to his work in the Archives. Yehuda developed and nurtured the Archives over the past twenty years as a hobby, having worked primarily as a construction worker in the kibbutz.

("For me," he says, "planning and building a kibbutz has always been a fascinating subject. The way a settlement develops is the same way that a society evolves. In a kibbutz, one must organize to preserve and encourage communal living. It's not a simple problem.")

I was born in 1909; soon I'll be seventy. I was born in Russia, or perhaps Poland—with all the shifts of the borders there, who knows. Anyway it was a tiny place, about a quarter of the size of this kibbutz. When I was four, World War I broke out. All I remember is the night our town was completely burned. It was Yom Kippur, I remember. The Russians ordered us to evacuate the town on the eve of Yom Kippur, and we all moved out of our homes into the forest. The next night, we saw the town burning down. They had started to retreat, and, wanting to leave only barren land, they burned down towns behind them for the advancing German enemy. Anyway, from then on, we became vagabonds of sorts. I remember being on the move during all the early years of my childhood —within Russia, from one miserable village to another, staying with different branches of the family. The only good thing about it was finding out firsthand about my roots, my great-grandparents, and about many important chapters of Jewish history, prejudice, and self-sacrifice. It was, however, very hard, and it was a pretty miserable childhood. Our wanderings finally brought us to Poland, and from there, at the end of 1924, we immigrated to Eretz Yisrael.

My family settled in Tel Aviv, where conditions were, at the time, as harsh as those in Europe in many ways. My father started a small business, trying to make a living in trade, the classic occupation of the Jew. For me, it was a continuation of the past, of the Jewish-Diaspora mentality, which I have always deeply resented. But, in spite of their poverty, my parents provided all their children with an education, and that is where my story actually begins.

I enrolled in Herzelia High School, which was then the most advanced educational institute in the country. My grade had two classes; we were about one hundred youngsters. Many important people came out of this group later on, but at that time about 90 to 95 percent of the class were planning to go abroad to study in institutions of higher education, since we had no universities or higher technical schools in Israel at the time. Only a small minority of those who went to study abroad, then, ever came back, you know. I, too, was seriously considering the possibility— I wanted to become an engineer, which was my parents' plan for me as well.

However, in the tenth grade, other thoughts began to stir us. We started looking for our own solution. We certainly didn't know what we wanted—we only knew what we did *not* want. A bunch of kids from the two classes of our grade organized themselves as a *chug,* * which started to meet regularly. Understand, the situation in the country at that time was a very strange one. On the one hand, Jews were immigrating to Israel; there was a pioneer movement whose aim was agrarian life and the establishment of kibbutzim. We knew very little about this movement— it didn't develop within Israel. On the other hand, we, the Israeli youth, were thinking mostly about leaving the country to study abroad. We shared very little of what was happening around us, outside the city. It was a very difficult period, with a high rate of emigration, poverty, and a sense of aimlessness. It was a "train station" population—people coming, people going, and we were in the middle of it all.

*Literally, "circle"; a group of people with a common interest.

Some of us youngsters were concerned with this situation. A girl who studied a year ahead of us wrote an article titled: "Youth: Where to?" or something like that, making the point that the Israeli youth was not playing a role in what was happening in the country. This was truly the case. We invited her to some of our *chug* meetings and received further support and advice from one of our teachers. We started to read about the first *aliya*, we read eagerly a lot of classical Zionist literature—things nobody reads today—and we discussed what we read and its implications for our lives. We also invited important people from various political factions to talk to us. All these activities were concealed; even the existence of the chug was kept secret. I guess it's common for teen-age groups to require secrecy—it heightens the intensity of the experience. Furthermore, we were influenced by other secret organizations, such as Bnei-Moshe,* which also kept its movement secret. This secrecy bound us close together. At the beginning, we didn't have any definite focus; we were simply searching for direction. Gradually, we got closer to the ideology of physical labor, and the idea of the commune—but this was a process which took some time.

The school was relatively supportive of our *chug,* when its existence became known. We used to meet at private homes, constantly reading and discussing our ideas. We were in the tenth grade when all this started, and by the end of the eleventh grade we felt quite sure about the idea of personal actualization through productive work. At that time, teachers active in the Jewish National Fund helped us; through their connections, they found ten or twelve jobs for us in agricultural settlements in the Yizrael Valley for the duration of the summer vacation.

At the end of the next school year, we returned to agricultural settlements, this time as an organized group, a *garin* of seventeen members, twelve boys and five girls. We debated constantly over our destination— not our geographical destination, but our ideological one. Some were in favor of joining an existing settlement. We were just high-school graduates and had very little experience, so this seemed the most sensible path. All the existing kibbutzim were in the early stages of development, so they were willing to accept us and we could make significant contributions. Some of us wanted to do just a *hachshara*** in a kibbutz, then start our own settlement. A completely different opinion was to join a *moshava.* † A *moshava* at that time was different from those today. The *moshavot* were suffering from tremendous work shortages, and, if anything, they preferred cheap Arab labor. This was the time of the struggle

---

*A secret Zionist association functioning in Poland and Israel at the end of the nineteenth century.

**A preparation period, especially referring to preparation for an agricultural settlement.

†A non-communal agricultural settlement. Plural, *moshavot.*

for Jewish labor, what we called Hebrew labor: the struggle to wrest the monopoly on manual labor from the Arab workers, who were cheaper and considered better for manual, agricultural work. Jewish farmers of the *moshavot* preferred the Arab workers, and the struggle to change this was of major significance at the time. The members who supported this tactic argued that as workers in a *moshava,* we would really be joining the working class. To belong to the working class one must be exploited, one must work for a boss, and doing so was central to our ideology. If, on the other hand, we were immediately to enter a kibbutz or start a settlement, we would have no chance of joining the working classes or establishing a firsthand relationship with them. This was the central argument among us; we were not just interested in experiencing manual labor—that we would experience either way. The crux of the matter was the firsthand experience of the current social struggle.

We finally decided to join a *moshava,* as a unit, and to work for a boss, a foreman. And we wouldn't go to a young *moshava* that had already accepted Hebrew labor; we went to Chadera, where the struggle was still at its height.

Chadera at that time was something impossible, impossible to describe. It was the cemetery of all the former *aliyot* that attempted to build the place. It was a disaster. Terrible malaria and swamps. The only available work was seasonal work in the citrus groves. That's where we were heading then, accompanied by a great deal of anxiety on the part of those adults interested in our activities.

In Chadera we received an empty hut, which we furnished with beds, linen, and clothes that we brought from home. At the beginning, only five of us got work, and the struggle for a "day's work" was continual. Looking for work was mainly my responsibility during our early stages. We worked in the citrus groves, and also for some public-works projects, drilling and taking part in other manual tasks. Soon people started to catch malaria. The winter was very harsh. Our income was insufficient, yet we insisted on living off our own work and refused to take anything from our parents. It's a long story, those days in Chadera, but it was the beginning of our group.

Obviously, some people had it very bad then. After about a year and a half, we felt we had to leave Chadera. Too many of us were sick with malaria and unable to live there, and the unemployment level was too high. Something had changed, in the meantime, around us. We were the "old *chug,*" and several younger *chugim* had formed in the towns. A youth movement was established in Jerusalem, joined by the Scouting Legion —we were suddenly the avant-garde of a growing youth movement. Some of these new members from Jerusalem joined us in Chadera at the end of 1929. We then got an offer to move to Kefar Yehezkel in the Valley of Yizrael. There had been a working company there that had just disbanded, and we were offered their places as workers in the *moshav.* The

Valley had been our dream, and we accepted. We saw this step as progress towards our goal of founding a settlement of our own. This was the second phase. Our group was growing, people were joining constantly, and a few had left. We worked in the fields, and the women occasionally did domestic work in the farmhouses. We had a camp there, and it was during our stay there that we eventually decided to join the Kibbutz Hameuchad* movement, which gave us some moral support but no financial aid. We stayed in Kefar Yehezkel for over a year. Then, one of the older kibbutzim of the Valley moved up the hill to their permanent location. They abandoned an entire camp of huts and tents near the water fountain, and a huge wooden dining hall. Our group asked to move there, and the request was approved by the Kibbutz Hameuchad, to which we already belonged. So this became our home, the third stage, which we simply called "the Fountain."

The time at the Fountain was great, exhilarating and creative, but also difficult for many. There were suicides, very tragic events that profoundly affected us. It is hard to analyze the reason for them and I am certainly not an expert in psychology. It seems to me, though, that throughout the country there were more suicides committed then than now. This was quite typical of the socialist revolution era: Many famous people—revolutionaries, poets, writers—all over the world as well as here committed suicide. Of course, each case is different, but when you consider them comprehensively, you have a social phenomenon.

There were three suicides in the early days. One as we were moving out of Kefar Yehezkel; two more in the beginning at the Fountain. One has to take into account the conditions of our life at the time. Firstly, here again the group suffered from a severe shortage of work. This was depressing—people were sitting around and we didn't know what to do with them. Our future was unclear, and we weren't sure we were going to make it. The people who committed suicide were relatively new in the kibbutz; they didn't belong to the original *chugim.* I remember one in particular, a very intellectual boy. This kind of intelligent youngster frequently meets a dead end in his search for purpose in life. It is difficult to separate the various factors: the conditions within the group, the lack of work, and romantic reasons, of course. Failure in love was always a common reason for suicide. The dead took their secrets with them.

Hardest of all was the fact that this phenomenon became an integral part of our life. More depressing than the number of suicide incidents was the atmosphere that prevailed in the group, the anxiety, the suspicion that there were more tragedies to come. This was what shook us very deeply.

There was something else: New people were constantly joining us. Some of them came from backgrounds different from ours, and we didn't

*A centrist kibbutz movement that tended left after the division from the Ichud.

know them that well. Perhaps they had problems which we didn't under-stand at the time. Also, the poverty of our life was too demanding for some. Many left us, though rarely did anyone mention material condi-tions as the reason for his decision to leave. When I look back at that period, this is how I summarize it: We set out to create a fundamental revolution in our lives, both as Jews and as human beings. We succeeded more or less in this. As in life, there is the dream and there is reality. Often they're not that similar. That's it.

Three months ago, we were celebrating our Jubilee, the fiftieth birth-day of Makom. I had to make a speech then, something I very rarely agree to do. I talked about our hopes in the past, the idea of the kibbutz. I don't consider myself a fanatic, but I believe that our way is the solution. The kibbutz represents a real hope for us Jews in Israel and for humanity in general. But it is clear that the events we are now undergoing, both as Jews in Israel and as members of the kibbutz are far from utopian. I wouldn't say that I am confident that the form of life my generation created is permanent. The strength of our movement is not increasing. Who knows, we might witness a deterioration of our ideal. But even if that is the case, I believe that eventually our ideas will return with greater force, for the premises of the kibbutz are essential for the future of human society: cooperation and equality. We did manage to create such a society in our lifetime. We arrived, but where are we heading from here, where is the train going, who knows? Naturally, it's easier to ask than to answer. Makom is a strong and securely established settlement; actually the whole kibbutz movement has achieved more than anyone thought or expected. There are, however, questions from within, and anxiety is our constant companion. I am not afraid of changes in our life-style; many changes have already occurred, and I welcomed them. I think that just as an individual changes, as he grows in body and mind, so do changes occur in the life of a community, and it's a good sign. Some things, though, we shouldn't touch: Those are the basics and if you change them you're cutting off your roots. These basics are what concern me most.

Take, for instance, hired labor. I am very anxious and critical about this development. In Makom we actually have very few cases of hired hands, but that is the result of a long and difficult struggle on the part of a small group of members who objected to this as a violation of our total life-style.

Some people say that it's an obsession of mine, my objection to hired labor. But for me it *is* a violation of our basic life-style. Once you hire workers, you become a boss and you just supervise; you let all the difficult jobs be done by outsiders. I see manual work, physical labor, as one of our basic principles—primary, productive work, both in the field and in the factory. This is the Jewish problem: all of the traditional Jewish occupations! And this was our revolution: We wanted to send roots into the soil! And then you see someone, who for twenty or thirty years worked productively in his branch, suddenly showing his other nature, that of the Diaspora Jew, looking for easy ways of making money, becoming a merchant. We haven't changed his basic identity as much as we thought we had. This is what I am fighting against. Some kibbutzim have huge factories, run by administrators who are members, while all the workers are hired from the outside. To me it seems horrible that the kibbutz should become the employer. Thanks to our constant efforts, we have prevented it from happening here, although we still have some hired hands. Some of them are quite old now, and will soon retire, and I hope the whole thing will be over soon.

There is another matter which greatly concerns me: the problem of external sources, or means, of income. This has bothered many kibbutzim. What do you do when you inherit a sum of money, or receive a money gift? You're supposed to hand it all in to the kibbutz.

I see these two things, hired labor and external sources of income, as very central to our social structure. Sometimes it seems as if a richer community has more problems than a very poor one. Take warehouse A, where in our early commune every item of clothing was shared by all. . . . I'm not for technical equality, for I don't think the kibbutz has to supply every single person with exactly the same things. People are different, their needs are different—but the kibbutz should be the sole source to supply these needs, not external sources. Take education—if one wants higher education—it costs a lot, but we probably would grant it. That's his or her individual need; it isn't everybody else's. Everybody gets the same personal budget; children have equal opportunities to be educated; we all receive the best health services—that's equality.

There are other aspects of our life that trouble me. One is the relationships between kibbutzim, even within the same political movement. We can have equality within a kibbutz, but, if one kibbutz is well-off and its neighbor is relatively poor, then again we have social classes of sorts.

Finally, I want to tell you that the kibbutz is a certain philosophy, a way of life. A kibbutz is not a static institution, and I do not support stagnation; I welcome changes. But I would like members to cooperate with the rules and policies, and not to produce slow change by deviating from the rules. There are too many unplanned developments, and we may eventually arrive at a point where we hardly recognize ourselves. I'll give you an example, a very minor one: As you walk around our paths, you see those small motorbikes. Or take TVs, that's an even better example. Someone brought a TV to his room—it was probably a gift; then a second and a third person had a television. We asked some questions, but we couldn't throw the TVs out, could we? So a pattern was established: It was decided to buy TVs for everybody, by seniority of course. The same thing happened several years ago with refrigerators in private rooms. The kibbutz lagged behind the fact that some individuals had acquired refrigerators; then the kibbutz gave in and supplied everyone with refrigerators in order to maintain order and equality. Sometimes these decisions were way beyond the economic means of the kibbutz, or, at least, weren't high on the priority list of investments.

For the most part, these are deviations which have to do with improving the standard of living. But there must be limits to that, too. What worries me, about all this, is that the kibbutz as a movement does not protect its ideology, its doctrines, and its philosophy of life; it does not teach it to its children. The school in the kibbutz does it only minimally, teaching a little about the history of the kibbutz, but very little about its basic principles. We do have experience, as well as doctrines that proved themselves during our history, and these should help guide us in the future. And of course, as in Judaism, there is always room for change and innovation. But our heritage needs serious study, which isn't currently being done properly, though we now have a higher-education center which attempts to do so. But that is only for adults.

The greatest influence on children is the room: their parents' room, the family. Today many parents aren't very enthusiastic about their son's becoming a cowman, a worker. They want their son to be a doctor—you see, the Diaspora mentality is returning, it's returning. I also would be personally satisfied if my son got a higher education, but first he should be a worker for a while; it's better that way.

But sometimes the parents' room is influential in the opposite direction. The danger is, therefore, that our children, the second and third generations, will be actually ignorant of the underlying principles of the kibbutz way of life. They live here; it's their home; they love the landscape; they have their roots here. But, to me, something is missing—I wouldn't call it ideology, but simply an awareness of the basic values underlying our way of life. Our values might be neglected over time. And then, imagine: I live here; I love the place; I hire workers and live as an employer; I use the money I receive from outside sources, and—what next? First you don't recognize yourself, and then who knows? One might decide on a division of the property, tearing the whole thing down. . . .

This is a real danger. It happened to communes which were tested elsewhere in the world. They were destroyed by the second and third generations. We need to study, teach, and actively preserve our ideology and way of life. I myself have done this. With another *chavera,* * I have collected and published our assembly decisions concerning the way of life of this kibbutz. We printed a booklet, and it's made in such a way that pages can be easily added. This, too, is very significant.

I myself have four children, three daughters and a son. Two are here,

*Feminine of *chaver,* literally, "friend," "comrade"; refers especially to a member of a kibbutz. Plural, *chaverim;* feminine plural, *chaverot.*

and the other two are in other kibbutzim. This is natural—they followed their spouses. But they did not abandon the kibbutz way of life. Naturally, this is very satisfying for me.

So this is my position. We have talked about the past and about the future. The sum total of my feelings is positive, there is no doubt about it, no doubt at all. We had a dream; we started from zero. We arrived at what you see here—it's certainly better than the dream. But my anxiety never leaves me, in spite of all our achievements. I feel that this uneasiness is much more typical of my generation than of the younger ones. It's like a parent's concern for his children.

D A V I D   I L A N   (age 64)

Many of the Israeli kibbutzim can "show off" a minister or a member of Parliament who belongs to the kibbutz. The famous man of Makom is certainly David, Shulamit's husband, who was an important figure in the War of Independence and, before that, in the Palmach. *His figure appears in the Israeli Wax Museum, raising the flag during the capturing of Eilat.*

Presently serving as the chairman of the regional council, David is extremely busy and frequently away from the kibbutz. It was quite difficult to schedule an interview with him, but when we finally talked, very late at night, David was very pleasant and eager to contribute his share to the story. His wife, Shulamit, was present in the room with us, and often corrected David, adding her point of view.

I was seventeen and a half at the end of 1932, when I graduated from high school in Jerusalem and went through a *hachshara,* as a member of the Machanot Haolim.** The main purpose of this *hachshara* was to learn to work in an agricultural environment, but no less important were our constant conversations and debates, our nocturnal discussions about our future, our direction, and what kind of kibbutz to become. We were a good, large group of youngsters, about twenty or twenty-five of us, and many of the existing kibbutzim courted us in an attempt to get us to join them.

We were a well-known, cohesive group, the Jerusalem circle, which had been formed when we were twelve or thirteen, and, even at that early stage, we had begun to make plans for the future. When we were fifteen, or so, we formed a commune in a rented house, where those who had dropped out of high school lived together. They worked as gardeners, electricians or plumbers, sustained themselves, and even managed to save money for the Jerusalem circle. We, the students, worked with the commune during our school vacations, often finding jobs doing construc-

---

*The military branch of the Hagana, the Jewish defense organization in Mandate Palestine.
**Youth movement aligned with Mapai.

tion work or gardening; all the money we made went to the commune. With that money, we bought work clothes and various tools, as well as some pistols for our future settlement. We were rich and accustomed to work, two definite advantages. In addition to that, because we were far-sighted youngsters, we encouraged several of our members to study in Mikveh-Israel, the best existing agricultural school. There, another small group formed around our members, all well trained in agriculture, and we were all supposed to join ranks when we completed our educations. All this explains why we were so sought after as a promising group.

While we were at our *hachshara,* the three kibbutz movements were forming and defining their different ideologies. Each of these movements sent delegates to persuade us to join its camp. The main distinction between them was the question of the structure of the commune. The Chever Hakvutzot* was for "the small group"—they conceived of the commune as an extended family, based on closeness and intimacy among the members. They envisaged the kibbutz community as consisting of no more than fifteen families, and believed that at this size maximum intimacy would be ensured. This concept was embedded in the real conditions of that period, when the "work companies," which were small communes of workers, roamed the land and searched for work together.

The Kibbutz Haartzi,** to which the Shomer Hatzair† movement belonged, presented the ideal of the "organic group." They saw the kibbutz as consisting of a cohesive group of youngsters who had all received their education within the youth movement and grown up to-gether before forming (or joining) a kibbutz. Common background was of utmost importance to this concept, and the idea was that such a kibbutz would grow by the addition of younger groups from the same youth movement, providing ideological cohesiveness and continuity. The kib-butz was to consist of fifty to sixty families, perhaps allowing this number to grow to a hundred, not more.

Finally, the Kibbutz Hameuchad movement had the idea of the big, open kibbutz. They saw themselves as a task force, the continuation of the former work troops. The bigger the force, the more could be accom-plished. The idea of the work troops was to attain employment in road construction, stone quarries, or swamp drainage, and to transfer the group wherever it could find work. It was a popular movement, nonselec-tive and appealing to a large public, both individuals and groups.

Our youth movement, Machanot Haolim, joined the Kibbutz Hameuchad a year later, so we were still free to make our own choice. Around that time, the group that had settled at the Fountain decided to

---

*Former name of the present Ichud movement.
**The left-wing kibbutz movement, which was closely aligned with Mapam, the United Workers' Party.
†The youth movement aligned with the Kibbutz Haartzi.

join the Kibbutz Hameuchad, and we, after endless debates, decided to follow suit. On the question of joining the group at the Fountain we had a "sexual" conflict. [*David laughs.*] We, the boys, wanted to start a kibbutz of our own, to experience all the aspects of a true beginning. For us, the group at the Fountain was already too well established, an old kibbutz. Our girls, however, said we were mere babies, and couldn't be trusted with such a responsibility as founding a kibbutz. In fact, however, I suspect they were looking forward to meeting somewhat older and more mature men, say twenty years old rather than eighteen. . . . The debate went on and on, and the point that finally decided the question was the security aspect of our joining Makom. At that time, the area of the Yizrael Valley was very uneasy; kibbutzim had been shot at from the Gilboa several times, and Makom's delegates, who had come to persuade us to join them, exploited the security argument for all it was worth until Makom won us over. Two of our members, however, rebelled against the decision to join an "old" kibbutz and left us. (Shulamit says there were four dissidents, not two.) So we were twenty-two in number when we arrived at the Fountain, and since the whole population consisted then of about forty to forty-five members, our annexation made an immediate difference to the settlement.

Sheer number was not our only contribution, though. As I told you, we were well equipped and I remember arriving at the train station with a whole car full of boxes, like a bride with a rich dowry arriving at her poor groom's house. The clothes we brought were used for years to come, and our experienced members immediately spearheaded an attempt to provide the kibbutz with some kind of agricultural foundation.

At the time we joined the Fountain, in the early 1930s, some German immigrants were existent members, but the majority of the Yekkes* arrived later. Since we came as a group, we had no problems of social integration whatsoever, and physical labor was something we had been well trained to do. I don't remember having any crisis or difficulties of assimilation at the kibbutz.

The majority of the men were assigned to work missions outside the kibbutz, making money to build our own community. I was a construction carpenter in a village; then I worked in drilling for the electricity line, then in the stone quarry near Haifa, and later, as a porter in Haifa port. One of my jobs was paving the road from Afula to Beit Shean, and from there I got myself into the transportation business. These were my major occupations until 1941, when I became seriously involved in defense.

Until 1941 I served, as did everybody else, in various guard duties within the kibbutz. In 1941 the first Palmach companies were started, with the full cooperation of the British authorities, who wanted to prepare military forces against the advancing German Army. The German forces

*Nickname for German Jews.

were advancing from two directions. They were threatening us on the South, from the African desert, while the government of Occupied France had taken Lebanon and Syria and could invade our country from the North. In case of invasion a retreat plan was set, according to which all the Jewish inhabitants of the country would gather in the Carmel Mountains. This plan involved preparing food, water, and firearms facilities in the mountains.

Theoretically, we and they were fighting together against the Nazi enemy. Meanwhile the Palmach had taken upon itself undercover goals, protecting the Jewish settlements against *all* dangers. So, at the same time that the Palmach was in touch with British Intelligence, which served as a liaison with the military command of the Allied Forces, it was also part of the triangular conflict between the Jews, Arabs, and British. It was like two independent spheres, following Ben Gurion's slogan: "We'll fight the Mandate as if Hitler didn't exist, and we'll fight Hitler as if the Mandate didn't exist." It was a highly complicated situation, with legal and illegal arms changing hands and directions—quite confusing.

The kibbutz movement was closely associated with the Hagana.* But, while membership in the Hagana involved part-time, after-work occupation, such as training at night or over the weekend, membership in the Palmach meant total mobilization. The various kibbutzim had, therefore, established quotas for members to be mobilized by the Palmach, as well as other quotas for draftees into the British Army, another channel of mobilization. I was approached by regional organizations and asked to join the Palmach, but the kibbutz considered my work in transportation essential, and prevented me from leaving. Three other members of our kibbutz joined the Palmach then. A few months later I was approached again, this time by Yigal Allon, the Palmach commander, and I began to organize a company of local kibbutz volunteers, originally doing this in addition to my work at the kibbutz. I was then sent to take a course on reconnaissance and sabotage techniques, and by the end of 1941 I was already working full-time for the Palmach. I stayed in the military forces (later, Zahal**) for nearly ten years. I was released with the rank of lieutenant colonel.

I never thought of the Army as a career—it was a job that had to be done. I didn't feel that I had volunteered as an individual, but that I represented the kibbutz, or even the entire kibbutz movement. At that time, serving in the military forces was taken into account in the daily work schedule, as if it were simply any other task, such as working in the orange grove or with the cattle. Those years of military service were an interruption of my home and family life, and I always looked forward to

*Literally, "defense"; the Jewish defense organization in Mandate Palestine.
**Israeli Defense Force (IDF). The Israeli Army, which replaced the Hagana with the establishment of the State in 1948.

their end and my return to a more pleasant way of life. Throughout that period, I maintained as strong a relationship with the kibbutz as I could.

Here Shulamit interrupts, commenting: "He was married to the kibbutz, not to his wife and kids."

Well, I was glad to return home; but in general I think it is a responsibility of the kibbutz, at present as well as then, to encourage able individuals to serve in the Army. Throughout the years, our kibbutz adopted this attitude—and, indeed, we have always supplied the Army with military pilots and Army commanders at various levels. After the Yom Kippur War the kibbutz assembly passed a resolution to retain continuously five men in the regular Army, and I think that's about the situation today. My son was in the regular Army for nine years and he, like me, sees the military not as a career but as an obligation one has to fulfill.

Since I returned from military service I have served as work coordinator, secretary of the kibbutz, and twice as secretary of the Kibbutz Hameuchad Movement. Professionally, I worked in our metal factory for some years and in our construction projects. One of my "babies" was to start a herd of cattle for meat production, and I worked at that for a long time; naturally, I have worked in the fields for years. . . . It's really difficult to remember everything I've done. Presently, I'm the chairman of the regional council. This is an elected position which I have already held for two years. I represent the Labor Party—in our area almost everybody is in the Labor Party today. The council includes about 15,000 people, among them several of the Valley's oldest kibbutzim, some newer immigrant villages, and five Arab villages. It's a responsibility, but I'm used to responsibility. . . .

When I compare my adolescent fantasies with the present reality, I have to admit that reality has surpassed all our dreams. Look, we came here as young hooligans, paupers, and tried to push ourselves in as a new settlement among the already established giants, the kibbutzim of the Valley. We used to roam around these kibbutzim like hungry dogs searching for a proper dinner. . . . And now it's us, Makom, the biggest kibbutz in the area, the fourth largest in the whole country! But our size is not the main thing. What's so special about our kibbutz is its human composition. The group of Israeli founders, as well as the later groups such as ours, were deeply rooted in the Jewish heritage and in the new Israeli culture, and this left its impact on everything that followed. The German immigrants who joined the Israelis brought a wonderful element to the society. We provided the Hebrew language, and they introduced music. We brought Israeli ways—and they introduced the big world, literature and history. They were all highly intelligent people, those first settlers of the 1930s, and as a result we're now one of only two kibbutzim to have maintained a local school of twelve grades. We have what are perhaps the best kibbutz archives; we started the Kibbutz Holiday Archives and the National Society for the Protection of Nature. We have many artists and writers. We have a very rich cultural life. The main index for our success, I believe, is the high percentage of our children who choose to remain here with us. We have about 650 adult members, and I estimate that two-thirds of them were born here. In comparison to other kibbutzim, we have here the highest percentage of children who have chosen to remain.

The main problem facing us now, as a kibbutz, is how to live with our wealth, how to avoid becoming ugly because of material abundance. . . . When we came here as paupers, my main ambition was to make a profit—firstly, in order to build the place and, secondly, in order to prove to my parents and to the capitalistic society at large that people could work devotedly even if the money didn't go directly to their private pocket. Today, people still work hard, but their aim, I'm afraid, is to improve our standard of living. I'm not against a decent standard of living, but it shouldn't become our sole aim in life. That is tasteless. This is what worries me: Do we have to remain paupers in order to maintain the kibbutz spirit? We must find a way out of this dilemma.

Now, fifty years after the formation of the three kibbutz movements and their different ideologies, I think it's time to ask which proved to be right.

Shulamit interrupts: "They were all right. A thousand flowers can bloom."

I think that each one of the approaches pointed to an important and necessary component, yet history has proved that some of the principles contradicted each other. . . . Take, for example, our size: Size is a condition of power. Our large size is what allows us to keep our own school, which is a sign of our social power. Our size provides for greater economic, social, and cultural power; it enables development in many areas that a smaller community couldn't afford. But friendship, or what we used to call intimacy, can't coexist with this size, nor can selectivity. In other words, the problem is to find a harmonious combination of the various elements. I don't regret our choice of the Kibbutz Hameuchad ideology, because I'm in favor of a powerful system. Yet I would like to find a way to introduce the close friendships of the "small group" and the political-ideological unity of the "organic group" into our system. We ought to find a way to blend the advantages of these three types of communities about which we argued so much in our youth.

S A U L *(age 61)*

Saul is considered the farmer of Makom, almost inseparable from the big tractors and other agricultural machines cultivating the fields of the kibbutz. Saul's wife, Amalia, appears in "Absorption."

I joined the kibbutz in 1935, at exactly the same time it was arriving here from the Fountain. How did I join? That's a long story. My parents immigrated to Israel from Poland in 1919. I was a baby then, and today I don't remember anything of Europe. By now I consider myself a Sabra.* My native tongue is Hebrew; I learned Yiddish in Makom.

After emigrating from Europe, all my family settled in Jerusalem, in one neighborhood, Kerem. One branch of the family came to Jerusalem from Plonsk, before World War I. They had some property and opened a button factory, producing buttons made of seashells. The shells were brought from Aqaba, the Red Sea port—nobody even dreamed about Eilat at that time. Gradually, the rest of the family made *aliya* and settled around this factory in Jerusalem. Most of the men worked on public-works projects: some on the railroads or in well-drilling, but mostly in road construction. They wandered around the country with the other workers. I remember when they were building the road to the Dead Sea and my uncle worked with that team. And my father participated in the construction of the old Mozza Bridge on the way to Jerusalem.

Later, my father accepted another job in a new neighborhood that was built in Jerusalem—Beit Hakerem. They had just started building the area; it was still a barren mountain far away from town. Now it is right in the center of town, but then—one had to walk three kilometers to get there. It's funny to think about now.

Father was a jack-of-all-trades. He did guard duty, repairs, jobs with the water supply—all those things. My mother and I moved out to Beit Hakerem with him and lived in a tent. I remember when my sister was born, and they brought her home from the Hadassah Hospital to that wide-open tent. Imagine, in Jerusalem, with its winds, storms, and cold. It even snowed, I remember.

But we lived there, and I was in the first class of the new Beit Hakerem school. I had wonderful teachers, many of whom are today distinguished scholars. That's where I joined the Scouts, when I was in the third grade. At the beginning there was a whole troop coming from my neighborhood, though the distance to town kept many away. I continued Scouting, however, and I stayed with them when I went to high school too.

In the Scouts I met an older member who was moving to Ben Shemen as a teacher, and organizing a group of children to join an agricultural school. I was fourteen at the time and decided to join this group, but I didn't announce it to my parents immediately. Actually, from a very young age, I had wanted to study agriculture, to be a farmer. I really don't know why. If I look for the roots of this desire, I think they were developed by a teacher in Beit Hakerem who exerted a great influence on me, instilling me with an unusual love for nature. I will always remember him for that. In fact, my father, although now a city dweller,

*Literally, "cactus fruit"; a nickname for a native of Israel.

had managed a farm in Poland for a Polish landowner. I had also heard stories from him about his family, who had owned and had maintained a big livery stable.

When I told my parents about my decision, they weren't very enthusiastic. They wanted me to finish high school in Jerusalem; it hadn't occurred to them that I'd become a farmer. I had a talent for drawing; they thought, perhaps, I'd be a painter. Now my son paints as well—look at all these pictures.

To make a long story short, I studied at the agricultural school of Ben Shemen for two years, earned my diploma, and then stayed on as a journeyman, specializing in nursery growing and citriculture, planning and hoping to work in this profession in the future.

While I was at school, the Scout troop to which I belonged joined another Zionist youth movement called Machanot Haolim, formerly the Chugim movement. This was the movement that had previously started Makom. Together with a friend at school, I started corresponding with an acquaintance at the kibbutz, and he invited us to join. We asked permission, received a positive answer, and have been here ever since.

I remember our arrival at the place. We took the train and then had to walk some distance. I arrived on a Thursday night, and by Saturday night I was already enrolled for guard duty. When we joined, the group was in transit, moving from the Fountain to an old, abandoned Arab village, a little to the west of our present location. When the village was destroyed, one building remained—a big house which we used as a barn. All the cows were kept in this house, and on the roof we built a wooden hut, where we lived: two or three shepherds, two or three cowmen, and two men who worked in well-drilling nearby. We shared the guard duty among us. And this was all there was. This was my beginning at Makom. The kibbutz had about two hundred members at the time, but there was a tremendous turnover. People used to come and go all the time—new *aliyot,* from Germany and elsewhere—and most of them stayed just for very short periods.

I was a watchman and a wagon driver. At that time, tractors were a very rare commodity. We had just one—now we have about forty. [*Saul laughs.*] So, we had one tractor—and it was a small one, too—and we used to work it twenty-four hours a day. Still, for much of the field work we used horses—for plowing and for cultivating among other things—and that was my job.

During this period, I worked outside the kibbutz for a year with the salt company in Atlit. Every second Saturday I used to come home to the kibbutz. Things were good in Atlit, but we worked very hard. We were about thirty men there, sometimes even sixty. The group was divided into two units: one of farm workers, those of us who had some agricultural background, and another group, who worked in the salt factory. All summer, I worked in the vineyard, and when winter arrived I joined the salt group.

I spent a whole year there, It was '36, I think. The reason that a large group of us had to work outside of the kibbutz was that we didn't own enough land to provide all the men with work. We were quite poor during those first years, and, if some members hadn't provided the kibbutz with income from their work outside, we wouldn't have had enough to eat, and certainly not enough to build the kibbutz.

After a year in Atlit, I got married, and I didn't want to leave the kibbutz and work outside anymore. One year was enough for me. So I came back to Makom. At first we lived in tents, and later in small huts. I worked briefly drilling wells, and then returned to agriculture, working at first with cattle and then with tractors. That's what I'm doing to this very day.

During those first years, I didn't feel that our life was difficult. But now, thinking back, I realize it was terribly hard, terribly cruel. [*He speaks with emphasis.*] For example—when new people came. It's impossible to fathom the difficulty of the initial adjustment they were required to make. I have no words to describe it. You just came—and you found yourself at storehouse A. This was a clothes storehouse to which you submitted everything you owned—every single thing, from shoelaces to whatever, and on Friday you came in and received from the stock clerk a package of clothing for the coming week—whatever she had arranged for you. This was storehouse A, a total commune. So imagine people coming from abroad, from wealthy homes, in expensive suits and dresses, and within a day everything was taken away from them. This used to shock these people, it would really break them. Even I, who knew what to expect, remember this feeling. When I joined the kibbutz my parents, who worried about me, supplied me with all the best. They bought me a new leather coat, and on my back I carried a new bed and mattress, walking all the way from the train station, several kilometers away. A day later— not a sign of it was left for me. [*Saul says this laughing.*] Everything became common property—out of which you get what you are assigned. I, who was prepared for this, reacted in a relatively moderate way; but the new-comers who arrived from abroad—it broke them down, ruined them. It depressed them terribly, storehouse A.

As the years went by, people saw there was no sense in this system. Since everybody needed their own individual sizes, getting a standard package really did not answer one's needs. All that had mattered before was that everyone should get one pair of pants, one shirt, etc.—that everybody should get the same things.

The situation with housing wasn't any better. At first we lived in tents —which I was accustomed to from years before in my parents' home, when we had lived in a tent in Jerusalem. Here, however, I didn't even get a bed for myself—I had to share one with another guy for a while after

I arrived. Then, during the summer, we built little tree houses in the trees, which was fun. When we moved to our present location, we, as a married couple, had a tent first and a little hut later. The hut was 4-by-6 meters and shared by three couples; it consisted of three tiny rooms with thin partitions between them. The width of these rooms was not more than this sofa here—a door, a window—that's all. No restrooms, no showers—nothing. The distance to the showers—don't ask me what it was, it was quite a walk. It was really hard, but I didn't feel it then.

We had a malaria epidemic at the kibbutz, which was awful. I don't remember any swamps in the area, but we definitely had malaria, even without swamps. Only about one or two of the men were spared this disease. I caught it, too. We all suffered—malaria is a disease that completely drains you. So we started sleeping under mosquito nets—imagine, in this heat! To sleep under a net was a nightmare. At night I felt as if I would suffocate, and I couldn't escape.

To complete the picture: the food. I can't even start to describe it for you. But we didn't mind then. We had lots of bread, oil, and sugar. Half an egg sometimes. We used to get jam in a tablespoon, smoothed out by a knife so that you wouldn't get too much. Butter appeared rarely. A piece of cake or an egg was a whole day's ration for a working man, a man doing hard physical work outside. It's no wonder that people ran away so frequently. Work was terribly hard, too. Many members worked at the quarry. Where do you find a Jew doing such work? I worked in the fields most of the time, which wasn't easy either.

Women, too, had it hard then. Taking care of children was a very difficult job. I didn't understand it then. I thought: Women! What kind of work can they do!? But now, when I hear our young women complaining about their working conditions, I keep thinking about the young women of my time. They had neither warm water nor heating in the homes. And, worst of all, there were no roads or paved paths within the kibbutz. If you have never experienced rain here, you cannot imagine it. You sink and get stuck in the mud up to here [*Saul points to his thigh*]. You really cannot walk—and we had just one pair of shoes. Our children grew up on our shoulders. My first daughter, who is forty now, used to sit on my shoulders all the time until she was eight years old. I carried her to the family room, to the children's home, to school, back and forth all the time because she didn't have the right kind of shoes or boots, nor a warm coat. Now, there is no problem. You can wear sandals in the winter and walk on the paved path, and it's fine.

What kept us going (those of us who did) during that period? I really cannot tell you. I personally never wanted to leave; I don't know exactly why. I remember how heartbroken my parents were whenever they visited me here. They said: "What keeps you here? What do you have here —no food, no housing, nothing. Our hearts bleed to see you here." They were devastated by our poverty. But I didn't feel badly, and I never felt tempted to follow my parents back to Jerusalem.

Maybe I kept going because of the conviction that we were building something out of nothing. And this is, apparently, something of great significance. The constant planning of what is to come, the ecstasy of the beginning! I remember when the first buildings, such as our first barn, were erected here. We dug the ground, which is all basalt rocks and heavy soil, with our bare hands. Now we have all the necessary equipment. Yet all of us competed with great enthusiasm to see who would be the first one to reach the basalt, to get deep down to the foundation. This gave us tremendous satisfaction.

This stubborn will to build the kibbutz, to settle the area, is what inspired us. And for me, my work kept me going, too. I always loved working in the fields; to this very day I derive a great deal of satisfaction from it. I just now came back from our experimental field where we reaped a new strain of wheat, and the positive results have given me a boost that will last for a long time to come. We always try to learn; we use new methods, try new kinds of seeds.

It's true, I still sit on the tractor for eight or nine hours; someone might say it's dull, but for me there is never a dull moment. I understand the importance of what I'm doing and I know what will follow. I plan ahead and take all the right precautions; I know that I'll get results. Some years are better and some are worse; there are many factors involved. Working the earth is not just a profession for me—it is an ideal as well. To learn to drive a tractor takes about three days—that's not the main thing. The agricultural problem in its totality is something you never cease to learn. And my aim is very simple: to achieve the best results, which, given the conditions of Makom, is not easy. And from time to time I think about my work in terms of Zionism as well.

For example, when I see the *moshavim* in the area leasing the land to Arabs—it really kills me. First we took these fields from them—we took them in war and many kibbutz members were killed in those battles, mind you. Now these very same Arabs are employed as hired workers in our own fields! I myself have heard Arab day laborers saying: "This used to be our land, and now we come to cultivate it as hired labor." This is very serious. I am strictly against hired labor in the kibbutz, and we have never hired anyone to help out in agricultural work. In our metal factory we have several hired people. I don't like it, but it's very unfair to fire them now, after so many years. We all regret it. Because, if we become employers, the kibbutz becomes an employer, our children become employers, and they will be like employers all over the world in spite of all our education. I have no doubt about it. And this will be the end of the kibbutz.

But let me go back to the Arabs. As I keep saying, my main job in the kibbutz was always grain crops but I also had a second concern, and that is security. I was never a general or a colonel—my concern with security is deeply rooted in my work. To understand that, we have to go back to the history of this place. Our fields, the way you see them today, all together, huge blocks, kilometers of land—in the old times it was different. Herbert Samuel, the British High Commissioner, distributed the land to the Arab inhabitants in the villages of this valley. He divided the land into strips, which is something unheard of: long strips of 1 kilometer by 6 meters. This prevented cultivating these fields by tractors —even a horse-drawn plough could hardly remain within the limits. What we got at first were 3500 *dunams,* * land which had belonged to the abandoned Arab village which was all in one piece. In addition, a Jewish company started buying land from the Arab owners, as much as they could buy—some owners sold the land, and some did not. They bought it all, in strips, Arab, Jewish, Arab, etc. Later it was acquired by the Jewish National Fund and given to us to cultivate. So this was our land, Jewish, Arab, Jewish, Arab, etc.

This started a series of continuous fights. The Arabs used to graze their livestock on our cultivated fields. Some of our fields ran right by the Arab homes, and at night they would let their cattle out and destroy everything. So there was terrible fighting between us, and these constant quarrels were part of our daily reality until the War of Independence. We constantly had to guard the land, day and night, so that it would not be stolen and destroyed. This was part of my job.

I knew intimately all the Arabs of the neighboring villages. I spoke Arabic freely with them, and I fought with them all. They respected me —in fact, some years after the War of Independence somebody told me he heard a song played for me with regards from an Arab in Irbid** on the Jordanian radio station. I myself didn't hear it. We had good relations. But, for me—with Arabs it was always respect mingled with suspicion. In the daytime we were friends, while at night they would steal from me. Even during the daytime, if you left your food in the field and walked away, it would, somehow, vanish right away. But especially nights—all nights, Saturdays and holidays, in heat or rain, we were on guard or waiting in ambush for thieves. For me this was a second occupation for a long time. Every two or three days, local quarrels would develop. Some of them were extremely violent, involving hundreds of Arabs against tens of Jews. Mostly these fights started because of Arabs trespassing on our fields. Also, when new land was bought from an Arab, it was done secretly. But, eventually, we had to come and plow the field, so we used to come with a tractor at night, to plow. When they detected us, they would attack us, and a fight would develop. Naturally, people were hurt; the Arabs used knives and stones, and I remember some serious head wounds. Nobody from our kibbutz was killed on our land then, but

* 1,000 square meters.
** A city in Jordan.

several members of neighboring kibbutzim were. Frequently, the three kibbutzim of the area were involved against all the Arab villages, and the fighting lasted from morning to night.

When the War of Independence reached our area, all this stopped in one single night. I remember it vividly. It all happened during the night between the fourteenth and the fifteenth of May, 1948.* On the fifteenth of May I was reaping our fields near the Arab homes. I was alone on the combine, and a whole company of thirty men were watching over me with two machine guns and rifles. They were spread out somewhat farther away, keeping guard, while I worked the field. Suddenly I saw an Arab, the *mukhtar*** of the village, leaving his house and heading towards me, making a big detour so that he wouldn't be seen from the village. I signaled to the men to leave him alone. I knew he had something to tell me. He approached my combine from behind and mounted it, and offered to sell me his crops. That's when I realized that the end of the struggle was near.

Just the day before, just one single day, the same Arabs were so sure of their victory, so sure that they would soon be looting our property, that one of them said to me: "See the Arab-Iraqui army up there?" They were really closeby. On the hills, I could see 300–400 men. "Their commander has maps of Tel Aviv." That's what he told me on May fourteenth. Of course, that's not how it turned out.

And, after all this, after the Six Day War, when the borders were opened, some came here to visit. It was interesting to see them, to talk with them. They had made tremendous personal progress in Irbid. They opened stores—this is their special talent. And, most interesting, their sons, the little ones whom I remember as babies, have all gone to college. They studied in East Germany, Yugoslavia, all over Eastern Europe, and today they are physicians, engineers. And all this, from a tiny village which hardly had a primary school. This development stems, perhaps, from their forced escape from here. Sometimes I tell my men: "Look what became of our children, they are farmers and laborers—while *they*, they are all doctors!"

S H L O M O *(age 62)*

My conversation with Shlomo took place in the Holiday Archives, a wooden hut packed with books, posters, and files of material concerning the Jewish holidays and the manner of their celebration in Makom. This institute, which is the creation of Shlomo, is beautifully organized and pleasant to work in. Shlomo and another member of the kibbutz, Moshe, work here full-time, serving the cultural and educational programs of many kibbutzim.

*This is the same day on which Israeli independence was declared.
**The local leader of an Arab village.

Shlomo is the oldest teacher in Makom. He was the teacher of one of the first school classes, and educated many of the young adults who presently live in the kibbutz. In our conversation I asked him to concentrate on his role as an educator and his memories of teaching in the old days. (Shlomo's daughter, Nima, appears in "Individualists.")

Shlomo prepared himself carefully for our interview, wrote down notes and used them in our long conversation.

I was born in 1916 in Russia. In 1921, my father, a physician, was murdered while serving as a military doctor. After my father's death my mother, a nurse, immigrated to Palestine. At the age of six, I was reborn in Israel and became a native in all respects. When I was eight, my mother brought me to Mount Carmel in Haifa, at that time nearly void of houses and people. We lived in an old Arab house. The scent of pine trees, the splendor of the mountains, the narrowness of unkept country roads, a giant red sun descending into a blue lagoon—that was the Carmel as an unspoiled forest, uninhabited, and deeply engraved in me as my personal and unforgetable Israel.

I went to an excellent high school in Haifa. My mother wanted me to continue my studies so that I might become a physician like my father, but I joined a pioneering youth movement, and saw my personal actualization in settling the land on a kibbutz. I understand self-actualization to mean: Ask yourself what the country needs at the moment, or what the most important thing you could do for your people is—and when you find the answer, get up and do it. This is also the finest translation of the concept of *mitzvah* * in Judaism—to take upon oneself, out of one's own free choice, the burden of duty. Not for an hour or as a solitary effort, but as a life-style and for a lifetime. The year was then 1935–36, marking the beginning of the Arab riots; homes and crops were burned, Jewish settlements were attacked, and the British had closed the borders to Jewish immigrants—it was a rough period. I felt the kibbutz was where I could contribute most. I explained this to my mother and she understood and blessed my decision.

If you ask me whether or not I regret the way of life I have chosen, my clear and sincere answer would be that, were I able to start my life all over again, I would take the same path. I have been here from the time of the first tent and the first tree. This heavy red soil with its basalt rocks was shadowless. During the long hot summer, your own shadow was the only existent shade. Barren land, simple huts and tents, and the joy of creation. The tents were round, conelike; inside were two or three iron beds, and mattresses stuffed with corn leaves which were cultivated in our fields. The closet was a vegetable box, two shelves for our one pair of pants and single shirt—a set of clothes for work and a set for rest. (All

---

*A religious command or good deed.

clothes were issued from the common store then.) A Van Gogh print decorated the central pole. An oil lamp, a vase, and an Arabian clay jug to hold our water supply were among the meager belongings which were later moved from tents to huts and finally, much later, to real rooms. Old sacks embroidered by our women were turned into bed covers and curtains. Working shoes were left outside the tent or concealed under the bed, and, during tense times, a rifle was hidden under the mattress.

In summer, the tent flaps were constantly turned up to allow the wind to blow in and cool our sweating bodies. During our midday break we used to supplement this cooling system by pouring water on the wooden floor and lying on the boards to take a nap. Living in tents was even harder in winter when rain and storms would tear the ropes of the tents, frequently causing the tents to fall, wet, on their sleeping inhabitants. As an experienced scoutmaster, I took it on myself to repair the tents every morning, using a shoemaker's sewing machine, and adding patch upon patch until I could right the tent again.

The word passed around that Bracha and I were moving into a family tent, and our marriage was joyfully celebrated by the whole community as the first wedding in the new dining room. The bell sounded, friends brought wine bottles from their tents, and the women made wildflower bouquets. My own wedding present to my bride was a new tent, with windows opening to the sky, which I sewed by myself and erected at somewhat of a distance from the common camp. This is where we lived for ten good years, where our two children were born. When the War of Independence broke out, I used to sit in the tent listening to newscasts in Russian and Arabic, as well as to those of our illegal Hagana network. From this information, I issued an update news bulletin three times a day. The same tent served as a small zoo; under the bed, I collected, in various boxes, lizards and snakes, scorpions and all sorts of bugs which I used for teaching about our environment.

My educational work always centered around two themes: love of the land—acquired by walking and feeling it—and the study of the Bible. These two elements characterize many of us Israelis who were educated by the Machanot Haolim Youth Movement. In long outings with my fellow students we learned to love the landscape, near and far, listening together to the whisper of nature and to the echoes of our past. Our Bible studies were attempts to bridge the gap between the distant past and the meaningful present. Biblical scenery was everywhere before our eyes and the Bible became alive in the hearts of our children. We would study the books of Judges and Kings in the fields and mountains described in these books. With Bibles in our camping gear, we went forth to explore where Gideon rested under the oak tree in the village of Ofra. From there we scouted our way to the spring of Harod, and visualized the events described in Judges 6:7. The Gilboa Mountain was our neighbor, and we knew that on it fell King Saul and his son, Jonathan—and members of our kibbutz in the War of Independence. As we ascended the mountain, we understood David's curse: Mount Gilboa—be without rain or dew. The ancient heroes became our living models.

Another of our educational goals was to teach our children to know and respect the Arab inhabitants of our land. I myself grew up among Arabs in Haifa and spoke Arabic fluently. As an educator, I tried to cultivate every contact of educational value with the neighboring Arab communities. Visits to Arab villages became a tradition, as did hosting Arab children in our kibbutz.

In 1970, I contacted the new principal of a neighboring Arab school in hopes of continuing our exchange program. One winter night, this principal knocked on my door and by way of apology explained that the current political climate was no longer conducive to the continuation of our previously successful exchange programs. Such visits, he clearly intimated, would cause him, as well as his family and village, discomfort. It was a time of tension and no longer like the past. I thanked him for his frankness. But, in spite of the fact that actual contacts are severely limited now, I am convinced that the seeds of respect that we planted in educating the second and third generations will be fruitful in terms of better understanding between the two nations.

I believe that the kibbutz is a unique Jewish creation, perhaps more so than any of the former Jewish creations. We, in Makom, like most other kibbutzim, are sitting on land which belongs to the Jewish National Fund, land of the people. We don't own it, nor does it belong to any rich noblemen. We cannot buy or sell the land, or decide to change the use of the spot: to convert it into a hotel or a business enterprise of some sort. People returned to this country, poverty-stricken, without a government or any national organization, with the sole idea of settling the land. They were not to become merchants or bankers as their ancestors had been. The land was given to these pioneers by the nation. Paradoxically, the vast majority of the nation was spread all over the globe, putting coins in blue-and-white tins to buy soil from the Arabs. So, whenever a kibbutz was started, it received its most valuable gift from the nation: the soil.

This historical process is in complete accordance with the Jewish conception that neither man nor the land can be subjugated: They are forever free; they cannot become private property since they belong to God. This principle, which finds its expression in the Biblical law of the sabbatical year and the Jubilee, has found its finest realization in the fact that a kibbutz doesn't own its land, but cultivates it as a gift from the nation.

These principles have gradually become clear to me during my long years in the field of education. Since its inception, our school has educated more than twenty-five classes, about six hundred students, 30 percent of them children whom we absorbed through the Youth Aliya as well as children of broken homes, children from Syria, Russia, Latin America, all corners of the earth. Many of these children have stayed on at Makom, married our children, and enriched our community. Our second generation has contributed its own tremendous strength to our society. It has given us our greatest gift: the third generation of our kibbutz, about three hundred fifty sons and daughters. Makom is known for its large number of offspring, and I see in this a sign of optimism and security. The second-generation families are far larger than our own, and having four or five children is fairly common now. We have our own local school; we're perhaps the only kibbutz that still operates its own elementary and high schools, all run by local teachers and administrators. This school is the center of our community and I hope it remains this way for a long time to come. My wife and I have two children, a son and a daughter. Both married other kibbutz children, and presently I am a grandfather to six grandchildren, all of whom are living here in the kibbutz.

I think that the social structure of a three-generation society living together has added a sense of stability to our life here. Three generations living so close together from birth to death is something rare in most societies, and I think it's the healthiest phenomenon for a family. A child needs the closeness of his extended family, and grandparents want to remain close to their younger offspring. For me personally, I think that this alone would make the course of my whole life worthwhile—the fact that I live in the same community with my children and grandchildren.

R A C H E L *(age 60)*

Rachel has a deeply lined face and the agility of a fifteen-year-old. In the Jubilee celebration, I saw her dancing barefoot on the stage. Her story could be titled "The Life Cycle of a Kibbuutznik Woman." At nineteen, Rachel joined the relatively new kibbutz of Makom; at sixty, she is joining forces with a group of youngsters who are starting a kibbutz of their own in the Golan Heights. In between, we hear about a "career" of a person who, starting from the laundry and kitchen, through many years teaching in a nursery school, became an expert in organization development, providing counseling for entire communities.

I'm going to be sixty this year, and I came to the kibbutz when I was nineteen years old, so I've been at Makom for forty-one years. I came from Haifa, from the Chugim Movement, and I joined the kibbutz when it was about eight years old, just when it moved to its present location.

My first job was at the laundry. The laundry was a tin hut that didn't even have a sewage system for the water we used. There were some large boilers heated by wood; the clothes were scrubbed by hand, using special wooden boards, and then were put to rinse in another tank. To take them out, we had to turn over this rinsing tank, with all its contents. The water spilled all over the floor and we just stood there, knee deep in water. Sometimes we used to stand on wooden boxes so as not to be soaking wet. There were no boots at that time. Then we would carry a container with the clean laundry to hang on lines outside. All this carrying and turning was a tremendous physical effort. When I came I was the only woman who was not pregnant in the laundry, so I was put in charge, and naturally I carried heavier loads than anyone else. Not to mention the fact that I didn't know the first thing about cleaning and washing. Outside the laundry it was incredibly muddy. If we dropped a clean garment, it immediately turned black with mud, and we never knew how to bleach it again. It was some job. It's hard to imagine today.

I lost a lot of weight because of the hard work, and my mother, who often came to visit, couldn't stand watching my state of health deteriorate. So, on advice of an older member from the health committee, she decided to take me home for a week to recover my strength. Two days later I received a letter from the secretary calling me to come right back. If I really needed convalescence, and perhaps I did, it shouldn't be at my parents' expense!

It was a big issue in those days, the question of whether to accept gifts from parents, and a real attempt was made to enforce the rule against it. I came back and I was reprimanded in the assembly. I stood there, and heard the reproach, and I felt like a baby, although nobody was more than eight or ten years older than me. I almost left after that, I felt so bad. It was pretty common, at that time, to reprimand people in public for any minor deviation. Today it's very rare, it hardly ever happens.

I remember another case, before. When my mother came and after she saw my working conditions, she sent me a pair of rubber boots as a present. Although the boots belonged to the whole kibbutz, that too wasn't allowed, because we shouldn't live off gifts from our parents. But although there was a norm of not accepting gifts, I remember several exceptions to the rule. My parents visited here a lot and became very friendly with the kibbutz members. When my son was born, my parents donated the first electric water boiler for the infants' home. Also, the road to the kibbutz was paved using money contributed by parents. I'm not sure whether or not those were the only cases.

Discipline was much stricter at that time. I hadn't really wanted to join Makom, because my *hachshara* group went and started another kibbutz of the Chugim Movement. But things like who goes where were decided by the movement then, and not by the individual. When the big shots came to visit us in the *hachshara*, they pointed their finger at me and said: "She goes to Makom." Why? Probably because they liked me. I was a pretty girl. One of those two visitors actually became my husband several years later. But they had a good cover story—that my father owned a textile factory, as did Makom at the time, and I probably knew the job and could contribute my expertise. In fact, I had hardly worked in this factory, which was closed down anyway pretty soon afterwards.

I kept hoping to join the other kibbutz, and for two years I didn't apply for membership in Makom—which was very uncommon at the time. Whenever I wanted to join a company working outside of the kibbutz, my request was turned down. "You won't return to Makom," they said. This made me feel popular and much wanted here, probably because I was young and nice, but also because I am a good worker. A little later I lost my interest in the other kibbutz. I married Y., who had been one of the founders of Makom, and I settled down here.

The main point I'm trying to make is how things were determined for us. The collective decision obliged the individual in many cases. The norm was that one must unconditionally accept the decision of the collective. People adjusted to this norm somehow, it's true. Yet many left because of this. There were some who tried to stay and rebel, but not many. We used to have very frequent assembly meetings to try and solve the problems caused by this strict discipline.

I remember, for example, in the early 1940s, when people were recruited by the Palmach. Many young men wanted to volunteer and go, and they rebelled against the kibbutz's decision which prevented them from leaving. It was impossible, of course, to empty the kibbutz of all the men, and staying in the kibbutz was important for the country as well. But every young man in town was free to join the Palmach, if he wanted, and here our men felt strongly restrained. I remember many assembly meetings on this subject, and I vaguely recall people who decided to leave the kibbutz and volunteer for the Palmach, but I'm not quite sure of the facts after all these years.

Look, a few weeks ago I was working with a young man who was born here. Suddenly, he asked me: "Tell me, all those years ago, did you imagine the kibbutz the way it is today?" We were doing a night shift, it was very quiet, and I really felt like thinking about his question thoroughly, not just answering it offhand. Finally, I said: "You know what? I believe we didn't think the kibbutz would exist at all." He was amazed. "You? The dreamers, the idealists, the founders!?" But I really think so, now that I look back, with all the so-called wisdom of my years. Because in those early days, for every minor deviation we had a formula reaction: "This will destroy the kibbutz." If complete discipline weren't enforced—it would destroy the kibbutz. If we built private bathrooms near the rooms, it would destroy the kibbutz. No, I'm not joking, this was really an argument then. "A private shower will destroy the kibbutz"; I remember its being stated in exactly these words. And later, an electric kettle in the room would destroy the kibbutz, and a radio in the room would certainly do so, too.

I remember how I resented this argument, since I didn't see the kibbutz as such a fragile institution. But it was the motto of our life then. Today one doesn't hear this claim anymore.

I remember the case with the dining hall. My second job at the kibbutz was in the kitchen, where I worked with Na'ama. This wasn't easier than the laundry. The dining hall had wooden floors and we used to scrub them with such vigor that the wood grew thinner by the day. Most difficult was serving the food. When the first gong sounded it meant that the meal was ready. People came in at their leisure, and sat wherever they pleased. I, near the kitchen, had to watch out for whoever had just sat down, and run with his or her tray of food. I ran all the time. Later I made a decision that people have to take their seats in a systematic fashion—starting from the corner table, filling all the seats around it, then starting at the next table, etc. This made our food serving somewhat more efficient. It was considered a radical change.

I tried to install self-service meals in our dining room. This wasn't a decision we could make by ourselves in the kibbutz, so I went "upstairs," to the administration of the kibbutz movement, and I started to fight for the self-service system. The reaction I found, the opposition, was our familiar motto: "It will destroy the kibbutz." Why? Because there wouldn't be a home atmosphere anymore. That was the argument; we had to have a home atmosphere in the dining hall, and this atmosphere is based on being served by somebody who hates his or her job. . . . I argued that I don't feel at home at a restaurant, where I'm served, and on the other hand, I feel very much at home in my room, where I take my own portion. All I asked for was a small loan to try the system out. But I was turned down by a decision made in the movement that the self-service system was against the kibbutz way of life. Someone had even said to me, "Hair will grow on my palm, before the kibbutz will switch to self-service." Well, several years later, we did switch to self-service. It was started by the Ichud, and we in Makom were among the last ones to install it. Anyway, by now it's pretty clear the kibbutz wasn't destroyed by this innovation either.

Now that I look back at these past events, I think that they were the manifestation of a type of defense mechanism, without which we couldn't survive. We had to erect so many restrictions in order that we shouldn't be—God forbid—restricted. This strict discipline gave us a strong feeling of togetherness, a deep group solidarity. But I always fought against it. I rebelled. There were others who also saw things my way. Today this rule of discipline is much weaker; it's not as pronounced in our life. If someone is elected for a function, for example, and he truly doesn't want to accept the nomination, there is no way he could be forced to do it against his will.

As a worker I was always satisfied. I developed severe back troubles when I was still pretty young—perhaps as a result of all the loading and carrying I did in the laundry and the kitchen in those early years. So I had to switch to teaching. Early education was my field. (Actually there is a children's book telling about me and my class, written by Shulamit, and using my real name, even.) I loved the creativity involved in this work, and I adored the children. But I think I could find something interesting and challenging in every kind of work. This was certainly true of the kitchen work—I love cooking. Even as a sanitary worker, when I had to clean, for six months, our common showers and bathrooms, I got some pleasure out of my day's work and I found something to innovate there as well. You see, it's part of the kibbutz ideology that all work is good and respectable. For me it isn't just an abstract idea—it's really how I feel about my work, whether it was dishwashing, bathroom cleaning, or teaching.

I worked as a teacher for many years, until my husband died twelve years ago. Later I was elected secretary—something that was extremely difficult for me. While I was secretary I heard about the first O.D.* courses offered to kibbutz members who held different public roles in their kibbutzim.

The program involved theoretical studies and field experience in conducting groups and workshops. Personally I didn't think it would suit me at all. But some people, who knew me well, convinced me to go and I'm now very much into that field. For example, two of us who graduated from that program have been invited as consultants to a kibbutz that suffers from a large percentage of dropouts and is, generally, in a state of crisis. Our aim was to reinforce their self-image, and to try to identify the sources of their problems. We did a survey of the whole community, we ran different groups with the members and we felt some improvement there. Of course, it's difficult to assess the success of such a project, at least so soon afterwards.

I'm no longer as involved with this kibbutz as I had been, since I have joined Ginat, and this is probably my last story for tonight. Ginat is a young kibbutz in the Golan Heights, which we have undertaken to develop and support. It's a complicated story. The former secretariat had actually initiated the whole thing. They saw it as an important mission, a pioneering deed, which was all well and good. So they went to the secretariat of the Kibbutz Hameuchad and suggested that they adopt a young kibbutz, and they managed to pass this beautiful decision in our assembly. The next step was, naturally, to mobilize people to help settle this kibbutz. Usually new kibbutzim are started by *garinim*** which are formed by the various youth movements in the country. But we all know that the stream of young settlers has been slowly drying up, so besides depending on *garinim* from the Scouts movement, a new method of recruitment was invented, called *"chavura."*† The *chavura* is made up of young people who, after their Army service, endeavor to start a new

*Organization Development.

**Plural of *garin.* Literally, "kernel"; a group of people brought together for the purpose of settlement.

†Hebrew for "group."

kibbutz. They frequently come from a background which is very remote from the kibbutz and its ideals; they represent a population different from that of the youth movement. Makom was among the first kibbutzim which took part in this program. We took it upon ourselves to host the first *chavura,* which was to settle in Ginat, and to educate them for the kibbutz way of life, and all that. You need good people to do the job, and I wasn't sure that we had the manpower to carry it out. We have the right people, of course, but they are all heavily burdened with work as it is, without any new obligations. At the assembly, I raised the question: "Who will man the necessary positions?" The answer was that there were people for the job. I thought they didn't want to mention names, perhaps, and I accepted this vague answer.

Well, to make a long story short, there is a popular joke about a soldier who gives his friend a rock, saying: "Hold on to this for a moment," and walks off forever. The same thing happened here. The former secretaries finished their term, and the person who was behind the whole project went to Tel Aviv to work for the Movement. A new secretariat was elected, and I was among its members, and it was quite ambivalent about Ginat. But the deed had already been done. The first youngsters had already settled in Ginat and now they desperately needed adults, more mature people, to accompany the new kibbutz both for economic and social leadership, and for consultation. To state it in simple terms, we wronged these young settlers, since we could not find the proper people who would be willing to go up there, join Ginat at least temporarily, and serve in the necessary functions. Not that we neglected the thing and didn't search for candidates. The opposite is true. In every meeting of the secretariat, Ginat was on the agenda. Finally, the social secretary of Makom volunteered to move up there himself. This was ridiculous, since he had such a central position right here. I, on the other hand, as the secretary in charge of services, felt that I could be replaced more easily, so I said I'd join Ginat. Nobody pointed his finger at me saying: "You go." I personally felt the situation was unbearable—but still I don't think I would have volunteered if I hadn't been in the secretariat.

So now I am defined as the social companion of Ginat. I'm there all week and I return to Makom on most Fridays for Shabbat. In the mornings I work at my hobby: I cook. It's pleasant to cook for forty people instead of a thousand. I don't even cook, really—the girls do that. But I'm in the kitchen, just in case. In the afternoons I take driving lessons as a "reward" for Ginat. I drive the lovely roads of the Golan and I enjoy myself immensely. All day long, the secretary and other people approach me freely to talk to me about various matters, but my formal working day starts at 6.00 P.M. I sit in on all the committees, in the assembly meetings, in the secretariat, and I do what I can. There's one evening in the week, Tuesday, which we've named "an evening with Rachel." It's an informal conversation, the only occasion that these people have to talk publicly about what is bothering them, what they want. I teach them to listen and respect each other, while they have the opportunity to get to know each other more intimately. It's an open group operation; whoever wants to come, comes. My professional training and experience in O.D. help me a great deal in performing my present role.

I have good feelings about what I'm doing. I'm the only adult living in Ginat right now. We have many problems there, as in every new kibbutz. The primary problem is to find meaningful work for each person. Then we have to go through the first stages when, due to their different schedules of army service, there are currently many more girls than boys. I do hope that a serious leadership will develop there. Sometimes I'm quite pessimistic and I tell myself, "If only there were five serious people there!" But they are children, you see.

I don't see myself as a great pioneer in doing this job. It was simply . . . that out of the things I saw, I simply couldn't stand the position Makom was in vis-à-vis Ginat. I simply wanted to save our honor. Furthermore, I personally can't bear a situation when people implore you for help and you don't react. These were my two motives. It's not pioneering, it's more like humaneness, that's the way I see it. Luckily, I can find satisfaction and pleasure in everything I do.

N A' A M A *(age 63)*

Na'ama is a grandmother, but she looks much younger than that: tall, with dark hair and a pale complexion. In her behavior, in her manner of speech, in the way she walks on the path, alone or in company, she impressed me as someone distinguished, an aristocrat of sorts.

On my first visit to the kibbutz, she invited me over to her room for a friendly conversation. She was easy to talk to, smiling, and very positive in her outlook. As I knew that she had lost her beloved husband in an accident fourteen years ago, I was prepared for some signs of loneliness, bitterness, or self-pity. Of these I did not find a single trace. I emerged from the meeting overcome with admiration for her, admiration I also felt for her late husband, Oded, about whom I had read before. He had been one of the chief operators of the Ha'apala* in Europe, and, as his letters showed, a most sensitive husband and father besides.

Our recorded interview, on which the following account is based, took place several weeks later, and other aspects of her personality were revealed. Yet, although difficulties and criticisms were the main themes that came up in this conversation, these were expressed, once again, without a trace either of bitterness or pride. It is as if everything is accepted, understood, and taken for granted by Na'ama.

People say that Na'ama is a person of great talents and abilities, but that her perfectionism keeps her from doing many things that she could do. They say of her: "She used to be one of our best teachers"; "Her husband was a great person."

---

*Literally, "ascent"; the illegal immigration to Mandate Palestine.

She has three children: a son and a daughter in the kibbutz, and a second daughter in a different kibbutz. Elisheva, Na'ama's eldest daughter, appears in "The Young Generation."

I joined Makom in 1938 shortly after I met Oded, who was a member there. Just a few weeks after my arrival, Oded came to me and said that the Hagana and the kibbutz movement had asked him to go abroad and work for the Ha'apala. I remember that conversation very well. There we were, a young couple who hadn't yet had a chance to live together. And we weren't that young either—he was twenty-seven and I was five years younger. There we were, finally, on the verge of our life together. And then . . . we didn't know how long the job he was taking was going to separate us from each other, and we were both aware that it was illegal work and dangerous, that he might be caught and put into jail. Who knew what would happen?

You can't imagine our position; even my children can't understand. He simply said: "Look, I'm going to save Jews." I was twenty-two and somewhat weaker than Oded. Still, I understood him perfectly, and I let him go. My son, for example, cannot understand it—he thinks of his father as a martyr. But that's a horrible mistake, a mistake that the generation gap cannot bridge. People of the second generation cannot see the point of what we used to call "an obligation to the Movement" or even "the command of the Movement." Today all these concepts seem ridiculous. Who can believe that the Movement was such a priority in our lives?

We had a completely different order of priorities then. It frequently saddens me to see how we have changed, the kibbutz changed, the whole country changed, in this sense. Again, I remember Oded, a short while after his return from his second mission in 1947. The State had just been established, and he was offered a very important position in the government. That's when he refused. He said: "You won't have any problem filling that position—people will come running for a job like that. Me— I went only where I knew nobody else would be willing to take my place." Personally, I think that this is a disaster, this running after prestige, after administrative positions. And who will do the real work, after all? The whole country suffers from this trend, not just the kibbutz. Actually, it still hasn't happened in the kibbutz, but I'm afraid it will.

Let me return to my first years in Makom. Oded was off on his mission and I was a kindergarten teacher. It was a horrible time for me. Conditions at work were terrible, and we didn't realize that we could take life a bit easier. For example, one *metapelet* and one teacher worked with a class of twenty preschool children; today this same class would have three *metaplot* and a teacher. It's true that we were short of people, but the real reason for functioning this way was that we simply thought that this was normal. And the housing: In the same houses in which we have eleven or twelve babies today, we used to keep twenty-four babies, six in a room, with six mothers spending half the day in this tiny room, breast-feeding their babies. Nobody used formula then; we thought this was the right way. Moreover, our methods of child-rearing were simply ascetic—bathing children in cold water the year round, for instance, because we thought it was healthy, that it would immunize the children. How they suffered, the poor things; they hated to take a shower, as if it were the worst thing in the world. Feeding as well—a child had to eat whatever was put on his plate, whatever was cooked that day in the kitchen. We sat with them and made them eat, and, if they refused to eat, they were given the same plate for their next meal. At night, they slept on wooden boards, which was considered healthy for their posture.

Today, I feel as if I were talking about the medieval ages. I'm not normally a strict person, far from it, so the whole time I was raising children this way, it was out of a sense of duty. For me it was a long, ongoing nightmare. I loved the children and I used to try to compensate for the strictness with games and stories, by showing my love. I really felt we ought to change the system somehow, but I didn't know how. Nor did my friends. This was the atmosphere, full of strict rules and demands, both from us, the educational staff, and from the children.

The parents also believed that this was the proper way. One thing I must admit is that, in general, parents then were much more involved in their children's upbringing and education than they are today. Everyone participated in discussions about feeding schedules, diets for the babies, educational problems—it was considered the social responsibility of the whole community. You can find proof of that in the old newsletters, in which every new development of the babies—who walked, who had new teeth—was an item of news. Naturally, there were fewer children at the time, and they were all infants. Today, there is a growing trend of detachment. Parents keep out of the school; some parents don't even know what their children do in the nursery or school all day long. I disapprove of that; yet, generally, the development in education, especially in early education, is very much what I had hoped for as a kindergarten teacher.

A gradual liberalization took place; the strict attitudes were abandoned and new approaches were adopted, whereby children were considered as human beings, treated with more concern for their individual preferences and needs. We now feel that love is not enough; one must take an interest in the needs of the individual.

I suffered for two years though, writing terrible letters to Oded about my sufferings, and then I could take it no more. In the meantime, while I was still in the nursery school, Oded returned to the country, but he had to remain in hiding. He didn't return to Makom for even a single day. We quickly got married at my parents' apartment and he went to another kibbutz, in the Negev, under a false name. Once a month I used to go there to meet with him. It was a nerve-racking situation. I had to live with my ongoing stress as nursery-school teacher. In addition, I had the continuous tension of separation and reunion. I think that the time he was abroad was easier for me than the tension of waiting for this monthly meeting and the immediate separation that followed. Again, today I can't see how we could have been so stupid—since we aren't stupid people, indeed. We considered this setup fair and normal, as if nothing else was possible at all! You see, how could I go to him every week? The year was 1941 and transportation was bad—just getting to this southern kibbutz took me a whole day, and another day to return. Who could allow oneself to lose so many days of work? Who could replace me at school?

And those visits. . . . It was all undercover, since Oded wasn't supposed to be associated with Makom in any way, while I was known to come from there. The cover was that I was coming to visit a girlfriend of mine, and we would sneak out separately, he and I, to meet at a third place—always looking for a place where we could be together for a moment of privacy. Imagine, a young couple. . . . My parents' apartment was out of bounds for us, since we were sure that British Intelligence would get Oded as soon as we set foot there. I think we greatly overestimated them at the time.

My nerves were wrecked, I cried whole nights, and finally I arrived at a decision, which was awfully difficult for me: to oppose the kibbutz decision, and to refuse to continue my work with the children. It was shocking for me to arrive at such a decision, breaking the kibbutz discipline; it was like a betrayal. But I did it, and the secretary, a woman, understood me perfectly, and it was decided to search for a way that Oded and I could be together. The kibbutz gave me a leave of absence of one or two years until things cleared up.

This was in November, 1941. Another kibbutz was found for us, and we moved there under a false name, as a young couple joining the kibbutz from the city. We lived there incognito, and people often wondered at how quickly we adjusted to the kibbutz way of life. And it was such a happy time! We received a tent, like all newcomers, and we lived among these very young people. Finally we were openly together, and very happy, I must say. That's where our first daughter, Elisheva, was born in 1942, and to this day her birth certificate is under the false name we used then.

We lived in this kibbutz for a year and a half, until it was considered safe enough for Oded to move back to Makom.

Oded was here with me until 1945, and then he went on his second mission to Europe. This was after World War II, when the gates were opened for the remaining Jews of Europe—opened from that end, but not here, since the British restricted the *aliya*. It was a period of great enthusiasm and devotion, with many joining the effort to save as many as possible of the remnants of our people. Oded had experience; he knew about buying boats, equipping them, running the illegal operations—and he was in charge of many important and successful missions, of Exodus of which you've heard, and many others like it. When he got the order to go, there wasn't a moment of hesitation on our part—he went to Europe and stayed there for two and a half years.

We had two daughters at the time; the youngest was just three months old. But who thought then of the possibility that a delegate of the country might be accompanied by his family? It was simply unheard of, although this norm was changed pretty fast later.

Well, anyway, I and my little daughters stayed behind. I have all these letters from Oded from that period; many of them were published after his death. It was pretty tough here alone, with two infants. In the winter, everything was terribly muddy. There were no boots, and we had to carry the children on our arms so that they should not sink in the mud. My older one was three, and, to carry two children, a friend of ours had to help me—he came with me to the children's home every day in the winter and carried the older one to my room. But there were many other difficulties, things we didn't even try to solve, because with our unconscious martyr-complexes we didn't even think about how to ease hardships. Some things still bother me very much.

Makom had a rule that children weren't allowed into the dining room. They ate their dinner at the children's home before they were brought to the parents' room and later at night, before we put them to sleep, we would give them a snack in the apartment. The usual practice was that one of the parents stayed home with the children while the other went for his meal, and then they switched. But I was alone, so what could I do? It hurts me to even think about it. But who had the sense then to rebel against the rules?

First, I used to put the baby to sleep, since her bedtime was still very early. Then, I'd leave my elder one, who was three when Oded left, alone in my room to wait until I had returned from dinner. There was no way to eat in the room then; there wasn't even an electric kettle to boil water in. Who imagined that someday we would be cooking whole meals in the room? So my daughter used to stay alone in the room every evening, when I went to dinner. And she, such a quiet, obedient girl, never protested or said a word. [*Na'ama is crying softly now.*] I cannot forgive myself. Only years later did I find out how frightened this little girl was, how she lay in my bed, trembling, afraid of snakes, afraid of all sorts of things, watching the door, watching for the moment I'd come in again. To this very day it hurts me terribly. Why did we not understand it then? How was it possible that I couldn't see what I was doing to my daughter? There was no one else in the same situation then. Oded was the only delegate abroad; there were no widows, I think, nor wives of enlisted men. I don't quite remember when this rule was changed, and children were finally allowed to be with their parents in the dining hall. Anyway, it was too late for me.

As I said before, all our rules and regulations were very strict then, even cruel, one might say. Some of them were the result of our difficult conditions, but others we accepted as principles, of our own volition. Maybe that's why it didn't seem difficult at the time, because we were living with our own personal choices. We weren't bitter people at all. We knew fun and joy, pleasure and humor; we were, in general, happy people. What we lacked, perhaps, was foresight, the necessary vision to direct ourselves towards the improvement of our way of life. This began only after the establishment of the State in 1948. Every little personal comfort was something of a revolution for us. Take, for example, private toilets and showers. It was a revolution, for we found it completely normal to walk on a rainy night all the way out to the "America," our common toilets! When, finally, we put showers, little bathrooms, in the rooms, I remember that the assembly spent a whole evening discussing whether we should have warm water or not. I remember one of my friends making a big speech, starting with the words: "The working class deserves warm water to shower with!" It seemed like such a giant step forward—since it was the most natural thing in the world to heat up a kettle of water and pour it into a sink. What could be better?

Now I see a lot of materialism among my generation. I see a lack of politeness, of fundamental manners, and our children follow our example. We were a generation of revolutionaries; we wanted to liberate ourselves from all the norms and values of the bourgeois middle class. Manners were one of the things we scorned, and now our children don't even use the words "thank you" anymore. We were all the same age, so we forgot manners and respect for the elderly. Don't misunderstand me, we have developed an outstanding system of support for old people, but it's not spontaneous. You can see a child standing next to an adult who has dropped something, and the child won't offer his help, won't bend down to pick up whatever it is, even for an elderly person. Nobody would offer his seat to an older person in a bus. It's as if we have stretched the sense of equality to an absurd degree. Some of the adults encourage this by refusing any sign of special respect. Whereas, if, for example, someone does get up for me on a bus, I accept the gesture and thank the person. I think we ought to stress manners much more in our education.

Somehow, it's very easy, in the kibbutz way of life, to lose sight of the delicate line which divides right from wrong. The difference is sometimes blurred, which doesn't often happen in the city. Take a volunteer: if he's hungry between meals, he may enter the kitchen and take bread, a yogurt, or an egg; but if he opens the refrigerator and takes a piece of chicken, the workers in the kitchen would call it "stealing." How is he supposed to know the difference? Or, if a child takes a drink, any drink at all, in the dining room, it's acceptable; but if he opens a bottle of soda in the supermarket and drinks it, it's wrong. If I visit the nursery school and have a cup of coffee, it's all right, of course. Yet suppose I take the whole jar and put it in my pocketbook? Recently workers in the children's quarters have been complaining of the strange disappearance of coffee jars. Coffee for the room is something one has to buy at our local supermarket, so why not try to save a bit out of your limited budget? I feel that people disregard the distinction between private and common property, but the distinction is often difficult to make, since obviously everything owned by the kibbutz is mine, in a way. Finally, it can lead to very unpleasant situations, such as what happened last year when a record company organized an exhibition in the kibbutz, and many records disappeared, or, to be exact, were stolen from the collection. We found out that some schoolchildren did it. So what can we do—expel them from our own school?

I believe we should find a way to educate the kibbutz towards better moral standards, to inculcate values that don't seem to come naturally to people. But many people object to my views, even among our secretaries. Some think it's well and fine the way it is: Let adults judge for themselves and set their own standards; one must rely on one's fellow kibbutznik— the right way is the natural way. I, personally, object to this view.

Absorption

A M A L I A *(age 64)*

Amalia's husband, Saul, appears in "The Beginning."

I joined the *hachshara* when I was eighteen, in 1932. The *hachshara* was in a town on the Russian border. It was a Jewish place, surrounded by Polish villages. The town had twenty-seven synagogues and four *yeshivot*,* and us, twenty Zionist youngsters, looking for work. We rented a three-room apartment and slept two to a bed. Frequently, only one or two of us out of the whole group found work, and we went hungry. The conditions were extremely difficult.

We continued our *hachshara* in this town for six months, and then we moved to a different place which had a lumber mill, and all of us had plenty of work. We had enough to eat, which was a great improvement, but our clothes were still ragged, and we looked awful. We lived in a commune, and we became accustomed to a life of work, which was our aim. All in all, I was content. It never occurred to me to go back to my family, although it wasn't more than two hours by train. What kept us in the group was the motivation to immigrate to Israel, the hope to get there. And we felt solidarity within our group, a close relationship. I think that the rules, which forbade us to eat or drink outside of the commune, worked to keep us very close together. We were young, we sang and danced all night, and we didn't care about our conditions.

After a year, a delegate from Israel came to meet us, and granted us some certificates to make *aliya*. There were sixty of us, and we received sixteen certificates, which we used for thirty-two people who traveled as fictitious couples. This enabled two of us to immigrate with a single certificate. People who knew some Hebrew, who were efficient workers, with the right attitudes about work and the commune, were approved for *aliya*.

I was one of the people chosen to immigrate, and I was given a fictitious "husband." We went to a rabbi, and he cooperated and gave us a marriage license. My "husband" was a man I disliked extremely, but this

Plural of yeshiva. The traditional religious institute of learning.

was the arrangement. We then went to obtain a passport as a couple, and I went home to wait for the papers. A month passed, then three months, then half a year—I heard nothing. Finally, I found out that my "husband" had been expelled from the Movement, and I, as a "married" woman, couldn't immigrate. He used to come and visit, from time to time, to see if I was at home. But when he found out what had happened, he refused to have this fictitious marriage annulled. My father wandered from one rabbi to another, and everyone said: "They're married—that's it!" After a year he finally found a rabbi who saw the point, and he gave me a document certifying I was single.

We sent my annulment certificate to Warsaw; two weeks later, I received a cable to come quickly, for I had a place in an illegal immigrants' boat. Luckily, I missed this boat, for it wandered for half a year between ports unable to obtain permission to let the passengers disembark. Eventually, they had to return to Poland. Anyway, I finally got a certificate in 1934. Again I had a "husband," and again I memorized a false name. There were twenty-seven women on the train; I had all the certificates and the password. Then, a young man came, gave the password, and introduced us to our "husbands." The men were mostly from the unsuccessful boat, and we women paid the fare for them, since they were completely broke.

We were on the boat for five days. It was stormy and I felt awful. But when we finally arrived I was the only one of the whole group who went to a kibbutz. Imagine, after all the *hachsharot* and things: I was the only one! Again, my "husband" didn't let me go easily, but I separated from him and joined the kibbutz.

I requested to join Makom, and they had, at the time, a working company in Ra'anana. These were people who came from the Fountain and worked and lived there. I arrived at the place alone. It was late in the evening. The secretary asked me a few questions, and sent me to sleep. I entered a dark room, and I didn't know if anyone was already sleeping there or not, for nobody answered my faint "hello." I felt around for the light switch but couldn't find it. Suddenly I heard: "Who is it? What are you looking for?" "I was sent to sleep here," I said, "and I'm looking for a way to turn on the lantern." I used this fancy biblical Hebrew, very different from the language spoken in the country. The voice roared: "What the hell are you talking about?" That was my reception. Well, I found a bed, and at 3:30 A.M. I was awakened to go to work in the laundry. "Where is it?" I asked the night guard. It was dark, and I had no work clothes, since my suitcase had not arrived with me. "You see the only light —that's where it is," he said. So I went there, quite disoriented. There, surprisingly, I found another Polish woman and she accepted me warmly. "Don't worry, it's all right, when the daybreak comes I'll take you to the storeroom and you'll get some work clothes." That's how my new life started.

In the commune in Ra'anana there were three distinct groups. There were the Israelis, who were a very closely knit group. Then, there were the Germans, the "Yekkes," as we called them, and, finally, the Poles. The Polish group was the smallest, then, with mainly women and very few men. I'm the kind of person who usually has no social problems. I sang very well and I loved to dance. But my Hebrew, my biblical Hebrew, was the laughingstock of the whole group. They used to say, "Speak Hebrew," but what else was I doing? This reaction bothered me. People said it was tough there, but I noticed that we had enough food, we had soup and vegetables every day—what was so tough? Compared to my *hachshara,* where we starved from hunger! . . .

I had a big trunk that my mother had shipped for me, full of linen and towels and dishes and clothes, very pretty dresses. She knew she would not marry me off, so she prepared everything that a good family gives a bride. My "dowry" was packed in a big straw basket. When I gave it all to the commune, I felt . . . I felt that I was liberating myself, getting rid of a burden, the burden of the Diaspora. Giving it away, sharing it, was no problem at all. On the contrary, it made me feel like one of the members; I belonged.

In spite of all this, my absorption into the group wasn't easy. They did not accept us Poles. Neither in Ra'anana nor later, at the Fountain, was the Polish group accepted. The Israelis were the highest social rank, then came the Yekkes who were admired for their education and cultural background. We—we came last. I don't know why. Well, for some reason the Polish group had always had more women than men; twelve women and two men, fourteen women and three men—that was always our composition. The young Polish women were short and plump; in Poland, this was considered pretty. Slim was sickly by our standards. Here, however, slim and tall was beautiful. I remember how I envied those Israeli girls for their figures. I had smart dresses from Poland, embroidered and well cut, and I saw how pretty they looked on the Israeli girls when we shared them. It made me happy to see my dresses making those girls look so lovely.

But we weren't accepted warmly by the group. I don't know why. I was very naïve; perhaps I didn't behave properly, either. For example, I shared a room in Ra'anana with two men. For about three months I never cleaned the room. Several times I came in and noticed that the floor had been washed, and I was sure that it was done by someone whose turn it was to clean the whole house. This was how we worked it out in my *hachshara,* and I just wondered why my turn to do it had not yet come. Finally, one day I saw one of the Polish women cleaning the floor and I asked her: "Is it your turn to clean today?" She replied: "What turn? Everybody cleans their own room." I was so ashamed. Nobody bothered to explain this arrangement to me.

Frequently, I had doubts about my future during the Ra'anana period. Most of my acquaintances were settling down in the city and often tried to convince me to leave the kibbutz. "Why should I leave?" I said, "I love the life of the commune. I'm used to being with people all the time."

What disturbed me most deeply was my longing for my family in Poland. I was homesick. I left home when my sisters were mere children, and I missed them and my parents very much. There were four children in the commune in Ra'anana. I was sometimes swept with a desire to hold them, to hug them. Once I ran away and cried and cried for hours. Sometimes I felt so sick with longing for my family that I wondered if I'd be able to live through this pain. I missed someone to be intimate with, someone to love.

Then a group of us had to return to the Fountain, and I was one of those sent there. I didn't want to go. Some of my closest friends were to remain in Ra'anana and there was talk of forming a separate kibbutz. I begged to stay, but the decision had been made. They were considerate of my feelings, though, and gave me a letter stating that if I didn't adjust to life at the Fountain after two or three months, I could return to Ra'anana.

The group which moved to the Valley consisted of eight women and three men. We had just enough money for train tickets, and in Tel Aviv we had to wait four hours for the train. People were hungry and suggested going to visit relatives and friends in town, eating there, and returning in time for the train trip. Somehow, I took the initiative and said: "No, we must all stay here together." I had a feeling that if people dispersed, their families would talk them out of going to the Fountain. We waited for four hours at the station, and after another four-hour train ride, we arrived at the Fountain. It was evening, but someone was waiting for us at the station. The year was 1935, and the absorption process started all over again for me. There were more Poles at the Fountain and I became a part of this group. In the evening, several of us Polish women used to sit outside on the steps and sing songs from home, sentimental songs. These songs expressed our longings.

Here, again, the Israelis were the distinguished group, although they mixed somewhat more with the Germans. The Israelis even had a special table of their own in the dining room! Anyone who didn't belong to the group dared not sit there, it simply wasn't done. Well, when we newcomers entered the dining room the first evening, we picked, of all possible places, the Israeli table. Being completely new, we didn't notice the significance of our deed, only the fact that nobody joined us. Well, when we finished eating, the table was cleaned and the Sabras sat down to eat. We didn't repeat this mistake.

There was a man among the Sabras who did try to get closer to us, to help us enter the social group. Later, he was killed in the Sinai Campaign of 1956. . . . One evening he called us to his room and asked us about our sad songs. We told him about our longings, and about our feeling of being looked down upon both by the Israelis and by the Germans.

Indeed, I don't know why it was like this. I remember a day when a new group of twelve women and two men arrived at the Fountain, all Polish Jews, and the secretary said: "If this group is accepted, I resign from my job." They were standing right outside the door, and when they heard this they wept. I called them into my room and told them not to pay attention to what they had overheard. I explained that it wasn't a personal rejection, but the result of the terrible shortage of work. I, myself, didn't feel absorbed yet either, but I managed to help these newcomers.

All this time, I carried my letter with me, the letter allowing me to return to Ra'anana. But life at the Fountain was somehow a challenge for me. I was stubborn, I refused to give in. I wanted to conquer the situation, as tough as it was. We had no housing; a friend and I slept outside all summer, under a tree. This didn't bother me at all. Physical hardships never made a difference to me. And gradually we penetrated the social system, and were accepted by the group, even the Israelis. Differences between Poles, Germans, and Israelis became less and less pronounced. After my first year or two, my adjustment period, I have always felt that I belonged, and that's what matters to me.

U R I *(age 60)*

I am a Yemenite, as you can hear and see, and I was born in Jerusalem. There's a story on my mother's side of the family about the arrival of my grandparents in Jerusalem in 1884. My grandfather traveled all the way from Yemen on foot, with my grandmother on the donkey carrying a baby, my mother. They entered the old Jewish quarter within the walls of the old city, asking for a place to stay. It was a cold winter evening, snow was falling, yet nobody let them in. Jewish Yemenites were not yet known in Israel. The Jews didn't believe that my grandparents could be Jewish, too, for the color of their skin was different, and they spoke with a strange Hebrew accent. Finally an Arab saved them from the freezing night and invited them into his home in Silouan, a village outside the walls. That's the story. They weren't accepted as Jews. Later it changed though, but they never lived in the old Jewish quarter. Gradually Jerusalem expanded outside of the walls and they found their place in one of the new Jewish neighborhoods. My father was an orphan and came to Jerusalem by himself when he was twelve or thirteen, on foot. So, all in all, I'm a third-generation Jerusalemite.

I grew up in one of the first girls' schools in Jerusalem, where our family lived because my father was the school janitor. My father died when he was very young, when I was only six years old; but my mother was allowed to stay on at the school, replacing my father as janitor. So I grew up with my three sisters and mother at the school, living in unbelievably inhuman conditions, all together in a tiny room. We used the school toilet, outside, in the courtyard. My mother had such a pitiful salary that we starved most of the time. We ate only bread, and we didn't even have enough of that. We used to rummage through the garbage pails for remnants of the pupils' snacks. There wasn't enough food; I keep asking myself how it could have happened. How did all the parents, educators, and administrators visiting that school—all of whom saw how we lived—allow such a situation to continue? When I was about twelve years old, I went to the principal and asked his permission to move into another room, outside, in the courtyard. Nobody used that room for anything, yet he flatly refused to let me move in. I don't know what sort of people they were, everybody was so cruel and unfeeling.

I attended a commercial high school, which was the cheapest means to obtain a secondary education available to a poor student. The education we got was dubious; it was, to say the least, limited and utterly superficial. I attended this school, though, and as I grew up I became increasingly convinced that I had to leave the city, get out of Jerusalem. I felt that Jerusalem as a city was too cruel; it gave me no rights, no opportunity to live a respectable life; it was the town which had let me starve. When I was twelve, I joined the Scouts. I was attracted to the glamor of the uniforms and the parades, and I felt a need to break out, for a while, from my miserable surroundings. The Scouts offered me a different life. I was very well accepted socially. We formed a tight group that used to go on many hikes together, using every free day on our school calendar; our favorite destinations were the Judean Desert and the Dead Sea. In the Scouts, I heard about another kind of opportunity; the message was: "Go to a kibbutz, start a new settlement—the country needs you." It was a great challenge as well as a promise of a better life. I was sixteen and I felt that the call was personally directed at me. I couldn't stand the city anymore, so I left school and joined the kibbutz at the Fountain.

It was 1934 when I arrived at the Fountain. My group from the Scouts was still in high school and I planned to live in the kibbutz until they had graduated, then rejoin them. We planned to start our own kibbutz, our dream being the Dead Sea area, and I intended to prepare myself as a useful member by acquiring several skills—driving a tractor, baking bread, and shoemaking.

What I found at the Fountain was the realization of a dream. The Valley enchanted me, it was so pretty. I didn't mind the shortage of food; it was a relative improvement over what I had known before. A new world was suddenly opened up to me, full of promise. It was a happy time, we were all young and carefree, and nothing else mattered at all. We had a combination of fun and work. In the winter we played games and danced every night in the dining room; in the summer we went on hikes, swam naked in the fountain, and slept outside in tree houses or hammocks. Nobody cared about proper food, dwelling conditions, or any possessions; these things simply weren't important. It was customary to invent all kinds of pranks and practical jokes. For example, when a new immigrant would arrive, we told him it was his turn to shine everybody's shoes, or to brush the cows' teeth—and everybody stood about, watching him perform these incredible tasks. . . . Some people got insulted, yes, but it was all done in good spirit. Besides the fun, there was also more serious entertainment—singing and listening to music were among the most popular activities, serving also as a way to bring the group together. Readings of poetry and literature took place on the grass every evening and anybody could join. If somebody disliked games and pranks, and couldn't find his place in the musical or reading circles either—well, he was lonely and depressed. But that was rare. I personally disagree with anyone who describes this early period as a difficult time.

On Friday we went to the storeroom and received packages of our clothes for the week, all neatly wrapped. Frequently the pants were too long and the shirt too short. So what—another matter to joke about!

We did work hard. So what? We knew working was an ideal. If somebody came only to have fun, then of course he couldn't take the work. But if you came to build a new society, then working was wonderful. I felt I was participating in an extremely important social enterprise, and within it I was rehabilitating my own life. This awareness made us into one cohesive group and we, the first generation, have been drawing from this source of motivation to this very day. (This is something our children don't have, and I see the difference, due to this, in their character.)

Well, as I told you, I came to the Fountain at sixteen, with plenty of plans for things I wanted to learn. Of all these, I managed to get easily into shoemaking and repairing; in fact, this is the only skill that I mastered while waiting for my group from Jerusalem. I did get to watch the baker at his work, but I didn't bake as part of my duties. As for a tractor—this was something only the high priests could touch! You needed to prove your excellence before you could even get close to the huge metal beast, let alone drive it! What an honor it was—although today such tractors can be found only in the junkyard! . . . I did sneak in at night and managed a few rides on that tractor, though.

Anyway, towards the end of the year, our Jerusalem group reassembled, and we moved to an older kibbutz for our *hachshara*. After that year we voiced our wish to go and start a new kibbutz in Ein Gedi, near the Dead Sea. You should have seen how we were reprimanded by the Movement! No, they didn't support our plan at all; the group at the Fountain needed us, and we were ordered to join them. I believe it was a real mistake, making us go to the Valley. They had no shortage of manpower, and they had plenty of new immigrants who wanted to settle there. Ein

Gedi was our dream, a fantasy born of our trips in our Jerusalem days, and only such a strong attraction could maintain a group at such a difficult location. Our Jerusalem people are frustrated to this very day, because we were prevented from realizing our dream. We wanted a kibbutz of our own, we didn't want to become juniors to the senior founders of an older kibbutz. But the institutions of the Movement bullied us with orders; they used their authority and actually frightened us into obeying. Nobody tried the gentle way of explaining or convincing. . . . It couldn't happen today, I'm sure. It was a shame and a great loss to all sides involved. Had they allowed us to settle in Ein Gedi, the border of 1948 between Israel and Jordan would have been different, and the Jerusalem youth would have done a wonderful deed.

Well, it didn't work out as we planned, and we joined Makom, which had been established as a kibbutz six or seven years before. Being younger than the founders, we were considered mere youngsters. . . . Actually, until very recently, we remained kids—especially Eli and I, who were younger than the rest and nicknamed "the orphans." Whenever a serious, responsible thing had to be done, it was obvious that we were "still" incompetent, and the function would be assumed by an older member. When the German immigrants came, they, too, were socially above us. With their assets of age and education, they managed to penetrate the founding group. But not we—we remained the kids. That's why we had wanted to start a kibbutz of our own, where we would be the "founders" and have to face problems independently and to cope with difficulties on our own.

Here, we missed our chance to grow up; we were always pushed aside to observe how the elders did things better. I don't think it was done intentionally, or with bad will; there were truly excellent people here— both the Israeli founders and the first groups of immigrants—so they assumed all of the crucial positions within the kibbutz and determined its direction and atmosphere. The leading positions of the kibbutz were continually passed among members of this elite, and we couldn't penetrate it. I think that many of us, of my group, felt inferior for a very long time. Eventually things did change though, especially when the founders got tired of their power. By that time I was out of the game; I had become a teacher, and teachers are usually out of the circle of people who are elected for various power positions within the kibbutz.

One thing I must point out, though, is that from the day I joined the kibbutz, my ethnic origin, my color, and my accent were never a cause for any kind of discrimination or negative attitudes towards me. Never. That has been my personal experience and the same is true for the other Orientals who settled here. In that sense, I really solved my basic problem by joining the kibbutz and I never again felt the discrimination I was aware of during my childhood in Jerusalem. The only test for a person in the kibbutz is his personal integrity—never his former background.

There are anecdotes about the reception given to the various immi-grant groups who came to the kibbutz; indeed we sometimes made fun of their strange accents, or different clothes, but all this was done without any maliciousness and, moreover, it didn't in any way determine the status of the newcomer within the kibbutz. If a German immigrant wanted to contribute, started a choir, or in some way enriched our culture, he immediately became popular and respected. Personality and talents have always determined one's position in our society; there was no ethnic prejudice.

I believe that the same holds true for the Israeli society in general. Furthermore, I believe that if someone comes expecting to be dis-criminated against, and begins his life in the country with demands, he will indeed experience a negative reaction. But that's due to his personal-ity and behavior, not to his origin. Some people immigrated with the slogan: "I'm a North African Jew, and therefore I deserve to get such-and-such." That's inappropriate, of course. First, let's see who he is, and, if he is a worthwhile person, his background, color, or accent will be irrelevant.

Although the kibbutz provided the Orientals with the best opportu-nity for social and ethnic integration, it's true that the kibbutz didn't absorb many Jews from the East. Many Yemenites and Iraquis lived with us but dropped out after a short time. There are several reasons for this phenomenon, none of which has to do with discrimination. I remember how hard it was for those Yemenites to live in the difficult conditions of the early years, because they had lacked ideological conviction and belief. They weren't educated and prepared ideologically by the youth move-ments, as we were, and without this idealism life here was pretty hard to take. They didn't understand our aims and values. When their parents visited, they were shocked by the difficult work their sons were doing at the quarry, the meager food, the hard beds, the tents that let the rain drip in; the parents easily talked their sons into leaving the kibbutz and joining the father in the small family store, thus perpetuating the old Jewish commercial occupation. These kind of people, especially their parents, wanted to be able to show something for their hard work. They needed concrete personal reinforcements, not abstract general ones. It seemed to them that they were toiling in vain, and so they left. This happened again and again. It didn't matter whether people were from rich or poor homes; if they had the ideological preparation they stayed, and if they didn't they left. This lack of conviction was what had differentiated the immigrants from the oriental countries from the Europeans we did man-age to absorb.

We, the "old-timers," didn't go out of our way to help newcomers overcome their adjustment period. There was no awareness of such a need. Newcomers were given work and some sort of housing, and left alone. We were young and didn't understand the psychological crisis taking place underneath the surface. We danced at night and fooled around, and didn't pay attention to those who didn't take part in our activities. This was a fault on our part at the time, but we were unaware of what we were doing, and we behaved in the same manner towards all newcomers, not just Orientals.

The Europeans who arrived, however, had come supported by idealism, as I said before, frequently cultivated during years of *hachshara.* Furthermore, they were uprooted from their home countries by the war and the Holocaust—they had nowhere to return to, they had to make it here. The Orientals, on the other hand, usually had some family and home basis in Israel, and the temptation to escape from our hard life was too great. Only a few individual cases did make it, in this kibbutz as well as in other kibbutzim. That dream didn't belong to the Orientals. . . .

For those eastern Jews who did remain, or still considered the kibbutz as a solution in the 1950s, the division within the kibbutz movement was yet another blow, perhaps the strongest blow. The Orientals saw the kibbutz as a source of hope for change in their private lives, a secure basis. And here, during the division, people were thrown out of their homes. The Movement told them: "You worked and toiled, but the place doesn't belong to you—go away, start all over again." They left with only the shirts on their backs, homeless again. This was a shock, particularly to people who had a basic feeling of insecurity and who went to the kibbutz to find a stable home environment. Suddenly they discovered they were sitting on top of a volcano! It was a shock for everybody, but again ideological conviction helped those who had it to cope with the trauma —and my brothers had usually lacked this.

Presently, I sometimes meet oriental Israelis, especially those from North Africa, who harbor profound hatred towards the kibbutz. People wanted to hit me when they found out I was a kibbutz member. "How dare you, as an Oriental, live within such a society?" Their hatred, based on disappointment, has no limits, none.

Well, to continue my own story, I was a shoemaker in the settlement at the Fountain. When we started to build the new point on the present location, I joined the construction team. Later I worked in the vegetable garden we planted there. For nine years I did physical work; then the kibbutz decided to send me to the Teachers' Seminary. The year was 1944 and, after all those years of growing up, I was ripe for learning. I attended a special seminary for kibbutz teachers in Tel Aviv, and its method was based on individualized learning. There were no exams or unwanted duties; we learned the topics we chose, at our own pace, choosing our own directions. I had not even finished high school, and to study at this seminary with graduate students who wanted to become teachers scared me at first. But, gradually, I discovered within myself a need and potential for studying, and I developed a deep interest in geology, in which I majored. Much of the credit should be given, however, to the great teachers we had at the seminary, teachers who really inspired us and taught us to maximize our abilities.

I returned to Makom as the second teacher acquired on the staff of our fledgling school. I tried to implant in the kibbutz the values of the seminary: individual work, self-discovery, learning out of internal motivation and not for external rewards. It worked miracles with our first-born children, who are presently the central figures in the kibbutz. I'm very proud of our achievements. I have dedicated my life to teaching, working for thirty-five years in our school. At first I worked with young elementary-school pupils, and then I moved up to high school and specialized in teaching geology. Acquiring knowledge and a love of the land, the flora and fauna of our country, have always been central values of our kibbutz education. We have passed them on to our children.

Recently, however, I have become somewhat anxious about the quality of our local education and its results. The level has gone down and the young teachers lack the enthusiasm we had. Many of the teachers are women, and they do mostly routine work. What I think our present education fails to do is to make demands on the children, forcing them to utilize their abilities to the maximum, to cope with difficulties by themselves. Nowadays children refuse to try. We used to mount the Gilboa Mountain with those children; they had to climb and identify personally various flowers and rocks. It was highly demanding, both physically and intellectually. I remember children crying out of frustration, yet we didn't stop for them; they had to follow and climb, and when they did they felt tremendous satisfaction: They had done it and it changed their self-image. Later they knew they could walk, knew they could solve difficult problems by themselves, knew they could rely on themselves. Today children are not willing to face the least difficulty, and they rebel if you make any demand on them. And the teachers accept this, give in. He didn't do his homework, didn't solve the problem—so what, it's all forgiven. He broke something, he wanted to break it—it's all forgiven. But why forgive? Education means learning to curb one's desires, to develop self-control. This is something rarely done nowadays; teachers and parents are too liberal, and I'm afraid they're wrong. Without benevolent yet rigorous control, people grow up soft and weak, unable to cope with all the problems life brings forth. Life is a chain of problems. One must swallow one's pain and go on.

It's true that the kibbutz still has a reputation for offering the best education. In the Army, for example, kibbutz children are considered the cream of the crop—able to cope and adjust, willing to risk themselves and lead others. It's true that we have sons of that nature, and on the average I still believe we do better than any other educational system. We have raised many weaklings too, only they don't make the headlines. I'm not interested in comparing the educational conditions of the city with our kibbutz education. But, compared to ourselves, we produced a much stronger educational result years ago. Our children today are terribly spoiled and unwilling to exert themselves. As young adults, they lack the ability to mobilize their endurance to the maximum, to make an effort for any length of time in order to achieve aims they set out for themselves. Their moral standards are lacking as well, and that's the final criterion for education.

Presently, I'm no longer teaching. As a biology teacher I was always inclined to do some research along with my teaching, and I developed a hobby of studying the ecology of the desert. I used to work in the Negev and the Judean deserts, until Sinai was opened to us in 1967, which gave me a tremendous push forward. When Sinai opened, many scientists were drawn to explore it, but very few of them could speak Arabic fluently enough to study the inhabitants of the desert. As the various authorities needed such people urgently, I was given many opportunities to develop my skills and gradually switched my interest from animals and plants to a fascination with the people dwelling in the desert, the Bedouins. For the last ten years I have spent all my vacations in Sinai, until I finally got a leave of absence and permission from school to live in the desert and conduct studies there. I discovered that my childhood Yemenite-Arabic was practically identical to the dialect of the Sinai Bedouin and that, with my ethnic background, I knew how to relate to these people, building trust and lasting relationships, penetrating the secrets of their ancient culture. Gradually I have become an expert on the subject, which I see as an extension of my interest in biology: namely, how organisms (people as well as plants) adjust to desert conditions. I've learned much fascinating information, and have written some papers and booklets. Recently, with the Camp David agreements, it's become clear that Sinai will soon be returned to Egypt, and it might be closed to research such as mine. So, many of us, historians, geographers, biologists, and anthropologists, have returned to Sinai with new zeal to complete our research. Currently, I'm down in Sinai most of the time, and although I don't expect to complete my study of the Bedouin culture, I have enough to write about for a lifetime.

R I V K A *(age 64)*

In her worn clothes Rivka impressed me as a remarkable woman. She ties her brownish hair in a loose bun at the back of her head. Her eyes are lively, her smile reveals a toothless mouth. She wears her false teeth only on occasion. Her face is frank and expressive, her voice loud and warm, and her story is accompanied with wide gestures.

I was born in Petach-Tikva in 1915. My family was rather poor; I studied for only eight years and then went to work for the farmers in the area. I was a good worker. I worked in the citrus groves and packing industry.

I used to walk an hour and a half to work. The farmers rode donkeys and the workers walked to work. Since many of the workers were Arabs, I was afraid to walk alone on the plantations, so I used to keep pace with the donkey. I ran the whole way, usually barefoot. It was no problem.

When I was about twenty I left home, planning to join a kibbutz. My boyfriend, who later became my husband, also had this in mind, but he was detained for a while by his parents. I roamed around the country, found my way to the Valley, and I fell in love with the Kinneret.* I found a small kibbutz with a temporary camp on the West Bank, which intended to settle permanently on the east bank of the lake. Simply discovering a desirable kibbutz wasn't the proper way to join, though; one had to apply to the Movement first. But as I was already there, I went to the secretary and asked whether he'd admit me into the kibbutz. I was met with suspicion. First of all, they thought I was in need of work, for there was a great shortage of work everywhere then. Furthermore, this kibbutz was established by a group of Eastern European Jews, all new immigrants, and what could a young, Israeli-born woman be looking for in their midst? I, however, had never worried about work, and I thought that the kibbutz should be based on the integration of the various ethnic communities. If I'd join, maybe more Israelis would join, and this would all be for the best. Basically, I loved the landscape.

The secretary told me immediately that he had no work for me. I requested to stay overnight; in the morning I walked to the nearby village, found a farmer who had a vegetable garden, and asked him for work. The farmer saw right away that I wasn't a pioneer, working her first day outside the kibbutz. He hired me for the day and then asked me to come the next day too. I went back to the kibbutz and told the secretary I had a job in the village. I gave him my day's salary as well as some cucumbers which I brought back from the farm. So he allowed me to stay in the kibbutz, and I maintained my outside job in the village.

But it was difficult for me. Not the work—that was completely familiar. But the mentality of these immigrants was so foreign to me. They did not speak Hebrew or Yiddish. They were suspicious of my behavior—walking barefoot and loading parcels on my head, like the Arabs. In the evening, unless I accepted the invitations of the young people from the nearby village, I felt very lonely. I felt that this was not the kind of life I wanted. A friend of mine lived at the Fountain and she finally talked me into moving there.

Socially, I didn't belong to this kibbutz either. The people there were all high-school graduates, either Israeli or German. Other groups, such as the Poles, hadn't yet come. The year was 1937. When I came, I felt there was no one I could talk to, there was no work, and they actually didn't want to accept me at all. It was the beginning of winter. I came at

*The Sea of Galilee.

dusk, walking with my suitcase from the train station, breathing heavily. I went to the hut where my friend was living, and I lay down to rest on her bed. People saw me coming and suddenly my friend was summoned by the man in charge of labor, David Ilan, who asked her, right under the open window: "Who is that young woman lying on your bed?" She answered proudly: "She's a friend of mine whom I brought to join our kibbutz." "Who asked you to do that?" he barked. "Why do I need more people lying in bed all day, more mouths to feed?" I felt very insulted. I went out and said, "Listen, man, I was never out of work, and I have work for tomorrow right here as well." He said some more nasty things, but I knew I had work waiting. On the train I had met a young man who had worked with me in citrus packing and knew me well. He told me that most kibbutzniks didn't know how to pack fruit, and invited me to come and work for him. On the train I didn't make any promises since I expected to get work in the kibbutz. But, after this exchange, I asked to make a telephone call and indeed I accepted a job for the whole season. Moreover I was the only one in the kibbutz who made thirty-seven and one-half *grush* a day, a highly respectable salary.

Though they let me stay, I was completely ignored. I worked packing oranges in different kibbutzim and villages in the Valley, and, although I gave all my salary to the kibbutz, nobody inquired how I got to my work and nobody made an effort to leave a warm meal for me at night. For two and a half months I walked miles back and forth every day, as I did during my childhood. It was always pitch dark when I came back. One evening a car stopped and the driver invited me to hitch a ride with him. I thought he was British so I refused, saying that I liked to walk. However, he was a Jewish policeman, and a few days later he met a man from our kibbutz and said: "Why do you let young women of your kibbutz walk all alone in the fields after dark? Don't you know that there are riots going on?" This opened their eyes. They inquired about this solitary walker and found me. Finally they asked where I worked and how I got there everyday. . . .

I think this was very typical of the social situation of the group during those years—actually it hasn't changed very much to this day. The Israelis were a very closed group, and so were the German immigrants, who were even more foreign and removed from my background. Nobody said hello or asked about your welfare. There was not even a minimal attempt to accept outsiders. When the Polish girls came, they were faced with the same atmosphere. And how many of them stayed? Ask Amalia about it. It was very difficult to stay here. I also felt quite disenchanted. But I had a strong desire to live in a kibbutz, to make a go of it this time after I had left my first choice in Kinneret, so I told myself: "Here you are, and here you will stay." And I did.

To this very day, however, I see the founding group of Makom as being closed, not willing to mingle with the rest of us. They did mingle in marriage, somewhat, and they formed family relationships. Also, with age and life's difficulties, they have mellowed somewhat; from time to time they, too, need some human support, but they're still not open.

But, as I lived through the first difficult period, I grew to understand the strength of this society, its richness in culture and its tradition of critical self-evaluation. I think our kibbutz is a wonderful creation. It was thus that we were able to withstand many very difficult crises.

So I think that Makom is one of the best existing societies. But I have plenty of criticism as well. The moment we say: "That's it, we've arrived," we actually cease to exist. It's my home, and I must respond to its short-comings when I see them. I used to complain a lot when I felt something went wrong. Recently, I've become calmer, more accepting—and I don't like it. Although many people around me are probably relieved, I see my restraint as a sign of fatigue. When is one quiet? When one stops believ-ing in one's ability to affect things, to improve the situation. It's a bad sign.

One thing I worry about is our attitude towards work. I think that our reluctance to settle down and work, really work, is the greatest fault in the Jewish people, and we didn't change much here ourselves. Look at the Gentile volunteers whom we regularly accept at the kibbutz. I watch these young women working in the kitchen; they're excellent workers. Jews never work like that. It's the Diaspora's legacy, probably, and it's difficult to reverse it within a short period of time. I'm different, though I don't know why. Perhaps because I started to work at a very young age.

Here, in the kibbutz, people did create a revolution and became workers. But as parents, many of the first-generation kibbutzniks would like to see their sons studying at the university to become engineers and architects. My son-in-law was a shepherd here. A few years ago, the kibbutz terminated their sheep raising and sent my son-in-law to study at the Teachers' Seminary. I asked him: "Look at me—what suits me better, a shepherd son-in-law or a teacher?" I was sorry he had to change his profession, although he's an excellent teacher. I know that teaching is not an easy job, but it's not manual work.

For about fifty years I've been getting up at 4:00 in the morning, doing work that might be regarded as completely routine. But for me, as long as my health allows, I enjoy every day anew. I get up very early. I hear the early birds on the trees. It's very quiet outside, just a single worker, perhaps, returning from his night shift, meets me on the way. I go and start cleaning vegetables for the day, and the other workers gradually gather too, and I think of the thousand people we'll feed today. I'm satisfied. Well, I have my moods, too, and if something per-sonal bothers me I can get quite angry with the others. But I forget easily, I smile at them again. I have a little apartment and a few years ago they offered to move us to a better house, like most people our age receive. But I refused to move. I like to see the Gilboa from this specific angle as I put on my working shoes on the little veranda every morning at 4:00.

N A T A N (*age 36*)

I arrived at the kibbutz in 1953, a few months after my brother's arrival. I was eleven years old at the time, and my family was still living in the *ma'abara** after their emigration from Iraq a year before.

The conditions at the *ma'abara* were horrible. It was terribly crowded, and, as there was almost no schooling whatsoever, thousands of children were wandering around aimlessly. My parents were rather helpless under these conditions, for there were eleven children in my family. So when delegates came and offered to send children to be educated in kibbutzim, my parents were glad to give their consent. My two eldest brothers went first, each to a different kibbutz; then my third brother went to Makom, and I, the fourth child in my family to take advantage of this offer, joined my brother at Makom. Somewhat later, one of my sisters was also sent to a kibbutz; of the five who were educated in kibbutzim, she and I are the only ones who have remained as adult members.

I see this project as an unsuccessful rescue mission for the population of the *ma'abarot* in the early 1950s. The kibbutzim opened their gates to the youth, wherever they came from, but due to the parents' attitude, their children weren't successfully absorbed in the kibbutzim. At the beginning, many parents sent their children to kibbutzim because they felt helpless within the *ma'abarot* to maintain their big families. But the minute that the parents' condition improved, they took their children right back home. I guess this was due to the mentality of oriental parents; they wanted to have their children under their control and close supervision until they matured, until they were sixteen or eighteen. They wanted their children to follow their own examples and traditions, the daughters as much as the sons, perhaps even more. Furthermore, Orientals have always been suspicious of the kibbutz way of life. The ideas of cooperation and the commune simply seem abnormal from their viewpoint. A normal human being takes care of himself, first of all. At first, oriental Jews thought that the kibbutz was exploiting their children. Later, they changed their attitudes a bit; today, you more often hear them express the view that the kibbutz is fine, but not for their children, because "my children have to make progress in their lives, they have to profit and own property of their own." A man without property is worth nothing. This is the Asian-African mentality, the main cause for the failure of the absorption of oriental Jews within the kibbutzim. People who came from Europe were much better prepared for the transition to a commune, but

*Temporary immigrant camps, known for their poor conditions.

this preparation was absent from our former culture.

To this day, very few Orientals try to join a kibbutz, or even serve in the Army within the framework of the Nachal.* I tried to convince some of my relatives to let their children serve in the Nachal and taste the kibbutz way of life. The youngsters were quite willing, but their parents objected, and continue to today. They say: "But my son has completed his matriculation exams—he must become something, he must achieve!" As if the kibbutz doesn't offer any avenues for personal development and achievement; as if I, the kibbutz representative, were nothing!

I have a brother who lives in town and struggles constantly with the economic burden of raising his children. He often says to me: "I envy you. You have the good life." I agree, and suggest that he, too, take his family and join a kibbutz. He has a ready answer: "But how can I? What shall I do with my apartment, my savings, etc.?" I can't figure out how so many people find their small private property more meaningful than their happiness and well-being.

People sometimes blame the kibbutz for not doing enough to absorb the Orientals or the underprivileged. I don't think this is true. When I came here, at the age of eleven, I was one of a class of fifty children from similar backgrounds. It's true that at the beginning we were scorned by the local children because of our different upbringing, and we felt somewhat rejected, but I don't think this was the main reason for the high drop-out rate of my group. (Actually, I see the same scorn, rejection, and feelings of superiority in our children today, including my own children here, towards the population of Beit Shean.**)

We were all *ma'abarot* children and were gathered in a special class of outside children. Most of us were new in the country and had hardly had any schooling before. For the first two years, we lived and studied separately, having little contact with the "real" kibbutz children. Within my group I felt very comfortable. We were a lively class; we had lots of fun together. Yet, I noticed the difference between us and the "real" kibbutz children, and I longed to be one of them, truly equal to them. It disturbed me that my parents weren't living in the kibbutz, too, and, unfortunately, I didn't get along very well with my first foster family.

Years later, I realize, however, that the policy of keeping us separate from the local children was, indeed, an extremely wise one. For two years we studied with excellent teachers, our social life was organized by the best adult leaders, and we developed greatly in terms of our social and intellectual skills, so that when we were finally mixed with the kibbutz

*The half-military, half-agricultural branch of the Israeli Army, which is organized to help settle border areas.

**A new immigrant development town near the Jordanian border, not far from Makom.

children the gap between the two groups had almost vanished. (In later years, attempts were made to absorb immigrant children into the regular school right away, and these attempts failed completely.) Our group had also grown much smaller by that time—I think that only about fifteen of us remained from the original group of fifty—and so we could mingle successfully with the local class. I, at least, felt good during this transition and afterwards. We were about thirteen or fourteen years old when we were moved into the kibbutz children's homes, and for me, at least, the feeling of being different had disappeared by that time.

My parents had a great share in my successful adjustment to the kibbutz. For some reason, they weren't like the other oriental parents. Their main consideration was my well-being, and when they saw that I was happy they didn't try to take me back home. They too, however, don't understand what makes me happy in the kibbutz, and to this day they often question me, wondering about it all.

Another factor in my adjustment was my second foster family. From the beginning, the kibbutz had assigned us to local families, but there were failures in this matching process. I was merely a child, and I remember how strange I felt when I had to visit, as if it were a duty, my original kibbutz family, a family with whom I had nothing in common. This happened to many children from my group. Going to my second family was sort of accidental. I became friendly with one of the kibbutz children and he invited me to visit his parents; at his home, I immediately felt comfortable. They were a big family of five children, and I felt really welcome. I felt especially close to my "adopted mother," and they all gave me the warm family life which, as a child, I still desperately needed. I am still very close to my "adopted mother." It's she whom I visited during my leaves from the Army, and later she adopted my wife and four children, too. Indeed, whenever we have a new baby, she's the first person I inform about the happy event.

By the time I finished high school here, it was completely clear to me that this was my home. I had no doubts about it at all. I met my wife in the Army. She's a kibbutz daughter, too, from a kibbutz not far from here. We got married when we finished our military service, and we decided to live here rather than in her parents' kibbutz.

I'm a music teacher here in the kibbutz. Right now I teach music three days a week; during the remaining three days I work at our metal factory or wherever I'm needed. For the last couple of years I worked as a leader of the first *garin* to settle in Ginat. For a long time, music was my hobby. I learned to play several instruments as a child in the kibbutz, and I have started to do some composing, too. A few years ago I was sent to the Teachers' Seminary to get some formal training as a music teacher, and since then I have been teaching here. I find my work unsatisfying, however. Children don't work seriously on this subject, nor is there any serious musical activity for adults here. With T.V., sports, and social

activities, there simply isn't enough time left for music in our life. Music
—singing in a good choir or playing an instrument—demands constant
work and discipline, and people don't seem to want this nowadays.

From time to time, for Passover or another holiday, I organize some
musical performance, or compose something new, but this isn't enough
to give me satisfaction. I believe I'll find some other line of work, or
perhaps I may find my way into music in a more satisfactory manner. As
things are now, I'm pretty frustrated, although perhaps it's partly my
fault, since I could probably put more energy into my field.

Then why are you so pleased with your life in the kibbutz?

I have a happy family, and this means everything to me. A person
must learn to see what's really important in life. For me, work is marginal.
I wanted to become a music teacher, and I made a mistake somewhere
along the line; I know that if I insist on not teaching anymore, I won't have
to. My main source of satisfaction in life is my family. I see my children
grow, what they're getting from the kibbutz, and the kind of relationships
we have within the family; this gives me enough to be able to stand any
frustrations I may encounter elsewhere.

*As a man who came from the lower classes, don't you think that the kibbutz
should do more for the underprivileged?*

In principle, yes, of course [*very angry and excited*]. But maybe it's too
late. Anyway, I, personally, am certain that if I volunteer to go and work
in Beit Shean today, it won't do anybody any good, and it will just cause
me a lot of pain. We used to go there a lot, working in youth clubs, visiting
families, doing volunteer welfare and teaching. Recently, especially since
the last elections, a profound hostility has developed in Beit Shean towards the kibbutzim of the Valley. I feel insulted by things they say about
the kibbutzim, so why should I go to Beit Shean to help? I was highly
motivated to help these people, but I don't know how to anymore. . . .
These are very painful things I wouldn't have expressed a year ago, not
until the last municipal elections. . . . We worked for the Labor Party in
town, and the town is mostly Likud*-oriented. Their hostility towards the
kibbutz was devastating and utterly unfair! They said that we stole their
lands and have turned them, the town dwellers, into refugees, and that
the workers who are employed in our regional factories (which had been
constructed with the interests of the town in mind, so that we would
provide work for their multitude of unemployed, unskilled laborers!) are
unjustly exploited by us. Generally, their complaints against the kibbutzim sounded very much like the P.L.O.'s complaints against the State of
Israel. I deeply resent this situation. I resent the fact that they don't see
their role in the situation, that they project all the responsibility on us.
And why? Because we're the kind of society that doesn't dirty the streets,
a society that knows how to plant a garden, even when its economic

*The right-of-center party now in power.

situation is bad, and then this garden becomes a source of jealousy for our neighbors.

I, as one who had belonged both culturally and ethnically to these subgroups, find it too painful to witness this kind of confrontation. My parents were never like that, anyway. The Orientals here—and perhaps it's a general trait of Orientals—simply can't stand anyone who's been successful in his life. They're envious and must hinder him. So I have personally decided to refrain from any contact with these people. If the situation changes somehow, I'll be more than happy to help again.

Security

S H A L O M *(age 72)*

Shalom's granddaughter, Dafna, appears in "The Young Generation."

I didn't belong to the Chugim Movement, but settling in the Valley was my dream, too. My youth movement, the Young Socialist Movement, debated whether to join an agricultural kibbutz, or to live as a commune in town and participate in the "conquest of labor." At that time, the authorities were letting Jews work in the train service for the first time, and we consulted with Ben-Gurion about choosing this work as our "actualization." B.G. said that the kibbutz was certainly important, but the trains were even more so. "We're going to have a state of our own," he said, "and the trains are run completely by Arabs." So we established a commune in Tel Aviv and we went to work there. I worked in the train service for five years, starting as a simple worker and ending up as an engineer.

In the meantime, I met my wife, who belonged to Makom. Because of my long-lived attraction towards the Valley, I decided to join her and settle there, at the Fountain. When we got married, I wasn't even able to stay for the whole wedding. I was there during the ceremony but then I had to do a night shift on the train, and the party took place without me.

Because my wife was pregnant, we lived with her parents for a while, for at the Fountain there were no children, nor any arrangements for infants yet. We returned to the Fountain when our daughter was eight months old. She was the first child born to the kibbutz.

There were about forty people at the Fountain when we joined, all very young—I was two or three years older than most. Since I was already a Hagana member, and I was trained and experienced compared to other people here, they made me a "general" right away. I became the regional commander of the area.

Personally, I don't think I was qualified for the job. This job was, in those days, like being . . . the government [*laughing*]. You were entrusted with a lot of responsibility. You had to organize for the eventuality that your settlement might be attacked and cut off, to plan for all aspects of such a situation: the women, the children, the lines of retreat—everything. I had some training with firearms, but all these organizational aspects were completely new to me. I had to learn empirically, out of my own experience, how to organize our security. Only much later did I attend a training course of some kind. With time I developed confidence, but the beginning was pretty hard.

I especially remember the year, very much at the beginning, when I was appointed cashier as well. It was the worst year of my life. I was always busy, doing my regular job like the other members, and, on top of all that, I was forever occupied with security, with things about which I had to maintain complete secrecy. After my time as cashier was over, I worked with the cattle for many years. This was much better, since I could be in the kibbutz area all day.

All my life, ever since I joined the kibbutz, I have devoted my energies to security matters. When my daughter was just a toddler, she already knew that Daddy worked with secrets, ammunition, weapons, and hiding places. Near our room I had installed a pipe, buried in the ground, which contained the different documents pertaining to my security job. She, as a little girl, was instructed that in case of trouble, she should burn these papers. This was her role. Somewhat later, I was officially appointed as a gendarme, and this job provided a better cover for my Hagana activities.

Actually, I had at least two roles: One was to prepare the settlement in case of an Arab attack; the other was to take care of the multitude of illegal guns, bombs, and ammunition we had hidden all over the place for the Hagana. It was some job, I'm telling you.

Security in the kibbutz had to do, firstly, with our own firearms. We had our own guns, kept in a locked iron closet—these included hunting guns, which we had legally received from the British for our defense, and guns that were smuggled from abroad or bought from Arabs. When the Jewish Police Units were established, we obtained another twenty-four guns from the British.

We trained all our members in the use of the weapons. I built a special training hall which was part of the sheepfold. Adjacent to the sheep's pen was a storeroom for straw. I added another four or five meters to the whole length of the building, and connected it with a hidden door to the sheepfold. We built double walls with insulation to keep the noise down, and that's where we practiced. I trained all the adults, men and women alike.

You see, security was a very important part of our life, then. The State hadn't been established yet, we didn't have a proper Army to rely upon, and the Hagana people were very few. We had to prepare seriously in the event that we'd be attacked, and might be isolated, in need of defending ourselves with our own limited resources.

We had around-the-clock guard duty, and all the adults took turns, women as well as men. During periods of tension, we had six to eight people on duty every night. Usually there were a pair of guards in each station, one awake and another sleeping, just in case. Moreover, we organized ambushes in the hills. We were constantly on the alert, ready for the Arabs as well as for the British, who might come to search. I organized our first defense system at the Fountain, and later, here in Makom. During our two-year transition period, I was in charge of security in the two spots simultaneously. Up here was a very dangerous site, completely isolated and exposed. Our two neighboring kibbutzim probably let out a sigh of relief when we settled this spot, right among the Arabs, across from Mount Gilboa. To the east there was nothing yet. First, we plowed a wide furrow around the new spot; and planned our defense from this line outwards. In the middle, we had pitched a few tents. As soon as we came here, before the first building was even started, we exchanged fire with the Arabs. I remember one of the very first nights, staying awake inside this furrow, and shooting at the Arabs who had opened fire. They knew of our presence here immediately.

The situation was very tense; it's hard to imagine it today. We exchanged fire frequently, but the Arabs never penetrated our settlement. We were well organized—we knew we had only ourselves to rely upon. Each settlement, village, or kibbutz had the same system. Each had a regional commander, like me, with firearms and a telephone, an intelligence officer, and a second-in-command. There was a communications system throughout the area, using Morse code with either lights or flags. This was our children's job. From the headquarters, we had a direct connection to the first-aid station where a doctor, some nurses, and some stretcher-bearers were always on the alert. In addition, our headquarters included a unit of firemen and someone who was in charge of civil defense, maintaining and allocating places in shelters. Moreover, we had an emergency food store, with basic products and ingredients calculated to suffice for a given length of time. Different people took care of all these functions, but it was, ultimately, my personal responsibility.

One of our responsibilities was the defense of members working in the fields that bordered on hostile Arab villages. Frequently there were attacks on our workers there; once a tractor was damaged but the driver escaped unharmed. When the British mobilized the gendarmes, we first appointed our tractor drivers to be gendarmes; thus they could legally carry weapons with them in the fields.

My second role had to do with a central Hagana arms cache here in the kibbutz. This was a top-secret activity, of course. The Hagana looked for young kibbutzim that were considered loyal to the organization, where they could install extensive central storages of firearms and ammunition. The main cache, which we named "Yankel," was built here by the Hagana while we were still at the Fountain. Even I didn't know at the time what they were digging here. It was built very quickly, and I presumed it was the foundation for some structure of the kibbutz. It housed a supply of weapons that were not currently in use but were being stored for real war and combat. It was an underground room six by three meters, and it was excavated very deep in the ground, more than six meters under the surface. This store contained a lot of things: thousands of bombs, mortar shells, guns of all sorts, and millions of bullets. Only one other kibbutz, besides Makom, had such a big cache. The security conditions were very sophisticated, even by present standards. The door was controlled by a hydraulic system. The entrance looked like ordinary concrete paving but outside there was a faucet that, when turned, raised the trapdoor. On top of this cache, we had our bread bakery and a flour store. Whenever the door was used, it was carefully spread over with flour, which made it indistinguishable from all the other tiles. Inside there was a tunnel and, farther down, the room itself. It had electricity and a ventilation system, but it was always terribly hot inside, nonetheless. The only trouble with this hiding place was that it couldn't be moved easily, of course, so we had to conceal its existence at all cost.

I practically lived down there, like a mole. I took care of the hidden treasure, so that it would be ready for use. But the burden was not so much the difficult work as the constant tension and anxiety for me as well as for all the others involved. There were four or five men who actually knew about the "Yankel"; they were the porters. We were all very young then, merely children, and we had such an immense responsibility. The Hagana officer in charge used to visit the place frequently and he always said: "I rely on you, you know." Actually, all our efforts succeeded, but what a responsibility!

The "Yankel" was our most problematic cache of arms, but we had many more. Our grounds were full of them. We had to hide our own guns and ammunition and, later, the Palmach's weapons as well. My concern with this situation was so intense that I suspected everybody of possibly leaking information, especially newcomers. When a new man or woman arrived at the kibbutz, he or she was immediately suspected of spying. We used to keep an eye on these people, even opening their mail for a while, until we got to know them better. Look, some of those "suspects" are among my best friends today, but, then, I always had to consider the area's security first. In addition to these measures, once a year I would conduct a complete survey in the kibbutz. I invited every person individually to my office, and tried to find out what he or she knew about our various caches and enterprises. If a hiding place was correctly identified by four or five people, we immediately relocated it. This was an incredible undertaking, but it was worth our while, since nothing was ever discovered in our kibbutz, not even on the Black Shabbat.

As I said before, besides the "Yankel" we had many different and smaller hiding places. We had firearms hidden next to every firing position. These were small caches, actually pipes with air-tight covers which were buried about ten centimeters below the ground, so that they could be easily dug out when needed. After some time we learned that the British were using mine detectors to search for hidden firearms. We were in trouble then, since the small caches weren't deep enough and, although well camouflaged, could be easily detected by mine detectors.

So we took all our schoolchildren out of school and we collected all sorts of metal scraps, thousands of tiny pieces, nails, whatever. These discarded scraps we buried in the ground all over the kibbutz, quite densely, and thus we hoped to mislead the British mine detectors.

Later we found out that the detectors couldn't find anything buried deeper than sixty centimeters, so during endless nights we reburied all of our hiding places, this time going down to eighty centimeters. I had completely switched to the night shift by that time; nobody saw me during the day. This solution was, however, good only for weapons we were hiding for future use. The arms for daily use were concealed in a different fashion. We built wooden boxes, and we put the guns in these boxes, just under the surface, with the wooden cover preventing detection by the mine detectors. All this excavation was done by hand, by a small group of people. We would work all night. Our methods proved to be very successful—in some caches we kept weapons underground for five years, and the moment we took them out, they were ready for immediate use, good as new. Of course we didn't invent all these methods by ourselves. We shared ideas with other kibbutzim who faced similar problems.

There was no end to our ingenuity in this area. We hid weapons in rooms and other places above the ground as well. In the children's homes, as well as in several private rooms, we built caches behind closets, where we could move several shelves out and walk into the hiding area. There were some great stories connected with these hiding places. A woman told me that early one afternoon she came home unexpectedly with a headache, and lay down to rest. Suddenly she saw a man entering her closet and, getting up to look for him, she realized he had somehow vanished inside her tiny closet. She swore that the closet had swallowed him alive! We persuaded her that she had dreamt it all. . . .

With time, and especially after the Palmach started training in our kibbutz, keeping track of the hiding places became quite complicated. The Palmach got permission to dig their own caches in the kibbutz area, but we asked them to coordinate their plans with ours. They really picked excellent locations, but found that all of them were already in use by us. I don't think there were a hundred meters that were not already dug, and it became very complicated. We then moved out to the fields and woods surrounding the kibbutz, and started to hide weapons there. There, we had another problem: marking and mapping these remote hiding places. It was a science in itself, but we never made a mistake in finding what we had hidden.

Everything was more or less under control until the Black Shabbat.

Then the British surprised us and surrounded the place. We sent some help to the neighboring kibbutzim, but the unit was caught and returned. The situation was very tense. We had organized a quiet demonstration. We all sat down in groups on the ground; when the British came to arrest us, we resisted passively and didn't submit unless pushed or dragged. We also sang as we sat there, and this deeply impressed the British.

We had so many weapons hidden all over the place here, I was sure we were doomed. We were very lucky, though, for they didn't find a thing. They killed a man in a neighboring kibbutz, and they arrested most of our men—but they found no weapons at all. It proves how right we were in our extreme precautions, which had sometimes bordered on cruelty. They didn't find a thing, and left. I think, though, that they were focusing on something else. We had a radio here, a pretty sophisticated one, one of the first instruments of its kind, and a member of our kibbutz transmitted messages with it. They picked up the waves, and followed their information to its hiding place. So they did find the radio, but nothing else.

With the establishment of the State and of Zahal, all these arms were, naturally, transferred to the new military authorities. But for a long time Zahal didn't possess any better storing places than our caches, so for about two years after 1948 many items just remained here and were gradually taken out by the Army. I remember that throughout the War of Independence our study room was full of ammunition, and TNT was simply lying around in very large quantities.

As long as these arms remained in the kibbutz, I was in charge of the entire defense. We also received new shipments of arms to store, and to these I added various guns which I confiscated from members who returned from combat with arms that they had obtained in various ways. Every man wants to have his own gun, and people used to hide their "private" arms from me. But I have managed to hand over many of these arms to Zahal.

Today none of these arms remains anywhere on our grounds. We merely have a formal arms station, like every other settlement. The station is used for guard duty, or for any possible emergency. There's still a regional commander here, but, naturally, it's a completely different role today.

As I said before, the Palmach was here for a long time, living with us and training here. They were never considered outsiders. The whole Palmach was developed through the kibbutz movement. The Palmach picked, for their training, young kibbutzim, in which they could mingle with the members and remain unnoticed. We had excellent relationships with them. We built a camp for them when we didn't have enough rooms for ourselves. They worked in the kibbutz whenever they weren't busy with training or on missions, and we all ate together in our dining room.

When I recall all this now, it sounds like a great adventure, an interesting life story to tell. But it's hard to describe the terrible tension, the continuous stress, the nightly vigils and duty, the endless tricks and secrecy. Whenever something happened, even far away, we were always apprehensive. It was an extremely heavy responsibility. I don't regret my work, though. People who participated in those enterprises are, somehow, fundamentally different from the people who did not.

There were two things which bothered me a great deal. One was that I was always short of people, reliable people who could carry out various military functions. All the good fighters and commanders were mobilized by the Hagana or the Palmach, serving elsewhere, not here. Me, I had to make do with second-rate people, so to speak, people who weren't mobilized outside, either because they were too old or physically unfit, and, of course, women. We were always short of people for our own defense. It was a burden to work under these restraints, short of firearms, short of men.

The second problem was that, due to my role, I myself could never volunteer to fight elsewhere, to participate in missions that I wished to support. I was glued to the spot. This made me feel rather bad, as important things were happening all over the country. On the other hand, frequently it was I who assigned men to various missions and operations. I sent men to places from which they never returned. . . . Take our three members who were killed in the attack on the Gilboa—I sent them there. I sent them because they were outstanding people. . . . Perhaps I should have been there in their stead, yet that was against my orders. It was a tough role.

When the State was established, I felt a great personal relief. I wasn't as responsible anymore; I didn't feel so alone. I knew there was a whole organization, Zahal, upon which I could rely.

During the War of Independence, it was pretty quiet here. Most of the men were mobilized. We ourselves prepared the shelters and frequently practiced what had to be done in case of an alarm, an air attack, or whatever. Luckily, we had only one air raid: Syrian planes came and bombed the kibbutz; we fired back with our guns, and hit one plane, which crashed nearby. . . . The bombs destroyed our carpentry shop and beehive, but nobody was hurt, for we were all down in the shelters—it proved how right we were in practicing. Every child knew his place in the shelter, and all the *metaplot* were perfectly trained.

In the Six Day War, twenty years later, we also sat in the shelters for a while. Our shelters were much more modern then, and the population much larger, too. These shelters are kept ready at all times. This is the role of our civil defense authorities. Today, however, we use the shelter space for other purposes, too. One shelter serves as our shoe store. Another is some sort of discothèque for the youth. I hope we won't have to use them for other purposes.

The Yom Kippur War was something else, again [*very excited*]. It's still too difficult to talk about. All our men were mobilized, of course, as well as most of our vehicles. Only old people, like me, were left here with the women and children. We immediately formed a headquarters to organize all that had to be done. There was simply nobody else to take over.

Then we started to hear the news—he was killed, and he, and he. . . . We lost eleven men, all outstanding people, within a few days. In order not to lose our spirits completely, it was decided that one of the kibbutzim of the Golan Heights, which had to be evacuated from its spot during the battles with the Syrians, would move in here. Suddenly we received instructions to prepare eighty places for the evacuees. Everybody was busy and the place was crowded so that, even if you wanted to do so, you couldn't despair. We had to carry on with all the daily activities and to take care of the evacuees, so that somehow we put our pain aside, we overcame.

But it was an extremely hard time, especially for people who were aware of what was taking place. I spoke to mothers of soldiers who, I knew, already had been killed; since the information was unofficial, I had to maintain normal appearances until the poor women would get the official announcement. We joked together. . . . So one lives with it, as I have all my life. There's simply no choice.

POSTSCRIPT

Chana * *read parts of the manuscript and added the following to Shalom's account:*
I would tell differently this last part of Shalom's story. I was the social secretary during the Yom Kippur War. People from this young kibbutz of the Golan Heights were not evacuated to us in order to boost our morale. Far from it. On Yom Kippur, at 11:30 in the morning, nobody in the kibbutz knew that war had already started on two fronts. Suddenly I received a call from the Army telling me to prepare space to accommodate the women and children of this kibbutz in Makom. I knew better than to ask any questions but I understood that something serious was going on, and immediately started our preparations for hosting the evacuated kibbutzniks. In the meantime our own men were mobilized and pretty soon the news started to arrive.

These women and children stayed with us for three weeks. It was a terrible period. Five men were killed from this kibbutz, while their wives and children were staying with us. . . . This, in addition to our own eleven losses. I, as social secretary, was the one who received the formal announcements about casualties, and it was my job to inform the families. When it became too much, our general secretary shared this role with me, and we alternated in going to inform the families. . . . It was awful. People were afraid of me when they saw me walking on the sidewalks, the bearer of bad news.

*For Chana's own story, see p. 86.

L E O *(age 64)*

Leo was very pleased to talk to me since he was sick and confined to his bed; our conversation broke the monotony of his day. He looked, at our first meeting, like a frail elderly man. The next week, however, I was sitting in the dining hall across the table from a man, in blue overalls and with an energetic face, smiling at me. I hardly recognized Leo; it was as if, with the change from pajamas to work clothes, he had shed twenty years. . . .

I was a gendarme till 1939, when World War II broke out, and with the war, there was a certain decline of Arab terrorism. Later, I headed the gendarme station until 1945, the end of the war. I was responsible for all the guns and ammunition, and commanded about twenty-five men. We did the nightly guard duty in the whole area and trained three hours a day. All the men were from the neighboring kibbutzim, although we occasionally had hired men as well. Whenever a settlement was in danger, we sent men to reinforce the threatened kibbutz. We fought this way in Tirat Zvi, as well as in many different spots. We cooperated with the Hagana; naturally, they were pretty active in this area. During the day, I worked a lot in hiding our illegal arm caches, "the slicks," as we called them. My official responsibility was to list all the firearms and their daily usage, by whom and for what purpose. This was pretty tricky; since I gave guns to many Hagana members who weren't enlisted gendarmes, I had to put down different names, of real gendarmes, instead. Every Friday a British officer came to my station to inspect the arms and my records. I was always caught in between, reporting both to the British authorities and to the Hagana people, and the reports weren't identical, of course. But my store was kept in perfect condition, and all the guns were as clean and sparkling as my tools are today.

As the British grew wise to our activities, their trust in us declined, and we felt a growing threat of being caught. We hid the illegal arms again and again, planning various diversions, such as burying metal scraps all over the kibbutz to mislead the mine detectors, which we heard the British were using in their searches. I was very busy in all these operations, and shared the anxiety of all the people involved.

The big search took place on the Black Shabbat. This is something no one will ever forget. It was Saturday morning, and I worked in the cow shed that day; it was just my turn to work there for the day. Early in the morning, we received a message that we were surrounded, and as we opened our eyes to the fact, we saw British soldiers and tanks surrounding us on the hills in all directions. Later we received the news by telephone and radio that they had stopped a bus on the road, were conducting a minute search of the other kibbutzim in the vicinity, and that some people had been killed during this search. One man had been shot for refusing to obey the soldiers. There was no reason for it, other than that. We knew that the situation was serious and decided to act completely passively, not to show resistance of any kind. This way we hoped to prevent violence. But we also decided to try and reach Molad, through the fields, and see if we could assist them. We were a group of twelve men, and we started to walk, openly, not trying to hide.

As we reached the hills between Makom and Molad, we were spotted by the British and surrounded by soldiers with machine guns, aiming right at us—it was pretty unpleasant. One of us, who spoke English, tried to start a conversation with the British. "Do you think," he asked, "that we plan to attack you or something?" "Shut up" was all the answer he received. "You behave like the Nazis, you know," he said. This aggravated the British and they pulled out their guns, so we decided to stop talking to them. Then their officer arrived and he said: "Go back home, the game is over." We started to walk towards another kibbutz, still planning to find out what was going on there. "No-no," he said, "not in that direction." So we went back home, strolling leisurely so that we wouldn't attract too much attention.

As we got closer to our kibbutz, we saw British tanks all over the place. It was afternoon already. Earlier the British units had finished searching the other kibbutzim, and now they were concentrating on us. We gathered the schoolchildren all together in one area, outside the dining hall, and we told them to stay there no matter what happened. We had a gate at the entrance to the kibbutz, a pretty gate, which we had locked; we had also put a tractor and a plow on the road right in front of the gate, creating a road block. Suddenly we saw a tank approach, and it drove right through the locked gate and over the tractor. I was with the schoolchildren and when they saw the tank getting closer they panicked and dispersed. We, the adults, were rounded up by the soldiers in the concentration area, an improvised prison. It was just outside our camp to the left of where the road is now. People were obeying, and going out there, but if the British thought they weren't walking fast enough, they jabbed them with their bayonets. The jabs were superficial, not serious, but they hurt nonetheless, and some people were bleeding. I saw a soldier stabbing a member in the buttocks, and I shouted: "Nazis! Fascists!" Though this made them very angry, they stopped. Finally we were all gathered in this makeshift prison, while the soldiers spread out and searched for hidden weapons, radios, whatever. What they had in mind, mainly, was to arrest the Hagana leaders. They had lists of names, and in our kibbutz they were looking for David Ilan and for Abraham, who had participated two weeks before in a big military operation in which bridges had been blown up all over the country. Abraham had been in charge of blowing up an important bridge in the north. It was an operation in which fifteen men were killed and Abraham slightly wounded. The British couldn't identify them, though. We got the two of them dressed up in white gowns, disguised as first-aid men. The British stood there, staring right into their faces, but they couldn't identify them. So finally they decided to arrest all the men, as they had in other kibbutzim. One of our members, a Jewish policeman, who spoke English fluently, said: "But wait, we need some men to take care of the livestock." They agreed, and an order was given: "All the men who work with animals—out!" I had been working with cows that day—this was my first day, mind you—so I felt justified in stepping out. Indeed I wasn't arrested. They took away about seventy or eighty men, who were kept in Rafiah* for about seven weeks. During that period, I actually did work in the cowshed, since that's where I was most needed.

It was very difficult to manage without the vast majority of the men. We received some help from the towns after a while. The Hagana organized volunteers to help the kibbutzim with the essential jobs. They were good people. Some of them are still friendly with families of the kibbutz today. But the Hagana activities did not cease after the Black Shabbat. We went right on with what was needed until Zahal took over. I, personally, fought here in the area. Before the war, I learned sabotage in the Hagana, and so I became a saboteur in Zahal in the Thirteenth Battalion. I remember this period vividly. We conquered Beit Shean by cunning, since we were very short of arms and ammunition. All night we frightened them using a single mortar, and at daybreak we let them catch sight of some camouflaged water pipes, which they thought were cannons. We managed to fool them, somehow, and in the morning they asked to surrender and immediately started to escape towards the east. This escape was a mass flight—there were about 10,000 Arabs there, joined by neighboring villagers. As they were leaving, we entered from the west and took control. I participated in this victory without any weapon whatsoever —and this was the case of many of the soldiers.

E L I (age 63)

From 1947 to this very day, my main job at Makom has been driving a truck. The trucking cooperative was started in 1947, and I've been with it ever since. Actually, I didn't want that job at all; I wanted to work in the garage and I drove only part-time. But in 1947, as convoys to besieged Jerusalem started to get organized, someone came to me and said: "You'll have to drive with the convoys." "But I don't want to be a driver," I protested. "I want to work as a car mechanic." Do you know what the reaction was? "Very well then, people will say that you're too scared to drive on the convoys." This was an argument I couldn't resist—that somebody might accuse me of cowardice—so I started out with the convoys. I did this dangerous route thirty times, bringing food and milk from the Valley to Jerusalem.

*A British prison camp in the south of Israel.

Our trip usually took us two days. On the first day, we organized the food and conserves from the various kibbutzim and drove, in daylight, through the dangerous zone of the Wadi Ara road. There were some Arab snipers in the villages along this road; as the Hagana patrolled the hills only during the day, nobody drove there after four o'clock.

Towards evening we arrived in Tel Aviv, where we had a parking area for the entire convoy. All of the trucks were checked there, and sometimes more things were loaded on. The next morning, we drove to Jerusalem in a convoy, each truck manned by two drivers. When we arrived, we sent off homing pigeons to the kibbutz with the message of our safe arrival. Very frequently, we were attacked and shot at by the Arabs, and several drivers were killed during these trips. During our first trips I did this route without any armor or protection. Then, a member of Makom invented a way to armor our trucks, with double iron plates separated by a wooden board which protected the driver's cabin. A shutter was built for the front window as well, and when the shooting started we pulled down the shutter and continued driving with our visual field confined to a narrow crack before our eyes. It was more or less like driving a tank. But at least we felt more protected against the Arab bullets.

Once, when food was very scarce in Jerusalem, an old, privately owned Chevrolet with a load of oranges joined us on our way up. This truck was in bad shape and it delayed the whole convoy. As we were climbing the hills, some drivers decided to speed up and not wait for this old truck, which didn't belong to the convoy anyway. One young assistant driver—a good man about seventeen at the time—noticed what was going on. He jumped out of his truck and ran up to the first truck. He pointed his gun at the lead driver, and said: "We're all going to drive at the speed of that orange truck. We don't abandon Jews on these roads." So everyone slowed down and entered Jerusalem together. Then, as we drove by the market, this same young driver ran over to the Chevrolet driver, and said: "You're not going to make money on these oranges, selling them on the black market. They're all going to children in need." And so they did.

Another thing I remember: The elderly father of a member of Makom who lived in our kibbutz at the time once came to me before one of the convoys left and gave me some change. "Give this to a beggar you meet in Jerusalem," he said. "The agent for a *mitzvah* [good deed] is protected from danger."* Maybe that is what helped me, who knows? It was very frightening. We were all afraid, although some of us showed it more than others. We weren't such big heroes. Once my assistant driver and I had to stop for a moment in Bab-el-Wad to fix something in the truck, and while outside we picked two cyclamens which we brought home to our wives. It was extremely dangerous to get out of the vehicles

*A Talmudic saying.

there, since you were a standing target outside, but we had to fix the truck. From then on, we brought cyclamens back every time, boasting they were Bab-el-Wad flowers. The truth is, however, that we later found cyclamens growing in a place near Haifa, which was completely safe, and picked the flowers there.

Well, after twenty-nine such trips, the work coordinator told me to quit a bit, to rest for a while. A new young driver took my truck in my stead. Before he departed on the journey, he came to my room to get the keys, and rested up in my room for a couple of hours. I gave him an extra pair of socks, for it was very cold in Jerusalem at the time. I never saw him again. On the outskirts of Bab-el-Wad he was shot by an Arab and died on the spot. My truck was completely burned. Seven cars of the convoy were hit and had to be abandoned, and several drivers were burned alive in their armored trucks. You might say that for me it was God's grace. The next day I got another truck and I drove up again. This was my last trip, for we made a detour to Kefar Etzion where I was stuck for six weeks. My family was sure I was dead, and I very nearly was. . . . I later took part in the War of Independence as well as in other wars, driving my car on military missions. No one ever talks about the heroism of drivers, but, I'm telling you, there are many stories to tell.

The
Eisman Family

INTRODUCTION

The first section of the book, dealing with Makom's early period, its establishment, its absorption of a growing number of people, and its struggle with the problems of security, will end with a presentation of five members of one family, all presently living in Makom.

The Eisman family is one of the central families in Makom. The individual histories of its members relate to many of the issues that have been brought up in the former chapters of the book. The additional profiles of the two young women in the family also serve as a preview of different issues concerning the younger population of Makom, issues which will be enlarged upon in the following sections of the book.

However, more than the individual stories, the picture of this family as a whole is of specific interest. The relationships which are revealed between the individual members of the Eisman family, between husband and wife, parents and children, may contribute to the understanding of the human element behind the stoic "front" of devoted kibbutzniks: the universal conflicts of human relations, as well as other conflicts that are perhaps indigenous to this particular society. Within the following stories are some hints about the structure of the family in the kibbutz and, specifically, about the development of a family in which both parents are deeply involved in the public life of the kibbutz.

There seems to be inevitable conflicts among the ideals that the kibbutz sets for itself. It believes that women should dedicate their energy and time to public concerns to the same extent as men do. It also believes that parents should be at least partially freed of their responsibility for their children's upbringing, yet the daily demands of familial roles still seem to follow a rather conservative model. The consequences of this situation are revealed both in the expressed guilt feelings of mothers (specifically in Chana's case) and in the ambivalent attitudes of their

daughters. Interestingly, it was usually women who expressed these conflicts and concerns, whether because of their greater awareness of such
problems and willingness to speak of them, or because men simply do not
experience the same problems.

The head of the family, Zvi, is one of the first German-Jewish immigrants who settled in Makom. He served in many different functions in
the kibbutz and the Movement, and is currently a student and a factory
worker. His ex-wife, Ester, and his present wife, Chana, both live in
Makom, and are both very energetic women who have served in many
central public roles throughout the years. These three first-generation
members may be characterized by their deep identification with the kibbutz as an ideologically desirable way of life and their lifelong involvement with its public roles and concerns.

Ester and Zvi have one daughter, Vered, now more than forty years
old. She too lives in Makom, is married to an immigrant from Iran, and
is the mother of four children. Chana and Zvi have four children. Their
elder son moved to another kibbutz; their younger son is serving in the
Army; one daughter lives in town, and the other, Iris, lives in the kibbutz.
Of the second generation, the stories of Vered and Iris will be presented
below. They are both mothers in the kibbutz and have worked, as most
women do, in its educational system. The contrast between these women
and their parents is dramatic. Both appear detached from their parents'
idealism, and their lives in the kibbutz are of a very different quality. As
will be seen later, this basic difference between the old and the young of
Makom is not at all unique to the Eisman family.

The different branches of the Eisman family live harmoniously in the
kibbutz. Ester and Chana seem to have a friendly relationship, as do their
children and grandchildren.

Z V I (I) (age 66)

*I met Zvi early one morning and accompanied him to breakfast after two hours of
easy conversation. In blue overalls, he was on his way to work at the metal factory.
He has a very pleasant voice and a warm, kind look in his blue eyes. Despite all his
years and experience, he impresses me as an unusually trusting man.*

I was born in 1912 in a little town on the border of Germany and Switzer-
land. Since my father, a doctor, was killed in World War I, I hardly knew
him. My mother, a truly remarkable woman, was thirty-six years old when
my father was killed; after that, she raised me and my brother, took care
of the family property, and rented rooms in our spacious house to students and tourists.

She wasn't a Zionist when my father fell in the war. After the war,
however, she was offended by the German nationalistic propaganda,
which claimed that Jews hadn't served their homeland loyally during the

war; she turned to Zionism. Once involved, she became a zealot in the movement, and our house became the local Zionist club. Many of the Zionist leaders stopped in now and again at our house, and in this way I got to know several of them quite intimately. The Jewish background I received from my family was, however, minimal, and this wasn't helped by the fact that I went to a non-Jewish high school in which most of the teachers were Catholic priests. I learned Hebrew from one of the priests and, later, something of the Jewish tradition from a scholar who used to rent a room at our house. Culturally, I was very much under the German-Christian influence; I actually breathed it in my native environment, in the music, art and literature, architecture and history of the place. I didn't feel any anti-Semitism during my childhood. The Protestant and Catholic students in our high school fought and cursed each other at least as much as they did the Jews. In fact, we were all fairly friendly as a group of adolescents.

A little later I became interested in politics, and was drawn, in particular, to the Communist Party. I was at that time a Jew, a Zionist, and a Communist, and saw no contradictions among them. Frequently I used to collect money for the Jewish National Fund during the day and attend meetings of our communist cell at night. My Jewish background didn't disturb me as much as my belonging to the upper-middle class rather than to the working class. I was ashamed of my big house and of the status of my family in town.

The final turning point in my youth occurred when I attended one of the Zionist Congress meetings, and met the delegates from Eretz Yisrael. Here, I felt, were real-life Socialists, while what I was doing in my communist cell was merely conducting sophisticated debates. I was tremendously attracted to these delegates, to the concrete reality of their actions; the insight of that encounter has actually remained something I believe in to this very day. I believe that we, the Israeli kibbutzniks, are actually the only true Socialists on earth. I don't know enough about China, but I think that, of all the societies I know, the kibbutz is the best existing realization of the communist ideology, both in the economic and the humanistic sense. This is notwithstanding the fact that we live in the midst of a capitalistic environment which, naturally, affects us in many ways.

Well, since my father had been a doctor, it was assumed that I'd study medicine, too. The whole family moved to Berlin, where I started medical school. My mother viewed her short stay with me in Berlin as a temporary station en route to Eretz Yisrael, to which she indeed immigrated two years later. I attended medical school for two years until—in 1931, I think —in the anatomy class, I found one morning that the Jewish corpse that we had been dissecting had been tatooed with two swastikas. This shocked me very deeply, and I decided I was wasting my time at the university and would rather go and work for the Zionist movement.

The Zionist organization was glad to accept me, and I was assigned the role of youth leader in the eastern part of Berlin. Here I encountered for the first time the Eastern European Jewish culture, religious and Yiddish-speaking. I also found a tutor who taught me the Talmud for the first time. A few months later I was sent to an agricultural *hachshara* in Holland.

Each pioneer was sent alone to a farm, to work for a farmer. On my first farm, I lived above the stables and worked from daybreak until night-fall. The transition was quite difficult—from the easygoing life of a student to the life of a farmhand. I used to reach my room so exhausted that I went to sleep immediately, neither washing nor eating. But gradually I adjusted and developed a close relationship with the Dutch farmer who had employed me and knew the Bible much better than I. I remember noticing that many guests used to visit the farmer during the day. Finally, I asked him about this, and he admitted, blushing, that his neighbors came to see his Jewish worker, the first Jew they had ever seen doing physical work.

Twice a month, we *hachshara* members gathered together on Saturday from our various farms for a meeting. Women members also worked on the farms, helping the Dutch women with their housework. We all worked extremely hard, but the Dutch farmers worked alongside us, so we didn't feel exploited. We were allowed to take evening courses in agriculture, which was of great importance to us. These years of my *hachshara* in Holland were the best agricultural schooling I could find, and laid the foundation for my future in the kibbutz.

Once, at our Saturday meeting, I met a delegate from Kibbutz Givat Brenner in Israel, Ancho Sireni (who was later killed in World War II when he parachuted behind the German lines on a rescue mission), and we walked together along the streets of the beautiful Dutch town we were in. The place was all green, abundant with flowers, and sparkling clean. "You see," said Sireni, "in thirty years, Givat Brenner will look like this." I thought he was crazy. I imagined a kibbutz as part of a biblical land-scape, a desert with tents and donkeys, while he was pointing to a Dutch town as a model. Well, look around. He was right and I was wrong; sadly, he died too young to witness his prediction's coming true.

In the winter of my second year of *hachshara,* when the Nazis had already taken over Germany, I got a cable saying: "Return immediately to Berlin." I wrote to my mother, who was already in her kibbutz in Israel. She answered that I shouldn't, by any means, risk the return to Germany at that time. But another message had arrived in the meantime, clearly stating it as a command from the Chalutz center in Germany. They needed me there, and the relationship within the organization involved absolute discipline, so I obeyed. The year was 1934, and again I was a youth leader in two different sections of Berlin, representing two Jewish worlds: the Western, assimilated sector; and the Eastern-immigrant, religious sector, with its rich Jewish heritage. Both sectors were, however, under the threat of rising Nazism, and our task was to prepare the youth for *aliya*. Actually it wasn't too difficult at the time, since the Germans were keen on having the Jews leave Germany, and helped us in many ways. It was, of course, quite profitable for them, because Jews paid heavily for their emigration permits.

I remember once giving a lecture, in a little town, about cooperation in the new economy of Eretz Yisrael. The audience was made up of the entire Zionist movement of that town, but right in front of me, in the middle of the first row, sat four Nazis, complete with uniforms and insignia, among them the local chief of police. I was worried about their presence, yet pretended to ignore them and delivered my lecture. Next morning, at the train depot, the chief of police showed up. He approached me, shook my hand, and said: "Rarely do we get to hear such an interesting presentation here. I wish you good luck—go to your Eretz Yisrael and may God be with you." Although I was, naturally, surprised, I encountered several similar reactions on the part of Nazis during that period.

Anyway, when I returned to Berlin to work for the Zionist movement, I met Ester, my first wife, who was also working for the Zionist movement. When she became pregnant, we sent her immediately to Israel, before her pregnancy began to show, since pregnant women couldn't get certificates. She was accepted and taken care of by my mother, while I continued my activities in Berlin. One day, in the middle of lecturing, I received a cable saying that my wife had given birth to a daughter, Vered, my first child. A week later, there was another cable, from my mother, saying that my wife was seriously ill and that I should make every attempt to come to Israel, too. This was indeed the end of my prolonged stay in Germany.

The fastest way to get a certificate was by using a tourist visa, which cost a great deal of money. I managed somehow to get the money from a Jewish gentleman, and soon enough I arrived in Haifa, where my wife was hospitalized with what was later diagnosed as a severe case of malaria. For a few weeks I remained with her, while our daughter stayed with my mother. Then one day my wife said: "Go to the kibbutz. I'll join you when I'm well," and I joined the group near the Fountain. Joining is a simple word . . . [*laughs*].

On the evening of my arrival, I walked alone all the way from the train station. The place was . . . the best term to describe it today is "hip," extremely hip. There were numerous huts and tents, and many people lived in the trees. The atmosphere was everything we labeled "hippie" in the 1960s—in appearance, manners, and language. I particularly recall the dining hall, as I saw it on my first evening there. Around one table in the corner, which could normally seat about eight people, were crowded some forty people, all making a vegetable salad. The noise and the filth reminded me of a marketplace; it was really shocking for me with my good German manners. Gradually I discovered that the noisiest of all were the Israelis. They were half-baked intellectuals who had completed, or partially completed, a high-school education, and were rebelling against the bourgeois background of their parents' homes, and against anything that could be defined as polite behavior.

I had several friends who had already settled in the place. I spoke good Hebrew, and was a trained worker—so I had absolutely no problems in adjusting and being accepted by the kibbutz. Although I did belong to the German sub-group, I personally have never felt the negative attitudes of the Sabras towards the Yekkes, something that many of my friends complained about. Indeed, the Hebrew of the new German immigrants was the laughingstock of the community, and many suffered from this ridicule. Furthermore, many Yekkes felt belittled and scorned, even discriminated against, in many ways. However, I don't think those feelings were justified. The Israelis knew that we were superior to them in our education and cultural background, and deep down they held us in high respect.

What really bothered me was the Sabras' complete lack of respect towards our common property or towards basic rules of order and organization. Indeed they were reacting against bourgeois values, but in some ways it was a very self-destructive revolution. I was, for example, very strongly in favor of our storeroom-A system—the kibbutz was a commune and this was accepted and understood. If we had coffee—it should be fairly shared by all; that was proper and just. However, the German immigrants had come to the kibbutz very well equipped, with fur coats, leather boots, and good dresses. They gave everything to the common store, and the next day they would meet an Israeli, in the sheep pen or the vegetable garden, in their coat or boots, ruining them immediately. Many valuable items were ruined just out of childish disrespect for property, as if to spite. Naturally, this hurt many of the German newcomers. I still remember that period as focusing around the issue of equality. The struggle then, among people who came from very different backgrounds, was much more painful and severe than anything that could happen today.

Some individuals really felt exploited, and the discord frequently concerned very elementary things. Like kerosene lamps, which were distributed one to a room, yet some members "managed" to get two, and it made a tremendous difference. Or food—frequently we were really hungry, and, if an Israeli member could visit his or her parents once a week, or every couple of weeks, and eat three substantial meals at home, it made a big difference. There is more equality today than in those days, although the kibbutz has grown much more liberal in these matters over the years. So today, perhaps a member does manage to retain a private bank account in town, against the rules—what do I care? We have similar apartments, we both get all that we need and much more. If he goes abroad to visit with relatives, I will go in my turn as well. Basically, we live alike, much more so than in the old days, I believe.

Well, I joined the kibbutz alone, since Ester was still sick. I worked very hard, mostly outside the kibbutz, in the stone quarry, for the electrical company, the water company, whatever. Physically, it was difficult, and we ate much too poorly for such work. A piece of bread, olives, and halva was all I got during the day. But I learned where to eat better—with our "richer" neighbors, the more established kibbutzim. Frequently, while working for the water company, I planned my route so that I'd "happen" to be in the right kibbutz at mealtime. I suffered more from heat though, and actually, to this day, I have not adjusted to the change of climate. I caught malaria, naturally, as everyone else did; frequently the fever had about 50 percent of the members in bed. When my wife joined me, we got a family room which was not much bigger than our bed, and the walls were thin, paperlike partitions. When I shivered with fever, the tremors were felt in the adjoining rooms and my neighbors came running in . . . but all this was considered normal. We knew that we were building our kibbutz by the fruit of our hard labor—there was no one else to turn to for help—and this gave us the greatest satisfaction.

Some people couldn't take this kind of life, though. We had many suicides in the beginning. They started before my arrival and continued; in approximately nine years we had about nine suicides. Two or three of them nearly destroyed the community. We were deeply affected by this. People had guns, and the most common method to kill oneself was by gunshot. Only men committed suicide in that wave. . . .

It's difficult to understand the reasons for that kind of desperation. It was a very young society; the majority of the people were eighteen or nineteen years old; the "elders" were in their twenties. All of us had drastically changed our life-style from that of middle-class intellectuals to that of homeless day laborers, often hungry and sick with fever. In the background was the awareness that with our kind of starting point in life we could have had important careers in the country, which we gave up by joining the kibbutz. It was a profound inner struggle. Work was the highest value in life, yet work was terribly difficult physically, especially in this heat. In the kibbutz, a person was judged by his working ability, and some of the people who were used to being popular and respected in their former environments were suddenly despised and scorned here, since they couldn't stand the difficult work. There was a great amount of friction. It's much more demanding to live constantly among friends than to meet them periodically. Some people who had been friends before became enemies or competitors, and the change was very painful. All this proved to be too demanding for some, and they simply couldn't cope with the situation. Add to this the romantic motivation of some of the suicides and the fact that going back home was unforgivably shameful; for some individuals there was no way out. A combination of these factors caused the suicides, and once they started they were more or less contagious.

Look at who the people were who had joined the kibbutz at that time. Both Israelis and immigrants were essentially people who hadn't adjusted to their original environments, who were in some conflict with their society, and the result of this conflict was often the decision to join the Zionist movement or the kibbutz. Who was able to endure the hard life of the kibbutz in its beginning stages? I believe they were individuals with outstanding strength of character, or people who had extremely strong ideological convictions, or those who had found social satisfaction in the kibbutz, for whom the togetherness, the fun, the dancing and the youth-movement atmosphere were very satisfying. A strong character was, however, the most important factor in adjusting, and those who lacked this couldn't cope with the situation.

The encounter with death in our midst was very traumatic, especially because of our youth and lack of experience. We felt it as personal failure. We were insulted, angered, and aggrieved by the suicides. They almost led to a disintegration of the whole kibbutz. For days following such an event, everyone would walk alone, hardly talking to each other. In particular, we avoided the people closest to the suicide—his wife or girlfriend, his parents when they came to the funeral. We didn't know how to relate to the disaster, and our reaction to the mourners was one of disdain, almost of ostracism, as in some primitive societies. It's very strange. At that time, we told each other that the relatives wanted to be left alone. . . . Today, as an adult, I know how far from the truth this is, how cruel it is to isolate bereaved people in their pain. . . . We buried these members, our first dead, near the Fountain. We buried them with mixed feelings of injury, anger, and pain, but we carried on. I think that other kibbutzim underwent similar traumas during that period. The phenomenon completely disappeared once the riots* started. There were, perhaps, one or two suicides later, but they weren't as directly connected to adaptation to the kibbutz way of life.

I can't make you a chronological list of the various things I did in the kibbutz, for throughout the years I've done almost everything; some roles I have even carried out twice. I have been an industrial worker, a gardener, a farmer, a secretary, a cashier, a teacher, and more. I have carried out many functions outside the kibbutz, in the Party or in the Movement's higher-education institutions as well. I have got them pretty much mixed up by now, but I am certain of one thing: Whenever I had the choice, I returned to simple labor again.

Right now I work in our metal factory. I'm "retired," so to speak, and

---

*In 1936 the local Arabs launched a series of riots against the Jews that encompassed the whole country.

work only six hours a day [*laughs*]. Nobody forces me to work, you know.
. . . Years ago I received a large sum of reparation money from the
Germans, and handed it all in to the kibbutz, naturally. I receive a
monthly pension from the Germans, as well—which goes directly to our
cashier; I don't even know how much it is. So I feel I'm a rich man, and,
after all these years of hard work and the extra income I brought into the
kibbutz from the Germans, I do only what I like. I like physical work,
however, and my job is an interesting one, not routine. But I know that
if I had requested to go study philosophy at the university for three years,
it would have been no problem to have my request approved. I do study,
though, in a part-time study program which I have organized for myself,
and I travel twice a week to the university and take advanced classes in
Judaism, especially in the Talmud. I, who received my cultural heritage
from the German Catholic teachers of my native town, am gradually
discovering my roots in the Jewish religion and its scholarly tradition. It
fascinates me, yet it often aggravates me as well. You see, I'm a Marxist,
a left-oriented Socialist and a kibbutznik, and with all my natural liberality
I take these words quite seriously. To work at integrating my old values
with Judaism is not an easy undertaking. But I'm working on it.

I'm content with my life. I think that the kibbutz in its present form
has fulfilled my wildest dreams. Actually, reality has surpassed all my
youthful fantasies. Personally, too . . . I'm not bothered by the problems
we still face; they are normal. Take the problems of equality or discipline
—I don't like to push myself into the private business of others, and I'm
not frightened by deviations from prescribed conduct. A kibbutz should
be a place to live in and not to suffer in.

Next Monday I am going for a visit to the States with Chana. We'll
stay there for six weeks, visit with friends and relatives, and on our way
back we'll stop at my native town in Germany, which I have not visited
since I left. From the kibbutz point of view there's nothing special about
this trip—it's finally our turn to go.

E S T E R (age 64)

*Ester is Zvi's first wife and Vered's mother. After she got divorced from Zvi, she
married another man, with whom she had a son. Her second husband was killed
many years ago in an airplane accident, and she has been living alone since then.*

Presently I'm a beautician here [*smiling*], but I have been anything you can
imagine since I settled in this kibbutz. I was a tractor driver in the fields,
I worked in the chicken coops, in the laundry and in the clothes storeroom. I have been in charge of the kitchen and I was the work coordinator. For years I worked outside the kibbutz for the Labor Party, especially
in its various women's organizations, and I specialized in education of
underprivileged young women. All this has given me opportunities to see

the kibbutz, and especially the women of the kibbutz, from many different perspectives.

When I worked for the Labor Party in Tel Aviv I took a course in cosmetics, thinking ahead to the time when I wouldn't be strong enough to run around, and being a beautician would be a nice, easy occupation. And indeed, I started working as a beautician two years ago, work full time now, and enjoy my work very much. I believe it's extremely important for women in our kind of climate, with tremendous changes of heat and humidity between day and night, summer and winter, to take good care of their skin.

Naturally, having a cosmetologist as well as a hair stylist, which we also have, may sound somewhat out of place in a kibbutz; it certainly doesn't fit the image of the simple life of the kibbutz. Actually, however, neglect was never part of our ideology. Years ago we were simply too poor to offer this kind of treatment to our women, and the ideal of living "naturally" was probably the outcome of this poverty. I remember, when I came to the kibbutz many years ago and was working in our communal clothes store, the famous storeroom A, how we used to sit, every free hour, and do fine embroidery on the girls' simple shirts, trying to give our extremely poor clothes the nicest appearance. I even thought then of developing an "Israeli kibbutz fashion." Well, this is something I haven't gotten around to, so far [*laughing*]. Now that we have the means to do so, kibbutz women take good care of their skin, body, and appearance, as it should be, and almost every kibbutz has specialists who work full time in these areas.

The women's situation in the kibbutz has been one of my major concerns. Presently, a vast majority of the women members work in the service branches: education, kitchen, laundry, sewing, etc. All these branches are extremely important, and in town people who use these services pay well to have them. You pay to send your child to a day-care center, to go to a restaurant, or to send your clothes to a laundry. So all these so-called service branches should be considered income-producing branches. This would make a tremendous difference in the self-image of the women working there. I believe that a change such as this is possible. It would require a system whereby members would get a higher personal budget and would use it to pay for the various services they get in the kibbutz. Perhaps it's just a psychological change, but I consider it of great significance for the status of women in the kibbutz. Take our child-care service, for example, which is completely operated by women. I think it's the most productive of all the branches in the kibbutz! We now have more than four hundred children, and more than a hundred of our adults have been raised here and they're now the main working power of the kibbutz! No doubt, raising children is the most productive branch we have, and it's good that people tend to have large families here. The only problem is how to change the system in such a way that the income of the women who dedicate most of their professional lives to child care and education will enter the records as "productive" and not merely "services." I believe that these misleading labels are one of the sources of women's frustrations in the kibbutz and I hope that someone will work on this problem. For me it's too late; I should have studied economics for that purpose, but instead I was more inclined towards politics.

I have the highest regard for women's work in the kibbutz. Working in today's laundry or kitchen demands very high technical skills—I know because I worked in our laundry recently. The process is completely mechanized, and the women who work there operate various machines of varying levels of complexity. Running these branches is no less complicated than running a big-city restaurant, a factory, or an agricultural branch—and it's all done by women. Therefore, I don't see why women think so lowly of their work here; it's just a wrong attitude.

Personally, I believe that women can undertake any job, can perform every kind of work. A woman should be directed in her choice by her talents and interests, and there should be no restriction imposed by her sex. As a child, I wanted to be a boy and preferred pants to dresses—and this was way before the era of women's pants. . . . I was attracted to the kibbutz, among other things, because of my belief that it would offer complete equality to the sexes, and I have always managed to realize this value in my own life, whether by working on a tractor or by working in politics. Therefore, I'm convinced it's possible.

In general, I wish that people in the kibbutz would be more aware of the basic problems and wider implications of their way of life. I joined the kibbutz and stayed here because I saw it as the best way to realize a socialist and a Zionist life-style, and never merely because it was a pleasant place to live. That's also the source of my dedication to politics; I believe that the kibbutz movement will perish if the whole country doesn't develop more in the direction of cooperation. The kibbutz movement can't be an island; it must be an avant-garde vehicle, an ideal for society at large. The decline of the Labor Party and the changing political climate in the country might endanger the kibbutz movement in many ways. Therefore, it is of primary importance that people who live in the kibbutz should see in it an ideological way of life, and not merely a clean, beautiful community, good for pets, children, and adults. . . . I'm afraid, however, that that is the outlook of many of our second-generation members, who live here just because they were born here and love this kind of existence. This is also reflected by the fact that the kibbutz has become more and more egocentric with the years, concentrating on its own internal goals rather than its ties with the society at large. As a result, its impact on society has greatly declined, and we maintain only minimal ties with the urban working classes with whom we should be affiliated. A kibbutz can't be an island; we're just 3 percent of the population in Israel and that's a small number, with a real danger of disappearing. We must grow.

I don't think that being a woman has stopped me from seeing these problems and being active in all those directions, although most kibbutz women do give first priority to their family lives. Generally, I feel that the family has become too central and important in the kibbutz, and it wasn't meant to be this way in our beginning. When the kibbutz was young, the group was more important than the family cell. When a couple formed, they felt awkward. They never walked into the dining hall together or left it as a pair; couples didn't want to stress their relationships as different from the communal relationships of the group. On the other hand, it isn't true that the kibbutz encouraged "free love." We were all young and unattached then, and naturally our relationships were relatively free but, once a couple formed, the family framework was as strictly observed within the kibbutz as anywhere else. With the normal process of growing up, the family has become an element as natural in the kibbutz as elsewhere. I believe there shouldn't be a conflict of interests between family and community; the two can and should work in harmony.

One difference between the family unit in the kibbutz and the conventional unit is that family relationships are not maintained for formal or technical reasons alone. Due to financial security within the kibbutz, families don't try to preserve their unity when the relationship has gone sour. There is no need to retain a framework which has become meaningless, because considerations of common property, livelihood, child care, etc., are much less significant here than elsewhere. It's quite easy to move out of your family room without otherwise disturbing your general lifestyle. It's highly personal, of course, but I do think that this was the attitude among the first generation. If there were a crisis or a conflict, separation was quite common, and, since people didn't make great efforts to live with an impossible mate, false relationships were relatively rare. In my time, there was no stigma attached to separation or divorce, nor any social pressure to keep the family intact if marriage was no longer to the benefit of both people. This trend has perhaps changed in the second generation. It seems that it is harder to make a decision to separate nowadays.

I personally believe that life isn't perfect, individuals aren't perfect, and promising couples often fail to cope with years of life together. I think one should face the fact of an unhappy relationship, and try to rebuild his or her life. Of course, it's a very personal matter, but I feel it's easier to make such a decision in a kibbutz than in town.

Zvi and I separated when Vered was about six years old. We didn't quarrel; we ended our relationship in full understanding. It was hard on Zvi, at first, to live in the same kibbutz with me yet be separated, so the kibbutz arranged a position for him with the youth movement in Jerusalem. Later, however, we both adjusted to our separation and remarried; now we're simply good, old friends. In some cases, divorce doesn't work as smoothly, however. I remember a case, here in the kibbutz, where the "deserted" husband demanded that his former wife leave the kibbutz with her new mate. This demand can only be personal, of course, since the kibbutz could in no way take a position on such a matter. They did leave the kibbutz temporarily and then returned, and now all the ex-spouses of this family live here in one community. Of the separations I now remember in Makom, this traumatic case was highly exceptional.

The kibbutz is also more tolerant of single mothers, who are very well accepted among us. We have in the kibbutz six or seven women—at least one is about my age—who at a certain point in their lives decided to have a child without forming a permanent relationship with a man. In some cases, the father's identity was not revealed; in others, the fathers were outside the kibbutz but did maintain special relations with their children. One rather exceptional case was of a single woman having a child by a prominent kibbutz member with the full agreement of his wife. This child even carries his father's name. Although it isn't a widespread phenomenon, in each case the mother felt safe and completely unstigma-tized, and the children proved to be normal and seem to have grown up without any unusual complications. I think it's one of the assets of our kibbutz society that, due to its communal responsibility in the social and economic spheres, it can allow and accept such phenomena. For me, it's an indication of our high moral level.

I, too, took care of my two children alone for the most part; and, although I hadn't chosen to do so, it didn't stop me from being as active in the community as I wanted to be. I went to a seminary when Vered was twelve or thirteen years old, and I used to return home every day towards evening. During that period, I saw it as completely natural that Vered would take care of her younger brother, who was then five, during the afternoons. On the other hand, I let them sleep with me in the room at night, and they often did. When I did have time to spend with my chil-dren, we did rather unusual things together. I drove a car before any other woman here, and on weekends we used to take a jeep and go on wonderful trips together. And we used to go fishing together. I felt no conflict between my maternal activities and other activities. The children spent hours with me in the various places where I worked, and seemed to be happy "working" with me; for them, it was their favorite game. The most difficult conflict of interests I remember occurred when I worked as a youth leader—probably because my own children resented my working with other children.

I think that the kibbutz is actually a place which enables parents to develop the closest and most meaningful relationships possible with chil-dren. People work hard until 4:00 or 5:00 P.M., and then can devote their entire attention to their children. While they're at work, adults don't have to worry about their children, because the kibbutz provides them with the best child care. This fact should free both men and women, even young mothers, to satisfy themselves equally in their work, each in his or her own area. And, above all, the afternoons are free of the housewife's chores of cooking, mending, or doing laundry, so that parents can really play with their children, tell them stories and relax with them. That, for me, is another special characteristic of the kibbutz way of life—really freeing parents for "parenting" by taking over all the technical aspects of the role. I see in this one of the greatest achievements of our society.

Furthermore, I'm one of the ardent supporters of the children's dormitory arrangement. I'm certain that it doesn't harm our children, and, at the same time, it frees both parents in the later evening hours for social activities and studies, which are such central aspects of our kibbutz life. If children were to sleep at the private home, this would completely prevent young mothers from pursuing voluntary or public activities—and they're not too active anyway these days. A few weeks ago I visited another kibbutz, which has recently made the transition to private lodging. I was invited, with other people, for an evening of questions and answers; before the public meeting took place, we were invited to the room of the woman presently serving as coordinator of cultural affairs. This woman had four children in the apartment with her, whom she had to see to bed, in addition to hosting the activity. I sensed terrible tension in the situation, but she denied it, saying she rather liked the idea that her children slept in. Well, I don't know. Maybe she has this attitude because she's a Holocaust survivor; her family is of utmost importance to her.

C H A N A *(age 56)*

Chana is among the busiest people in the kibbutz, presently running the school—a very central position. She is a pretty, white-haired woman, with bright blue eyes, yet her face and posture seem to be burdened by heavy responsibility. She is pleased with her kibbutz life, yet does not hide her deep disappointments, and, all in all, impresses me as a sad person.

I was born in 1922 in the border area between Hungary and Rumania. It was a region which changed hands several times, but the Jews remained loyal to Hungary, and Hungarian was my mother tongue.

Although my father was a highly educated man, dedicating a great deal of his time to Jewish studies, and very respected in town, our financial situation was quite poor. Father was a saintly type. He drove a horse cart around the countryside, selling vinegar in villages; he would be away from home for weeks, surviving all the while on bread and olives, since he ate only strictly kosher food. This hard work provided only an extremely meager livelihood; yet, when he asked to be employed in the local Jewish carpentry shop as a simple worker, the owner refused to give him work because he was ashamed to employ such a scholar as a manual laborer. We never went hungry, but I remember the constant atmosphere of need. I used to share a bed with my older sister, and I remember one night after we went to sleep my father suddenly arrived from his trip. Half-asleep, I felt his kiss, then saw him bending down by the bed, lifting our shoes and inspecting the soles with a sigh. "Again we have to make new soles," he said. It was a constant problem. We were five children— I was the second—four sisters and a brother, our youngest family member.

I studied at the local Jewish elementary school, and although both my home and school were strictly Orthodox, I never felt forced to conform to the religious rules. When I was drawn to socialism and gradually became non-observant, there was never an open conflict between me and my father concerning my behavior. At the basis of this liberality lay my father's gentle personality and his conviction that his way, the traditional Jewish life-style, was leading nowhere, whereas I perhaps was on the right track towards a better Jewish existence. He was pretty discouraged, aware of the approaching catastrophe, and therefore willing to let me experiment and try to actualize the new Zionist alternative.

I finished elementary school, but it was very difficult for the family to support me through high school, which was in the "big city." I studied there until I was fifteen-and-a-half years old, though; by that time, I was already deeply involved in the Zionist movement and didn't care too much about having to leave school for financial reasons. Back in our town, Father found me a job at a local Jewish store, where I worked as a clerk, and I dedicated all my free time to organizing a Zionist youth movement in our town. It was based on the Shomer Hatzair* ideology, directed towards the Kibbutz Hameuchad Movement, and it became the focus of my life. We were extremely active, trying to solve the problems of the whole world, discussing socialism and communism, reading a lot, and trying to mold our daily life-style in accordance with these ideologies. I remember how we made it a point to dress as simply as possible, and wearing silk stockings was one of the most disgraceful crimes imaginable. I found a lot of satisfaction in my work in the movement, and it was completely evident to me that, with time, I'd go on *hachshara* and immigrate to Israel.

I loved my parents and family, in particular my father, but it was unquestionably clear to me that their existence was hopeless. There was no solution to the Jewish problem in Europe, and if anything was right and proper it was my own direction. My older sister did accept the Jewish Diaspora destiny. She learned to sew and became a seamstress. I didn't want to go to a vocational school, yet my parents couldn't afford to provide me with an education, and the only alternative was, therefore, Eretz Yisrael. I think I pointed towards a hopeful solution for all of them, yet I was the only one in whom these hopes materialized at that time.

*Left-wing youth movement aligned with the Kibbutz Haartzi.

. . . It makes me very sad to remember those days of the late 1930s
. . . the despair I sensed on the one hand, and the beautiful, loving family
life of my parents on the other. I was sure—and yet, obviously very sad
—that I had to get away.

In 1939, when World War II broke out, I had already finished my
hachshara and had become a member of the secretariat of the Movement.
I lived in a commune in the city with several Jewish guys. They worked
in various jobs in factories since agricultural training was extremely difficult to find. Our physical conditions were very poor. I remember the cold
nights without sufficient heating, trying to warm ourselves up by lying
close together, using tents from the previous summer camp as blankets.
We ate almost nothing but bread, since one of our men worked in a
bakery and got bread for his salary. . . . Yet I don't remember minding
those conditions.

I worked at the office and, although I was only eighteen years old,
I held a tremendously responsible position. My main function was to
organize youth *aliya,* mostly illegally. Hitler was already in power, and
there was a great urgency about our activities. A lot of families wanted
to send their children to Israel, to rescue them from rising Nazism. Many
were too poor to finance the trip, so our system was to convince rich
families to send their children, and to make them pay twice the price, so
that the poor children could also be saved. I conducted the negotiations
with families on the one hand, and with the *aliya* representatives on the
other, and all the practical arrangements depended on me. Doing this
complicated work, I was driven by the conviction that our ideals were the
only solution, that a socialist Eretz Yisrael was our only salvation, and
work, the only worthwhile style of life. Jewish religion had become quite
marginal to my existence at that time. I didn't observe any of the rules.
I remember even working on Yom Kippur, I was so busy.

In 1941, I was still in Rumania, and it became urgent to escape before
the Germans advanced. The Rumanian government made a last gesture
of good will towards the Jews and provided us with four hundred immigration certificates for youngsters and their escorts. We drew lots to
decide who would go to Israel, and I was among the lucky ones. Everything happened in such a hurry that I hardly believed I was going, and
I had no time to say good-bye properly to my family. I talked to them on
the phone and I cried a bit. I felt that they were all heading for a terrible
disaster. Through my job in the city, I knew much more than they did
about what was happening all over Europe. I happened to be in T. during
the week that the Germans invaded Rumania, and the city was full of
German Army officers. One evening I went to watch the famous anti-
Semitic film *Jew Züs,* which was presented as free entertainment. I sat in
the audience, probably the only Jew, hoping that I wouldn't be identified.
I was shocked at the profound hatred, the sadism, which the film depicted
towards the Jews, and heard the audience—mostly Germans—cheering

loudly. I sat, holding tightly to my chair—but I made myself stay to the end. . . . I knew what was coming. . . .

Therefore, during this last telephone call, I implored my parents to cross the Rumanian border to Hungary, which seemed safer at the time. Father objected, however. He said that if God wanted to save him, he'd be saved wherever he stayed, whereas if he was doomed Death would get him on either side of the border. He preferred to stay where he was and, luckily, this decision saved him and my whole family. Later, the whole Jewish population of Hungary was sent to extermination camps, whereas the Rumanians saved their citizens.

For the first nine months in the country, I was trained in agriculture in a women-workers farm, and then I joined my friends from Rumania, who started a kibbutz near the Kinneret. It was a happy reunion, but it didn't last, since the ulcers I had developed during my tense life in Europe started to bother me seriously and I needed medical treatment and finally an operation. I met Zvi while I was convalescing from my operation in a special sanatorium, and this meeting changed the course of my life.

Zvi was already divorced when we met in 1944. He was a member of Makom, but he worked for the Movement in Jerusalem, and to help support himself he took a gardening job at the sanatorium where I was staying. Our relationship became very meaningful to both of us, and a few months later we got married. For awhile I entertained the idea of returning to my kibbutz with Zvi, but I realized it wasn't possible for him to leave Makom. His little daughter, Vered, was living there, and his mother had also joined Makom in order to take care of the girl. I understood that I had to leave my own group and follow Zvi.

So, in the summer of 1944, I joined Makom as Zvi's wife. It wasn't an easy transition. In my own group, there was so much intimacy among us that I felt close to and really loved by the whole group. Here, I was a stranger who didn't belong. I wasn't a Sabra or a Yekke. I came alone, and everybody was watching me, testing: How is Zvi's second wife? This feeling of not belonging to any group has remained with me to this very day (although I feel very much part of this kibbutz by now) and has given me a certain amount of freedom and independence within this society. I have always felt free to express my own views and to fight for my beliefs because I didn't owe any loyalty to a person or a group. This lack of commitment to a certain sub-group is characteristic of me at present as well, although I have developed deep friendships on a personal basis. Maybe I'm an independent type of person, and I would have been that way wherever I had lived—I'm not quite sure.

At the beginning, however, I felt a stranger, although some individuals became my friends right away—Na'ama and Oded, in particular. They were such a wonderful couple. . . . I was very much alone—Zvi was sent to a six-week seminar immediately after our wedding, and his former wife was away on some job as well. I often had to take care of their daughter Vered, and her younger brother—Ester's son—of whom she was in charge. I got along well with Zvi's mother, who was an extraordinary woman, and gradually I adjusted to the place.

From the beginning I have worked in the educational system. When I joined, several children from the third grade were sick with scarlet fever and were in quarantine together in a separate house. I became their teacher and *metapelet,* and formed a close relationship with their families. Later I became the *metapelet* of the whole class. I remember the hard physical work, the crowded rooms, the cold water—but all of the hardship was overshadowed by the positive feeling that I was getting to know the people of Makom.

At that time, children from the third grade were already assigned to daily work after school. I remember that they picked olives, for example, and the discipline concerning work was very strictly enforced. I have pangs of conscience concerning some of those memories—I'd presently evaluate some of our norms then as cruel and inappropriate for children. Yet those were the accepted standards at the time, and I didn't question them. I was 100 percent sure that this was the right way to educate our children.

I remember the winter that I was pregnant with my first son, and how difficult it was to walk in the mud when I returned from school after dark. I used to call for Zvi when I neared our room, and he would come out, carrying the boots that he got as a cowherd. I would take off my soaking shoes and walk the remaining distance in his huge rubber boots. In the evening, the other cowmen would gather in our room, spinning fantasies about the future, when all the paths would be paved and their grown-up children would treat them to coffee. It seemed so incredibly remote.

When I consider my life over the years in the kibbutz and all of the different roles I have assumed, one thing stands out for me—I have never doubted the way. I knew I chose the right path and was certain of it even when my family—my parents and sisters who escaped from Europe after the war—didn't want to join me here in the kibbutz. My children didn't seem to follow my way either. When my daughter left the kibbutz (that's Iris, whom you met, and she returned to the kibbutz later), I felt a terrible blow, and the pain was even harder to bear when my second daughter followed suit. I saw it as a trend. The first child to leave was my firstborn son, although his was a different story. He went to a new kibbutz after his military service, and decided to stay there. He lives there with his own family. When he left, he wrote me a long letter, explaining his decision. He said that he felt that he couldn't grow and be himself near us, his parents, and especially near me, since he saw me as identifying so intensely with the kibbutz. He did decide to remain in a kibbutz, though, but felt deflected by our central position in Makom. This letter hurt me immensely, and I cried when I read it and realized what he was saying.

We talked about it later, and I presently feel we can accept and understand each other.

My daughter, Iris, however, never managed to express herself to me. She's an extremely introverted person and we can't talk about matters of this nature; when she left the kibbutz, though, I guessed it was for reasons similar to those of her older brother. In her case, I really blame myself. Maybe if I had been a different person, a different kind of mother to her, she wouldn't have grown so remote and closed in her relationship with me. . . . My second daughter is, again, a similar story, but, with all the pain, I still truly believe that I did the right thing with my life, although we might have developed into a happier family had we lived in town. Who knows?

My difficulties with my children stem from the fact that I have always been very active publicly, expressed my opinions, and openly fought for my values. I have assumed, perhaps incorrectly, that family relationships would take care of themselves and develop naturally without any need of special attention. Zvi has always been busy with his own public duties and was away from home very frequently, leaving me in charge of our four children. After years of being a teacher, I, too, was elected to various roles —chairperson of our education committee, social secretary, etc.—and I never doubted my ability to perform these roles well, even though I was also a wife and a mother. So frequently, in the afternoon or evening, I used to put my young children in their baby carriage, and walk around the kibbutz with them, to my various meetings and errands. I didn't see it as a crime towards my children; I thought that children might eventually participate also in the social responsibilities undertaken by their parents. I never considered it a "must" to spend the afternoon playing with my children; as long as they were with me, I believed it was okay.

This dilemma, however, did bother me; it's the dilemma of my life. I couldn't have taken a different course, though. Whenever an actual choice had to be made, whether to stay at home with the children or to be active in a public function, I always resolved the conflict in the same manner—by taking the public role and carrying my children along. I have always been drawn towards participation. It's like a need, a need to take over all the necessary functions, to provide answers for all problems, all demands. I knew I wasn't perfect, that I couldn't carry out all roles in a perfect manner, yet I had this drive to be perfect in all respects, and often had the feeling that I might be approaching such a goal. People all around me, and my children as well, had, therefore, a great many expectations of me. Probably I have disappointed many of those expectations. . . . And, within, there was always this tremendous battle of where to go first, how to carry out all these functions simultaneously. Even today I'm still bothered by this: To be a good wife to Zvi and a good grandmother is frequently incompatible with all my other plans, yet I try to do everything and be everything.

I think that this is a woman's fate, if she wants to be an active and contributing member of the society. Zvi was also a public figure, and he lived for years outside the kibbutz, yet I completely accepted Zvi's goals as a most natural choice, and I never doubted that it was mainly *my* role to remain with the family, although I had other aims in life as well.

Generally, women in the kibbutz are much less socially active than I. They put most of their energy into their family life. I don't know whether they gave up public activity in favor of their families, or simply aren't interested in public activity—but in fact they are very passive members in the kibbutz. Women frequently believe they aren't talented enough to undertake public roles, while in fact, if they tried, they'd realize that quite the opposite is true. Take, for example, the driving license business: For years and years, women have accepted as fair the rule that any man has priority over a woman in taking driving lessons and getting a license because, naturally, women rarely need to leave the kibbutz premises for their work.

Many women are very powerful in our society, however, but they employ their power in an indirect fashion; they send their men to fight for a certain issue, or to perform a certain role. I have always been different; I didn't act through Zvi but came out publicly for or against the issues that interested me. Maybe their approach is a more efficient way, though, since public conflicts have much less weight nowadays, and most important decisions are made by a subtle game of give-and-take.

Perhaps I'm naïve, but I still believe in open debate and in direct persuasion. I have often fought against the mainstream of the kibbutz's tendencies. I have had my own idea on what a kibbutz is and what direction it should follow. Basically, I believe that the kibbutz should divide its energy equally, to say the least, between involvement in the problems of the country at large on the one hand, and improving its own standard of living on the other. I can't accept the idea that the kibbutz is nothing more than a collective of people working together towards the achievement of a better life, based on a high standard of living, highly developed aesthetic and cultural values, and the equilibrium between individual freedom and social support. This is certainly very nice, but I refuse to see it as our sole aim.

I have always seen the wider national involvement as essential. The way to integrate these individual and societal goals is by having *many* individuals in various missions outside the kibbutz. There should be as many participants as possible, not just one or two outstanding, token functionaries. I would like to see the kibbutz more involved in politics, within the Labor Party and the Histadrut.* We *do* have our ideas about the aims and directions the State should be assuming; so we have to fight politically for our views, for a better socialist society. We can't allow

*National organization of workers' unions.

history to be determined by all kinds of powers, while we ourselves sit still and tend to our gardens. It's not just an ideological stand I'm taking, because I'm certain that if we just attend to the beauty of our courtyard, we are bound to lose that, too, pretty soon. Had our life inside really been so beautiful, it wouldn't have been possible to raise and cultivate an individual who's so egocentric and insensitive to the social wrongs outside our fence. So, I consider these two aspects interrelated to a great extent.

I view this issue as central to many areas of our life. We face this issue in the shortcomings of our educational system. Our children grow up in an atmosphere of contentment. If they remain here, as the majority does, they don't have anything to fight for, nothing to improve. They never have to struggle for anything because they are very rarely exposed to the negative aspects of life. If you're not exposed to the negative, you can't really evaluate the positive either. In town, a child sees a beggar every day on his way to school and he tells himself: "That's not going to happen to me and that's what I want to change in my world." These negative encounters provide one with the energy and persistence needed to fight for constructive changes in life.

Here, children grow with just one side of the coin, a tremendous illusion which creates the false belief that everything is good; it doesn't prepare people to guard against the intrusion of the negative into our lives. Visiting Beit Shean for a day and walking through poverty-stricken areas is not enough. What it frequently leads to is an increase in the feelings of superiority and complacency that characterize our children, anyway. At the beginning, the kibbutz had a goal of improving life for the whole nation. As a movement, it aspired to eliminate the negative all around us; it used our financial ability as a means to free members and allow them to dedicate their time to public roles in politics, economics, and education. Today this is just an empty cliché.

Once my mother visited me on a day dedicated all over the country to the March of Dimes. She put 200 IL on the table and wanted to know when the ladies who collect the money would come by. I told her that we do it differently, that the cashier would send a big contribution for the whole kibbutz. She couldn't understand the arrangement, and I think she had a good point. People here are spared their own moral responsibilities, they don't face the negative, and therefore lack some basic ingredient for forming character. I don't want to introduce the negative into our own courtyard, yet, if we were more integrated with the world beyond, the daily experience of individuals would be wider and much more realistic.

Another area in which the kibbutz has disappointed me is on the subject of hired labor. It's indeed true that we have almost no hired labor within our kibbutz, inside our own fence, but we do share in the ownership of several large factories in which kibbutz members, from several kibbutzim, are the employers, and all of the workers are hired from the surrounding towns. These factories are primarily food-processing projects, in which we use our own agricultural produce. They developed from the idea that we could get much higher profit by marketing processed foods rather than by selling raw agricultural produce to a factory. Since many kibbutzim encountered the same problem, we joined in opening regional factories, building them outside the kibbutz. These projects have grown enormously; presently, they employ hundreds of workers. What hurts, of course, is that all the workers are townspeople who are hired by the factories for extremely low wages, while all the administrative positions—the bosses—are filled by the rich kibbutzniks. We might comfort ourselves by claiming that we're providing work for many unskilled workers who couldn't earn a living otherwise. I don't think that this sufficiently justifies the situation. We've become capitalistic, we've reestablished class divisions in our society, and we're on the side of the exploiters.

My own opinion is that if we can't maintain these factories with our own manpower, then we must propose full economic partnership with the workers. In other words, we must develop a cooperative system by which all workers participate in the administration and get their share of the profit. This is very far from what is actually taking place, and I know that the majority of our members, the young people who carry the central economic positions, don't see eye-to-eye with me on this matter. They feel quite comfortable in the shoes of big factory owners.

A few months ago, I brought up the subject for discussion with our high-school students, and I suggested that we take a trip to one of these factories and meet the workers. The trip, however, was vetoed by our kibbutz members, the executives of the company. They justified their refusal by saying that the children's visit might stir up trouble among the workers. . . . Well, the trip was canceled, but I feel we're playing here with fire. Unless some real steps are taken to arrive at a fairer arrangement, a big scandal will break out sooner or later between the exploited workers and the kibbutzim, and the image of the kibbutz movement will receive a terrible blow.

All these are issues beyond the limited local concern, and, as I said before, I believe that the kibbutz as an ideological movement must continue to fight against the erosion of its values by reality. We haven't yet accomplished our aims.

V E R E D (age 44)

Vered, a tall blond woman, is the daughter of Zvi and Ester. She was extremely helpful to me throughout the various stages of my stay and study of Makom. This readiness to be of help appears also as a central theme in her life story.

I have only vague memories of my early childhood. I was born in 1934 and in 1936 the riots broke out. From the top of Mount Gilboa, the Arabs fired the Fountain, at the former site of the kibbutz. There were ten or twelve children then, and we were placed in neighboring kibbutzim which were safer. This is also the time when our permanent land was acquired and gradually we started moving up there. There's just one experience I remember from those early years at the Fountain. I'm not quite sure whether it's fact or fancy, perhaps it's a story I heard later; it was a period of several suicides among the kibbutz members. I vaguely recall death; some members died—that's my earliest memory. Later I found out that a number of people did commit suicide then. Some had despaired of the kibbutz idea, and some had romantic disappointments. Somebody was murdered too, or killed in the riots. I don't know the details of these deaths, you'll have to ask some older members. But these are my earliest memories.

I remember later visits to the Fountain, the way it was then—not a pond, as it is today. I remember the thick raspberry shrubs, the fig trees, the clear water, the men's spring, the women's spring, nude bathing, ducks on the water—some images and a general atmosphere. There was also the old dining hall which still served the people who were living there.

My memories of the early days in our permanent location are some-what clearer. My parents lived in a tent for a while, and the children's home was in a wooden cottage. All around there were mostly tents, with only two buildings standing. There were no trees whatsoever. In the summer, it was terribly hot, since there was no shade, and in the winter it was awfully muddy, since there were no paved paths or roads. We always washed in cold water since there was no warm water nor electricity. We used kerosene lamps for lighting, and I recall the first time I was burned by one of those.

When I was three years old my parents got divorced, and my grand-mother left her own kibbutz and came to take care of me. She was my main parent figure, actually. My parents had their own problems. Father was quite devoted to me, but he left the kibbutz temporarily to work for the kibbutz movement in town, and mother was too withdrawn to mother me. She was a rather cold woman and never a very motherly type. She used to be very busy, working on the tractors in the fields. Later, she too lived in town, working for ten years for the party.* She never gave me much, nor my brother, who was born to her from her second husband. I always mothered him. She had her own problems.

In the children's community I was in a good class, it was very select. At that time, those who didn't do well enough in their studies were left behind a grade. Both Shlomo and Uri were my teachers. They were

*Mapam, Israel's left-oriented workers' party.

extremely demanding and we studied pretty hard. At the beginning of high school, in 1945, Holocaust survivors were added to our group. They adjusted quite well. Generally, the atmosphere in the children's community was good. Personally, however, I suffered from my family problems and I felt a need for a private corner of my own. We lived in huts, boys and girls sharing rooms until we entered the Army, at the age of eighteen. I felt that the togetherness was too intense, although others didn't react in the same manner. I needed my own corner, where I could spend several hours by myself. My roommates were two boys who were disorderly, dirty, and noisy. Actually, I didn't choose them as roommates. Since I was considered to be fairly organized and orderly myself, I was put with two messy boys so that their room might, thanks to me, retain some semblance of order. This was more or less how the roommates were divided. You see, when something was decided for us, we never said no, we accepted it as if it were one of the Ten Commandments. Actually, it was our class committee which decided on the rooming arrangements— we spent whole nights trying to figure out the best solution.

Besides my own room, the whole place was noisy and busy every night till two in the morning. We had a heavy load of homework for school, and on top of that, since I was always very conscientious, I took on many social duties such as editing the children's weekly paper, and being the counselor of the younger age group. I could never refuse any demand, whereas some others could and did, without being punished for it in any way. All this added up to a lot of pressure and responsibility, too much for my age.

As a result of all this, when I was seventeen I would sometimes run away from the children's home, and sneak out to my mother's room and sleep there. I desperately longed for silence and solitude, for a corner of my own. Whenever I felt that the noise and the stress were too much for me, I went to my mother's to sleep. That's where I could also concentrate on my schoolwork.

There were many other factors involved in this habit of mine. As I mentioned, when we were growing up, boys and girls used to share rooms. We used to take showers together as long as we weren't ashamed, till we were about ten or eleven years old. In some other, more left-oriented kibbutzim, boys and girls were supposed to shower together until they went to the Army. All this was part of the educational ideology then, although I don't quite understand the sense of it. Perhaps the idea was to stress the value of the equality of the sexes—you had better ask the older members about it. Since we shared rooms, there was also the problem of getting dressed. We used to do that under the blankets, or we would say "curfew" and the boys were supposed to turn around. My roommates, however, used to peep, or at least I suspected them of it, and I didn't like it, or them, particularly. That was another reason for retreating to the privacy of my mother's room.

Besides studies and social duties, we were also intensely involved in work and war. Kibbutz children always do their share of the work, but at that time we frequently also had to take adults' jobs due to various emergencies. I remember, for example, the "Black Saturday" of '46 when about ninety men of our kibbutz were arrested by the British authorities and taken away. Our studies were interrupted for about three months, and we filled the positions vacated by the missing men. I worked in the cowshed. We used to milk by hand, for there weren't any machines at Makom yet. The work started before daybreak with the first milking and went on until late at night—I was just about twelve years old! Actually, when I was eleven I worked in the infants' home with another boy of my age. We were responsible for the babies in the afternoon, bathing and dressing them. Imagine, one of the babies I took care of was only nine years younger than me; she herself is now a mother in the kibbutz—when I was eleven she was two years old!

Besides that, we were actively involved in the war, in rather responsible roles. When we were thirteen we had field training, and when the War of Independence broke out in 1948, we, the children, took charge of communications. We learned the Morse code, flag signals for daytime and light signals for night. Some of us were responsible for the communications between Makom and our two neighboring kibbutzim.

Our own kibbutz was fortified with trenches throughout. During battles in the area, it was my duty to run in the trenches between the two commanders' posts, passing notes between the two. All the children had runners' jobs between the army posts here. That was how we participated in the war [*laughs*]. In addition to that we had to work full time, replacing the adults who had been mobilized. I remember everything very well, the battles and the cease-fire periods, three of our members being killed in the battle for the Gilboa—these are my childhood memories. We were very involved in everything that was happening and it all seemed perfectly natural at the time.

Although children still, we were actually always treated as adults. We assumed our share of responsibilities in all the events taking place. Since we were the oldest children's group, we matured very quickly—too quickly, I think. Although I functioned rather well at the time of these events, I think that too much was demanded of me. Basically I was a frail child and these demands completely exhausted me.

The situation of our kibbutz children today is quite different. First of all, they are not as overcrowded as we were. Boys and girls sleep separately, and the living conditions are much better. They don't work or study as much as we did, so they're not so overburdened. There is much less social pressure today, on children as well as on adults. Children have fewer responsibilities in the adult community. As a result they simply have more time and leisure. My children often visit with us for two hours in the evening; at their ages, I was always on the run, never spending more than thirty minutes a day with my family. Both my daughters, although they're very conscientious, have more time than I ever had to pursue their own interests, hobbies, and such. My second daughter is extremely busy with our basketball team, which is her own hobby, not a duty that she has to carry out for the community. In my time, those of us who were socially involved and conscientious never had a minute for ourselves.

As a mother of four children I became quite critical of the communal sleeping arrangement in the kibbutz. I became aware of this right after my first daughter was born; I felt I needed to be close to her and couldn't accept the idea of her spending the nights far from me, in the infants' home. I couldn't abandon her. To this very day, I suffer severe anxiety concerning the sleeping arrangements of my children—although it's perhaps somewhat less acute now than it had been with my first daughter. I suffered a lot then, and couldn't be silent about it. I wrote a critical article about communal children's lodgings, which was published in the kibbutz paper, and I was severely reprimanded for it. Regular members as well as kibbutz authorities in education and psychology sent me letters: How dare I attack the communal lodging, which is one of the fundamental principles of the kibbutz idea! How can I deny its major contribution to the equal rights of women as well as to the well-being of the child and the community!

People who knew me personally reacted somewhat differently. They said, "Look, you've come from a broken family. Your parents got divorced and they both lived for long periods of time outside of the kibbutz; therefore you're more sensitive to the issue. You're not objective. Children who grew up in normal families don't have these feelings." My own mother reacted in a similar way. She said that just as I didn't suffer in the children's lodging, my children weren't suffering either. It was all in my imagination. But you see, my mother, as I told you before, was never keen on taking responsibility for her children; she would, in fact, support any arrangement that might free her of that burden. I would never want to be a mother like her.

These reactions didn't convince me. I still have my doubts and criticism in this area, and I know there are still others who share my concern. As the years went by, several other kibbutzim even switched over to family lodgings, and the children sleep in their parents' rooms. I raised four children here and have never resolved this problem. Often I would be anxious about my children, rushing over to the children's home to see if their blankets hadn't slipped off. On cold stormy nights I would wake up and run to see if they were safely covered and warm— and it isn't that close either. I would certainly prefer to have them sleeping with us.

This criticism and my anxiety have, however, softened over the years. I'm calmer now about my seven-year-old son than I was about my first three children. In spite of all this, I never seriously thought about leaving the kibbutz.

During my military service I met many people who came from an urban background, and I sometimes felt I ought to try living in town for a while to see whether I was missing something. But whenever I'd go to town, I'd get fed up with it after three or four days, and would long to be back in the kibbutz. It's my home and I feel bound to it. I feel secure here, since I'm used to this form of life. Furthermore, I think this way of life liberates us from the competitive nature of city life, from the constant race for a higher standard of living. Here our life is calmer and more relaxed. I'm satisfied with my work here. At present I'm the technical secretary of the kibbutz: My job is to take care of the kibbutz correspondence, to type the letters, take the telephone calls, keep the records of all the kibbutz residents, etc. It's interesting and never monotonous. But for almost twenty years, I worked in education, which wasn't at all satisfying. When I look back on my years in education, I see them as a long nightmare; it was terribly difficult for me. During all those years, I agreed to work in education out of a sense of duty, never as my own personal choice. I was even sent to the Teachers' Seminary for a year, supposedly to increase my interest and satisfaction at work, but it didn't change my feelings a bit.

At first I worked with infants. I was the *metapelet* of four babies, confined within four walls. I felt myself becoming increasingly frustrated, wearing myself out. I felt as if my intellectual level was approaching that of the toddlers I was tending. In addition to my physical exhaustion, I felt mental fatigue; my nerves were frayed by the children's constant screaming and nagging. I worked with them for eight and nine hours a day (now *metaplot* work only seven, I think) and I felt it was a continuous sacrifice on my side. I reached the point that I developed an allergy to babies and to their communal homes.

After many years of this, I tried to work with older children. This was a different kind of job, but it was also ungratifying for me. For a couple of years I was solely in charge of a class of forty-six children. We had children of another kibbutz here, too; that's why it was such a large group. My job was to wake them in the morning, to get their clothes ready and take care of their laundry, to accompany them to meals, to see that their rooms were neat and clean, to supervise their health and hygiene, and to help them with their psychological problems. Of course, I couldn't cope with so many matters in such a large group! At the end of the day I felt that I had seen each child for only five minutes, having only a five-word conversation with each, no more. Some of them I never reached at all on a more personal level, yet I was busy with them from morning to night. For about six years I was a *metapelet* of older children.

Throughout the whole time that I worked in education I felt badly about my work, especially while working with the little ones. In spite of my feelings I kept at it for many years just because of my sense of duty. I knew I had four children of my own and therefore must contribute my share to the educational system. I kept hearing people say, "We don't have enough educational workers, and we have so many children, so every capable *chavera* has to work in this area." Indeed, about 80 percent of the *chaverot* work in education. A *chavera* who has guts and can assert herself, who can say "I can't and I won't" may finally get another job. Or, if she has another well-defined profession, she may be excused from this work. But the majority of women, those who are more conscientious, or have a weaker character and can't say no, or have no definite alternative occupation for themselves—will remain in education for years and years. Of course, if a woman is unsuitable for the work, that's a different story; people won't give her responsibility over children and another job will be found for her. But if she's suitable—then it's too bad for her. This covers 70 to 80 percent of the women, since we now have 420 children, and, through the age of three, every four infants are assigned one *metapelet* and an assistant. We're always short of *metaplot,* there's a large turnover in this job, with women leaving because of pregnancies, for studies, etc. It's my impression that the vast majority of the women working in education feel personally unsatisfied, and this is a major problem for the whole kibbutz. Few women like this job—I wish there were more of those that did. I frequently hear people claim that in the kibbutz we have big families because, "It's easy to raise your children in the kibbutz." What nonsense. You work eight hours a day with children who *aren't* yours, you hardly have a minute to spare to look in at your own children during the day, and then comes afternoon and your own children are to be taken to the room, to be mothered, while you feel completely exhausted and fed up with children from your day's work. Isn't it absurd—and the kibbutz claimed it would liberate the woman from her traditional role!

On the other hand, suppose I were living in town: I'd still want to have my four children, and every mother in town raises her own children, somehow, for better or worse. Still, I believe that, had I lived in town, I'd be looking for some sort of a part-time job, to meet people, to be involved in something else besides being a housewife, taking care of the children, and cooking. I'd hire someone else to take care of my children—hoping I could find someone suitable. I have rather good, unproblematic children, while in my work as a *metapelet* I frequently had to take care of children who were extremely difficult to handle. Well, perhaps every mother has this feeling about her own children, that they're easy to manage, while a stranger's children are difficult. I'm not sure. A good *metapelet* can be rather objective, and I think that in spite of all my inner difficulties I was a good *metapelet,* especially towards the children. I never discriminated between children; I always treated them equally. I'm not sure I gave them enough intellectually, but I was capable of giving more after my year of study on early child development. I wasn't too efficient in my work, but I'm sure, at least, that I never caused harm to any child [*laughs*]. I also managed my relationships with the mothers quite well. My only problem was that I remained on the job for far too long, until I had exceeded my limit, and, to this very day, I'm allergic to the whole business.

I R I S *(age 30)*

Iris is a young woman, the second child of Chana and Zvi. She's married and a mother of two.

I'm a nursery-school teacher *(ganenet)* of children from three to seven years old. It's the system here to mix the ages of preschool children, so that the younger ones get more stimulation and the older ones have a chance to feel responsible as leaders of the class. Our educational team includes three *metaplot* and a *ganenet.* The *metaplot* are in charge of the physical maintenance, clothing, meals and cleaning, while I'm responsible for the children's activities. Actually, however, I try to share the educational work with my team so that their work won't be so mechanical and boring. I know how the *metapelet*'s work can get on your nerves, because that's where I started. It's only my second year as a teacher now —and I haven't been trained professionally. I was one of the *metaplot* of this class. The *ganenet* left on maternity leave and they couldn't find an experienced replacement, so I was recruited for the job. At least I know the children and some of the routines of their former teacher.

It was terribly difficult during the first year. I hated the constant need to control and discipline the children, and it still upsets me today, having to be on guard all the time. By now, however, I have acquired the children's respect and I don't have to yell, so it's much better. When I started, I received no guidance or supervision. Although we have six parallel nursery classes, the teachers almost never meet to share their plans and ideas or to discuss problems. At the beginning, I really felt lost. I felt I didn't know what to do and I had no one to consult. I felt completely isolated and inexperienced. At the same time, I felt I was constantly being criticized, although nobody confronted me openly. It was probably my own imagination, the feeling of social pressure, the expectations to be very good. . . . I would wake up at night with sudden panic concerning my work, nightmares about chaos in my class, or a disaster happening to one of my pupils. This is the famous kibbutz pressure which indeed made me leave the kibbutz eight years ago.

My husband was an outside child here, and after our Army service he returned to the kibbutz and worked as a bus driver for Egged.* When we got married, we left the kibbutz and went to live in a village. Actually,

*The national bus company.

my husband didn't want to leave Makom, but I put a lot of pressure on him and finally he agreed.

It's very difficult to explain why I had this strong wish to leave. . . . I don't see myself as belonging to the kibbutz; I have no close relationships with the people or the place. I knew that in the kibbutz I'd have to work with children all my life and the prospect didn't excite me. I didn't want to live according to the kibbutz way of life. The social pressure had always upset me and it still does, although to a lesser degree. I remember feeling this pressure from my early childhood onwards. The constant pressure to be okay, to fulfill the expectations of the society, of being always under supervision and control, and of being judged for every little thing . . . especially in work, but also in your private life. Everybody knows what you do or don't do and this made my life very difficult.

When we left, I got a job at a library, and took a course in library science; my husband worked for the bus company, as before. We lived there for three good years. I felt liberated. I was really happy, for the first time.

It wasn't a problem for me to leave my family and the kibbutz society. Actually, I think that I needed to put some distance between them and me. This was perhaps my reason for leaving in the first place: to get some perspective on myself and to put a distance between myself and my parents. I didn't even feel any longing for them. When I came back from the Army, I couldn't find my place in the kibbutz nor any close relationships with the people here. My classmates were never my friends, and I didn't want to have anything to do with them. The only thing I missed were the holidays as they were celebrated here, but even when I came for holidays, I felt like a stranger.

Well, our time outside lasted for three years. Throughout the period, we had problems with the apartment we were renting. There was an ongoing struggle between us and the owners. The whole time that this conflict was going on, my husband tried to talk me into returning to the kibbutz. I guess he was attracted by the economic security offered by the kibbutz, and afraid to face the difficulties of being financially responsible for a family, all on his own.

The situation was finally settled by the outbreak of the war in 1973. I was due to give birth at any moment, when my husband was mobilized for the war. I came to stay with my mother in the kibbutz, gave birth here and remained for a while, presumably until my husband would be discharged. But this took a number of months; in the meantime, we were evicted from our apartment in the village, and found ourselves here. I couldn't believe that it was final. I felt trapped and searched for ways out for a long time, until about a year ago. . . . Recently, however, I have felt relatively accepting about staying here.

My husband prefers it here; that's certain. He continues working as a bus driver, and much of the time he's outside the kibbutz. He has two hobbies, riding horses and sailing, and he can afford them both here, whereas in town it would be much too expensive for us. Right now he's organizing a sailing course for the high-school children and they plan to acquire a boat, so he's completely content.

Returning to the kibbutz as a young mother has added to my former criticisms of the kibbutz way of life. I have two children, and at the beginning I found it extremely difficult to accept the common sleeping arrangements. I think we miss a lot by not really raising our children by ourselves. We see them for a very limited time each day. It's completely different from waking your children up in the morning, dressing and washing them, cooking their food, buying their clothes, etc. What actually happens is that you get your child sort of ready-made in the afternoon, and all you have to do is bestow your love on him or her. There is no need to cope with educational difficulties of any sort, since it can all be passed on to the *metapelet* or teacher. So our role as parents is rather limited and superficial, and I think that the loss is ours.

Very often I let my children sleep with us in the room. But we have a very small flat here, and I'm frequently scolded by my children's teachers who claim that I bring them too late for their classes, and that it's difficult for them to get into the routine after sleeping in our room. (I myself never scold mothers of my pupils for taking them to sleep at home. I can see their point very well.) I know that many mothers of young children feel as I do, and I intend to start a struggle for private sleeping arrangements. We could get a majority vote for that, but the problem is that it would require rebuilding the whole kibbutz and it's too expensive. But I'm personally very concerned about the present sleeping arrangements. I think it's very bad for a child to wake up at night and see a strange face, a different face every night. A child needs his mother to comfort him if he wakes up suddenly, and, although my own children sleep fairly well, I'm worried about that. I myself slept very frequently in my parents' or grandmother's room during my childhood. I hated my classmates.

This is another thing that worries me about raising my children in a kibbutz. I belonged to a very bad class in my childhood. (This is not just my private opinion—you can ask anyone here and they'd agree.) Each one of us had his own interests and no social relationships existed within our group. We were labeled a bad group, and as a result I also felt bad as an individual. It was awful having to live all those years so closely with children I couldn't stand. When I became a parent here, I began to think of my own children in this respect. What if they happen to be born into a bad group like that? What if they don't find in their class the kind of social satisfaction they need? This is another reason I have for wanting to leave. In a kibbutz, you must spend the first eighteen years of your life with your class, whether you like it or not. There's simply no alternative. In town one can change schools, move to another neighborhood, but here you can't escape. I try to comfort myself with the knowledge that the age groups are much larger presently; this allows for a little more choice and flexibility, and one has a better chance to develop friendships within the class.

When I returned from the Army, and again when I returned after our three years of absence, I was hurt by the indifference of the community. Nobody pays attention to you, or cares whether you have found your place or not. People assume that, if you have a room and your meals are provided, the rest will work out automatically; nobody makes any attempt to absorb you into the society. I, however, had been very isolated here, and didn't have any childhood friendships to depend on for support.

Another point that bothers me a lot is the women's place in the kibbutz system. Women in the kibbutz have nowhere to go, they have little choice in life or work. All women know is that between twenty and forty they have to work in child care, whether as a *metapelet, ganenet,* or teacher—these are nearly all of the existing options. I want to be a librarian; I want to study library science in graduate school and to organize our different libraries in a more sensible way. I like to work with books and I prefer helping students find material for their papers rather than teaching them as a group. I know, however, that I have no chance of reaching that position until I'm forty or forty-five years old, and that's a long time to wait. We have several older women who take care of our children's, adult, and foreign-languages libraries. They're not professionals, and the job is considered a kind of retirement position from the difficult child-care work which younger women must perform.

Well, with all my criticisms and reservations, I feel somewhat more accepting of my life here than I felt before. For one thing, I feel more confident in my work, and I don't feel constant pressure and criticism any longer. After a long transition period, I have formed good relationships within my team, and our work runs more smoothly. I did manage, gradually, to establish some friendships here—probably because of my husband, who is much more relaxed with people than I am. I'm slowly discovering some aspects of our life here that I appreciate. I'm afraid of growing old in the city, of the loneliness of old people in town. Here I find growing old is a much less frightening prospect. I know that I'll be taken care of. I think that my children are getting a very good education here, and somehow I feel better about my life here as well, although I find it difficult to define the precise improvements.

One of the areas of my life which I need to improve is my relationship with my mother. Since I've returned, I've gone for counseling and have gradually allowed myself to realize the amount of bitterness and resentment I still carry with me from my childhood. My father and mother were both extremely busy people. In Father's case I could accept it much more, because many fathers were away or very occupied with their daily work. Furthermore, I remember that Mother was always busier than he was.

When Father wasn't away on a mission in town, he was very much with us, and was available to us when we were in the room. Mother was never present in the room with us. She always had something to attend to, and when she would go out she'd claim only to be away for a minute, and then not return until several hours later. . . . On the other hand, she was such an outstanding woman here that I felt that she was supposed to be a model for my behavior and attitude towards the kibbutz. The kibbutz—society—always took first priority in her life, whereas family life was somewhere below, in second or third place. Mother demanded of herself perfection vis-à-vis the society, while the family, she believed, would somehow manage on its own. This demand, to be first of all perfect from the public point of view, was something I couldn't digest as a model for my own life, and the conflict concerning this demand has upset me a great deal. Mother has always attended every assembly meeting, every committee session, etc.; I couldn't see the sense of it and felt personally neglected. This pattern disturbed me a great deal, and I think it has affected my younger sister, who also left the kibbutz recently. Our brothers were, somehow, less affected by the family situation.

This was certainly one of the basic reasons for my desire to leave the kibbutz. I felt that if I remained here I would always be compared with my mother, have to compete with her standards and realize her own ambitions in my life. I felt I couldn't be independent here, nor judged as a separate person, and this feeling has created a lot of tension in my relationship with my mother and, through her, probably with the entire kibbutz. Above all, I was afraid I might repeat my mother's behavior towards me in my relationship with my own daughter. That's why I sought counseling in the first place.

Well, gradually I have started to separate myself from my mother's strong impact. I don't like the other feminine model which I frequently encounter in the kibbutz either: the woman who devotes all her energy to her apartment and household activities. I think that this phenomenon is a result of the boredom which most women face in their kibbutz work, and the frustration of not being able to realize themselves in any other way. I, personally, hope to find a balance between my dedication to my family and some sort of meaningful occupation. Women have received more opportunities recently, and I myself hope to go study soon.

As to my mother's standards of behavior, well, I usually don't go to the assembly meetings and I don't feel as guilty about it any longer. When I do attend, I feel I have nothing to contribute, since many issues are beyond my comprehension. Anyway, I don't feel I have the ability to participate in the decision making because I have the feeling that things are determined elsewhere, long before they're even brought to the assembly. I think it's high time to do something to change the nature of our weekly assembly meetings, for they serve very little purpose now.

On the other hand, I did accept the nomination to our social committee, and it was important for me to be elected. I saw this election as a test of my standing in the community, and I guess I would have been insulted if I hadn't been elected. I haven't started to work on the committee yet, but I see it as a sort of personal challenge. I still feel I'd rather live in a village or small town, though—if only my husband would agree. . . .

Part 2

THE
DIVISION

INTRODUCTION

Uncovering the facts and feelings concerning the 1952 division of Makom
has been a fascinating process. The way in which this event evolved is of
great significance in understanding the present attitudes of people towards this event, which is often alluded to as "an earthquake in our
midst."

From the very beginning, members of Makom presented their population as subdivided into two large groups: those who have always been
in Makom; and those who had once belonged to Molad, a neighboring
kibbutz, and joined Makom after the division of Molad. Belonging originally to the Molad group was one of the first identification factors which
people used in their personal accounts. My interview with Ora, which was
among the first I conducted in Makom—and is presented as the first story
in this chapter—clearly opened the subject of the division from the perspective of those who had to leave Molad and joined Makom as their
second-home kibbutz. With the accumulation of additional versions of
this event, it became quite clear that the former members of Molad are
respected and very well integrated into the community of Makom. Moreover, they seem to have emotionally overcome the tragic event, which is
presented as a thing of the past that could never recur. As a group,
Molad's ex-members are proud of their present home in Makom, and
look upon their former kibbutz, which "has never recovered from the
blow of the division," with a certain amount of pity. They consider their
contribution to Makom a primary factor in the economic prosperity and
social success of their "new" kibbutz. The three individuals selected to
represent this transplanted group talk about the Molad division as an
isolated event in their past, and—as in other chapters—also refer to many
additional aspects in their personal accounts. For them, the division is a
finished episode, not necessarily a central stage in their personal history.
Several other individuals who belong to the former Molad group are
presented in other chapters of the book.

The fact that, prior to the acquisition of the Molad group, Makom
itself had undergone a division in which about a third of its members and
children left for another kibbutz, Adama, was hardly mentioned. Not one
of the central kibbutz figures whom I interviewed in my first visits to
Makom talked about the division. Some of these people, like Na'ama,
Shlomo, Yehuda and David, had played important roles either in the

rupture or in the attempts to prevent it, yet I only uncovered these facts months *after* I had interviewed them, while interviewing former members of Makom in Adama.

On the other hand, there was no attempt made to "conceal" this schism. I was told, from the beginning, that in order to get a complete picture of the history of Makom I should get in touch with the former members who have been living in Adama since 1952. Makom itself initiated the contacts in Adama for me, provided me with a list of ex-members, and advised me on their selection. My meeting with these ex-members of Makom proved, indeed, to be of profound significance.

I visited Adama for several days after conducting nearly ninety interviews in Makom. Adama is a kibbutz which belongs to the Ichud Movement. It is situated in northern Galilee and looks much smaller than Makom. The dining room is about one-third the size of the huge hall at Makom though the population of Adama is almost two-thirds that of Makom. Indeed, the dining hall is much too small for the kibbutz population, requiring that meals be served in two shifts. Adama does have an extensive cultural center, though, with another large hall for special occasions. The area around the dining hall is a marvelous park with unusual exotic plants and a huge lawn. The buildings look old but well kept.

I spoke with several people informally, and collected some background information. Adama is older than Makom; founded sixty-four years ago, it's the third- or fourth-oldest kibbutz in the country. It's difficult to attribute an exact age to Adama since the settlement had started as a workers' camp of tenant farmers working for Baron Rothschild in one of his agricultural enterprises.

Presently, Adama's main income comes from its orchards and a large guesthouse which it runs for tourists and travelers in the area. My impression was that the members are relaxed in manner, and seem satisfied, unhurried, and unharassed.

I have interviewed eight people in Adama. Three of them will be presented in the following chapter, and another two in the section about the Dor family.

In the majority of the long conversations which I had with ex-members of Makom living in Adama, I discovered traces of profound pain and dismay incurred during the 1952 trauma.

As my short stay in Adama drew to a close, I gradually realized that Makom's counterpart to the touching stories I heard in Adama was actually missing from my records. I then realized that in Makom, when people mentioned "the division," they were referring, in most cases, to the joining of the Molad group rather than to the departure of the Adama group and their own roles in the split within their kibbutz.

I returned to Makom intending to fill in the missing part of the story, and, indeed, I encountered resistance to reviving this painful issue.

Whether due to feelings of guilt, pain, or a sense of failure, magnified in anticipation of the present union of the two kibbutz movements that were then responsible for the division, or because most of the people who had been involved in the division had already spoken to me at length about their lives and could not spare more time for the study, it was extremely difficult to organize interviews when my specific purpose became known. I finally managed to talk to several Makom members about the division of their kibbutz, among them Zvi Eisman, who had, by then, become a friend and gave me a sincere and balanced account. In the Archives, Yehuda helped me find local newsletters and other written documents dating from the period of the division, all abundant with expressions of anger, sadness, bitterness, and disappointment. In a special issue of the newsletter on the day of the first departures to Adama, Makom's members wished their brothers and sisters good luck in their new home. Both through this written material and the interviews which are presented in the last section of this chapter, I discovered that in Makom, too, the pain of the past trauma had not yet been overcome. As will be uncovered in the following accounts—and in the story presented by the Dor family later—the common denominator of all the parties involved is puzzlement and dismay, the question: "How could we have particpated in such a chain of events?" This is most movingly voiced in a local newsletter from the end of 1951: "I feel like screaming, 'Stop, this is just a mistake! A terrible mistake.' For it should have been so totally otherwise!"

From Molad
to Makom

O R A *(age 45)*

Ora met me in her apartment, and later we went to the dining hall together for lunch. At that time, I was told she was a sick person, but I did not realize—and received no hints in our conversation—how severe her illness was. Several weeks after our conversation, she died of cancer. She died in Makom among family and friends.

I was born in Molad in 1933. Molad is an older kibbutz, started in 1920. As you know, in 1950 a deep division developed within the Kibbutz Hameuchad Movement. The cause for this division was conflicting attitudes toward Russia. Today, all of this sounds ridiculous and it's difficult to understand why it was so meaningful then. But that is the fate of many ideas, which start with a roar and die out with a whimper. I don't want to go into the fine details of the division, for it's too complicated to follow. Briefly, the conflict was whether to accept the dictates of the U.S.S.R., or to hold a relatively moderate position within the kibbutz movement under the leadership of Mapai. This was the time of the famous "doctors trial" in Russia and the Prague trials, and we felt we had to define our position vis-à-vis the official stand of the U.S.S.R. Bitter disputes ensued and a very deep division within the Kibbutz Hameuchad followed. Almost no kibbutz was spared. It was a terrible rupture, and it snowballed, dividing families and close friends; everyone was involved.

I belonged to the more leftist group in Molad and this controversy happened while I was in the Army. When the actual division took place, our group left Molad and joined Makom. The group consisted of some of the eldest of the second generation of Molad, those more ideologically-minded, and some of the younger first-generation members. Of the older pioneers of Molad, very few moved over here. I made the move with my family, but most of the sons and daughters of our group left by themselves, leaving their parents behind. This was the case with my man,* who joined Makom with his sister, leaving his parents and a younger brother in Molad.

All this may sound horrible today—dividing families and friends! But at the time the tension was so intense that it was a blessing to terminate it. What impressed me most deeply then was the thought that indeed we were still the same kind of wandering, homeless Jews, passing from place to place. If an ideological dispute could cause us to abandon our homes and our land, then we were still the same rootless Jews, always leaving and starting anew. The new image we tried to make for ourselves—of farmers, tied to their land, of a new Jew, ordinary people—was shallow and meaningless. We were still basically the Diaspora Jews, no matter how hard we tried to see ourselves otherwise. This was what really bothered me, not the actual division.

After all, what's the real distance between Makom and Molad? Nothing [*laughing*]. You can see it out of your window. Yet I had never set foot in Makom before the division. I didn't know a thing about it or its people. I had no friends or acquaintances there. Makom was a young kibbutz then, and didn't have children of our age; therefore we didn't meet any of them at camps or in the Army; there were no connections whatsoever. And mind you, I am the type of person who knew every nook and cranny of this country. In trips and hikes I had been everywhere, but not to Makom. So it was like entering a new world, which existed all along right under my nose.

The decisions as to who would go to which kibbutz were made in the kibbutz movement and not by the members. During the division, a large group of members of Makom went to Adama, and, from there, a large group moved elsewhere—and so on. It all happened in 1951–52, and in most cases it was a real boon! It was like an infusion of fresh blood. Kibbutzim were revived by this movement, by the new people. Adama has prospered since then, and so has Makom. Molad is perhaps the only losing party in the game, since we weren't replaced by an organized, cohesive group of people but only by individual families. They have not really recovered since.

So, from a certain point of view, it wasn't so bad at all. The division provided the kibbutzim with new blood, new energy. But I don't think that it would happen again, that people would get up and leave their homes because of an ideological dispute. Can you imagine leaving your house, your neighborhood, because of some political conflict regarding, say, the steps which should be taken towards peace in our area? Presently we have within the kibbutz people who hold opposing views on issues such as the preferred borders and the occupied territories—so what! We hold different opinions, we argue, but it would never occur to anyone to

---

*Kibbutz women often refer to their spouses as "men" because the Hebrew for "husband" has a strongly possessive connotation.

leave his home for that reason! Possibly all ideological controversies are shallower nowadays. Once, if you said, "We'll mount barricades for that," you meant it and you did it. As Alterman* once said, "What strange people. They say—and do!" Today, you say something—so what? You don't have to draw any conclusions. We have differences of opinions—so what, can't we live together anymore?

Personally, the move from Molad to Makom was very difficult for me. I simply loved the place and the people there, and it was hard to cut myself loose. I felt attached to the land, to the mountain I used to see from my window, to the garden I cultivated near my room—a multitude of elements that make one a part of a place. But most of my group didn't feel this as intensely; they would laugh at me for still longing for Molad.

This longing always disturbed me, although I was very active during the division. Not that I ever seriously considered returning to Molad, but I couldn't control my homesickness for the place. For many years, about fifteen I think, the settings and landscapes in my dreams were always those of Molad, even though the people and issues were those of Makom.

As a teacher I always tried to remember the anniversary of the establishment of Molad. I often took my class to the site of the first settlement, somewhere on Mount Gilboa, and we'd spend the day exploring, cooking out, and studying the history of the place. None of the other teachers in Makom ever observed this date with their pupils; they never even remembered it themselves [*laughing*].

All these years we have kept our close social contacts with Molad. My man left his parents and a younger brother there, and every single Saturday afternoon, for the past twenty-six years, at 5:30, we go for a visit to Molad—all of us who still have families there. And they visit us every single Tuesday afternoon at 5:30. There's a special car reserved for these visits. My man's mother is now eighty-three years old, and in rain, wind, storm, or heat, I see her walking over here every Tuesday afternoon. Sometimes I ask myself: How can she keep at it, it's such bad weather today? But she wouldn't ever miss a visit.

At first, when we used to come, they'd say: "The children have come to visit." To this very day we're "children" over there. "Did the children arrive?" They mean us [*laughing*]. At the beginning, they often said: "Come back home, enough of this foolishness." But this is not mentioned anymore. Twenty-six years is quite a period of time! Even the bitterness between us is gone; it's part of the distant past. There were two hundred of us who moved here from Molad, and this was approximately the size of the group that moved out of Makom. So in terms of work and lodging it wasn't difficult to accommodate us.

When we arrived at Makom there was almost nothing here. It was a funny sort of kibbutz [*laughs*], simply impoverished. They had neither

*N. Alterman (1910–1970): renowned Israeli poet and publicist.

land nor water, since they had started the kibbutz really from scratch, in extremely difficult conditions. Contrary to other kibbutzim in the area, which had political or other institutional support, Makom built itself on its own resources; they didn't get any material help from anyone. They established the kibbutz out of pure ideology, reinforced by the principle that this eastern block of land must be settled by Jews, that it shouldn't be abandoned to the Arabs.

Besides that, work wasn't the forte of the Makom pioneers. We in Molad were better trained, and more accustomed to physical work, to agriculture in all its aspects. Yet, with all its poverty, Makom established itself as an unusual settlement from a cultural and social point of view. Their strength was in the creation of cultural values: holidays, for example, and the ways to celebrate them in the kibbutz; a highly developed local school; and a very rich social life. The differences between Molad and Makom probably stem from the different sort of people who inhabited these two spots: Molad was built by Eastern European Jews who had hardly finished high school. In Makom the majority was Israeli-born with a good education, people who had finished the best high schools in the country, reinforced by a large group of German Jews who came with their rich European background and education, and brought into the kibbutz their long-standing tradition of European culture and music. The combination of these two elements was highly successful. Roughly speaking, we, the Molad group, enriched the kibbutz in the economic-material sense, while the Makom core enriched us in the social and cultural sense. We were absorbed like seeds falling into fertile soil. Practically speaking, we were tailor-made for Makom. They had two generations—the adults and their children, with nobody in between. That's where we fitted in and that's why there is no generation gap in Makom. While in large cities you aren't aware of it, this generation gap is sometimes quite problematical in small settlements, where there's roughly a twenty-year difference between the two generations. Here, however, the various age groups form a continuum, which is very convenient.

It's difficult to pinpoint a date, a period when things started to change here, when the combination of the two groups started to yield fruits. It was a slow process of growth, as more generations of children and newcomers gradually joined our community, while the first generation matured and grew older. There weren't any jumps or crises. The economic improvement was steady, marked by the addition of machinery and industry. Goals were achieved as we slowly pulled the cart uphill, working consistently and stubbornly together. And one day, lo and behold, we could look back in pride and say: "Look what we have achieved, what we have managed to do in the last four years, the last ten years!" This perseverence is a central trait of the old core of Makom—they never accept failure; they'd try again and again and, if it didn't succeed, they'd try yet again! It's very unique to these people.

The idea of a community is a central principle in our kibbutz. A community is made up of many elements. If some are eliminated, the whole will become unbalanced. Though it's true that not everybody wants to be a teacher, our local school provides jobs for many people, not only in teaching but in workshops, construction, many things which are interdependent.

Under the same principle, Makom works to provide additional supportive elements of the communal system, which in turn develop the kibbutz's branches of industry, agriculture, art, and welfare. It doesn't have to be that way. Take aging people, for example—some kibbutzim send their aged to special homes for the elderly; we don't. We are building here a whole welfare system in order to take care of our parents. We're also building a medical center for this purpose, and, even though that's not yet finished, we have started to train the professional teams necessary for its operation. Why do we go into all these areas? Because we're building a community. This is a word I'm not even sure you'll hear in another kibbutz. The idea of the community is that we would like to be as self-supporting as possible in all respects. We have our limitations, naturally, and we're aware of them. As we get older, we have two distinct populations in need of care: the children and the elderly. What remains in between is the middle generation, ranging from twenty to forty-five, let's say, and they have to carry the bulk of the economic burden as well as provide the personnel to work with the two extremes of the life cycle.

So people will tell you: "Well, Makom is a big kibbutz; therefore, they don't have many problems." Of course we have problems, and we don't try to avoid them. We want to provide our individual members with the personal security of knowing that whatever happens—when they have babies, are sick, or get old—they'll still remain part of our community. We don't ever want to reject our responsibility for each other.

This, you may say, is the unique theme of our kibbutz. It developed with time, and you may ask, "Why here rather than somewhere else?" I think there were several elements that contributed to this development: the warmth and cohesiveness of the family in Eastern Europe, where the old and the weak were always kept within the family; the cultural background of Western Europe with its respect for the individual as an individual; the openness of the Machanot Haolim who were always in favor of diversity and soul-searching; and the intellectual ability of Makom's founders. It's perhaps all of these components that produced the kibbutz's sense of community.

This soul-searching is especially typical of our kibbutz. We sit and think and ponder a problem almost endlessly. When we don't reach an agreement, we never cut the argument short; we meet again, search for new ideas, advice, and information, until a solution is reached. When a private issue is involved, the secretary may go to a member again and again to discuss the case with both sides, until a satisfactory solution is achieved, agreed upon by both parties. Where else can you find such consideration? In Molad, we weren't used to this style; a vote would be taken, and a decision made. The secretary sat in his office; he never had time to look for an individual, to talk things over with him. When I was the secretary here, whenever a member approached me I'd never reject him or delay our meeting; I found time to talk to him or her, even if I had no time. Having no time is relative, after all: Everything can be squeezed in if you're willing to delay something else for half an hour.

This is the essence of our life-style: maximum consideration for the individual. Not economically—in this respect we were too poor for years to offer much—but socially and personally. Another small detail: In Molad when two people meet they don't greet each other. Here it will never happen that I pass someone without saying: "Good morning," "Shalom," "Good evening," whatever. I see someone; he's a person not a tree! We used to have a schoolteacher in Molad who demanded that we greet him with a "good morning." What roundabout paths we used to take then, all around the kibbutz, just to avoid meeting him! It simply wasn't acceptable, there was no rule requiring it.

Now, when I visit Molad every Saturday, on my way to my parents-in-law, I say "shalom" to people I meet, out of habit. They are often taken by surprise, frequently stopping and staring at me bewildered [*laughs*]— what business do I have talking to them? Sometimes they do respond, though. It drives me crazy!

You might consider this just a question of manners, an external style —but I think it's indicative of something deeper. Why did we develop in such a different fashion? I don't know for sure, yet it's a fact that we're different. Somehow, in this kibbutz, we developed a humane idea which is beyond the worker, working the land; it is the antithesis of the Diaspora Jew.

Here we cherish much more than work and economic achievements. Let me give you another example. Many of us study in various programs of the open university. We also have an ongoing Talmud Study Group and other adult education programs here. Last year we added to these courses a new program that is studying the history and philosophy of the labor movement in Israel. It was initiated during the winter. Twice a week at 5:30 in the morning. I'd get up at 4:30 when it was still completely dark. Putting on the light, I used to see my mother, who's seventy-one now, also turning on the light in her room to get ready for our class. Before sunrise, this group would gather in the school building, together with some teachers we had invited for this purpose. All of us were pretty advanced in years; most of us were parents and grandparents, and we'd crowd into our children's classroom for an early-morning lesson. At the beginning we were laughed at—losing sleep to study A. D. Gordon!* But soon they stopped laughing. Frequently, our children, who start their

---

*A. D. Gordon (1856–1922): one of the founding fathers and spiritual leaders of the Jewish labor movement in pre-State Palestine.

school day at 6:30, come to class and see us still absorbed in our studies. Patiently they wait at the doorstep for their parents and grandparents to leave their classroom, and then they take their seats as we leave school for our day's work. It's just an example, but there's so much meaning in this single act of daybreak study of the labor movement ideology in our children's classroom, I can't even start to unearth it all. We all live and study here together. It is uniquely moving.

Lately, people speak a lot about equality in the kibbutz: Does the kibbutz still maintain the basic value of equality? Equality is, in my opinion, based on the sincere attempt to satisfy each individual's needs and develop each person's talents. If someone has musical talent, we'll give him the adequate training, even if it costs thousands of pounds. If another has a talent for mechanical work, we'll give him a job at the workshop. So, objectively speaking, these two are getting very unequal treatment in the kibbutz. That is the meaning of equality—to provide an opportunity to develop one's potential, and to satisfy one's needs.

C H A I M   *(age 69)*

Chaim is nearly seventy, and his upcoming birthday party is scheduled to take place in the large dining room. He was the leader of the Molad subgroup when it merged with Makom in 1952. "But he's completely one of us now," people say about him. He eulogizes the dead in almost every funeral in the kibbutz. His son, Yair, appears in "Administration."

When the British set up prison camps in Cyprus for illegal *olim,* * whom they wouldn't let into Israel, I went out to Cyprus and stayed there over a year. When I returned to Molad, in the fall of 1948, the kibbutz was in the midst of its division. For me, personally, it was a shock. The school principal, who used to be a very good friend, called me in and said: "You won't be teaching here anymore, since you aren't reliable." Reliable for what? A reliable Jew, reliable Zionist, reliable Israeli, I could not understand of what I was being accused. Just unreliable. My position in school didn't matter at all to me, but the principle mattered to me a great deal. I'm a member of the kibbutz; why can't I teach? Of what did they suspect us—that we were more loyal to Russia than to Israel? That we might betray our country, even desert it, and go to Russia? They couldn't have thought that; they knew us too well.

The deep meaning of the division wasn't our left-oriented ideology, our so-called loyalty to Russia. At least, I don't think so. The crux of the matter was differences in the theory of who controls the kibbutz. Is the kibbutz a subject of the State, and should it therefore take direct orders from the State, or is autonomy the basis of the kibbutz, as I personally

*Immigrants.

see it? Today we all know that the power of the kibbutz, its value, lies in the fact that it is voluntary. It is, perhaps, the only remnant of voluntary activity in the country, in addition, maybe, to the voluntary elite units of the Army. In the late 1940s, people were drunk with the idea of the State. We, however, believed in maintaining autonomous units such as the kibbutz or the Palmach, although we were, naturally, willing to accept the State's law and discipline. We wanted to keep our independence in terms of our values and style of life.

I think this was what threatened Ben-Gurion most of all, and he was the one who caused the division within the kibbutz movement. He feared our strength, so he had to break us up. He didn't want any strong autonomous organizations, because he considered them a threat to the new State. He wanted to atomize society into tiny elements that would all be directly under his control. Actually, this was a totalitarian idea, something very Russian, whereas he blamed *us* of loyalty to Russia. I don't think that Ben-Gurion himself suspected us, for a moment, of a dangerous link with Russia; he just used this argument to convince the fools. If people tell you that the division happened on that basis, they are naïve and don't see the total picture. Our so-called allegiance to the U.S.S.R. was nothing but an excuse. I remember Ben-Gurion's speaking on the lawn of Molad. He put the fear of God into the simple people of Molad. I remember a sentence of his: "All the tractors of the Kibbutz Hameuchad won't pull me out of here." What did he mean? What was he afraid of? It's a mystery to me. Yet, truly, we were anarchists of a sort. It's true, we believed in spontaneity, in voluntary action—and he suspected we might overturn the young State. He wanted to be the only source of the Idea, one Idea, and this was completely against our spirit. Despite all of this, I don't want to detract from Ben-Gurion's keen political judgment in other areas. When he wanted to declare independence, we thought it was the wrong moment —yet today it's clear that he was right while we were wrong. He understood that there existed a narrow crack in the international political organization, the only moment when the U.S.A. and the U.S.S.R. could join forces and help us establish the State. He saw it, and we did not. But in the case of the kibbutz, he was the one in the wrong.

Anyway, as I wasn't accepted back as a teacher, I moved ahead. Just at that time Efal was being organized, and its goal was to become an institute of higher education in the ideology of the kibbutz. It was extremely important to clarify the values underlying the kibbutz and its relationship with the State, and I gladly participated in this project. I worked there for four years, from 1949 to 1953, returning home every-other weekend and once during the week.

I was away from home for very long periods and my wife raised the children more or less by herself. Our firstborn was born in 1941, the twins in 1946. But I always tried to be a good father to them. I remember when a friend of mine came with his backpack to go on a hike with me, and my son stood at the door exclaiming: "This is *my* father, *my* father!" He was used to seeing me depart.

In the meantime, the process of the division in Molad was taking place. It was a long process, starting back in 1942, when a group of Molad members formed what we called "Faction B." We were a group of the more ideologically oriented people, whereas the prevailing atmosphere in Molad was of *mishkism,* namely, work and production for their own sake. They weren't closely associated with the Kibbutz Hameuchad, they were alien to its temperament, its enthusiasm, its socialist intentions. They were good, simple people, and excellent farmers. But during the division they became irate. They actually threw us out. They considered us a threat to their home.

Not all of them, though. There were some saintly souls, such as one older member who used to accompany tearfully every truck of our group as it departed for Makom.

Gradually it became quite clear that we would leave Molad, as similar divisions took place in other kibbutzim around us, but we were not of one opinion as to where to go. One thing we made very clear—that we would stick together and find another kibbutz that would be able and willing to absorb us as a group. The older members preferred to join an established kibbutz, where they wouldn't have to start all over again, building a home once again, at their age. The younger members wanted to start a kibbutz of our own, or to join a very young kibbutz where we would participate in creating the place from the start. I was for joining the split of Ein-Harod [Hameuchad], which was completely devastated after its own division. But the final decision wasn't our own; we followed what was decided by the Kibbutz Hameuchad, and we joined Makom.

Makom was materially poor, but rich in spirit. Just at the time when so many members, especially kibbutz children, left them in the division, they sent away ten of their best men to the secretariat of the Movement. They understood that it was a very rough time for the Movement and said: "If the Movement falls, Makom will fall with it, but if it stands the storm, we'll all survive." And that's what happened. By mobilizing ten members to the secretariat of the Kibbutz Hameuchad Movement, they gained great influence there, and they got the Molad subgroup, which was directed to join them.

So, we built Makom through our joint efforts. I'm not saying we did it alone; we all did it together. Makom lost some very good people, central people who moved to Adama. I believe that the ones who moved from here regret their action to this very day. Adama will never be like Makom, and they know it.

The Molad group is still a rather cohesive group. Not that we feel a barrier between us and the original Makom members, not at all. But we of Molad grew up together, we raised our young children together, we still share the happy or sad events of Molad, we go there for visits, some still have relatives there. These things bind us together in a special way. However, I have many intimate relations with Makom members, in particular with my students. All in all I was a member of Molad for fourteen years, and have been in Makom for twenty-eight years—twice as long. It makes a difference. It's sad to look at Molad today, though; it's very sad. They never recovered from the blow which they themselves caused. We were never replaced there. They have a good income, but many of their sons have left them throughout the years. I have heard that some are returning, however.

Well, as I look back at all this, I think I'm much wiser today. Now the two movements, the Ichud and the Kibbutz Hameuchad, are seriously considering reuniting. This should happen not only because Begin now runs the government and we're all outsiders now. That's not the only reason. It's time to admit that both sides, both of us who created the conflict, have actually gone astray. They were mistaken when they threw us out; we, in joining forces with the Shomer Hatzair,* which was in fact much more leftist than we were. Had we not done so, it wouldn't have been so easy to convince people that we were indeed the black sheep. I remember a very good and innocent Jew in Makom who had read in the Shomer Hatzair paper that we had two homelands, so he got up in the assembly and declared: "I have two homelands." And what was the outcome? Ten more families packed their belongings and left the kibbutz. So he made a declaration—so what? It was sheer nonsense, for he had no real loyalty to Russia, but it made the split much deeper.

Both sides made mistakes. We should have been more tolerant, live and let live. I remember a fable which was used by Tabenkin, one of our leaders, in that context. It was a Russian fable about the alarm spread among the oaks of the forest: Iron has penetrated the woods! They went to the eldest oak to ask for his advice and he said: "As long as you don't provide Iron with a Handle—no harm can come your way." But we, we gave the Mapai people the handle to harm us with. What I regret most of all are some of the basic mistakes in human relations, the ruined friendships, although in our case it wasn't as extreme as in some other kibbutzim.

Today I feel that the more opinions we have, the wider the variety of outlooks within the kibbutz, the stronger we are. Take for example, the issue of settling the Golan. I support it, and our kibbutz has decided to adopt Ginat up there, yet some of our members are vehemently against all this. I'm not trying to force them to accept my view, nor, God forbid, would I throw them out of our common home. We will live as a pluralistic society. If someone is against settling the so-called occupied territories, it's his right to stay here, and by his work here he actually frees another member to go up there. But once, in the 1940s and

*The left-wing youth movement aligned with Kibbutz Haartzi.

1950s, we didn't have this flexibility. Things were different.

The day we joined Makom we held a general assembly in the evening. All the tables in the dining room were arranged in a circle, we all sat around the hall, facing each other, and this togetherness impressed me very deeply. The togetherness, the intimacy between the members, and some ideological naïveté—these are my earliest recollections of Makom. In Molad the atmosphere had been completely different, and especially since we were constantly struggling with one another. There, ideology was a storm; here, it was poetry, a wish, a dream. I was enchanted by this atmosphere.

My second vivid impression was the poverty of the place. Respectable poverty. They really didn't eat enough. I think it's the only kibbutz in which the scarcity of means found expression in the daily menu. Other kibbutzim were perhaps as poor, but food was never lacking. I remember a visit by some functionary from the secretariat in Tel Aviv, followed by an order from the Movement that we must increase our food budget. Yet the cashier of this wretched kibbutz was accepted in the banks with total respect. Firstly, because it became known that Makom was extremely punctual in all its payments and that its word was the best possible guarantee. Furthermore, because of the manners its people had—their cashier came to the bank in sandals and with a rose in the buttonhole of his shirt. They were charming people.

When we arrived, we found out that each member here owned one pair of pajamas and one sheet. They washed them in the morning and reused them at night. We brought, I believe, four sheets per person, and as many for each child; simply sharing these increased the standard at Makom somewhat. Moreover, since we brought all our personal belongings—linen, clothes, and furniture—the Kibbutz Hameuchad gave Makom a loan so that they could buy some of these items and maintain equality among us all. This poverty was, somehow, of their own choice; they never took a loan unless they were sure they'd be able to repay it, never made an investment before they had the money in their pocket, and, most important, never agreed to accept donations from the rich. Take, for example, the plan to build a memorial center for illegal immigration, in memory of Oded; his wife vetoed it just because the money for it wasn't our own but was donated. This is very typical of this kibbutz; they never wanted to live by charity. That's pretty unusual in this country, pretty unusual.

Another principle they took very seriously was not to use hired labor. Their own work, as far as I saw it, was exceptionally dedicated; the ethics of work have been maintained at the highest standard. In the cotton branch, for instance, they work ten, twelve hours a day because they have this unusual motivation to maximize its potential. Or in our factories, you will see the lights on in the administrators' offices at all hours of the night. They feel this tremendous involvement and responsibility, while, obviously, they receive no personal profit from this, at least not in the usual sense of the word. Satisfaction—yes, that's for sure. This is something one must say about the kibbutz: If one doesn't make a constant effort to increase every achievement—economic, educational, whatever—it regresses immediately.

The Molad group contributed to Makom in three main areas. Firstly, we were a group of very ideologically oriented people. We had chosen the kibbutz as our way of life, not because we were born there or grew up there. This personal model was life serum to the second generation of Makom, who had just reached tenth or eleventh grades then. They saw in our group the flag bearers of the Kibbutz Hameuchad, and this influenced their development to a large extent. From my point of view, this was our most important contribution. Our second contribution was our ability to bridge the generation gap between parents and children at Makom. Finally, as everyone knows, our group had experience in farming and agriculture. Here, there were some excellent workers as well, but they needed some extra help. They simply hadn't been lucky before we came; the soil wasn't right, the water was salty, fourteen different agricultural and industrial branches had been attempted and had met with failure, and, above all, they were very short of money. But actually I think that, despite all our contributions, things started to improve here even before we came. Right after the War of Independence money started to come in from the State and, with the new budget, things started to move.

M I R I A M *(age 56)*

Miriam is a youthful, blond woman, who talks freely and seems unafraid of expressing whatever is on her mind. I invited her to be interviewed as one of the few women in the kibbutz who holds a central role in an agricultural branch. But, delicate and sophisticated, there couldn't be a woman who appears less like a "cowwoman" than she.

I've been here for forty years now and I still have a trace of an Austrian accent. I arrived in Israel when I was fifteen, in 1938, when the Nazis occupied Austria. The Jewish community in Austria organized youth groups, especially from the Zionist youth movements, and sent these groups to Israel, to safety. I arrived at Molad with such a group, and indeed this arrangement saved my life. My mother and brothers managed to escape to the U.S.A., but my father died in Auschwitz.

So I lived within a subgroup of immigrants in Molad, and, although this period doesn't directly belong to the history of Makom, I think it's quite important. Makom had also absorbed a youth-*aliya* group from Czechoslovakia at that time; I'm not sure whether their experience was different from mine. Young immigrants were not accepted then as they are today, that's certain. We lived completely separated from our peers in the kibbutz, and we weren't assimilated within the school or the children's society either. We lived in separate houses, and we ate in the dining hall with the adults, while the local children dined in their own dining hall. At that time, children were stuffed with food; they were forced to eat everything that was prepared and they received the best food available. Adults, on the other hand, lived on a very poor diet, and we received what they did. Our menu consisted primarily of bread, olives, and eggplants. Coming from well-to-do families, we were used to a very different diet; I remember hungering for something better, for sweets, or butter to spread on the bread. . . . We knew the kibbutz kids did get such things—it was no secret. As our sleeping quarters were right across from their dining hall, when the kibbutz children had eaten all they could, they'd put their leftover cups of pudding on the windowsills and yell: "Yekkes, come and get it!" My poor friends grabbed the food, although I don't recall that I took part myself. . . . This is my most vivid recollection of that time, followed by the awareness that I was, somehow, a second-rate person in the kibbutz. It was unpleasant, of course.

The same treatment was typical in other areas as well. Children of our age in the kibbutz studied in high school, and they all completed their secondary education, while we had a schedule of four hours of work and four hours of studies, daily. All we studied was Hebrew and some Jewish history, with very little general education of any kind. I must say that these things hurt me more in retrospect, whereas at that time we loved the kibbutz, we enjoyed our work, and later we became much closer to the local youngsters.

When I was eighteen, our group joined two other youth-*aliya* groups in an attempt to create a new settlement near the Dead Sea. This project failed, however, and the majority dispersed to various towns. It's a shame for there were many excellent people, well educated for the kibbutz life, yet almost nobody remained in kibbutzim. I didn't go to the Dead Sea settlement because I became attached to a kibbutz member, whom I later married, and we stayed in Molad. I bore my three children there, worked in the dairy farm and left for Makom during the division in 1952.

The division provided me with the opportunity to leave Molad, in which I had held a peculiar social status. I had associated with people who were identified as Communists ("factioners" was the term they used at the time), and although I didn't share their political point of view I was suspected of being a Communist myself. I wasn't a popular individual in the kibbutz, and for fourteen years I had lived in Molad without being granted kibbutz membership. When I applied for the first time, the secretariat declared that they wouldn't back my request because Communists were not welcome as kibbutz members; it wasn't even brought up before the general assembly. People then were very sensitive and suspicious of communism. Though my closest friends were indeed Trotskyists and later emigrated, and though I have always held progressive opinions, I never belonged to a party. I was hurt by this suspicion, and didn't try to prove my "innocence." Years later, just before the division, the tension over communism had calmed down somewhat; I finally received membership by an uncontested vote, but I never felt at home socially in Molad. I found the people there very simpleminded, with a provincial mentality and limited cultural interests, whereas I longed for, and had been used to, a different milieu. I had heard that Makom was different. Therefore, when the dissident Molad members decided to join Makom, I joined the departing faction, although I felt very little identification with their political position.

I moved here with my family. From the very start, it was an extremely well-chosen step. To this day, when I compare the two kibbutzim, I see how fortunate I was in taking that step. While Makom is flourishing, both economically and culturally, Molad is slowly dying away. They lost their best people during the division, and were never able to replace them. Today, if you walk into the dining hall of Molad you might think you were in an old-age home: More than half of the population is over seventy years old.

Anyway, I personally felt very well in Makom from the moment we arrived. I felt liberated here, although I was put in the kitchen right away —I, who had always worked with cows and didn't even know how to boil an egg! Contrary to other Molad members, I didn't find the conditions here worse than in Molad. I had a room without a shower in Molad, and I received the same thing here. The food was indeed less plentiful here, but this had never bothered me.

Two months after our arrival, I was elected the coordinator of women's work before I even knew the names of all the members. It wasn't an easy job then—there were four hundred children for whom I had to arrange the care-taking and educational teams from the adult community of three hundred members! But people were very cooperative then, their work habits were good, and I don't remember ever being refused assistance when I was in need of a worker. When I finished my term arranging women's work, I was elected as supervisor of the menu and food supplies, which is another central role in the kibbutz. It's called the "kitchen economist." The kitchen economist is a "middle man" between the members, who want a lot of good food, and the secretariat, which wants to cut down expenses.

Well, many things concerning food and eating habits have changed completely since my time as kitchen economist, as have so many other aspects of our life. Firstly, I'd say that about 70 percent of the population, especially the young families, eat in their rooms every evening, and most people take Saturday breakfast at home, as well as various meals here and there. Women cook and bake in their private kitchens, and therefore have all sorts of food stored at home. This food comes from three sources. All items that are offered at the dining hall—bread, margarine, white cheese, eggs, etc.—can be taken freely from our food store, as well as many other food staples, such as ingredients needed for baking. The second category of food is obtained with coupons which are provided to the members: cream, hard cheese, sausages, fruits and vegetables. The rations are generous, and a member can dictate his or her own combination, but they're not completely unlimited. Both rationed and free foods can be obtained from our local food store, which actually replaces the dining hall in many ways. It's much better that people don't come into the dining hall and pick things out to take to their rooms. Finally, there are luxury foods and sweets one can buy out of one's personal budget at our supermarket. I don't buy anything there except for coffee and tea, which cannot be obtained elsewhere.

This freedom and abundance of food has taken much of the pressure off the kitchen economist's position, which I held until 1961, during pretty rough years. I can still remember quarrels with women who came to the locked food store in search of a few eggs with which to bake a cake for Saturday, and I couldn't afford to satisfy their needs.

You'll find the same relaxed trend with clothes nowadays. We used to wear very simple clothes, and getting a new dress was a very rare event in a woman's life. Today, if you enter the dining hall on Friday night, you might think it's a fashion show. I'm for dressing well, but . . . I often regret that we have lost so many of our simple ways of life. I think that the peak of the dressing-up phenomenon is already behind us, and women have gone back to some moderation recently. The emphasis on clothes and personal appearance characterized our community three or four years ago, when we initiated a personal-budget system. Suddenly people realized they had a certain amount of money to spend, and this freedom turned the heads of many young women who ran to the city and spent their allowance on fancy outfits. The personal budget covers all the individual's expenses—clothing, furniture, presents, books, concerts, travel, etc.—and it's up to one's own discretion how the money is spent. But you needn't rush off to the city to buy clothes; good clothes can be purchased in our local store as well.

In 1961, I was approached with the proposal to help save our dairy farm. I gladly accepted the position; in Molad I had worked with cows for thirteen years, and I was more than willing to finish my work with people and return to working with animals. This is what I'm doing to this very day. I'm one of very few women in kibbutzim who play any agricultural role, and am probably the "last Mohican" in my age group. When I returned to the cattle branch in 1961, I reestablished the breeding business; today it's a very important department in our kibbutz. I personally enjoy my work very much and I hope to continue working there as long as I'm able. My work is my hobby.

I work every day from 6:00 A.M., and although I don't have to work more than five hours a day, I often stay for eight hours; frequently I'm back again at the dairy at night. My job is to receive the newborn calf right after birth; I put him in a clean cage, and I take care of his nursing, which is a complicated process. Our arrangement is to separate the calf from his mother, who is then milked immediately. The calf gets his milk from bottles, but it's important to nurse him with his mother's milk since this provides immunization against future disease. In winter we have about thirty-five or forty newborn calves each month and I receive help in tending to them. I may have between 100 and 150 young calves under my supervision at a time, and I care for them for four to five months.

In addition to this, I am in charge of the record book for our cattle, an international, computerized project. This book provides information about the genetic pedigree of every cow, the amount of milk it produces and its fat proportion, its offspring, and other important details. It is an important source of information for buyers all over the Western world, and involves competitions and prizes. Without going into details, I can tell you that the situation of the Israeli herd is excellent, and our cattle are very sought after. Our cattle are now serious competition for the Dutch cattle, which used to have the top reputation.

So I have headed these two activities in our dairy, the breeding and log keeping. In the latter, I am the only person with all the technical expertise, so I remained in charge of the records even when I went to study at the university.

Young women today, however, don't take advantage of their opportunities. Their aims are extremely limited. If they wish to study at all, they only want to learn arts and crafts; as it is, there are already too many handicrafters. It's a very stereotyped, feminine choice.

From Makom
to Adama

YAAKOV PORAT (age 64)

Yaakov came to our interview directly from the synagogue. "Yes," he answered my question, "we have a synagogue and it's pretty active. I'm a regular member, and I see it as very important for the community, especially for the young generation, to have one in the kibbutz. Makom doesn't have one yet, does it?"

I asked Yaakov to tell me about the division, but he said that he must start somewhat earlier.

Makom was founded in '28, and I joined in '32. However, I knew all of the founders and I lived through the settlement's most critical stages. Actually, when I arrived from Jerusalem, the group consisted of very few members, and the place was on the verge of disintegration. The group had undergone a most acute crisis, involving several suicides; there was complete unemployment, and the probability of settling down permanently in the spot was almost nil. Yet, within three years, the situation had totally changed. Personally, living through that critical period in Makom gave me a proper perspective when facing other crises I have encountered in my life.

But the Makom/Adama division was a crisis of a completely different nature. One of the greatest errors in telling about the division today is in presenting it as the outcome of a sudden upsurge of passions, or as the result of a chain of events caused by external intervention of some sort. I think that this is erroneous because the division was actually the climax of a slow process of change which had begun in 1936. World War II, the Holocaust, the struggle against the British, the attitudes towards Russia, and the debate concerning the establishment of the State all played a part, in one way or another, in this internal political dispute. For that reason, I have always objected to the absurd claim that Ben-Gurion himself planned and directed the division within the kibbutz movement.

This is the exact opposite of what really happened. Actually, B.G. was a very careful person, and he constantly pressured the Mapai faction to be moderate, to restrain ourselves and not to escalate the conflict, since he foresaw the coming division within the Mapam camp and believed that in a short while the whole political constellation would change. Ben-Gurion became the scapegoat of the whole story, and this provided a simple version which helped people deny the deep processes which had slowly been splitting the kibbutz movement for approximately twenty years.

In the country, the leaders of the labor movement, B.G. and others, gradually assumed wide national responsibilities and they viewed the kibbutz movement within the context of their wider perspective. The Kibbutz Hameuchad's outlook remained narrowly within their own parochial framework. This created tension between the Kibbutz Hameuchad and the entire Labor Movement, similar to the friction formerly felt between the work troop and the Histadrut.*

In addition to this process, a growing enchantment with Russia was developing within the Kibbutz Hameuchad. It started quietly and grew in intensity, until, in 1936, I remember an important speech which stated: "He who doesn't support communism cannot be loyal to the establishment of the commune." We felt a growing discomfort with what was happening within the Kibbutz Hameuchad Movement.

As you know, there were two separate kibbutz movements at the time: the Kibbutz Hameuchad and the Ichud Hakvutzot. They were both affiliated with Mapai in the 1930s, and therefore it had always seemed natural that they unite. In '39, two months before the outbreak of World War II, a meeting of the Kibbutz Hameuchad delegates was called to discuss the possible union of the two movements. Although the majority of the delegates would have voted for the union, under the pressure of the old leadership a decision was made against it. You must understand that the actual spirit of the period supported a union. It was the time of the riots, people were being mobilized for various national tasks, they fought together and fell together, and they were aware of their common fate. Yet, apparently, a minority still opposed this trend. That's when Faction B got organized, consisting of people who considered themselves truly loyal to the spirit of the Kibbutz Hameuchad. They conducted secret meetings in Haifa and tried to conceal their activities.

At the same time, a parallel crisis was taking place in the youth movements. There were several different movements, and there were forces trying to unite them all, especially since we were facing the threat of war and the Holocaust. On the other hand, there were forces that tried to keep them apart. In '45, the Kibbutz Hameuchad decided against the union of the youth movements as well. I, as a man who was deeply

*The national organization of workers' unions.

involved with the youth movements, couldn't understand or accept this attitude. It was especially unconscionable when one considered the terrible condition Jews were in after the Holocaust, and the urgent need to rescue the remnants of our nation.

Simultaneously, immediately after the war, a conflict developed regarding the proper educational aims of the youth movements. Some members claimed, to my utter dismay, that the youth must be educated according to the principles of *The Communist Manifesto.* I belonged to a group which thought that we should focus on the Holocaust and its lesson for our nation. This debate was tied to general political attitudes concerning Russia and the communist world. Since Russia had become a major power after World War II, some people in the country believed that it would also be the crucial power in the Middle East; therefore, the question of the proper orientation towards Russia seemed to be very important.

Probably even more relevant issues to the vast majority of Israelis were the questions of the political future of the country and the best methods of struggling against the British. I think this was our most severe conflict. I was shocked to discover the opinions of some of the people I had considered my friends, people with whom I grew up and was educated! Their point of view was that we should struggle for the replacement of the British mandate by an international mandate. Instead of British rulers, we'd have Americans, Russians, and Chinese as well. . . . Every child could understand that such a situation wouldn't advance the Zionist project even one step forward! On the contrary, it would lead to greater risks and complications for all of us.

I think that since some people had developed violent animosity towards Ben-Gurion, the situation was such that, if he was *for* an independent state, the opposition had to be against it. Any idea coming from B.G. would have arbitrarily received a negative reaction. Things were carried to such extremes that to speak out in favor of the creation of a state was to be a traitor to the kibbutz and towards "Greater Eretz Yisrael" as well. They inscribed that slogan on their banner and fought against the partition plan (between Jews and Arabs) with all their might. The truth is that this strategy was basically developed to stand in B.G.'s way. Look at these people today: How many of them are for a "Greater Eretz Yisrael" now?

So all these issues, the union of the kibbutz movements, the U.S.S.R., the "partition borders," and the establishment of an independent state were tearing apart the internal fabric of the kibbutzim long before the actual division took place. In the meantime, Mapai itself split and separated from Mapam and this naturally affected the kibbutzim as well.

Well, as I said before, I was a delegate to the youth movements most of the time, while my wife and my three children lived on the kibbutz. In 1947 I was called to go to Europe to work in the Jewish refugee camps to organize the youth; it was undoubtedly a noble mission. In the kibbutz, however, everything was done to prevent me from going. They were afraid I'd be a missionary for the Ben-Gurion camp. I did go, but I hadn't stayed long when I received a letter from our secretary urgently calling me to return since my wife was seriously ill. This indeed was true, but my wife, in her letters, had concealed her disease from me so that I might continue calmly with my important work; the secretary, on the other hand, was of the opposing camp and took the opportunity to share the news with me and induce me to return right away. . . . I did return, and I don't regret it, but the secretary's motives soon became quite clear to me. The Palmach wanted to draft me to do educational work with their troops, in preparation for the approaching establishment of the State; again, the kibbutz stood in my way and decided that I must stay in Makom. This was too much. I disobeyed the kibbutz decision and joined the Palmach, and the kibbutz formally retaliated by withdrawing my membership. This was, however, so absurd that after outside intervention the decision was repealed and I continued in my work with my original kibbutz status.

Well, the climax of it all was perhaps on the night of November 29, 1947. Being in charge of our cultural committee, I was listening to the sole radio. At midnight, with tremendous excitement, I heard the final U.N. vote and decision. I ran out, planning to ring the bell, and to wake everybody up in order to share the news and celebrate. Near the bell I met some members.

"What are you going to do?" they asked.

I told them.

"Who told you to ring the bell? Did the assembly decide, did the secretariat decide? No, you won't ring it, no way."

It was a very tense encounter, and I felt that I had to give in, or else I'd be physically prevented from ringing the bell.

In the morning, I took flags out and was on my way to hang them on our public buildings and the kibbutz center, when I was stopped again.

"Where are you going?"

"To hang those flags out, just like everywhere else in the country."

"No, you won't. First let's call the secretariat and make a decision."

Again I submitted, but after breakfast I called for a special meeting of our cultural committee. I said, "Last night, while the whole country was joyfully celebrating, we didn't do a thing. We can't ignore what's happening—let's plan something for this evening." I suggested a party; it was immediately voted down. Being in the minority, I suggested a general meeting for a discussion of the events instead, and demanded that the dining hall be decorated with white tablecloths and flowers. "Absolutely not!" was the reaction.

"We'll never forgive ourselves for letting this historic occasion pass in such a manner," I said.

And the famous reaction to this was: "If a woman has a miscarriage, does she celebrate the event?"

I argued and failed to convince them, and I finally withdrew. Others took over, and a little note was put on the bulletin board:

"Tonight—a meeting to discuss the current events."

That was the exact wording. . . . A huge audience gathered, nevertheless—adults, adolescents, and children. The speakers opened by lamenting the event. Yehuda said in his speech: "I was in Haifa today, and I saw the masses going wild in the streets, and I'm sure some blood has already been shed in this great commotion, for this fantasy of a State." People continued in this vein until someone jumped up and yelled: *"Gewald!* * We want to celebrate and you want us to weep!" A dead silence followed. I didn't know what would happen next, the air was so tense. In the corner, however, a single member got up and started to sing the national anthem, "Hatikvah." Gradually the whole audience joined in, and then tables were moved out of the way and a Hora dance was started and swept everybody in. You might say that it's just a story, but it expresses a lot, and I will never forget it.

On the personal level, one must add to all the above the growing awareness that, from the 1930s on, people were being elected to various roles and missions, advanced in rank or blocked from activity, according to the concealed criterion of their "loyalty." There were three questions underlying the definition of loyalty: whether you were for or against the union of the kibbutz movements, B.G. and his political view, and the U.S.S.R. as our main ally. "Loyal" were those who were against Ben-Gurion and the union, and for the U.S.S.R; no one else deserved this title.

I, for example, was by profession a teacher and youth leader, yet in Makom I was considered "unqualified" for educational work. Once I was approached by a group of high-school students who had organized a study group and wanted me to instruct them in Judaism, which was known to be my special area of interest. I agreed willingly, but the moment our school administration heard about it they vetoed my participation, even though they couldn't find another teacher to take my place. . . .

Things like this, coupled with the open political antagonism, embittered my life. Later we decided to divide the kibbutz, as you know, and I moved to Adama. For history's sake I'd like to add, however, that I'm now sure that, had we been able to postpone the division of Makom for a year or two, we might have spared ourselves this trauma entirely. There were global events which prevented the whole kibbutz movement from delaying but here, locally, we could perhaps have waited a bit longer. Our side had indeed offered just such a temporary solution, namely, that every camp would establish a *modus vivendi* for our common life within the community. All we demanded in return was minimal satisfaction in the

*Exclamation of grief.

sense that our identity and viewpoints would not be totally negated—but the majority rejected our terms. Today, I know how right we were then. Two years later, another political split occurred—Achdut Ha'avoda* separated from Mapam, and this completely changed the position of Makom on the political map. We sensed that process, and played for time as long as we could, but the other side didn't cooperate in our attempt to save the unity of Makom. I couldn't grasp it then, and it took me some years of study to understand the roots of their intolerance.

People who identify with bolshevism and the U.S.S.R., either rationally or emotionally, can't accept any deviations from their way. There's a saying that the most dangerous reactionaries can be found inside the revolutionary movements. They have their clear conceptions, and they won't allow for any deviations from them. One example is the idea of the local school, which was one of the basic tenets of the Kibbutz Hameuchad. We have to have complete control over our children's education, from nursery school to high school, all run by ourselves. The regional school is, however, so much more practical; it offers the students greater flexibility, can maintain full-size classrooms and a complete curriculum! Gradually all Kibbutz Hameuchad settlements accepted the regional-school system, except for Makom, which still insists on the old concept, though I estimate it's not for long. People should be flexible enough to admit their mistakes once in a while. Nobody is right forever—but this was so characteristic of Makom when we split!

When we finally decided to move, we adopted the principle of not fighting for anything material, not even for our basic rights. We were 250 individuals—including children—and even though Adama was in pretty bad shape economically, and it was quite difficult for them to accommodate such a large number of newcomers, we took only our clothes and furniture. We didn't demand anything from the common property, because we sensed that such a demand might cause a struggle, and we made it a point to sacrifice property in order to save the spirit. Again, we were proved right: Kibbutzim that attempted to divide the common property got into terrible, ugly fights, which ruined any vestige of human respect in both factions.

However, one of the most encouraging phenomena also occurred during the division. During all the commotion that characterized this period, no family left the kibbutz for civilian life. Actually, it would have been quite conceivable for someone to say, "If after so many years of toiling and sweating I'm thrown out of my home, why do I need this whole idea of the kibbutz again?" Our departing group was socially heterogeneous and not ideologically fanatic (Mapai was never extreme). The majority of Makom said mockingly: "A third of you will soon return, a third will move to town immediately and the remaining third will move

*Union of work. Left-of-center party, now part of the Labor Party.

to town eventually. . . ." Yet nobody took that step. Not one family left the kibbutz during the move and we all remained in a cohesive group. I think that what gave us this strength and solidarity was the knowledge that truth and justice were on our side, and the fact that we hadn't soiled ourselves in petty material fights.

Now that we are considering a union of the kibbutz movements after all these years, I think it's time for some soul-searching regarding our past. I don't want to sound as if I blame only the other side for the division, but from the point of view of the history of the kibbutz move-ment, the Labor Party, and the whole State, it's hard to think otherwise. I myself was a scapegoat in these events. People of the Kibbutz Hameu-chad considered me a leader; they deluded themselves, thinking that if only I could be put aside the whole process could somehow be stopped. They didn't recognize the depth and seriousness of this historical devel-opment, in the same way that they didn't imagine in their worst dreams that most of the old kibbutzim would align themselves with the Ichud, that the greater youth movements would favor our point of view, and that we'd emerge from the division so strong. This whole series of events is certainly one of the most difficult and upsetting in our recent history, and I imagine that future historians won't be able to understand how such pioneers, people who literally sacrificed themselves for this land, could have misjudged reality to the extent that these people did.

I have been fighting for the union of the kibbutz movements for forty years, and am gratified that this union is finally taking place. It's a shame we had to wait for it so long, that we wasted so much energy on our internal struggles and so much money and manpower on maintaining separate organizations for all these years. But it's better late than never.

To end my story, I'd like to add a few words about Adama. A home you haven't built is never the same as one you've erected with your own hands. In spite of the fact that the earlier members have accepted us extremely well, certain friction has existed between us from the very first day, friction I can understand but cannot justify. It all boils down to a statement frequently heard here: "From the day that the Makom mem-bers joined Adama, a period of prosperity started for the place." This hurt the local members' pride a great deal, although it wasn't we who started that saying. A period of prosperity did start in the 1950s; many factors contributed to this: The kibbutz got more water, land, and funds —and, of course, also more working hands. Naturally, we tried to intro-duce some of our Makom traditions into this community—I remember that it struck me as odd that here, when the children still slept in common quarters, their homes were named "lodgings" and the parents' rooms were called "home." I thought it signified an attitude, and I suggested changing it. People were puzzled by my intrusion, however, and the suggestion was never accepted. On our first Passover here, we wanted to introduce our own version of the ceremony, but, feeling that our tentative attempts would be insulting to the local tradition, we set them aside. In spite of our tactful behavior we were often accused of arrogance, while actually we were truly respectful of the local habits and now, twenty-seven years later, the antagonism still exists. I have never felt really at home here. An uprooting is an uprooting and there's no way to change it.

S H O S H A N A (age 69)

To the present day, in my dreams, I'm always in Makom. I have one recurring dream in which I see all the members, all the rooms, contained within one big hall, and this hall is Makom. I think that this is highly significant, because in Makom the kibbutz as a whole was more important than the separate families or our private rooms; the whole always came first. In Adama, it's the other way around. My home, my family take utmost priority, and the kibbutz is the assemblage of all these individual cells.

I keep dreaming that I'm in Makom [*tearful*] and I have many slips of the tongue reflecting that unconsciously I'm still a part of it. Often I write "Makom" as my return address on the back of my letters. Would you believe that? As if my soul has remained over there. It's strange, since I've been in Adama for twenty-seven years, and I was in Makom for only fourteen. . . .

The division affected me very harshly, in spite of the fact that, politically, I was completely convinced that we had to leave. The fact is, however, that our political split did not change my mind about the social quality of this community. I'm a great admirer of Makom, probably giving it more credit than it's due. Whenever I see something sick or basically wrong here, I say to myself, "This couldn't have happened in Makom, because the quality of the people is so different."

What, for example, do you call "sick"?

Somebody, for example, got caught stealing from the room of another member. . . . Makom has remained for me a point of light in a dark reality. This is probably because, as I do *not* live there, it can remain an ideal for me. I am, by nature, an idealist.

Politically I clearly identified with Mapai, and I remember several very traumatic episodes from the period prior to the division. I'll give you some examples. It was right after the War of Independence, during the period of austerity in the country, when food was very scarce and a black market flourished. This same wonderful, idealistic Makom momentarily lost its head, and decided to make some extra money by selling wheat at a higher price than the official government price. It wasn't a large quantity, just five tons, I recall, and all the difference it made was about five pounds per ton, but when we found out about it, we felt terribly aggravated. I got up at the assembly meeting and exclaimed: "Even if we didn't have bread to serve, I wouldn't have done this." Another, a highly respectable member, retorted: "As long as this is our government, we have to knock it down." This was something I couldn't take. All of us, the Mapai people, got up, and a great storm broke out, and I can't even tell you how it all ended.

The other episode had to do with the way the declaration of independence was accepted by Makom. This remains one of my greatest traumas. People gathered in the dining hall in the gravest mood, and an important *chavera* got up and said: "This new State is an abortive State"; someone added: "We aren't equipped to hold out against the Arab attack, and we'll certainly lose in the battle." A great sense of defeatism enveloped the whole audience. This is how we experienced this historical moment, while the rest of the country was flooded with joy and every square was full of dancers.

After an hour of lamentation, another woman got up, knocked on the table, and shouted: "If you don't want this State—get out of here and go back to your rooms! I want to dance here!" So people moved some tables out of the way, and the dancing started. I'll never forget or forgive ourselves that night.

There were other events, of course, but they were more reciprocal. In other words, I don't blame the other side; I have never believed in one-sided responsibility for a conflict. We contributed our share to the friction, especially when we all became indignant and lost our self-control. Now, in perspective, I can take many of these episodes in a more tolerant manner. When a man like Shlomo said that Russia was his motherland—how could I have taken it seriously! How could I doubt the deep Zionist loyalty of such a person, or of the others who said similar things? They were wonderful people, they sacrificed their lives for this country! Yet, the moment I heard Shlomo, I flew into a rage and I thought his statement was unforgivable. I probably reacted in a very offended way, flaring up and escalating the quarrel. I can attribute my reaction to the fact that I came from a middle-class home and very early in my life I absorbed my parents' resentment towards Russia, communism, and all the leftist movements. I'm Israeli-born and I was educated in the youth movement, but Mapai was as far left as I was willing to go.

Personally I had undergone a terrible period right before the division. I had been pregnant, and had given birth to my third baby girl and was nursing her, and I felt very feeble and depressed at the time. When people started to talk about moving to another kibbutz, and then started visiting the possible relocations in order to inspect the society and the conditions, I had just one thought in my mind: "If we have to leave, let it be to a kibbutz with private lodging arrangements, so that our children will sleep in our rooms." In Makom, just prior to the division, we won a vote to switch over to private lodgings, but this decision was never carried out because of the pending division.

D——, a kibbutz we considered joining, had private sleeping arrangements then, and therefore I wanted to go there rather than to Adama, and I presented my argument at our assembly. The reaction of the male members was, however, completely unsympathetic. One of the men said: "Shoshana, what are you talking about! When such important issues have to be decided, how dare you bring up trifles like this? We'll go to Adama and we'll see; perhaps we will be able to win a vote for the private lodgings that you want." (He was right—with a delay of twenty-five years . . . alas, it was too late for my daughters.) I was very weak and exhausted after my delivery, and I felt that perhaps he was right, and I was losing my judgment. So I didn't persist. Later, however, other women turned to me regretfully, saying: "You were so right! Why didn't we have the courage to support you?" But it was too late.

I had other objections to Adama; from hints and rumors I formed the attitude that it was a bad, hopeless kibbutz. I remember saying [*bitterly*]: "Adama would be the last place I'd set foot in." That turned out to be really true, only not in the sense I had in mind then.

Well, I didn't want Adama, and there were many kibbutzim I could go to, but I had decided that our family decision would be made by Benjamin, my husband. I believed that I'd be able to adjust anywhere— I'm like grass, I put down roots very easily. Benjamin is quite different, so I thought that he ought to find the place that *he* preferred, and we'd follow him. I'm not usually that kind of a wife, but in this case I said: "You pick your place, and I'll follow blindly."

Benjamin went to visit Adama, formed a fairly positive impression; also, he didn't want to separate from the whole group. I think he was right in joining the rest because, as an emotionally worn couple with three babies, we were both too tired to cope with the adjustment alone. . . . So I agreed to the move. It seems, however, that I was suffering greater distress than I myself admitted. A few hours before we left, as we were packing, I got a crying fit, and I couldn't stop crying for three days. I arrived at Adama weeping. I saw everything as totally dark and hopeless, and I refused to unpack or to take my daughters to the children's homes. All I could say was, "No, this isn't my home." My sister rushed in, but it was a real breakdown, and for three days I completely lost control of myself. On the fourth day I recovered somewhat and I asked Benjamin to take me for a walk. I said to him: "I'll let the landscape make my decision. I can live for a landscape. If I find something to love in the view around here, then, okay, I'll stay, but if not—we'll have to search for another place."

It was winter, a very rainy season here. We put on rubber boots and walked in the mud, on the swamplike ground outside the kibbutz, with no path, heading north. Benjamin walked beside me, silently, through the orchards, on and on. Suddenly, as we reached the edge of the orchards, I guess Heaven had mercy on me, and the sky cleared up. The sun came out and lifted the fog; before my eyes stretched the wonderful Chulla

Valley in all its splendor. The far mountains were covered with snow, the valley was green, and the lake was sapphire blue; it was a picture of incredible beauty, and it captured my heart. I stopped crying, returned to our room, and said: "Let's unpack."

Only some time later could I understand the depth of my traumatic reactions to the division. Makom was such a dream for me; I had fought my father and mother in order to join that place, and after fourteen years of total involvement, it all exploded right in my face. I'm the type who forgets quite easily, though, and I didn't resent the people of Makom, because, as I said, I understood that we all had played our roles in the split. My closest friends, people who grew up with me in Haifa, remained there. I started to visit as soon as my daughters grew up a bit, and my friends have also visited me frequently, especially in times of trouble. Actually I haven't formed intimate relationships here like I had in Makom. My best friends in Adama are people who came from Makom. With the others here I have comfortable, superficial connections, that's all. I could easily pack my suitcase and leave this place. I didn't reestablish the deep attachment I had formed in Makom, neither to the place nor to the people who live in Adama. An attachment like that is probably created only once in a lifetime. In Makom, I could walk blindfolded, and I knew every rock, every tree [*crying*]. Here it's impossible, I'm emotionally detached.

You must understand, though, that on the surface I'm a very active, even central, member of this kibbutz. I was a teacher until twelve years ago, and, since retiring as a teacher, I've been the editor of the local newsletter. I'm also in charge of our Friday night reception, of which I'm very proud. A few years ago, when Makom decided to introduce this ceremony too, the woman who was in charge came to me to learn from my experience.

My absorption into Adama, once I had overcome my initial shock, was relatively smooth. I remember that I mistrusted the *metapelet* who was assigned to my middle daughter, after I saw her forcing a child to eat something he violently disliked. I went to the coordinator of the educational committee and complained, and she immediately transferred my daughter to another class. It made me feel better.

It was, however, even harder for me to help my daughters adjust to the common educational system here, because they didn't know the children, and I didn't know the staff. You see, none of my three daughters remained in the kibbutz—probably because I myself don't feel deeply attached to the place. I often think that, had we stayed in Makom, at least one of my daughters, the middle one, would have probably chosen to live there, too. Yet, when I wrote her about this (she lives in Los Angeles now) she answered: "Mother, forget it. I couldn't fit into any kibbutz. . . ." The three of them have unusual artistic talents, and they're highly individualistic women. One of them, to whom I feel closest, talks with me a lot about what she still remembers as her "horrible childhood." She resented the common education, the strict framework, the attempt to mold all children into a single form, notwithstanding their special talents or traits. I still believe that, had my daughters been allowed to sleep with us at home, to spend the nights with us, they'd have grown up happier people. Too bad. . . . This is something we didn't manage to introduce in Adama then.

We were, however, one hundred adults who arrived from Makom, and we had a great impact on the community. I remember the first three decisions which we brought to be approved by the assembly: that parents of members be entitled to all rights (housing, etc.) that were due to members; that the open porches of the children's homes be closed by glass windows to block the cold winter wind; and that manpower and a budget be allotted to plant a garden in the community's courtyard. (There was no gardening whatsoever here, and the common courtyard was terribly neglected. Look at it today, it's one of the loveliest parks in the whole country.) Adama's people consented to all these proposals, and our cooperation started out auspiciously. We brought with us much idealism and experience, and what we found here were wonderful people, real pioneers, in body and soul. It isn't their fault that my heart still longs for Makom.

A H A R O N *(age 67)*

This big man broke out in tears several times during our conversation. It seems that he still feels profoundly much of the pain of the division.

I want to begin by saying that this is the first time I have agreed to render my version of the division. Several people have asked to interview me on this topic in the past. Even quite recently, Shulamit came to me with the same request, yet I have always refused. I guess it's because I still feel so deeply attached to Makom, in spite of the fact that twenty-seven years have passed. Not a year has passed without my visiting there, and pretty soon I'll be visiting there once again. I managed to separate personal feelings from the political split, and my best friends still live in Makom.

I arrived at the Fountain in 1934, after my *hachshara* in the Netherlands. I belong to the same early Yekke group as Zvi and Ester, and I had to live through all of the difficulties of those first stages. It wasn't easy. I remember one episode which symbolizes my early reception: On the third day after my arrival I was working on a drilling project. David Ilan was in charge. I was doing my best, although it was hard work under the blazing sun. David thought I didn't understand Hebrew, and, passing by, he said: "Here's another Yekke we'll have to support." I felt devastated by this comment. To my own amazement, I overcame the absorption crisis pretty quickly and I acquired a respectable position within the group. My last job at Makom was as a youth leader of a childrens' group of Holocaust survivors who were studying in the kibbutz. This was, for me, a holy service, and I was devoted to it with all my heart and soul. The best people in the kibbutz were dedicated to this job, and that's where I became so close to Shlomo, Shulamit, and the others, even though we often had differences of opinion.

I loved Makom so much. . . . My sole intent was to prevent us from ruining that place. Therefore, when things started to get unpleasant, it was I who suggested a public vote, to count the followers of the two parties and to have it all out in the open. Until that moment it wasn't even clear which camp had the majority of members. When the vote was about to take place, it was understood that the minority would have to leave. As it turned out, we, the Mapainiks, were the minority, and I knew we'd have to find another place to go. For me, however, the most important consideration was to rescue Makom from a civil war, because this is what an ideological struggle implied at that time. Staying and fighting it out would have led to degradation and abasement for all and some kibbutzim did reach that stage. Makom was my—our—creation, I felt that I had participated in building it since its very first day; my major concern was that it remain whole, even if I myself would have to leave. There was no other alternative: Either we could prolong the struggle and ruin the kibbutz and its society, or we could separate at that point and save us all from a greater disaster.

Though I wasn't among the leaders of our faction, that's how I saw this development. There were other reasons involved, and actually, at the time, I voiced them more clearly than I voiced my basic consideration which I just explained. I said that I had to leave because I refused to let my three sons be educated under the leftist banner. It disturbed me that they were being educated to admire the U.S.S.R.; I felt that it was my duty to save them from this. This was my public position.

What I didn't take into consideration was, however, that I was uprooting my three sons from their home environment (*very emotionally*). My eldest son was fourteen at the time, and he suffered so badly from the fights within the children's society at Makom that we finally decided to send him away ahead of us, and he moved to Adama about six months before we did. He had told me: "Father, I can't stay here. Children won't play ball with me, and they say the worst things about you. . . ." Children have no mercy, and they exaggerated what they understood from the conflicts in the adult society; so our firstborn was the first of us to leave. Our two younger sons were seven and five, and they arrived with us. . . . Now, only one of my children is living here in the kibbutz, and I don't know why it turned out this way. I often tell myself that it is the result of the fact that I uprooted them from their true home, a place that was very dear to them, and they could never feel the same way about this place. Perhaps that's why they left; I can't really tell.

I, too, feel cut off from my roots to this very day. I'm a teacher, and even today it often happens to me that in talking about our kibbutz I'll say "Makom" instead of Adama. . . . And so many years have passed since that time! My deep roots are still there, because I was very young when I came to Makom and I was reborn there. I built a kibbutz from scratch and I created a family there, and in this way I established myself there too.

When it was decided that we had to leave, I managed to isolate my disappointment from my daily activities and relationships. I was work coordinator at the time, and I continued my job, talking impartially to everyone, calling people to order, ignoring any differences of opinion among us. I'm proud of my behavior at that time; I didn't get into any sort of personal clashes and I kept all of my feelings to myself. I convinced myself that politics was just politics, and that the rest of our life had to continue in its normal course, even if in a short time some of us would be leaving. People admired me for my attitude, and often wondered at it. I remember somebody from my own camp telling me I ought to have my head checked! Thanks to my behavior, no one considered me an enemy, and I was the first one who felt he could visit Makom after the division. This was a very personal reaction, though, since the majority of the people did get carried away, and burned some bridges on their way out. I don't believe that I would have been able to act as I did if the transition period had been longer. It took us six months, all in all, from our decision until its realization; I was the last one to leave.

I left with tears in my eyes, but I was convinced that there was no way to bridge the gap and make us into one community once more. The division had swept the whole country by that time. I know that some people who were actually closer to our view did decide to keep their mouths shut, keeping a low profile for awhile, and thereby stayed in their homes. But I didn't feel that I could deny my beliefs in such a manner; it was like Jews in Europe concealing their true identity, and therefore I couldn't take this path.

We were more than two-hundred individuals, including children, and we decided to continue together and relocate as a group. As former Makom members, we had a good reputation, and many Ichud kibbutzim wanted us. There were three suggestions that we seriously considered: Y—, which was a new kibbutz that was being established by the departing minority of one of the biggest kibbutzim; D—, which was the oldest kibbutz in the country; and Adama. I was for Adama because D—was a well established place with its own traditions and life-style which we would have had to fit into, accepting it as it was. Y—, on the other hand, was a completely new kibbutz, but it was flooded with Mapai money and didn't need our help. Adama was about fifteen years older than Makom, but it still hadn't accomplished much. When we visited the place, I felt I could be of use there, building, changing it, improving it. If I had to leave my own home, I thought, I could find satisfaction only in a creative and productive existence, and I felt that Adama offered me the best chance for that. Other people might have had different reasons, I guess, but the final choice was indeed Adama.

Here, at Adama, a division had also taken place. As far as I could gather, the community had consisted of two alienated subgroups of Polish and German descent; almost all the Germans had identified with the Kibbutz Hameuchad and left. Our group was, however, larger than the departing one, and there was some overlap in the transition period (we arrived and they had still not departed) so the housing conditions at the beginning were very poor. With the aid of external budgets, donated by Mapai, which was then in power in the government, an extensive building project was inaugurated almost immediately, and within six months we were all much better off. We had plenty of work in the orchards, which are still the main branch of this kibbutz, and we developed the landscaping, since the grounds had been neglected for the most part before we came.

On the surface, I have adjusted to living here. But, as I said before, the pain of my departure from Makom has remained alive, though buried deep inside me. At the beginning, I used to talk readily about Makom, using it as an example both in personal encounters and in the general assembly meetings. I wasn't completely aware of what I was doing, until I realized how hurt the Adama people were by this; then I stopped.

We're pretty much integrated by now, and the younger generation, which grew up here together, has certainly forgotten our different origins. Among the older members . . . I want to be very careful here, but I have noticed that the older Adama members may still be more tolerant and understanding when a personal problem or request concerns someone in "their" camp rather than "ours." It might be my imagination, though.

Both Makom and Adama have made a great deal of progress since the division, and both have done very well economically and socially. However, Adama will never be Makom; there's no comparison between the two at all. Economically, Makom is better off than Adama, because during the division they didn't lose any of their "brains" in the economic area, or their central organization people, and in terms of working manpower they were greatly reinforced by the Molad group. Adama is, however, also very well established economically, and this isn't, in my view, the main dimension of our life anyway. In the cultural dimension the difference is much greater. Look at their weekly newsletter as compared to ours, their holidays and various study activities—they're incomparably richer than ours. Makom is a more intellectual kibbutz; they have many talents and they brought into their life a deep Israeli background and identity, since their first founders were Sabras. We don't have here personalities of that stature, no Yehudas, Shulamits or Na'amas. Politically too, the atmosphere here is shallow, and the involvement in the general political scene is minimal, whereas at Makom, I believe, it's different. The part that ideology plays in their life is much greater than in ours, and this is probably true of all Kibbutz Hameuchad settlements as compared to the Ichud. This is evident in one simple example, namely, that we rely quite a lot, and without misgivings of any kind, on hired labor, while Makom's people have always fought against this deviation from formal kibbutz ideology. Indeed they haven't introduced hired labor into the kibbutz. Significantly, this devotion to ideology was passed on to the second generation of Makom and they, too, object to hired labor in the kibbutz. Here, people have even ceased talking about it, especially among our second generation, who accept hired labor as an inevitable fact of life. Furthermore, I have the impression that the younger generation at Makom has a greater sense of identification with their home, of "patriotism," and of constant concern with the image and future direction of their kibbutz. I don't think that we have a higher proportion of people who leave the kibbutz here than in Makom, but people here are more concerned with the material aspect of life; they're not as austere and self-critical as those in Makom. We're a kibbutz of the proletariat, I'd say, and that sums up everything in my mind. . . . We ought to remember, though, that the kibbutz of today is not what we had dreamt it would be years ago. Reality never follows the script of a dream.

Makom's Version

S H I M O N *(age 62)*

On a sweltering hot day, typical of the summer in that region, I interviewed Shimon in the sickroom. He was lying in bed with a broken leg, and was being treated for high blood pressure as well. The room was air-conditioned, which helped considerably; nevertheless, the inner temperature periodically ran pretty high, as Shimon's excitement over the division mounted.

I was born in Russia in 1916, and I immigrated to Palestine at a very young age. I completed my education (a technical high school) in Haifa, and joined the group at the Fountain at the end of 1934. So I've been in this kibbutz for a very long time [*pausing*]. I've done all kinds of jobs. I worked outside the kibbutz for a while, as most men did, and then became a truck driver. For the last twenty years I have been a teacher, teaching mechanics to our school children. Between these various jobs I chaired our education committee in the early fifties, and functioned as cashier for five years a bit later. Presently, as a partly retired person, I work in my former profession, doing fine metalwork in our metal factory.

I was told that you want me to concentrate on the time of the division. . . . I was from a family of four sons, and each one joined a different kibbutz. One son was killed defending his kibbutz in the War of Independence, so there are only three brothers now. I can tell you that, if it was left to the three of us, we could unite the various kibbutz movements within five minutes. The differences between the movements are so picayune and meaningless in my opinion that I can't really grasp why we went through all those events leading to the division in 1952. Frequently the human and social character of a settlement is quite independent of the slogans that a movement has inscribed on its banners. I can tell you that from firsthand experience, because as a driver I knew many kibbutzim well.

In our kibbutz, I felt that we had a socially homogeneous group, and for years I didn't notice any conflicting political viewpoints within our community. From 1935, I lived with the people who eventually left us in the division, and I knew them very well. One of their leaders was my next-door neighbor, and throughout the years I didn't detect any sign of political conflict, didn't notice any of us becoming more right- or left-oriented, communist, or whatever. There wasn't the least hint of any of that. In the division I lost some of my best, my closest friends, people who grew up with me, people for whom I would give my soul, in work, in health, and in sickness, in times of happiness and in times of sorrow—everything. I used to drive trucks with some of them—we always drove in pairs when times were rough. We drove daily from Afula to Jerusalem, returning at night during riots and battles. Our job was also a question of security, keeping the roads open, until the Hagana forbade us to carry on. I can't tell you how close we co-drivers became; "brothers" would be too weak a term to describe our mutual feelings. . . . Some of those "brothers" of mine later defected to Adama.

They couldn't explain to me why they were leaving. They received an order from above, that's all, and some of them were influenced by friends without having any political opinions of their own whatsoever. Their departure took me by surprise. I had talked to each one of them, trying to understand what bothered them, what had upset them so profoundly in our life here. I didn't find an answer. They were like people following a prophet from the outside.

The division of the kibbutz movements followed the earlier division in the youth movements. I remember that we recalled a member, Yaakov Porat, from his work with the youth movement in town, because we didn't understand what was going on, and we had started to feel that he wasn't representing our views anymore. He was following Ben-Gurion blindly. We suspected that Ben-Gurion was probably interested in dividing the Kibbutz Hameuchad, for it represented rising young powers; B.G. was afraid of its potential strength and threat to his authority. That's what some of the people who left us later said: "It's an order of the party. We can't disobey the Movement."

Sometimes the Adama group spoke of the old debate between the big, open kibbutz, the model for the Kibbutz Hameuchad, versus the small intimate group, which was the model for the Ichud. But this was so unreal! I grew up in the Yizra'el Valley, I saw some of those "small groups." I never saw any real differences between them and us. I had very good friends in some of those settlements and they too wanted to grow in number and strength, just like us.

Later, I thought that there were economic reasons involved for some who left us. Most of them were German immigrants, and they followed the pot of gold, looking forward to living in Adama in order to improve their material situation. There were other kibbutzim in which similar developments took place, especially following the whole issue of the German reparation money. Different kibbutzim made different regulations concerning these monies.

In our case, Makom had decided that all the monies should be used collectively. The individual, upon signing his agreement with the kibbutz, got a bottle of wine and a piece of cake. . . . We later decided to show the kibbutz's gratitude by a more material gesture—we were changing the mattresses of all adult members to a new, foam-rubber type at the time, so we gave them first to those Yekkes who had donated their reparation money to the kibbutz. The people who left for Adama were, mostly, Germans and I believe that they thought that in Adama they would get better terms concerning the money. I can't say for sure—I don't know what was finally decided in Adama concerning the issue, and anyway there were also several non-Germans in the faction that left us.

But even if we don't take that aspect into consideration, I'm pretty certain that the people who left us for Adama had material considerations in mind. They knew that their new kibbutz was economically much better off then, and that their standard of living would probably go up. I don't know how well off they are now, or have been ever since, because I have never set foot in Adama since the division. . . . I have very good friends there, and I have received many invitations for weddings, funerals or other personal events there, but I have never attended. I can't make myself go there after what happened. I feel as if I'd received a terrible slap in the face, even today.

There were two things that were mentioned by several people in Adama concerning the reasons for the division: different attitudes toward Russia and toward the establishment of the State of Israel. Do you remember anything concerning these issues?

First, about Russia. Maybe there's a grain of truth in that claim, although I personally never seriously believed in Russia as our ally. I have a large family in Russia, and, through them, I knew about communist oppression long before it became known to the whole world. I don't believe there were any members here who were great followers of Russia, as you claimed. The major principle we tried to hold onto was nonidentification, neither with Russia, nor with the U.S.A., nor with England. We believed in maintaining some sort of ideological independence between the two big powers, and objected to becoming a satellite of the U.S.A. This was the issue, and not so-called loyalty to the U.S.S.R.

As to the establishment of the State, I don't quite remember, but it might be true that we didn't celebrate very warmly the U.N. decision on November 29. I was away from the kibbutz that night, driving my truck, and I saw great celebrations all over the country. In Afula all the houses were lit up and people were dancing in the streets. When I reached the kibbutz very late at night it was, however, dark and quiet, and I thought that the dances were already over. I personally felt very happy, and blessed the moment in my heart. I didn't know what had taken place, but I realized that the Kibbutz Hameuchad leaders thought that the timing of the decision was poor. So we did put a flag up or we didn't: What does it really matter? What does a celebration mean? The meaningful fact is that the majority of our men were mobilized at the time, in the Palmach, working and risking their lives to establish that State [*very excited*].

I don't know how anyone can claim that we weren't good and devoted Zionists; it really maddens me! What is more Zionistic than building the State, wandering all over the country achieving Jewish national goals? Our members put in the pipeline near Iraq, and worked in the salt factory at Atlit. We dug for water and started a stone quarry; we built the spot with our own sweat and blood in order to open it for new helpless immigrants and refugees. Could there be a better demonstration of our Zionism? Our members filled many important positions in the organization of the illegal immigration and in the struggle against the British. I myself was a driver for the Palmach, and it infuriates me if someone calls me "anti-Zionist." If Yaakov Porat could stand in front of me and tell me to my face: "I left your kibbutz because you weren't enough of a Zionist," I could only laugh. I'd ask *him* what he did for the country that was more important than what I did. We and the people who later left for Adama had all shared collectively in the struggles and activities which made the establishment of the State possible. We did it all together.

What about the social atmosphere, hadn't that become quite unpleasant towards the end? They say, for example, that the friction was even more acute within the children's society.

Even if ten people tell such stories, *I* know better since I was in charge of the education committee and was deeply involved in everything that went on within the children's organization. Actually, I lived among the children all day. I was in charge of the whole transition, the departure of the children to Adama and the absorption of the new group of children from Molad. Throughout that period there was no violence in the children's quarters. Parents from different factions could sometimes argue while putting their children to sleep or they could create tension with the *metapelet* if she belonged to the other camp. We never removed a teacher, *metapelet,* or child from his place just because of the developing division among us. I remember that some of the Mapai people demanded that the more left-oriented teachers be removed from the school, or that more of their people get teaching positions so that the children would be exposed to both sides. So there could have been some tension here or there, but if someone talks about violence, outbreaks, or an ongoing unpleasant atmosphere, it's just an exaggeration. We shared the dining hall to the very last day. We never put up a partition to divide it as some kibbutzim had done—we all sat at the same tables to eat. There was perhaps one case of physical aggression when a member was caught eavesdropping at a secret meeting of the other camp, but that was really an isolated event.

When they [the Ichud people] decided to leave, they voted on their decision in an assembly of their own. Then they submitted to the secretary a list of the people who planned to leave and there was no further confrontation or debate concerning the matter. The Ichud sympathizers went around for a while trying to convince more people to accompany them in their step, and indeed several people who didn't have any strong political identification with either side decided to join Adama with them for various personal reasons. On the other hand, we made the rounds among our friends trying to persuade them to stay. . . . It was all quite peaceful and sad, nobody forced anyone to leave or expressed any hatred.

With this departure we were left with a gaping hole in our midst. There were about one hundred people who left us, with as many children. At that time the Kibbutz Hameuchad faction of Molad, who already knew that they would leave their home, had to decide which kibbutz to join. They visited several places, including Makom. Many kibbutzim were interested in absorbing them because the Molad faction was a big, strong, and young group. They were the same size as the group that had left us. They were caught in the same conflict as our departing faction, the conflict between hard work or the fleshpot. Joining us certainly meant hard work for the Molad group. Economically we weren't well established yet since we were never supported by the authorities and had to do everything by ourselves. We ate very poorly and dressed like beggars. (Just at that time a central committee of the Kibbutz Hameuchad came to inspect our clothing situation, and, following its visit, we were given a loan to buy pajamas for all the members. . . . We gladly accepted the loan but immediately invested it in a production project and continued to sleep without pajamas.) For the Molad group, joining us meant a striking decrease in their standard of living, and it was therefore natural that some of their members had wanted to go to a richer kibbutz. Finally they did join us, however, and they did it knowingly, expressing their willingness to toil with us and to build our home together. Indeed, with our combined forces, we improved our economic situation a great deal within seven or eight years, and by 1960 we were doing quite well.

The main contribution of the Molad group was in bridging the age-gap between our first and second generations. Frequently it is said, however, that they gave a tremendous boost to the economic stability of our kibbutz. This, I believe, is more a legend than the exact truth. The Molad group was known as *mishkists,* namely, good workers. When we were courting them, we believed that we would get about seventeen new cowmen to help develop our own branch [*laughs*]. The truth is, there was hardly one. Furthermore, their people weren't trained to work with modern, mechanized equipment; they were accustomed to simple manual work. But of course the added manpower we did receive was a help, and it was reflected in all our agricultural branches and gradually in our industry too. The young women were immediately channeled into educational and child-care jobs in which we had suffered a severe shortage before they came, and this was a significant relief.

There was, however, a minor problem of cultural integration between the two groups. Our own people, whether they were Israeli born or immigrants, were all Israeli in a cultural sense. We all spoke Hebrew and adopted the youth-movement culture with its deep Israeli roots. The Molad group, mainly of Polish origin, was—how shall I say—more Jewish than Israeli. They retained a Diaspora, ghettolike mentality. They spoke Yiddish, for example, something that was very foreign to our ears. (To this very day, if you happen to hear two people conversing in Yiddish, you can be sure they're from Molad.) This different background wasn't, God forbid, scorned by us, but it did provoke smiles quite often. We didn't repeat our intolerance of the first years when the Germans came, when we simply didn't let our newcomers speak German, even to each other. At that early period the slogan was "Jew, speak Hebrew," and, although the intention was certainly positive, I think that we were rather insensitive and intolerant in our demand vis-à-vis the Germans. In spite of the fact that they couldn't express themselves in Hebrew as yet, we actually forbade them to use their own language. It used to happen that a Sabra, passing two Yekkes conversing quietly in German, would snap cruelly, "We don't want to hear any German here."

We certainly didn't show the same intolerance towards the Yiddish-speakers from Molad twenty years later. But we noticed the difference, and on Friday nights, when we had to organize cultural activities, it wasn't easy to find a topic or performance that would be equally pleasing to both groups. By the way, our attitude towards Yiddish, and whatever it represents for each of us, has remained ambivalent to the present day. Sometimes a guest actor is invited to present something in Yiddish, or Jewish poems are recited, but such events would never be scheduled to take place in the dining hall, only in the club, which is a much smaller space. The club would, however, be packed with people, both elderly former-Molad members—who enjoy such performances tremendously—and young Israelis, who enjoy watching the older people's joy.

Today, however, these two groups are very well integrated, and I think that of all the sides involved in the division, the Molad group has the least misgivings. This is probably due to the fact that, in a relatively short period, they participated in our transition from poverty to plenty. They witnessed the two periods, our lack and our overcoming of it, and they often attribute the change to their help. Well, I don't think we sat and watched idly. After all, we weren't good-for-nothings before their arrival! I don't know if the Molad people are at all aware of the tremendous difficulties we faced in our early years, how everybody and every authority objected to our settlement here and therefore we couldn't get any kind of assistance. Yet we clung to the ground by the skin of our teeth and built the kibbutz with our own hands. There's no other kibbutz that I know of which established itself under similar conditions; they were all funded by the Jewish Agency or some other source. Then we had the terrible water shortage; our own water was found to be too salty and we had consecutive years of drought which ruined our fields. And our ongoing struggles with the Arabs, their stealing of our meager crops . . . Many things happened simultaneously which led to the improvement of our situation—the addition of the Molad *mishkist* group was certainly one factor, but perhaps not the crucial one.

Let me tell you one thing: I've been a member of this kibbutz for forty-five years now, but I have been living in a two-room apartment for only the last seven years. And why is that so? Because when the Molad people joined us we gave them the best possible conditions. Naturally we calculated their seniority—including their years in Molad in addition to their ages—and many of them came out at the top of the list. So when the new houses were completed, they received better housing before I did; I'm not complaining about it, but it was quite difficult to raise three children in our one tiny room. What I mean to say is that we did everything we could to accept the Molad people as well as possible.

I know that our own people were also well accepted in Adama. There were some very good and efficient workers among them and they immediately occupied central positions in their new place.

Their kibbutz is also pretty well off nowadays, but I believe that much of their economic success is based on hired labor, while we have always strictly forbidden this in our kibbutz.

Well, looking back upon all the old conflicts, they seem today even more senseless than ever. I look at current leaders of the different kibbutz movements, all second-generation people, and ask myself: "In what way are we different today? Who is 'right' and who is 'left'? Who's for Russia nowadays?"

The entire party line has completely changed with the years and I don't know why we had to go through such a trauma in 1952.

Z V I (I I) *(age 66)*

In spite of several rational explanations I could give for the division which took place in the 1940s and 1950s, I think all that happened then was basically irrational. I feel that both sides involved—and perhaps there were even more than two sides—fell into a trap, although at that time we understood the events in ideological-political terms, and the underlying problems seemed to us very serious, even essential.

Before putting forth my version of the story, I'd like to introduce those things for which I cannot forgive myself, as I was clearly an active agent in all that took place. I think that there is no forgiving the fact that while the Holocaust was taking place in Europe—and it can't be denied that we already knew about it—the Labor Party of those days occupied itself with inner struggles and even split over those problems. It proves that we were severely alienated from the suffering Jewish world at large. However, those problems in which we were involved at the time were indeed fundamental and very serious for such a small population to face. They involved the establishment of an independent State and its borders, and this was certainly a major issue.

I worked in the youth movement, in the Machanot Ha'olim, where the division started. Actually, one might say that the division was planned and started by our side, the more left-oriented side. Another version would be that we got caught in a trap—but we certainly did it willingly, with our flags flying. The underlying problem was, however, the direction which the Labor Party had taken; it had evolved from a clearly defined workers' movement to a large popular party which was losing its ideological underpinnings. We, the Achdut Ha'avoda faction, wanted to hold on to the old nature of our party and were afraid of this obscuring of our identity. We felt that the leadership wasn't insisting on such basic labor principles as productive work and cooperation, which we considered the basis for the merging Israeli society, more important than even the settlement of the land. This was the inner struggle in the country and was represented by two people—Ben-Gurion on one side and Tabenkin on the other. Since the kibbutzim were the core of the left, and had an extremely high level of political awareness, the conflict became quite acute within the kibbutz movement. We considered ourselves the flag bearers of the Zionist-socialist movement, and we felt that our identity was endangered. Although Ben-Gurion had been a very loyal Marxist in the early stages of his development in the 1920s, we felt that he was leading Mapai too much towards the West and the U.S.

We thought that this was a dangerous trend and this was how our attitude toward Russia developed. Remember, this was during World War II, in which Russia was an extremely important power. Furthermore, Russia had been deeply involved in the struggle against the Nazis and was the first and only country which supplied us with arms and ammunition. While most of the Arabs took sides with the German Nazis, we considered the Russians our allies. The Russians had their own interests, naturally, in wanting to have the British out of the Middle East, but our interests seemed to lie in the same direction, and the proof was the massive supply of firearms with which the Russians later provided us through Yugoslavia, Czechoslovakia, and other communist states. All these were highly practical considerations which, it appeared, Ben-Gurion was ignoring in his growing inclination towards the U.S.

To this you have to add a certain ideological proximity that we, as workers and Socialists, felt towards the U.S.S.R. The red flag was a very common symbol in the kibbutz—in all factions—and May 1 was one of our most important holidays at that time. We felt that the political leadership was still using the same symbols but was robbing them of their original meaning.

Actually there were two distinct opinions within our camp. One was openly pro-Russian and the other, more neutral, was for maintaining our independence in order to play off the two great powers. (This was the political position taken by Egypt many years later, a position which they used very cleverly to their benefit.) The "neutral" group had also, however, stressed Israel's alliance with Russia in order to counterbalance the growing tendency towards the West.

This brings us to a third factor in the developments leading up to the division, namely, the opposing views concerning the declaration of independence. Ben-Gurion was in favor of the establishment of the State right then, within the limited borders ("the borders of the partition") offered as a deal by the British and the West. We were afraid of declaring independence with such narrow borders, and we thought that if we delayed our consent and played our position cleverly between the two great powers, which both had their interests in the Middle East, we might attain much better and safer conditions. This was, naturally, a very controversial issue, and the inner conflict revolving around it was extremely painful to both sides.

This, by the way, is something which I find pretty hard to explain today, with the completely different political map of the parties of the country. In the 1940s, Mapam, to which I belonged, was on the one hand pro-Russian (what would be termed "left") and on the other hand we were in favor of an enlarged Eretz Yisrael as against the narrow "partition borders." Mapai, the minority camp in our kibbutz, was more right or West-oriented in their international outlook, yet more dovelike (in today's terms) on the internal level and willing to accept a state within very limited borders.

As a result of this debate, on November 29, 1947, when the U.N. voted for an independent State of Israel, Makom did not celebrate the occasion. There was no joy here. Much later, somebody brought out some wine and a few people danced, but it wasn't a spontaneous burst of joy as most of the country felt that night. Here people felt that the joy wasn't justified. The newly declared State was compared to a premature baby whose chances to live are questionable.

After the establishment of the State in 1948 there were other events which contributed to the coming division. Ben-Gurion had to make a political state out of the country, and to do so he had to take several severe steps. One of these steps was to break up the Palmach, and, although it was a very hard step to take, I know that he had no alternative but to do it. It's impossible to have within a State different military commands, none of which completely accepts the authority of the central government.

This is a good example of the tremendous task which B.G. had undertaken, namely, to establish a State out of a disorganized people who had not previously acquired the habits of statehood owing to the fact that for two thousand years they did not have a state of their own. It was an extremely difficult task, and it had to be done through sheer force and discipline. This nation was abounding with various voluntary organizations, some of them extremely powerful, and each driving towards its own ends. A party wasn't merely a political party, as it is elsewhere; it was an authority with agricultural settlements, with banks and factories, with its own health-insurance system, educational network, and many other such institutions, some of which were kept very inconspicuous. (I believe that this is a phenomenon peculiar to Israel.) Besides the parties, there were also other voluntary organizations, such as the Hagana (and the other underground military organizations), the Histadrut and others. These organizations undertook most of the functions that a State requires for existence, but since they weren't centrally regulated the outcome of their activities was often anarchistic, with both overt and covert conflicts among them.

Ben-Gurion understood that if he wanted to establish a State, he had to restrain these groups and organizations. One of the most serious powers was the kibbutz movement. Within it there was a faction which had accepted B.G.'s leadership, while several factions were opposed to him because they felt he was denying the spirit of the kibbutz. He couldn't leave the great pioneering power as a voluntary organization, so he tried to establish a State-controlled settlement organization instead. This failed right away, yet it remained quite clear that he wanted to cut the size of the kibbutz down to suit his own needs, and he certainly didn't reinforce its tendency to grow.

There were several instances in which the kibbutzim felt really deprived of their just due, in various ways. Mostly it concerned the fact that the kibbutzim weren't given the means to actively participate in the absorption of *aliya*. We had a strong drive to grow and to open our homes to the new immigrants. However, we needed a budget from an outside source to house and supply these people with the basic needs, and in receiving this allowance we were always pushed to the end of the line. It could be that we didn't demand loudly enough since we had been used to being self-supporting for so long, but certainly our weak attempts were turned down.

Looking back on this issue, I find it really quite difficult to judge things from today's perspective. I'm not certain that many of these *olim* (immigrants) could have adjusted to kibbutz life, and I'm not certain that we had the understanding then necessary to make it easier for them to adjust. There was a group of Holocaust survivors which we absorbed before 1948. When they came, we, the veterans, moved out of our rooms into tents so that the new arrivals would get the best available housing.

Many of them later left us, though, and I remember one of the good-bye conversations when somebody said: "When you moved out of your houses for us it gave us a profound shock. We asked ourselves, what is the value of such a style of life if in three or four years *we* would have to move out of our houses for somebody new!" This was their mentality and it was something beyond our grasp.

The resistance to funding our efforts to absorb immigrants made us feel that B.G. was trying to weaken the kibbutz movement as he had the Palmach and other organizations, and at this point the conflict within the Kibbutz Hameuchad gained in strength. There were among us people who said "Amen" to every act of B.G. and others who were highly critical of him. The political life of the young State in the early 1950s was terribly intense, and the arguments escalated easily into fights, most of them focusing on this one point—being for or against Ben-Gurion and his method of government.

Although I was then in the "anti-B.G." camp, I see today how right he was in most of his decisions. I think he was right in leading towards the declaration of independence when he did, in abolishing the Palmach, and in the painful step of sinking the Altalena. All these actions are part of a noncommunist Bolshevik conception of centralizing all powers under one hierarchy. At the same time, he was unfair towards the creative, voluntary powers in the country, powers which couldn't be squeezed into any formal framework, and which he felt stood in his way, the path towards statehood. The kibbutz was such a force. By his overemphasis of statehood and centralized authority, Ben-Gurion accustomed us to being supported and aided by the State, an attitude which had been completely alien to our way of thought beforehand. He broke the great independent voluntary spirit of the kibbutz, and we are suffering from this to the present day. The conflict around this point was one of the immediate causes of the division within us.

There was also a completely different factor which had to do specifically with our kibbutz. A great number of people who left us for Adama belonged to the German group, to which I belong as well. Here again I have serious misgivings. I, as a German immigrant, was very close to many of those who left, and I blame myself for not doing enough to prevent the rupture. I wasn't active in the escalation of issues leading to their departure, but I don't think I used my personal position enough to prevent it, either. I don't know, perhaps I'm being too strict with myself. I kept my friendly relationships with these people, visiting them and working together to the very last moment. Many of us who were identified with the majority tried to talk them into staying, and we succeeded with about four or five families. Although they felt awkward about remaining in the beginning, their previous intentions gradually were forgotten by us all. We should have done more in that direction but we were all so irrational. . . .

Well, as I said before, many of the Germans left us during the division and I see it as an outcome of their feelings that they couldn't reach complete expression and fulfillment in our community. They complained that their attempts to reach positions of power in the social and economic structure of the kibbutz were thwarted because all those positions were occupied by the Israelis. I myself never felt that way in Makom; it seems it's a personal feeling. In many other kibbutzim as well, I found out later, the division followed ethnic or social lines, with a certain homogeneous group leaving together. The truth is that many of those people who left us grew markedly in stature the minute they reached Adama. They received highly responsible positions and could fully utilize their talents in organization and leadership. This partly proves their complaints against us. . . . The fact is that Makom was blessed with many leaders in the original Israeli group (even if they weren't as advanced in their education as many of the Germans) and, as a result, those who later joined the move to Adama had felt suffocated when here, in need of breathing space. But, of course, there were others who left, Israelis, who didn't have that particular reason for their move.

With all these struggles, Makom is certainly among those kibbutzim that had no physical violence prior to the division. The most insulting remark was, "So when are you leaving, finally?" and even that was rare. Attempts to bridge the gap went on until the last minute. I think that what finally made up the Adama sector's minds to leave was one assembly meeting in which we discussed the educational system and our educational goals. One of our members said: "We want to establish a Leninist-Marxist school." And someone added: "We have to educate for two homelands, Israel and Russia." These extreme statements completely divided the community and, for many members who were uncertain until that night, the decision was made to leave. I myself was shocked at these statements; I was never in favor of terms like "motherland" or "Father Stalin," nor any other form of idolatry. I didn't stand up to protest though, nor did anyone else of our camp, and this again is something that I see as one of the greatest sins of Makom.

The tension and confrontation were most extreme in the school and in the children's society. Firstly, because among the teachers were some of the most radical extremists, and, further, because children are more blunt and aggressive in their behavior than adults. Children often attacked their friends saying, "Your parents are traitors," and tempers would flare.

This is what I can tell you about the background of the division. I also remember the awful moment of the actual departure. We said good-bye as friends do. I cried. Many cried, from both camps.

Makom was in a terrible situation after the division. We were terribly poor then, the poorest kibbutz in the whole valley. We had daily problems of simple survival. There are two symbols of that situation—the half-an-egg and the single pajamas. The Adama people improved their conditions by leaving, though the fact remains that we stayed in our home and they were thrown out of theirs. Nobody kicked them out, as I told you, but, as in a case of divorce, the party who ends up outside, even if it's by choice, always feels kicked out. In other words, their trauma was much more painful than ours. I didn't break off my friendships with them and they too, after a year or two, started visiting us here, but the same feelings still exist. For them—their home is here, their forsaken motherland; they suffer longings and pain much more than we do.

Later, we received the Molad group. Molad was the richest kibbutz in the area then, and in joining us their members did something akin to moving from a fancy private home to a slum dwelling. We acted wisely though in letting them immediately participate in all the important positions and committees, in giving them complete freedom to choose their areas of work and development, and, indeed, together we soon pulled our cart out of the mud. Today Makom is one of the richest kibbutzim and Molad is deteriorating right next door. It hurts me a lot to see this condition. . . . It reinforces my feeling that the division was a disaster. That kibbutz members could actually hit each other, that a kibbutz would have to call in the police to intervene in their fights—this is one of the severest traumas suffered by Israeli society, which had always taken pride in the kibbutz as one of its exemplary creations. The division dealt an awful blow to the prestige of the whole kibbutz movement, and it took us years and years to recover.

The
Dor Family

INTRODUCTION

The presentation of the Dor family closes our section about the division. It includes representatives of three generations. The grandparents, Lea and Levi, emigrated from Germany to Makom, and moved from Makom to Adama during the division. They have adjusted well to the move to Adama, in spite of the fact that they left their firstborn daughter, Sara, behind in Makom. Sara, a second-generation Makom-born woman, maintained her loyalty to Makom. In fact, among all five members of the Dor family, she is the only one who has lived all of her life in this one place, and is content with this situation. Years ago, she married Yosi, who had been born in Molad and moved to Makom with his family during the division. Sara and Yosi have four children, and Anat, their eldest, represents the third generation of the Dor family. Anat is twenty-two years old and is living with her boyfriend in Makom. Although she is personally happy with her life in the kibbutz, she plans to leave Makom, together with her boyfriend, in order to try to live independently in town.

As in the case of the Eisman family, the comparison of the members of the different generations is of great interest. Levi, the grandfather, who joined the kibbutz movement for ideological reasons, saw his political affiliation as a central aspect of his identity, strong enough to bring about the decision to leave the kibbutz during the division. (This was not so for Lea; she followed her husband in the move to Adama despite no great ideological conviction.) Their son-in-law Yosi, now fifty-one, is still an idealist of sorts, although he is shy about his beliefs. The daughter Sara denies the importance of any ideological political considerations whatsoever, and accounts for her rather unusual personal history only by her deep love for Makom. The granddaughter Anat seems to go one step further and reasons that, in order to make a decision about where to live, she has to try living elsewhere in a different life-style, first.

These representatives of the three generations demonstrate the decline of ideology and of political involvement within the kibbutz, and the development of a different type of kibbutznik who seems to seek personal development in a private—one might say, even egocentric—manner, rather than through orientation towards the communal aims of the State or the kibbutz.

There is, however, a certain parallel between the three generations of women in the Dor family, all of whom seem to be remote from public life and the ideological dimension of the kibbutz life. Lea and Sara did not express any more ideological interests than their young daughter-granddaughter Anat. Is it a feminine trait to be more involved in the practical aspects of one's life, with an emphasis on the familial roles? While some of the first-generation women did try to change this more conservative image of the mother-wife, not all women of that period did, and it seems that this "revolution" was not carried over to the younger women of the kibbutz, either. The men have suffered no such break with the goals of the first-generation men. Naturally, one family is not enough on which to base generalizations on all these important issues, but more material regarding these matters will be presented in other chapters of the book.

L E A   A N D   L E V I   *(age 68)*

Lea and Levi showed up for the interview together, a jovial couple with a deep German accent. He did most of the talking, while she expressed, facially, her approval of his version of the story.

LEVI—We were part of the German immigration, as you can surely detect by our accent. My impression is that the division in the kibbutz movement followed the lines of the ethnic origin of the members. Most of those who relocated here were German, and most of the people who left Adama were also German. There were basic political conflicts, of course, but the ethnic aspect also played its part.

In Makom, we, as newcoming Yekkes, were accepted in the 1930s by the Sabras, the high-school graduates, the idealists, who considered themselves the cream of Israeli society. I wouldn't say that they were snobbish, but they did exude a sense of pride and superiority, as if they considered themselves better. This attitude had its effect on us: Although our situation somewhat improved over the years, we Yekkes felt inferior and oppressed.

Here, in Adama, we encountered the reverse atmosphere. The members here were good, simple, people, mostly of Polish origin; but they had one problem—self-esteem. They felt that they weren't good enough, especially since their own Yekkes were leaving them. This atmosphere provided us with a very fertile ground for our own growth and for the parallel development of the whole community. I want to make myself very clear: This was altogether a psychological phenomenon, it had no basis in reality. The members here were wonderful people, there was no reason for them to feel inadequate. The fact that they absorbed a large group of Makom members, the "cream of the Israeli society," significantly changed their self-image. For our part, we felt liberated from the constant criticism of the "Israelniks," and also became much more self-confident. So both groups ended up feeling better than they had felt before the division. I don't believe that *we,* the Makom arrivals, built the kibbutz here, as some claim; what we built was a better image for all of us, and this, in turn, created an actual change. We could never have arrived at our current prosperous state without the vital contributions of the original members. There was also another benefit in our move here: Age-wise, we fitted neatly between the older founders and their offspring. But I think that this factor was secondary in importance to the change in esteem which I mentioned.

So you might understand why I don't speak of Makom with great nostalgia, or about the division with profound pain or sorrow. This might seem strange, since we left a child there; of all the people who left Makom we had the best case for bitterness and misgivings. One hundred and twenty-two children moved to Adama with us, but one was missing—our eldest daughter, Sara. She was sixteen when we left for Adama, and you might say that we lost a daughter in the division. (We came with two young children, and our fourth was born here.) On the other hand, due to this fact, we have maintained a closer relationship with Makom than others in the group. Frequently we visit our daughter, who is married to a man from the Molad group, and our four grandchildren, who all live in Makom, and we feel quite comfortable returning for visits.

The division itself was a tragic event. We felt obligated to leave. We identified with Mapai, but, moreover, we felt that the Kibbutz Hameuchad faction negated Zionism as we understand it. Furthermore, a power struggle had developed in Makom concerning control over the resources and various central positions, and this ruined the interpersonal relationships to the extent that, finally, our only choice was to leave, even though our daughter stayed behind.

I'm an accountant by profession, and numbers are very much my hobby and interest. I want to tell you that the numerical proportion was such that we, the Mapai group, very nearly had the majority in Makom before the division. The numerical difference between the two factions was rather small, and this, of course, added to the tension we all felt.

Here, too, the situation was very tense when we arrived. At that time the faction that was leaving Adama was still living here, and they behaved in a most unpleasant manner. They actually tried force to prevent our entering the kibbutz. They ran to ring the bell, calling for reinforcements from other Kibbutz Hameuchad neighbors, to help them block the gates to the kibbutz. This was extremely unpleasant. They were deeply attached to this place and bitter about having to depart. We had to live in the kibbutz together for some time, though, before they finally left.

Although strife wasn't as obvious in Makom before our departure, there were some very unpleasant episodes there, too. I personally participated in one, which I call "the spy in the shoe barrel." It happened after the two factions had already become very hostile, and each maintained its own secret meetings. One of the most fanatic members of our group went to spy on one of the leadership meetings of the other group which took place in a private room. He hid in a big old shoe barrel that was placed just outside the window of that room, and listened to their discussion until somehow he was discovered. He then tried to escape as fast as his legs would carry him, with the angry crowd chasing after him. All this happened near our room and I clearly heard them screaming, "Kill him, kill the bastard!" I'm not exaggerating, I swear. Since the pursued was my friend, and I was a witness to the escapade (not that I'm such a hero), I joined him in his flight and we both managed to lock ourselves inside his room. From the outside I heard somebody ask: "And what about him?" (meaning me, of course), and a soft feminine voice answered: "Let's kill him, too."

Well, it sounds funny now but it wasn't at the time. Things calmed down, however, and we both emerged unharmed, but this incident indicates the emotional intensity of the experience for both sides.

In ideological debates, people frequently used rough language and terms that they themselves didn't understand. Twice I was called "a Fascist," which was really irrelevant to the whole issue. Another sentence directed at me was: "You'll leave this place on a stretcher." This suffices to describe the atmosphere just before we left. Actually there was a slow, quiet process of a growing rift between us for about seven years before the final division.

LEA—In some kibbutzim the final stage of the division was prolonged, lasting even one or two years, during which highly hostile camps still lived together. In most cases this was due to a wait for new dwellings to be completed in the kibbutzim to which these people were planning to move. This prolonged crisis produced absurd situations. Some kibbutzim had two dining halls, duplicate classes, even two clothes storehouses and secretariats. We were lucky because we left Makom almost immediately after we voted to divide. For this we must thank Adama, because they understood our situation very well and offered to absorb us immediately, even though they had no vacant place. In many cases they left their own rooms, and lived in abandoned huts and cottages which were no longer being used as living quarters, so that we might begin our new life in their kibbutz with decent housing. I will never forget it. Taking in one hundred adults and more than one hundred children is not a simple matter at all. A few months later, after their own departing faction had left, we had more space at our disposal.

LEVI—During the transition period in E.C. [a neighboring kibbutz], there was a common dining hall that had been divided by a partition; two separate kitchens provided the meals for the two factions. Before the partition was erected, there was just an aisle dividing the two eating areas; I was once visiting there and I saw the two groups sitting separately in the huge hall, each camp completely ignoring the people who sat across the room. It was shocking, especially since I knew that in E.C. people had lived together for more than thirty years before the division.

Molad and E.C. set the scenario for the divisions in all other kibbutzim. After the violent conflict which both kibbutzim underwent, other kibbutzim felt almost as if they had no choice but to follow suit.

Our division was relatively humane. We all worked together until the last moment and we even managed to smile at each other sometimes. We had a common secretariat, and, actually, the last secretary was one of our group, a man who left with us for Adama. During the very last days in Makom our children studied in separate classes, however. I believe that the growing tension was a result of the fact that the size of each camp was so close in number. I felt that with a slight change of mood, we, the Adama group, could have become a majority. The fight over each "neutral" member was, therefore, crucial, and both sides tried to win people over to their camp. Although I was known to be a Mapainik, Yehuda came over to our room one night and tried to convince me to stay. "You're a Socialist," he said, "your place is with us." We, on our side, also tried to enlarge our camp by trying to persuade those who were still indecisive that they'd feel better with us than with the other, more extreme group. Indeed we succeeded in convincing many neutral families to join us, especially after the atmosphere had become rather ugly within the kibbutz. There were, however, five or six neutral families who decided to remain. Basically the choice was between the ideological rift and one's attachment to the place we had built, to the land and the landscape. For a while, it seemed as if we were getting as large as our opposition. I never thought that we might turn the tables on them, causing them to leave, but I believed that if the two forces would assume equal strength we might declare a "truce" in the political struggle and give priority to the maintenance of our united society, as at least one other kibbutz had done at the time. This solution wasn't, however, accepted by the majority.

LEA—The actual departure was very poignant. On the last day, we went as a group to the cemetery, to say good-bye to our dead. Somebody had even suggested moving "our" dead with us, and reburying them at Adama. This wasn't done, but it showed how melancholy we had all become upon leaving. We didn't have enough time to be immersed in these feelings, though. We worked incessantly until the last minute, and for the actual move to Adama we only received three days of vacation, for packing, traveling, unpacking, and all the various chores involved. Right after those three days, we were all working in our new jobs in Adama.

LEVI—Luckily we had very little to pack since we took very little with us. All the property of four families, including all our furniture, fitted into one truck. And how we packed! Books were placed in old vegetable boxes and clothes in powdered milk containers. These we had to unpack as soon as we arrived, so that the next set of families could make the move after us.

LEA—Our relationships with those who remained at Makom continued through and after the division.

LEVI—In my case it wasn't exactly like that. Following the events, I felt persecuted by some members of the opposite camp and I cut off all further contacts with them. Even when I visited Makom and happened to encounter them, I didn't say hello to them. It's all over now, and I can tell you about it with a smile, yet at one time there were very painful feelings involved.

LEA—Now we visit Makom frequently; we're invited to many of their events.

LEVI— . . . especially to funerals.

LEA—No, to weddings and celebrations as well.

LEVI—Well, now that the two movements might be reunited, we'll see what feelings we'll experience then. . . . I'd like to finish with another statistical observation—as I told you I have an accountant's mind. There's a high rate of intermarriage between kibbutzim, marriages conducted through our great matchmaker, the Army. People rarely marry within the kibbutz. ("Yes, I know your son married within the kibbutz," he says mockingly to his wife, "but that's still a rare occurrence.") Following a marriage between members of two kibbutzim, there's competition between the two kibbutzim-of-origin, the winner being the one that manages to attract the couple to live in it. Well, I counted the cases and compared the results of mixed Ichud and Meuchad weddings, and I found out that we, the Ichud movement, win at the rate of 8 to 1. Young "mixed" couples highly prefer our Ichud kibbutzim to the Meuchad. There's an additional interesting fact: In all those years, I don't remember one single couple bridging Makom and Adama. There is no more animosity between us, and we're not reliving the Romeo and Juliet tragedy, but that's the fact, just the same.

LEA—Except for our daughter who remained in Makom and still lives there, our remaining three children live in Adama with us. They all got married and tried to live elsewhere for a while, but they all returned, bringing a big dowry (their spouses and children), and settled here. This gives us a great sense of achievement and satisfaction.

LEVI—You can add to this satisfaction the fact that we are both responsible and active members in this society; we feel loved and respected here, and we lead a better life here than we could have in Makom. There's no nostalgia in our story as I said before. I know that some members of our original group do feel completely different. Perhaps the main difference is, indeed, in having our children and grandchildren here with us, as my old wife just said. . . .

S A R A *(age 43)*

I was the only child whose parents left for Adama during the division and who decided to stay in Makom. Actually, I have often wondered whether there's a similar person in the entire kibbutz movement. I was in high school when the kibbutz split and I arrived at my decision with another girl who was, and still is, a very close friend of mine. She also decided not to leave Makom, but hers was a different case; she was a child who had survived the Holocaust alone and had no parents at all. In the kibbutz she had been adopted by the Porat family and had wonderful relationships with them; still, she too decided to stay here.* We were like two sisters, and the fact that we both stayed behind helped us a lot during the first stage of separation from our families.

We didn't decide to stay here out of any political or ideological considerations. We were both very remote from all of the controversy. We were, however, very attached to the place and to the children's society and this was our only reason for staying. Our class had absorbed many outside children, children who had no parents at all or whose families weren't in the kibbutz, and they had all managed alone without families. So separation from our parents wasn't so exceptional in our class and to a certain extent we joined this group of outside children.

As a child, I had been very close to my parents and I must have suffered because of our separation, but I don't think I had any motive to cut myself off from my parents. My decision wasn't the result of a conflict or any sort of particular tension within my family. My step hurt my parents a great deal, of course. My father took it very severely and he was ready to cut off all ties with me when he realized that he couldn't convince me to join them. My mother, however, was more realistic. She respected my decision and influenced Father to accept it too. He was awfully angry at the beginning, but I told him: "Let's not ruin our relationship by fighting. Let's not talk about it at all, since you can't accept my viewpoint. I'm staying here anyway, because I love the place and the people and I don't want to start a new life elsewhere." That settled it. After all, he is my father and has always wanted to see me happy.

In a similar manner, my girlfriend's adopted family agreed to let her stay and still maintained their good relationship with her. In their family, too, the father was more extreme and the mother more willing to accept.

Anyway, I joined my family for the departure and helped my mother settle down in her new room. It was a difficult time for her because she had to make the move with two babies, my two young sisters, and so I stayed for several days to help her out. Then I returned

*The Porat family left for Adama (see p. 128).

to Makom. I went to visit my family quite often at the beginning, and then gradually less frequently. As my sisters grew older, my mother started to come and visit me here, too. My father didn't come for years though, and even now he rarely visits. I can sympathize with him very easily and I'd probably have reacted as he did. He left our kibbutz with very bad feelings, after losing a political struggle, and felt defeated. It's hard to overcome such feelings.

You talk about a struggle, but people from Makom tell me that the departing faction didn't have to go.

Today that's easy to say. . . . Indeed, some friendly relationships were maintained throughout the period—and up to the present day—and people kept working side by side up to the very last day. . . . I was just a child and I don't remember much serious friction. What I remember better than anything else is the line of buses ready for departure in the courtyard, many people with children on the buses and at least as many people around the buses, with tears in their eyes.

The people who left were a mixed group; like any group of people, some were better and some worse. But I remember those who stayed saying cruelly: "Don't worry. The bad ones left—the good remained," or, "We didn't lose anything by *their* departure." Of course, I can't agree with that, and not only because my parents were also on the bus.

For my father personally, leaving Makom turned out to be a very fortunate step. Here he would never have reached the position he now holds in Adama where, since the very beginning, he assumed the responsibilities of a central figure. Here the Israelis occupied all the important positions and didn't see any of the new immigrants as suitable candidates for any major roles. My father came from Germany after a *hachshara* period in the Netherlands. Here, somehow, all that group was belittled and prevented from filling any of the positions of power. My father is an extremely clever and sharp man; he can also be stubborn and blunt, but there's no doubt that he has a great deal to contribute as a public figure. In Makom he used to be an accountant and that was also his first job at Adama. Within fewer than three years in Adama, however, he became the cashier and a member of the secretariat and to this day, they won't make any move in Adama without consulting him first. I don't think that the society of Adama is on a lower level than ours. The fact that my father obtained such a status in Adama can be attributed mainly to the fact that they didn't have any prejudice against Yekkes there. The absorbing core wasn't as snobbish as the core people at Makom.

My mother had a different experience. She's a nurse, as I am, and she's a very warm person and easy to get along with. She would be as happy and socially successful here in Makom as she is there, perhaps even more so. She has many friends in both places and has maintained her social contacts with her friends in Makom throughout the years. I think that women generally are more adaptable, and, since they weren't as involved in the political conflict as the men, they could forgive, forget and come back to visit more readily than their husbands.

My father was very active in the political debate. He was an enthusiastic Mapainik and didn't hesitate to fight for his opinions. I remember as a child how unpleasant this was for me. In the children's society I was made to feel ashamed of him and his views, as if he was a criminal or a traitor. But I suppose that if the pressure had been really unbearable, I would have left with my parents. I didn't leave because, in spite of all the ongoing conflicts, I managed to remain a popular and central member within my class. When it became known that I was considering staying on alone in Makom I even gained respect, as if I were a heroine of some kind. People frequently pointed to us as an example of the strength and higher conviction of the Kibbutz Hameuchad ideology—well, I think it's all nonsense. I wasn't interested in ideology or in politics, and I stayed out of no conviction other than my love for this place.

Furthermore, I want to stress that I've never been able to understand why the division took place. Even those who seemed to understand the dispute in the 1950s have by now lost their certainty about it all. I didn't understand it then and I still don't understand it. Or perhaps I knew something which I can't recall anymore. . . . I think that there is a psychological tendency to follow a banner, a mass phenomenon which makes people act without exercising their personal judgment. Somebody just raises a flag, and he's got followers. And waves of people also join the cause for social or personal motives of their own. That's the way many people jumped on the wagon and used the opportunity to move to the city as well. Everybody was on the move. As things were quite chaotic, everyone could go their own way pretty much unnoticed.

I got the impression during my visit to Adama that many former members of Makom still carry the scars of the division. It's like an open wound for them. As someone who knows both kibbutzim, do you agree with my impression, and, if so, how do you explain this phenomenon?

Yes. . . . There are people who are still angry and others who are still in pain. I think that these people originally belonged to the Israeli group here and still miss the atmosphere of the old Makom group. Indeed, by their very presence there, they made a change in the cultural atmosphere of Adama, but they still couldn't overcome their longings. Shoshana and Benjamin particularly represent this group. Shoshana tells me that every time she visits here, walking along the tree-lined path to our kibbutz, she has tears in her eyes. Perhaps she doesn't feel it daily when she's at her home and her work, but returning here is still very painful each time. They visited several times during the Jubilee celebrations and I know those visits were difficult for the Israelis. They miss our holidays, the cultural events, the social atmosphere they imagine we have. My father, however, and others from the German group do not feel this way, as far as I know.

Someone here told me something that would probably be unpleasant for you, but I would like to hear your reaction just the same. He said that some of the Germans left Makom because they believed that in Adama they'd get a better arrangement concerning the reparations.

This is completely wrong as well as totally unfair to that group and to my parents in particular. My parents could have become millionaires had they kept their German reparations. In addition to a large initial sum, they receive high monthly payments to this very day. Yet they didn't and don't see a penny of any of this, nothing. In Adama, as in Makom, every single penny goes to the common budget of the kibbutz. It's just viciousness on the part of whoever invented that story! Furthermore, it's also wrong historically because they left the kibbutz *before* the reparation agreement and, therefore, they couldn't have considered this among their reasons for leaving Makom. Not only did my parents not keep a penny of all the reparation monies, but later they inherited a large estate and donated it all to their kibbutz, which built a vast modern infants' home with the money. Here, however, I know of several individuals who didn't give similar inherited money to the kibbutz, but called it a gift and used it to cover trips abroad instead. It's true, as I said before, that not everybody left due to purely political convictions, yet the reason you just mentioned didn't play any role whatsoever in the whole chain of events. My mother, as I said before, went just because she was following my father. She wasn't interested in politics any more than I am.

This political indifference is actually very typical of us, the second generation of the kibbutz, today. Therefore, I'm convinced that another division couldn't happen in our time. We're a generation without an ideology. We received little political education in the kibbutz, since our school taught nothing on this subject. Our children, who are quite old by now, are even more indifferent than we are. They don't participate in any political activities, they are completely uninvolved. This trend is also evident in the greater tolerance within the kibbutz now to various political viewpoints. For example, we have people who hold extreme and opposing attitudes concerning the conditions of peace with the Arabs—whether or not to return territories for peace—and they all feel free to express their different views.

This plurality of opinions and general political indifference has perhaps gone too far, though. Our daughter, Anat, plans to leave the kibbutz and live in town and this is something I'm willing to accept as her legitimate right. But she also claims that if leaving the country, emigrating, makes somebody happy, it's all for the best; this is an opinion which I won't accept. We have an older son, however, now twenty-four, who is a devoted kibbutznik and an ideologist, exactly like his father, so it's unfair to make any generalizations.

Some people of the third generation have claimed that they don't see much they could contribute here, and that, therefore, they'd rather settle in a young kibbutz. Isn't that a return to ideology?

That remains to be seen. I personally object to the whole idea of joining a young kibbutz. I think that our children have a lot to contribute right here, and it's only due to their naïve perspective that they don't realize this. We won't be able to survive without an incoming generation of support. We keep growing and developing all the time. Actually, the kibbutz is the only society in which parents prepare a place for their children to live right there with them. In town, children look for a livelihood wherever they can find it. In the *moshavim,* most of the children have to leave because the limited arable land can't support all the children of a family. The kibbutz is the only way of life which lays the foundations for a home for all its children, and I wish the majority of them would decide to stay here with us.

Y O S I *(age 51)*

Yosi is Sara's husband, a blue-eyed, suntanned man, easy to be with yet difficult to talk to. In general, he's a quiet man and answered my questions with extremely short answers.

I was born in the Valley, in Molad. When the division took place, I was about twenty-five and deeply involved in the political conflict. This determined my decision to move to Makom. I was identified with the Kibbutz Hameuchad movement and could not continue living in Molad while maintaining my views about what was taking place in the country and the kibbutz movements. Moreover, I was pleased to move to Makom, which was known to be more ideologically oriented. Actually it wasn't as dramatic a step as it sounds today, because I moved here with my parents and brothers, as did the majority of my age group. The group that moved here consisted of 120 adults and many children, so we felt pretty much at home right from the start, even though the economic conditions here were so much worse than those we had known in Molad. Actually— perhaps this is indiscreet to say—Makom looked like a children's kibbutz when we came, and I believe that it's mainly due to our contribution that the place has changed so dramatically, although there were other factors involved as well.

I got married here to Sara, a daughter of the first graduating class of Makom. She has an interesting story to tell because her parents moved to Adama during the division and she stayed here, although she was only sixteen years old.

When I came, I started to work in the cultivation of our crops, and I have remained in this branch to the present day. We grow wheat and hay primarily, crops which don't need irrigation. Due to the sophistication of agricultural machinery, the same branch that employed fifteen to twenty men in the past is now maintained by six or seven men, and it's even possible to increase the production of the crops. We work as a team and although we have a branch coordinator, a position which we rotate amongst ourselves, most of the decisions concerning our branch are taken by the whole group when we meet at the dining hall during the morning and evening meals. We don't make a lot of profit, but we have a very limited amount of water for irrigation, and can't grow more of the other crops, such as cotton, which are more profitable but require irrigation. Actually its a strange situation; we are now the biggest kibbutz on the eastern side of the Valley. Yet, since we are relatively young, we don't get the largest water allocation.

I consider myself an active member of this kibbutz. I have served in various roles and committees, and I always attend the general assembly meetings. I see it as my right, not as a duty.

A N A T   *(age 22)*

Anat is of the third generation in the kibbutz and the oldest daughter of Sara and Yosi.

I was born here, I grew up here, and I've been away for only three years: two years in the Army and one year of service in a young kibbutz, before I was drafted, which is mandatory for all kibbutz children. Now it's been nearly a year since I came back to the kibbutz. I live here with my boyfriend, also a kibbutz child, and I'm fairly happy.

Returning to the kibbutz as an adult after those three years of living outside is really one's first test of accepting the kibbutz way of life. Most returning soldiers go through some form of crisis, or at least have difficulties in adjustment. I believe this is due to the fact that the life of a child growing up in a kibbutz is completely dictated by various rules and regulations. A child knows what he or she is expected to do every single hour of the day. There's a routine of meals, school, work, planned social activities (being a leader of another group or participating on a committee, for example), home visits, etc. All these are fixed and determined by an external system. The same holds true for the soldier while engaged in active service; his duties are dictated from above and occupy all of his time.

Upon returning home, a kibbutz child at twenty-one or -two is suddenly faced, for the first time, with freedom of a new kind. He can choose his place of work, even if it's not an entirely free choice. He or she has free time from the early afternoon until the next morning to dispense with as desired. This can be disconcerting: Frequently one wants to do too many different things and it's difficult to begin any. Sometimes everything seems empty and meaningless and one doesn't know how to use all this free time. Socially it's strange, too. I can stay alone in my own room for hours; it's both a luxury and a threat which I never experienced before. The tightly knit social group, the school class, slowly dissolves. Some people return from the Army earlier, some later. Some get married and keep to themselves. Its a confusing period; for some it's even a "shock."

There are additional problems. The early twenties are a time to consider the future and, in our case, this means deciding whether or not to remain in the kibbutz. Then there's the choice of work, which is easier for men than for women. Men often become attached to a certain branch before they enter the Army. Mostly, they find satisfactory work, they work a long day, and return home exhausted. If they are happy at work I'd say that their adjustment problem is more than half solved. Women, however, have extremely limited choices. The vast majority work in the various services—kitchen, children, laundry—that's about it. It's hard to find satisfaction in this sort of job.

When I returned from my service, I didn't want a permanent job at all. I volunteered to be a "substitute," one who substitutes for missing people and works wherever it's necessary. For a while it was very nice to be in different places, among different people, every day. I became reacquainted with a lot of people after being away from the kibbutz for three years. Thus, I have avoided taking any responsibility in a permanent place. I think what I tried to avoid most was a permanent job in the children's homes. After a while I did get a permanent job, however, in the dining hall. I decided it wasn't such a bad deal, since everyone has to do a stretch of ninety days in the dining hall. I don't know if it's done once or twice in a lifetime, but for the moment I've fulfilled my obligation. After that, I moved to the kitchen and I've been working with the cooking team since then. I used to love cooking, but the huge quantities of food and the machinery have completely disillusioned me. I don't enjoy the food we prepare. But it is a comfortable job. I start at 6:00 A.M. and I'm done by 1:00 P.M. and when I'm done I'm truly done, nobody bothers me after I finish. I can go my way for the rest of the day, whereas if I had any sort of job which has to do with children, it's never really over. Parents question you whenever you meet them, there are always meetings and conferences, you must take turns putting the children to bed at night—it never ends. So my job suits me rather well. I don't pay much attention to it and I'm not required to do more than I'm willing to do. Maybe I take it so easy because I know its only a temporary place for me and I'm not going to do it for a long time.

Actually I plan to leave the kibbutz quite soon. Perhaps I'll stay for another half year, at the most. This knowledge helps me not to feel confined here, you see.

When I came back from the Army, I already knew that I'd leave the kibbutz. I thought I'd return for a year or so; I'm not too well organized with my life and haven't set a definite date for my departure as yet. Actually, my instinct was to leave the kibbutz immediately after my military service, but I thought that wasn't a fair choice since I had only experienced the life of a child in the kibbutz and I realized that I must try the adult way of life for at least a year. But knowing how transient I felt here, I never even applied for membership in the kibbutz, and I'm formally, therefore, not a member of Makom. I thought, however, that I had to try, at least for a limited period, what we call the "sixty-year cycle." This is the kibbutz sixty-year routine of work, family, children, functions and committees—very much a predetermined route.

So I returned to test it out for myself and I decided I'd stick to it for a year, although I would have allowed myself to leave before the year was over if I had really felt miserable. Surprisingly I have been very happy for the last year. Not just because I was aware of the time limits of this period —I have simply been personally happy. Nevertheless, I still intend to leave.

Why? Well, firstly, because I don't want to live here out of inertia. I want to test myself out in other life circumstances and then I'll be able to make my choice. There are plenty of disadvantages to living in the kibbutz. They're mainly centered around the fact that in the kibbutz my life depends on others, on the public norms and the decisions of the community; I have a need to live privately, on my own terms, to decide for myself what I can or can't do, to move my life in my own direction. At least, I'd like to try to live independently for a while. I want to know that, if I work hard and save money, I can later travel or spend the money the way I wish, that it's all up to me.

Frequently I feel that Makom could be like a bed of roses for me, for everything is guaranteed and available. I could, at the end of this year, ask to go and study whatever subject I want, and I'm certain that within five years I'd be granted my request. Even a crazy idea, perhaps with some compromises towards the needs of the community, would probably eventually be approved. (I'm not sure this is true for all kibbutzim, but Makom is very open to individual wishes.) Or, if I wanted a trip abroad, I could obtain it eventually as a kibbutz member. There is a recent suggestion to enable newly discharged soldiers to go abroad according to a special waiting list, and if that is approved every young person could go within five years after his or her service.

So I don't feel that in the kibbutz I'd be blocked from achieving my aims; that's absolutely not the point. All I say is that I'd like to achieve my aims independently, on my own. I'd like to test myself and see how I'd survive in the real world, outside this ivory tower.

One thing really frightens me and that's staying here out of inertia, out of circumstance. There are many people like that here. They were born here, they returned from the Army, and, not quite knowing how, they suddenly found themselves married and with four children, and they never think again about other possible options. It becomes a no-choice situation, and this happens especially to women. I don't want to belong to the kibbutz in this manner. Therefore I want to leave, to sever my formal ties completely—not to take a year of leave or some other half-way arrangement like that. And if, while I'm outside, I arrive at the conclusion that the kibbutz way of life is better than whatever else I've tried, I'll probably come back. It's quite possible, but it would be a completely different sort of decision.

This is my present situation, and since I haven't applied for membership, it's not a secret and a lot of people here are aware of my plans. They know too much, actually. Often I'm stopped on the street and people inquire: "When will you be going?" or "Are you *still* with us?" I don't know how the news spread so widely. It gives me the feeling, although I know it isn't true, that soon people might say, "What are you still doing here, since you said you were leaving?" or even, "Go away." But I don't think this would happen. I work like everybody else and I don't exploit the kibbutz by staying.

I know that people outside are surprised to find such reactions. There was a time when the kibbutz felt terribly threatened by people leaving it. People who left were considered traitors. But that is part of our past. What has remained of those attitudes is the parents' fear that *all* of their children might leave. In that case the parents are regarded by everyone as really miserable. I don't know why people don't see that this is natural. All over the world children leave their parents, each in his or her direction, to find their own way. A big kibbutz like Makom isn't threatened by departures, but the family unit within the kibbutz is. Interestingly, people outside think that families are of no importance within the kibbutz, while in fact the opposite is true. Big families are very powerful here.

Nobody seriously tried to talk me out of carrying out my plan. Surprisingly, many people have even encouraged me, saying that if I have my doubts it's better to leave now and gain perspective on it all. Indeed, many people have said that it's a positive step that I'm taking. I myself was amazed by this reaction, because only four years ago, towards the end of high school, when I expressed similar views, I was seriously criticized for my deviation.

My parents also approve of my decision, although naturally they express some concern about my future and feel that my best place is still under their wings. I guess that their concern is partially based on the fact that I don't have a well-planned alternative in mind. I dislike long-range planning. Some people leave to study on a certain program, or to go to an awaiting job. I, however, plan to leave and see what happens as time goes by; whatever comes, comes. My boyfriend intends to leave with me. His parents are in the States right now and have an apartment in town, where we're planning to live. He wants to work at a photography store and learn the profession, whereas I'm thinking of becoming a housemaid, which will make good money. We'll save and then travel and go to visit his parents in America. All the rest remains to be seen. I have lots of time. I don't want to rush things.

Now that I compare the life of adults here to the children's life, I think that kids live under much more pressure than adults. From the seventh grade, which is when one joins the children's society, children study, work, and must also be very active socially. Children work seriously here, doing a great part of the mass seasonal farming work. They also work very hard preparing cultural events. Every season has its holiday or central event for which the children's society must prepare. In the summer it's camps, in the spring it's field trips—an endless chain of social events, each one prepared to perfection. You can never relax. And, of course, there's homework and visits with your family; you never have a moment for yourself. When you are finally in your room, it's shared with two other kids and it's never quiet. It's very crowded in the children's dorms; that's why every kibbutz child dreams of the private room he gets upon returning from the Army.

Constant fatigue is one result of this sort of life. Socially, a very unique network is created. The class you grow with develops unusually close relationships, very much like a family, like brothers and sisters. It's very difficult to explain to anyone who hasn't grown up in a kibbutz. These people have shared rooms and showers with me since we were babies! It's a very strong feeling. Even if I don't see a classmate of mine for a very long time, or even if there's a classmate I don't like, a very deep bond still exists between us, something impossible to explain. The larger social group of several classes is a different network. Since it is formed later, it doesn't have this "bonding" quality. Here, it's a matter of choice; you get friendly only with people you like. It isn't automatic.

Within this whole network, however, deep and intimate friendships between two boys or two girls are very rare. I never had a girlfriend to whom I could talk about everything, sharing feelings, etc. It's very rare among kibbutz children. Intimate one-to-one relationships develop only on a romantic basis, between a boy and a girl who fall in love. It's also true that love affairs or sexual relationships rarely occur within the class; perhaps a class is indeed more like a family. My parents say that in the early times in every class there was one couple who did form a romantic bond within the group. Usually, one member of the couple was an outside child. Today it never happens at all. Boyfriends and girlfriends are found either in younger or older classes, if not outside the kibbutz altogether.

Sexual relationships between adolescents have become fairly common. This was an area the strict social norms didn't refer to and people naturally did what they liked. It seems to me that we grew up with sex; it was always accepted and natural, there was nothing to hide, gossip over, or frown about. Girls were entitled to as much sexual freedom as boys, although some people are still not at all open about it. A girl can ask for the pill at the clinic, or through her mother or the *metapelet*—they'd all supply it on request without any questions. There's nothing to it, really.

Part 3

THE
PRESENT

Administration

N O A M *(age 41)*

Noam is the current kibbutz secretary. His hair is completely white. What he presented is, in a way, an overview of the kibbutz society, followed by his own short history.

I'll begin by telling you about my current work. The kibbutz is run by a team of functionaries, each one in charge of one area: work, economy, monetary matters, society, school, etc. These functionaries are elected members whose administrative work is a full-time job. There are eleven people who have such positions and seven of them (the general and social secretaries, economic coordinator, cashier, work coordinator, services coordinator, and school administrator) are in the secretariat. In general, my main responsibility is to coordinate this central team. I participate in two of the secretariat teams, one which deals with services and consumer needs, and another which deals with economic issues. Since I am the only person who sits on both teams, I coordinate their activities and see that they don't make any decision which rightfully pertains to the secretariat.

Besides the two teams on which I actively participate, there are two more active bodies: one for matters of work, which includes the two work coordinators, and one for overseeing our educational system. The latter two teams are more autonomous, and can make their own decisions on daily matters, or on any issue that doesn't involve monetary expenditure.

There is a new team which we created recently, the monetary team, which helps the cashier make financial decisions. These are the secretariat teams. It's an organization that is fairly unique to our kibbutz, based on our traditional organization, which was established years ago. But recently I have had thoughts about whether or not this structure fulfills our present needs and size. Some of us of the second generation, such as the social secretary and myself, feel that our organizational system is too centralized and we'd like to decentralize it a bit. I think there should be an economic committee whose role would be to propose long-range economic policy decisions. It is of vital importance to start such a committee, not operating on a full-time basis, but meeting after work, as most of our committees do. I have spent a lot of time trying to implement this idea and gradually more people recognize the need for such an institution. In a way, this new committee will parallel the social committee, which was started about four years ago in order to deal with all personal matters. Although this team is chaired by the social secretary, it is fairly autonomous and independent of the secretariat. If we establish this new economic committee, I would like to give it a broad field of responsibilities as well. In this way we may decentralize the present organization.

However, it is not easy to carry out this design since decentralization is against our tradition, which claims that, since almost every major decision involves both social and financial aspects, it's preferable to have one central decision-making body that would see the comprehensive picture. We have many specialized committees for housing, furniture, transportation, etc., but each has little operative power; this is frequently manifested by the fact that a member may have a problem or request in an area under the jurisdiction of a certain committee, but refer his appeal directly to the sovereign secretariat. Consequently, these lesser committees make only minor decisions and refer any serious matter to the secretariat. As a result, they have limited authority while the secretaries are flooded with work, serving every function from acting as a personal wailing wall to purchasing new tractors.

We aim to change this trend. My ideal is our social committee, which is elected directly by the assembly and reports directly to the same body. It's the only committee whose decisions don't require the approval of the secretariat but of the assembly, instead. It's often difficult to decide which committee should deal with which issue; therefore a lot of coordination and flexibility is necessary. Many things are simply settled between me and the social secretary. Luckily, we have an excellent relationship. Yet fairly often there is friction between the secretariat and the social committee. A recent example was the issue of whether or not to install private telephones for our war widows. After many debates, the social committee was in favor of the move while the secretariat was against it. It was a full-scale fight but later we called for a joint meeting of the two bodies and this *ad hoc* forum voted for the telephones. The issue was complicated because it is a strongly social and personal issue on the one hand, and it involves a serious financial investment on the other. This is fairly uncommon; in the last two years we have allocated a certain budget to the social committee and it decides independently how to spend it, according to its own priorities. Older members of the kibbutz, however, oppose this arrangement. They would like to limit the power of the various committees to an advisory capacity. It's a shame that more of these opponents are not willing to participate actively in the various public roles.

So this is the kind of administrative problem with which I deal daily. I have to see that this complicated structure runs smoothly, that the different teams work in spite of frequent conflicts of interests. I aspire to efficiency and improvement, but I prefer gradual change to revolution.

It's vitally important that we have good human relations within the teams. Once I sat on the secretariat as the work coordinator, and the tension within my team was so intense that loud fights were common occurrences. It became so difficult to run the group that we asked for the intervention of the kibbutz human-relations experts. Therefore, I am very pleased to be the coordinator of the present secretariat, which is basically quite friendly. We have our conflicts, naturally, and some anger is often expressed, but all of this is legitimate when you run such a project. One of the issues that has been the cause of arguments on our present team is the priority of financial versus social considerations. We, the two secretaries, are sometimes accused of being too socially oriented, neglecting the economic aspects of our proposals or decisions. But all arguments take place within the framework of normal, even friendly disagreements.

Recently the secretariat finished its first year of service. Both of us secretaries will be replaced next fall and the elections of our successors are already taking place. For the occasion of our one-year anniversary in the secretariat, we held an open discussion reviewing our activities and our plans for the next year. The main issue to surface was the conflict between our service and leadership responsibilities. One may view our role as that of civil servants, trying to solve the daily problems, which vary from sewage disposal to immediate personal pressures. Another image, however, is that of the leader trying to lead the community towards some goal, giving its development a certain direction. These two orientations, if not actually contradictory, determine the method of our time allocation. According to the civil-service orientation, the secretary should be free and willing to accept people at all hours, for all reasons. If, on the other hand, he is to be a leader, he must limit his availability to people to make time for higher purposes, so to speak. The question is, basically, whether a society like ours can be led in a certain direction, and, if so, what that direction should be. I think that this dilemma is highly significant to all people who have central positions within the kibbutz. Personally, I am convinced that the secretariat has to lead the society in addition to, and not in place of, all its other routine functions. I have no doubt that the unplanned change within the kibbutz is detrimental. The initiative championed by the members is a positive development in the areas of production, whereas in the social and consumer areas it frequently has a negative effect. This is partly due to the fact that almost everyone capable of leading our society in social and ideological spheres is already involved in a central public function, whilst the remaining people, who are not elected for these roles, are primarily concerned with their own materialistic needs. Take my partner, Amos. If he weren't a functionary, he would be a teacher in our high school again, and in this position he would constantly be proposing ideas which would raise the level of our social-ideological life, suggesting challenging goals and being the pioneer in realizing them. For example, as a teacher of the twelfth grade, he took his whole class and went to live with them for the entire year in an underprivileged immigrant town. This exposed our sheltered youngsters to the tough reality of Israeli society and gave them the opportunity to contribute to a community very different from ours. I think that it was a wonderful idea, and it appears completely different in spirit if it arises as an initiative from below rather than as a decision from above, from the secretariat. Sadly enough, when people such as Amos and myself are within the administrative system, we cannot contribute to the society in such a spontaneous manner. There aren't many people who remain free to assume this voluntary leadership, and generally people in the kibbutz are content with their lot; in a way, they even tend to be passive because for every problem you have an established recourse. So, whereas city-people learn to rely more on their own initiative and ability to cope with problems, kibbutz people learn instead the appropriate committees or teams to go to for a solution to any tiny difficulty which may come up in their lives.

I have also found that the more functionaries or committees one has, the more problems are brought to the public sector to solve. We must limit this endless process and instead present the community with an important project, some broader social issue, to which we'd all give priority even if it detracted from the time and resources available for meeting the individual's needs.

What goal would raise our community above their daily concerns? Last year we had our Jubilee celebrations. It was a great undertaking and it occupied many people for the whole year—planning and performing, exhibitions, publications, group discussions, holidays, and miscellaneous activities. But the year is over now, and a certain emptiness remains after all that activity. Another target which we have and which is highly problematic concerns Ginat. In a way Ginat's problem demonstrates our situation, the level of the present ideological awareness of our members. And we are considered to be outstanding in this area! When I meet members of other kibbutzim they often say, "Well, if *you* have such a problem, think what would it be like in our kibbutz!" That doesn't comfort me. The situation is indicative of the second generation's attitude towards settlement and their self-involvement in realizing their beliefs.

The first generation was highly ideological in that sense, but today they're old and tired. They could be very instrumental in helping a new struggling kibbutz such as Ginat. The settlers there are mere children and they lack life experience, particularly the experience of people who have lived through the crises and problems of a kibbutz in its fledgling stages. The strength of the first generation was in their confidence even while facing a crisis, whereas the young ones up at Ginat are threatened by every changing wind. They feel that their existence is shaky and may dissolve into nothing at any minute. That is what Rachel does up there. She moderates things, gives them proper perspective, and this is of utmost importance for a new kibbutz. In addition, the first generation is, in many ways, easier to transfer, for they don't have schoolchildren who need classmates and child care, nor do they play such central roles in our economy. But they aren't rushing to realize their ideals any longer, and I can't blame them for this. The second generation simply lacks the necessary ideological awareness and concern; this is our problem and our challenge. They're used to our very high standard of living and they say to me, "Look, I'm happy here, I have young children. Ginat doesn't mean much to me. Why should I go?" Just the other day, I asked a man to go and become a leader in our youth movement in town, and he said, "But I have a small boy and I hate to be away from home from Sunday to Friday every week." Our parents would never have voiced such an objection, and I don't think we suffered because of their frequent absences. I myself worked in the Movement in Tel Aviv for a year when I was already a father of two small children, and indeed it was quite unusual for my generation. The second generation is very devoted to the family and has been spoiled by our standard of living. We hardly know yet how the third generation will turn out.

I'm very concerned about our moral obligation to Ginat. It's an example of what I described before as an initiative started from high up. The former secretariat initiated this beautiful project without testing the readiness of individuals to fulfill the necessary roles. And then, when they finished their term, we were left holding the bag.

It's not so difficult to mobilize a first wave of enthusiasts, but it should have been obvious that a second and third wave of volunteers would be needed to maintain the responsibility. In fact, the little enthusiasm that once existed cooled off quite quickly and we now must do a tremendous amount of work in order to maintain our minimal obligations towards this young kibbutz. I believe this could have been foreseen and that steps should have been taken to make sure the project would be realized, and if not—well, perhaps it would have been better not to start the project at all.

Another line of activity which I see as a possible challenge to our society is political involvement within the Labor Party. This is something I refrain from mentioning to others, because I realize that its immediate result would be that two, three, or four central members would be taken out of the community to serve the party. Again, the three who were willing to go to Ginat would probably volunteer to work for the party, while the kibbutz would suffer seriously from their absence. Actually there is no one from our kibbutz who is presently working for the party. I realize how important it is for the kibbutz movement to gain more impact in national politics, but on the other hand we can't spare the people who could succeed in this kind of activity. Basically there is a very small group of capable individuals who would do well in whatever direction they might choose to take. The same people come up again and again as good candidates for all the many necessary roles to fill. This is the crux of our problem. We don't have enough talented people, motivated people (talent and motivation do go hand in hand here, as far as I have observed), to place in all these important roles supporting new settlements, the party, the Army, and also to carry out central responsibilities within the community. I don't know why it's like that, but a vast majority of our population are simply—I hesitate to say this—mediocre people.

As a result, a certain kind of elite has developed within the kibbutz, a group of people who are elected for one role after another. They have no extra privileges, only more duties to carry out, a harder and longer day of work. They, or rather we, find satisfaction in these positions, that is true, but it's not healthy for the kibbutz. I'd rather go back and work in a productive job at the factory when I finish my present term than be elected or sent to fill another public function. They want me to become the manager of our food factory, but I hope to go back as a worker first.

The work of the secretary is a twenty-four–hour job. No family, no entertainment, nothing. Frequently, when I go to bed at night, I ask myself: What did I do all day? Nothing, just extinguish a few fires. My day is very busy, but I think about half of it is spent in meetings of all sorts, since I belong to so many teams and committees. Once a week, I'm supposed to be in Tel Aviv in the general secretariat of the Kibbutz Hameuchad, but this is something I often neglect to do. Most of the kibbutz's outside connections are taken care of by our cashier. Anyway, my day is full of meetings, my schedule is packed even before I open my eyes. In addition to the regular weekly meetings there are many specific ones. Once a week, the central people of the kibbutz meet in a small hidden place which we've named "Golda's Kitchen." For three or four hours we discuss the problems of the current week, consulting each other about possible solutions. Naturally, we don't make any decisions in this forum. In my free time, I prepare for my coming meetings, especially for the general assembly and for the weekly secretariat meeting. The truth is that Amos takes over in many ways. I'm lucky to have him as my partner. Amos has an independent nature and he often acts on his own judgment. It has even happened that I have reproached him for it, but he said: "What do you need this trouble for?" All he wants is to take some of the load off my back.

Besides all these activities, I'm supposed to have time to see individual members with their requests or problems. Although members of the secretariat have specific areas of responsibility, people come to see us according to their convenience; they talk to whoever happens to be free, or to the person they feel most confident with. I often listen to a person whose problem I really can't solve because it's not within my jurisdiction. "What do you want," I ask, "that I be your telephone? Okay, I'll be a telephone for you." If it's an older member, I don't even mention my objection. I take my hat off and do what I can. If it's a younger person,

I could refer him or her to the proper functionary, but this would create bureaucracy, and since the conversation has already taken up my time I try to solve the problem myself.

People arrive at all hours of the day. They open my door and start talking, whether I'm alone or with somebody else. Amos is actually the person who handles all personal matters. He has a special private room, and he has made it known that he receives people every day for the first two hours of the day. But people come at all times, even in the dining hall while we are eating—that's what they elected us for. We don't try to restrict our contact with the public, we rely on the members' good sense. If someone stops me on the way or appeals to me in the dining hall, he probably feels really pressured.

I don't know how it was all done by one secretary years ago. For the last fifteen years or so, there have been two secretaries, and recently we hired a social worker to take care of many of the personal and family problems. But we all have our hands full. In spite of this pressure, I have taken it on myself as a personal project to prepare the ground work for the financial committee which I mentioned before. I have worked on it for a whole year, and the probability of a positive decision is very high.

There are, however, some plans which we haven't been able to realize yet. For example, when we were elected, Amos and I, we decided to organize informal gatherings in the kibbutz. This is something we thought of as a means to increase the involvement of a wider circle of people in the community, but we still haven't managed to put this idea into operation. You have perhaps noticed that deep friendships among people within the kibbutz are rare. I think of it as a structural disadvantage of the kibbutz, probably related to the common education. I have many superficial friendships here, but my intimate friends are outside the kibbutz, and it's the same for others. I think it's a fascinating phenomenon. This may be attributed to the fact that such a vast portion of our existence is together; we work together, eat together, live in a closed community together, so naturally, when one has the choice of how to spend one's limited free time, the preference is to be alone or with one's close family. As an adolescent, I yearned for my private corner. I led an intense public and social life, and, when I had a free evening, I didn't long for friends but for quiet and solitude. Today, too, I'm constantly with people, and most of these encounters are defined by a common task we have to perform. I'd enjoy meeting these same people informally, without this task on my mind, but there's hardly time. Moreover, due to our daily pressure, there's hardly any motivation. On Friday night, my only free evening, I enjoy staying in the room with my wife and kids. Yet I miss friendship.

What I visualize is not simply letting spontaneous friendships develop. I want groups to talk over kibbutz matters and to form some sort of public, or "street," opinion which would affect our life. Because, you see, many things here are determined by this street opinion. The kibbutz is a form of life which doesn't have any sanctions. We have no material rewards for good behavior. We have no punishments for wrongdoing, except in the most extreme cases, when a member can be expelled from the kibbutz or his candidacy terminated. But in the vast majority of cases, even when a great financial loss is suffered by the community, the individual remains unaffected. Take a case where, as a result of criminal negligence, a tractor was completely ruined by someone. In town he'd feel the results of his deed immediately—at least as a financial loss. Here, however, he can awaken the next morning as if nothing had happened at all. That's why our only weapon for maintaining proper behavior is the atmosphere of acceptance or rejection, public opinion, the response of the "street." It is, therefore, extremely important to develop this instrument.

I believe it would be healthy to have people talk and exchange feelings and experiences. Since things like that don't seem to develop spontaneously, I had a plan to organize informal groups. For example, for the forty-year-olds. It's often said that the kibbutz is great for children and old people, but the middle-aged group which carries the burden of running the kibbutz both socially and economically does not fare as well. This is the hardest age here, the forties. I, for one, feel that I could have flourished in many directions outside the kibbutz. To remain in the kibbutz and forego all the opportunities outside is an ongoing decision that is not always easy to make.

My life as an adult has been comprised of periods of deep involvement with the kibbutz and periods of life outside it for various reasons, in the Movement, in town, or abroad. If I were a private person I would probably study further, but as a kibbutznik—I don't know. This is perhaps the most difficult problem in being a kibbutznik. You must give up a lot.

I don't feel I have in any way sacrificed myself for the kibbutz. I made my personal decisions with open eyes. Today, I still frequently entertain serious thoughts about leaving the kibbutz. Not because of daily friction or frustrations, but because I believe my personal and professional development could have taken different courses in the city. But whenever I sum up all the factors—my wife and children, my work and environment, the quality of life and the culture as well as many other considerations—I always end up seeing the positive side of kibbutz life.

A M O S (age 36)

Amos is the social secretary of the kibbutz and, in this role, he served as one of my hosts during my visit to Makom. It was, however, difficult to find time to talk to him privately and quietly. He is always on the run, and people stop him with new business every time he steps outside. Accompanying him many times to the dining room or during meals, I have been impressed by the warm smiling greeting he offers whoever approaches him. He reacts to the constant demands made upon him with unbelievable patience and a wonderful sense of humor. Finally, we did set a time and place for a formal interview. At the appointed hour, however, a woman arrived: "Amos sent me to be interviewed in his place. An old kibbutz member has just died and Amos is busy with all the necessary arrangements." Two hours later he arrived, still smiling, telling me how happy he was to be able to talk with me for a couple of hours, where nobody could track him down.

I started by asking him about the arrangements that had detained him.

When a member dies, the kibbutz has a specific procedure which the secretary puts into operation. First, it's the secretary's role to inform the relatives about the death if it happened at the hospital or elsewhere outside the kibbutz, since I'm usually the one who gets the message. In today's case the family knew before I came, yet I did contact all of the relatives, to make sure they were informed, and to see how they were responding to the news, and if there were any immediate needs. Then I issued a public announcement. I ran to the person who makes the mourning posters, then to the dining hall to clear the bulletin board of all other announcements, posting the mourning notice at the center of the clean board. Next, I asked all the people who are in charge of the various activities tonight to cancel the scheduled activities. It's Friday and we had planned a public seventy-year birthday for some of our older members; now we'll postpone it until next Friday.

Then I got in touch with our cemetery committee which is in charge of the technical arrangements for the burial. When this was done, I returned to the family, to talk about the funeral and how they wanted it done. We try to help the family by making as many of the necessary arrangements as possible, frequently even making the necessary telephone calls for them. Today, the family preferred to do it by themselves, and I offered the secretariat telephone to one of the relatives for use in making arrangements.

All these are the more technical aspects, but there's a more personal angle, too, concerning the funeral ceremony. We do not use the Jewish Orthodox ritual; instead, we recite a poem and read two paragraphs appropriate to the deceased. It is my duty, as social secretary, to find the suitable material for the ceremony and the people to read it. That's just the beginning of the process; later we print a memorial pamphlet; we hold a memorial after thirty days have passed, and then once a year—it's very complicated. We thought of appointing a committee to take care of this, but I feel that this kind of activity cannot be carried out by formal appointment. The secretary, however, is familiar with most of the individuals in the kibbutz and it makes sense that he should deal with these matters. Even on my way here, I stopped in at some of the deceased's friends and asked them to write something about him. I just have to start the wheels rolling.

Our attitude towards death and mourning in the kibbutz is indicative of the situation in many other areas of our social life. The process is highly institutionalized, yet frequently without deep emotional involvement. First of all, we are a large kibbutz, and every year we have about ten to twelve deaths. It's impossible to maintain a high level of emotional involvement on the part of the whole community for such a frequent event. Not everybody is truly involved in the pain of the relatives, and that's something one shouldn't expect. Yet I'm deeply disturbed when only a handful of people arrive at the funeral or memorial ceremony. (It upsets me much more than the poor attendance in our general assembly meetings, for example.) I believe that attending such events expresses our solidarity in its deepest sense, not towards the deceased but towards his living relatives. I used to go to all the funerals even before I became secretary, even to those of people I hardly knew. It's much more important than participating in holidays or other joyful celebrations!

This is the result of institutionalized society: The more formally organized we are to meet every individual's needs, the less spontaneously we express solidarity in our lives. We are a big community, no longer an extended family, and we can't rely on spontaneous support in cases of private crisis or hardship. So we organize the support through functionaries and committees, and this, in turn, reduces the need for spontaneous involvement even more. People who live here know that somebody else will take care of the unpleasant business, and after a while they cease being interested in their roles or contributions as individuals. Frequently I have asked someone why he or she didn't attend a funeral and I receive the answer: "Well, do you want me to lie and pretend that I care deeply? I hardly knew the person." This is one of the prices we pay for our size, and many miss the intimacy of the old days, when the whole kibbutz resembled a large family. But I think that spontaneous solidarity is something we might foster, even though I don't think it is feasible to stop the process of bureaucracy, the planned organization of our welfare system.

The same phenomenon occurs in many areas. Take, for example, our care of drafted soldiers or hospitalized members. We don't rely on the family or close friends to visit and maintain contact with these individuals; we appoint special committees to regulate these things. These appointed people serve as a collective superego, one might say, thus freeing the individual members of their own moral responsibilities. Often, you forget to visit hospitalized friends, unless somebody from the health committee has put a note in your box and supplied transportation. That's not good, I know, yet I prefer this situation to a system that relies on spontaneity, which might or might not exist when it's needed.

This has to do with my view of the kibbutz. The kibbutz is not just an idea which has materialized into a reality—it's a society of people, real-life people with real-life needs that must be dealt with. It's not a lark, a youth movement, or a summer camp. We have people with all sorts of serious problems, many old or sick people, people who need welfare; it's not a game anymore.

We must, however, find some place in our society for free, spontaneous interaction. The trouble is that people get so spoiled by the mechanism of the kibbutz, they rely on us, the secretariat, to initiate things and divide the various tasks fairly so that nothing remains unattended. Take a tiny example. Last Friday, I started a meeting of so-called intellectuals, ten to twenty people who share intellectual interests, to discuss a certain article which appeared in the paper. We met in a private room, with some tea, and we had a very interesting discussion, instead of the usual waste of time on gossip or small talk. It was very successful, yet I was the one who put the notes in people's boxes, mimeographed the article, found the host. . . . At the end of the meeting I asked that somebody else take over the organization of the evening for the following week. I found a volunteer, but I haven't heard anything to date, and I keep wondering: Did he pick an article, issue the invitations? I intend to find out today. You see [*laughing*] I can't let the baby walk by himself; I'm not willing to gamble —that's my Achilles' heel. This was a group of people who come from various branches and sub-groups, aged twenty-six to seventy; the only thing they had in common was that they enjoy an intellectual discussion rather than horseback riding or watching a football game. I'm not afraid of establishing an elite within the kibbutz, because I'm sure that such a group, even if it develops, which is highly unlikely, cannot gain any special privileges, only extra duties. This could become a leadership group and I'll be pleased if such will be the case. It is, however, highly improbable, for a kibbutz is a completely democratic society, where the complete ignoramus has as much to say as the most learned professor, and the criticisms of both are equally significant. So a real elite, in a sociological sense, cannot develop here. If we do have a set of potential leaders, they can't form a defined group with a network of social interrelationships, because they are diffused throughout the sub-groups, age groups, and branches in the kibbutz.

It's been my experience that it isn't difficult to find people willing to fill various public roles in the kibbutz. Refusals do occur from time to time, and receive a lot of our attention, yet the majority of people we turn to are willing to cooperate. Our basic administrative problem, I think, is that the kibbutz is run in too centralized a fashion. Centralization is a tradition here. It's a good way to maintain strict control over the budget of the kibbutz, and it is fairly convenient for the individual member who has one office to turn to for the satisfaction of all his needs. Yet I find it inappropriate today. As a result, many of the existent committees are devoid of real responsibility and cannot alleviate any of the pressure on the secretariat. This may, in turn, discourage people from participating in committee work, for no one wants to spend time on insignificant activities when real decisions are made elsewhere. Many former secretaries have perpetuated this problem, though, for it has been more effective for them to act directly, without delegating authority to committees. I share the opposing opinion with Noam, the general secretary, and we would both like to revive the different committees, even if it entails some friction and conflict within the administrative structure. I support allocating budgets to various committees, and giving them the authority to conduct their own business, even if there are differences of opinion within the administration. Some risk must be taken. Presently, too many things require my personal attention, since the committees which should deal with them are frequently rendered helpless. I particularly resent having to deal with the mundane problems of possessions, decorations, items in the private rooms, things with which I can't really sympathize. Yet often I have to go into such matters, because nobody else does and I think it's important to take prompt action on members' appeals.

As social secretary I chair our committee on social affairs. It's a nominally autonomous committee, but it has no authority in monetary matters. It deals with every kind of personal matter. Let me give you an example of our agenda last week. First we heard the request of a military pilot who asked to take a leave of absence from the kibbutz for a year. Indirectly this is a financial decision because, although our approval doesn't *cost* any money, it represents a financial loss for the kibbutz since this pilot's salary will go, during that year, into his private bank account and not to the kibbutz. We heard his reasons and approved his request, which will now be brought to the general assembly for its approval. If there are no objections, then our decision becomes final.

Our second case concerned rules for travel abroad. There had been a set of rules, but during the last few months we have been revising it and now it's ready to be brought before the general assembly. There are two more steps I have taken regarding this matter: I have passed the document to the secretariat and to the travel committee and asked for their comments.

We reviewed a third matter: A member wanted to work outside the kibbutz. This request was first discussed by our work committee, which is very active and central. In that particular case, the decision of the work committee was negative since the man was considered indispensable in his branch. He didn't accept the decision, however, claiming that he had a deep personal need to work for a while outside the kibbutz. This became, therefore, an issue for the social committee. We heard the man's case, though we still haven't made a decision on the matter.

Many cases we deal with are appeals against former decisions made by a specific committee. Another recent problem: An apartment was renovated and the owner wants a window here and not there. (It frequently drives me crazy to have to waste hours on such trifles!) The building committee rejected his request and since he insisted on his plan, it came to the social committee's attention. We agreed with the building committee. In this case, the man still has the right to bring his request before the general assembly. Here I enter the problem more directly, because I firmly believe that the general assembly of a big, established kibbutz like ours shouldn't have to deal with the problem of a single window in a renovated apartment! I see this as a counterproductive step, a process of trivializing the value of the assembly. Besides, the discussion of a matter like this by such a large forum can be neither efficient nor constructive. Furthermore, its mere occurrence implies that all the former committees that have tried to arrive at a decision are totally impotent.

So I talked with the man several times. He said to me, "But I want to bring it before the assembly," and I said, "And I don't want this to happen." "It's my legal right," he said. "Of course it is," I consented. Still, I visited him again and finally convinced him to accept the decision of an *ad hoc* forum comprised of three institutions: the secretariat, the social committee and the building committee. We all sat together one evening and finally closed the issue. . . . But think of all the time I dedicated to this matter!

I care a great deal about the welfare of our general assembly. You hear a lot of talk about it; it's a sore point with many central members. We have about six hundred adults, yet rarely do we have more than one hundred people present at the assembly. When two hundred are there, it's a remarkable occasion. Many people have searched for remedies for the situation, which also occurs in many kibbutzim. One solution is fairly simple: Introduce personal topics to the assembly's agenda. Having a hot debate about a window, or a quarrel between two families about whose turn it is to enter a newly built apartment is sure to attract a large number of members who don't normally attend. Routine meetings about the annual budget, school problems, or long-term building plans are much less interesting. But if it's a question of attracting people, why not go a step further and show a pornographic movie for the first ten minutes of the assembly meeting? People will stay for thirty minutes after the film due to sheer inertia!

I don't agree with such a remedy because I don't want to pretend that the general assembly meeting is something it isn't. It's just an instrument; either it serves its function or it doesn't. People don't view their attendance as a symbol of solidarity within the community or as a requirement of our democratic structure. Young people especially don't feel they have to participate. In some large kibbutzim, an alternative institution has been introduced, a counsel of delegates, perhaps fifty people, which is elected to replace the general assembly made of the entire community. It might not be such a bad idea, but here in Makom it hasn't yet been accepted. In the meantime, our shrunken assembly of about one hundred people who voluntarily attend the weekly Saturday night meetings is a very efficient tool. It's easy to make decisions there, and some decisions which would have taken months to be approved in the old days are voted on immediately. Some would say that it's a destructive efficiency, though. . . .

When I was elected social secretary, I was determined to carry out this impossible task and to finish my term in one piece. Theoretically, I knew I could do it, yet it was an important test I wanted to pass in real life. This job is considered one which shortens one's life expectancy and costs one many friends; therefore, one is presumed to hate every moment of it. When elected, the secretary becomes, in a sense, a victim of the society. I don't agree, however; it needn't be so demanding or traumatic and I set out to prove this to myself. The secret is in seeing the role as a personal challenge. If you do so, then you can cope with all the daily insults and frictions that the role entails. In this way, the pettiness, the ugliness become marginal phenomena which might even make one smile. Now that my second year as social secretary is almost over and my term will be up soon, I can say that I have faced my personal challenge. I could even go on for another two-year term, but I no longer find it interesting, so I'd prefer to relinquish the job. Furthermore, I have realized that one has a greater impact on society outside the role than in it. The role is confining, it makes you too responsible, whereas social changes require risks, a type of abandon. Besides my personal target, I have also had some more public goals. I was disturbed by the atmosphere of constant criticism and discontent within the kibbutz; I consider this a lack of pride in the kibbutz, which is dependent on solidarity. I have noticed that when members appear outside they present a rather positive, even proud facade, but inside the community, at home, they complain about everything. This was something I wanted to change, but how? I decided to put up an optimistic front, smiling even if it's often artificial, always to talk about things positively. Some close friends of mine thought I was bluffing, but I'm sure there's an element of truth in my bearing. A kibbutz is a place where the public mask frequently sets the tone. In many situations the atmosphere one creates may increase the morale, and this in turn produces real change. A kibbutz may suffocate in its own atmosphere of self-pity and pessimism, even though objectively it may be as well off as another, more cheerful kibbutz. I assumed that the social secretary would be a key person in this process. Because people expect me to lament and sermonize constantly, I have made it a point to behave in a completely different fashion. Smiling made it easier for me as well, and what began as a mere front has become a real part of me. I haven't gotten into serious fights with anyone and, even if there were bursts of anger, I have been able to shake my opponent's hand a week later. Perhaps I am lucky, because I have always been the kind of person for whom it is easy to communicate with other people, even on touchy matters, and communicating is about 70 percent of my job.

Sometimes at the end of a long day of listening and talking, I ask myself what I have accomplished. People may say I deal all day with extinguishing fires and making compromises, that I don't even start to direct and initiate more important issues. Perhaps I'm naïve, but I believe that my daily occupation with trifles is probably more significant than highly organized and planned activities.

When I finish my term as secretary, I want to work at Ginat for a year, with my wife and children; afterwards, I'd like to return for a while if possible to physical labor—to the fields and the open sky. I still have a dream of finding a channel for creative expression, although I don't see how I am going to realize that dream. Above all, I want to return to the rank and file of kibbutz members, because I have realized that beyond the confines of one's appointed role, one can contribute to society in a much more profound and even revolutionary manner. As long as I'm secretary, I cannot focus on socialism and spiritual drive when the plumbing is leaking.

People say of Amos: "He's an excellent man as well as an inspiring teacher. What this community needs is ten more people of his caliber. We can't allow him to go to Ginat, we need him here."

M E N A C H E M (age 70)

Menachem was born in 1908 and immigrated to Molad from Poland in 1934. During the division of 1952, he joined Makom and was immediately given the job of economic coordinator in his new home. Later, he also served as kibbutz treasurer. Although we spoke about the division also, I will concentrate on Menachem's analysis of the economic situation at Makom.

Presently I am the cost accountant at Makom and I understand that you wanted to learn about our economic state of affairs. Very well, I'll give you my version of the situation, but I want to tell you a little story first.

Several years ago I was arrested in Russia and was sentenced to fifteen years in a labor camp in Siberia. I don't want to go into the circumstances of my arrest, but, anyway, I was released after a few months and returned to Israel. I want to tell you one minor episode, however, which is of great significance from my point of view.

I was in a prison which served as a way station for convicts who were en route to Siberia. While most people stayed there for two or three days, my detention there lasted three months. I had the chance to meet hundreds, perhaps even thousands, of people and I tried to pass the time by listening to their stories and telling and retelling mine. So it happened that day after day I was telling prisoners about the kibbutz and how it works. I couldn't avoid it because there was always one prisoner from the day before who told the newcomers: "He's from a kibbutz in Israel; ask him to tell you about it."

Well, there were two reactions to my story. It's amazing how many times I heard these two reactions from so many different people. People would say: "We believe every word you say, of course, but tell us two things: Do you have a police station and a prison in your kibbutz? And can you buy a liter of brandy there?" If I answered no to one of these questions, people frequently added, "Then your story must be just a fairy tale. You can't maintain a village without a prison and police and no one wants to live in a place where you can't buy brandy."

Well, let's forget about the brandy, but the first point gave me much to consider. I repeatedly ask myself whether they perhaps were right: How can we live without any formal law enforcement? My conclusion is that in the kibbutz the disciplinary tool is the atmosphere which is created by the total community. If a person cheats me once or twice, I don't care. But I wait until it becomes known and then the social atmosphere will take care of the matter, and the individual will either have to change his behavior or leave.

All this is to say that our economic success is just one part of the story, while the social and personal factors certainly play the more important role.

As cost accountant, I compile all our costs and profits. I compute each individual branch, then determine the finances for the whole kibbutz; as a result, we can measure the profit of every branch in the kibbutz and use this data for future planning. Administratively, I am under the authority of the secretariat, to which I submit my accounts and reports.

Makom has two main productive branches, agriculture and industry. Our industry centers primarily on the cannery (what we call the "olive factory") and metal projects. These enterprises make much more money than the agricultural branches. Among our agricultural endeavors, the most profitable one is the cotton fields, but this area requires irrigation throughout the summer, which is a serious problem for us. The amount of land we allot to the cotton is in direct proportion to the amount of water we can spare in the summer. Since it's a highly profitable crop, we try to conserve water in many different ways—by digging artificial lakes, etc.; still, all we can allow ourselves is three thousand *dunams** of cotton. With our expertise, land, and manpower, we could double the size of this branch.

Other agricultural branches are also problematic because the State sets certain production quotas, and, as long as the kibbutz stays within the limits of these quotas, it is subsidized by the State. This applies to our cattle and poultry farms; we try to stay within the limits because, without subsidies, these branches wouldn't bring in any profit. So, in all branches of agriculture, development is severely limited.

On the other hand, the kibbutz cannot depend exclusively on industry—no way. A kibbutznik doesn't like to work on the line in a factory;

*One *dunam* is equivalent to 1,000 square meters.

it simply doesn't agree with our mentality. Take a young man who has just returned from three years of military service; you can't put him into industrial work. If you put him on a tractor, combine, or a cotton-picking machine he is content, even though he knows that agricultural work isn't very profitable. Nobody can pinpoint the red line which separates economic problems from social problems. The most valuable resource of the kibbutz is its people, and this cannot be ignored. One cannot take only purely economic factors into consideration and ignore the fact that most men want to work in agriculture. The human satisfaction is, from our point of view, at least as important as the profit we're making. Although these human factors cannot be conventionally calculated, they're nevertheless an important component in our general formula.

In practice, we try to help those people who do work on the assembly lines by allowing them one to three months of agricultural work per year. This works out well because agricultural work is seasonal and demands extra people for short durations; however, it still doesn't solve all the problems generated by routine industrial work.

For the same reason, we try to improve the technological efficiency of our factories, so that we can increase productivity without adding more workers. Another method we use is rotating personnel within the division. After two or three years of administrative work, we rotate, so that the chief administrator becomes a regular worker again and vice versa. Actually, we have no problem in filling the administrative and scientific positions in our industrial divisions; these jobs are indeed a challenge and many of our offspring have the degrees in engineering, economics, and other necessary fields of expertise. Our factories are also clearly different from urban ones in the way that all workers participate in the decision-making and planning processes, so they don't feel exploited by the system.

In spite of our problems of manpower we don't use any hired workers in our factories, with the exception of about ten experts who have been working on our metal project for years. The lack of workers is especially severe in the food industry, since our production depends on raw materials which have very short life spans. We produce pickles, for example, and have to treat all the cucumbers and onions within two or three weeks. In order to cope with such seasonal pressures we draft workers from all divisions of the kibbutz: School teachers (this season is during the school recess, anyway), secretaries, everybody is mobilized. The food factory usually employs about seventy workers; in the "hot" season it needs about 170. We also mobilize all the temporary residents we happen to have at the time—Ulpan students, volunteers, and *garin* members—and introduce night shifts for people who volunteer to work after their regular work is done.

The harvest, although also seasonal, is somewhat easier to organize, for various reasons. Until recently, we used to buy a large portion of the vegetables that we preserved. Lately we have been growing most of the vegetables on the kibbutz, which increases our profits. Harvesting is done by sophisticated agricultural machines or, in the case of olives, by our schoolchildren. The important fact is that we avoid employing hired labor. I believe that this is one of the factors which keep our sons from leaving the kibbutz. People feel more at home and more involved in our autonomous economy; they would feel completely different if they met strange workers in every corner of the kibbutz.

Sixty percent of the adult kibbutz members work in the service divisions—education, administration, kitchen, laundry—and 40 percent work in the productive branches. Of that 40 percent, two-thirds are employed by industry and the remaining third by agriculture. Actually, very few people work in agriculture because we operate no branches that require any manual labor. With the aid of mechanical innovations, we've been able to increase production while using a smaller number of workers. We have excellent farmers here, I can assure you of that. It's incredible what we have been able to accomplish in such a short period of time. . . .

I still remember the Valley when I came to Molad in 1934. It didn't resemble the present place at all. Going out at night, for example, you now can identify all the settlements by their electric lights and it's impossible to get lost around the area. When I came, however, the Valley was completely dark at night. I used to drive our milk cart at night to the central dairy plant, which was situated in another village, and it wasn't unusual at all to lose the way, especially on rainy nights. . . .

Makom was built under particularly difficult conditions. When the group moved to its present location in 1936, it thought it could profit from the experience of the other settlements which had been living in the vicinity for several years. The early beginnings proved, however, that the climatic conditions of Makom, although so close to other settlements, were entirely different. The land needs artificial irrigation for almost every crop; the soil is heavy and somewhat salty, and the local water is salty as well. These conditions caused the settlers immense difficulties; in addition to the agricultural drawbacks, Makom's settlers had to support themselves independently from the beginning. Actually, agricultural experts who inspected the land greatly discouraged the settlers by concluding that the local conditions made it impossible to undertake any intensive farming. Add to this the fact that the more established neighbors refused to share their water with this intruding kibbutz—and what else do you need for failure? Indeed, I have studied the early stages of the economic development of Makom and I found that no fewer than thirteen different branches were started and abandoned after they proved unproductive. Pomegranate orchards, a textile factory, shoe making, and sheep raising were just a few of the abortive agricultural experiments. People who stayed here, and managed to achieve what you see now, must have had exceptional faith and dedication to overcome all these obstacles!

From 1952 on, several factors combined to contribute to the great economic success of this kibbutz. The first sons of Makom graduated from high school and returned from the Army and they were of immense help to the kibbutz. Also, we suddenly received a much greater water supply when several good wells were discovered in the Gilboa area and we reached an agreement to receive a fair share of any newly found water. A loan from the agricultural center was also granted for the first time at about the same period. (The agricultural center of the Jewish Agency had particularly taken upon itself to support five extremely poor kibbutzim, and Makom was amongst these five. This enabled us to get loans and credit under reasonable terms.) The German reparation money started to pour in at about this time. The original decision was to use this money only for special public purposes, such as memorial buildings and cultural projects, but later, due to the economic situation, it was decided to use it for the current budget of the kibbutz. Last among the contributing factors, I'd put ourselves—namely, the new group that arrived from Molad. It's true that we were experienced workers and our younger members bridged the generation gap in Makom, but I don't think that it's fair to say that it's due to us that the kibbutz suddenly started to flourish. All the factors I have mentioned were at least as important.

I want to complete my little economic history by returning to my story from the Russian prison. I don't think that our economic intuition is our secret charm; it's our social spirit which preserved us. I believe that our most profitable undertaking is rearing children. The core of people who first settled this location were an outstanding intellectual elite, much more intellectual than the average kibbutznik elsewhere. Every single one of them could easily have become an administrator or a branch coordinator, yet this kibbutz decided to allocate its best people to education and child care. Furthermore, whereas several years ago the average birth rate in the kibbutzim was .80 children per member, in Makom it was 1.25 children per member. So we have had many children (and still do), and, although people complain about the crowded childrens' houses, the difficult physical conditions and the number of adults who have to work in child care, I think that herein lies our success. We suffered a lot, we ate only half an egg, but we raised a lot of good children and provided them with the best possible education. This is our kibbutz talisman, our secret. As the result of all this, today 60 percent to 70 percent of the adult members are sons and daughters who were born or educated here (including their "imported" spouses), and it's this second generation who today carry the entire social and economic responsibility of the kibbutz. So, if you want the formula for our "economic miracle," our secret, it's all here in a nutshell, as formulated by an economically oriented accountant. . . . That's what we started with then: a personal-social factor which became a major determinant in our economic success story.

Y A I R *(age 32)*

Yair is Chaim's son. He is presently the work coordinator of the kibbutz and most of our conversation centered on this very central role in Makom's structure.

We have two people who function as work arrangers: a woman responsible for the work of women members and a man who organizes the men's work. The main job of the work arrangers is to provide substitute workers and to organize the daily work schedules of temporary residents and children. The work coordinator is in charge of the long-range problems; he steps in when an arranger encounters fundamental problems that he can't solve. The coordinator is elected for two years and he participates in various activities of the secretariat. I have been in this role for six months now. Before that, for ten years, I worked in the cattle shed. My new job was a drastic change for me. At my regular job I used to wake up every day at 5:00 A.M., fresh and happy to face the new morning and the coming workday. Now, I open my eyes with a sigh, asking myself: Again? I wish I didn't have to face another day of dealing with the same problems. Actually, I don't consider my present job as work at all; I just spend my whole day talking, which I don't enjoy at all.

Half of my time is spent as a go-between, pleading with people. I have to take care of our most difficult work assignments, namely, the work in the dining room and the kitchen, where people take turns and usually don't work on a long-term basis. I go to those branches in which the arranger couldn't complete his business by himself, pleading with people, trying to convince them to move where we need them most. You see, it's not an army, where I, as a commander, have power over my men, nor is it a private enterprise where I can threaten people with dismissal or some other sanction if they don't follow my orders. My only method is persuasion, and if that fails I can call the work committee and ask for their advice. In severe cases we can oblige someone to obey; but, in fact, our decisions have very weak teeth.

Let me give you an example. In the kitchen we usually have eight workers, mostly women—four of whom are regular cooks while the others, usually more temporary people, help with the routine work. Recently it so happened that two young women who were regular cooks left to study and we couldn't find replacements for them. Pretty soon, two more women notified us that they, too, wouldn't be continuing their work in the kitchen. So the entire regular team had left within the span of a week. We did manage, somehow, to serve the food, but don't ask me how it tasted. Well, in this emergency situation, we went over the whole list of women, noting possible candidates for kitchen work. These women were working in other branches, naturally, and if they agreed to transfer to the kitchen, I first had to convince their present branch coordinators to let them go. The branch coordinators were far from sympathetic. Each branch is a kingdom in itself, guarding its own workers. I know, however, the kind of pressure our branches face, and, indeed, it's incredible that they can accomplish so much with such a limited work force. We're always short of hands, and transferring people from one branch to another is my most difficult task. Well, I found two or three women who were capable of both cooking and organizing the team (it's a bad business to organize an all-women team, I'm telling you), and we devised ways of replacing them in their current positions—but all of the women refused to work in the kitchen.

It went to all the possible institutions—secretariat, work committee, social committee—and in spite of all the decisions, they refused to obey. Each one of the women involved was talked to four or five times individually, but nothing helped. Finally, we had to assign a man to run the kitchen, which is something we were reluctant to do since men are so urgently needed in the production branches.

This is a good example of the role I play. Our manpower grows 1 percent a year (in other words, six people are added to our work force each year), no more, and the services keep demanding more and more manpower. We're lucky that our production is so high that we can maintain all those services. Five years ago, the division between services and production was nearly equal in terms of annual work days. Today, however, only 38 percent work in production. The services continue to grow in proportion to the rise in our standard of living. Surprisingly, it's not child care which demands more workers, because our birth rate is pretty stable. It's the other services—care for the elderly, selling in our stores, etc.—which have grown bigger recently. Our main problem is demographical—we have a lot of children to take care of and a growing number of old people, too. The middle age level is relatively small.

I think we have about 250 people between the ages of twenty-five and forty-five, and they have to take care of all the rest. The older members, even after sixty, work hard, and I hope we'll be like them when we reach their age, but they no longer take positions of responsibility and they can't be placed in the most demanding areas of work. It's very rare for a woman after forty-five to continue working in a child care or teaching position. They work in various stores, in sewing workshops, or in similar fields. We have another difficult age group—the young members between twenty and twenty-five. This group consists of about one hundred people who are pretty indecisive and haven't yet decided whether or not they will remain in the kibbutz. After the young people return from the Army, they usually enter what is called the third year of service (actually it is the fourth year for men now that their military service is three years); then they usually take a year on leave, try to make money, and travel abroad before settling down. It's a long transition period before about half decide to come back and settle in the kibbutz. The others find their places elsewhere.

Generally, however, my greatest headache is with women. It is much more complicated to organize them as a group. We have about two kibbutz women for every man enrolled in a university or college. Other women, who are in the kibbutz, are also very frequently absent from work —they have different courses meeting on different days each week, they're sick more often, they go to doctors outside the kibbutz for different treatments, or they just take a day off here and there. Most of them work with children and, therefore, *must* be replaced during their absences. It was therefore decided that every woman who works in a managerial position or in various jobs outside the kibbutz has to give one day a week to the work arrangement of the kibbutz, so that she can be used to replace those women missing in the children's homes or the kitchen. In addition, we use *garin* members as replacements, but we don't always have a *garin* here. This is a constant source of difficulty for the women's work arranger, who frequently comes to me, tearful, after having been rudely rejected by a woman whom she approached and tried to send as a replacement somewhere. Some women are known to be so rude that the work arranger won't even attempt to get their cooperation! Interestingly, it frequently happens that I go to the uncooperative members and solve the problem in five minutes, right after the arranger's attempts were flatly refused. My intervention works, however, with problematic men as well, not just with women. It works in about 90 percent of the cases. I don't attribute this to my charm or talents of persuasion —traits which I think I lack anyway—but to the mere fact that I wield greater authority than a work arranger.

So, generally speaking, arranging the women's work schedule is a much more difficult task than arranging the men's. Women are absent a lot. According to my statistics they work five days a week, no more, and they work in places which can't be left unattended. Their working habits upset me on two specific points. First, they don't coordinate their absences among themselves in their branches, so that it won't happen that two of a team of four nursery-school teachers will be absent on the same day—they just notify the arranger, without any concern for the consequences. Secondly, when they take time off to attend a class or seek medical treatment, although they may be back by 11:00 A.M. or at noon, they don't return to help in their branch but take the remaining time off as well.

Men are more responsible. Yes, I know I'm generalizing, and that there are exceptions to the rule amongst both sexes, that's true. In the cowshed we had one worker who was obsessed with horse racing and had to attend all the races, and another who made a hobby of skin diving. They never took leaves simultaneously, though, and they privately arranged to substitute for one another without even bothering the arranger. Because of independent arrangements such as these, the men's arranger has about five replacement problems a day, never more, while the women's has ten to fifteen replacements on a typical day. It's partly her fault, too, because she ought to be more strict and less tolerant of women's whims. Being a woman, though, it's difficult for her to see the system from a different perspective. I think that it would probably be more effective if a man ran the women's work arrangements too, but we can't spare another man for that job—we'd have to take him out of a productive branch. That's my opinion, of course, and the women arrangers don't agree with me on the matter. Men have the problem of military reserve service but that's more manageable, especially because of the higher number of private reciprocal substitute arrangements that exist in the productive branches, in which most men are concentrated.

In terms of longer-range work arrangements, our main problem is that it's very difficult to move people between the branches, because naturally each branch tries to protect itself from losing its workers. This situation manifests itself in frequent conflicts within the secretariat, where the services and social secretaries might refer to me and the economic coordinator on such issues as placing yet another man in one of the service branches. The composition of the secretariat is such that it's predictable who will take which side, but the candidate has a voice in the matter, also. A recent example concerned a young man who has just graduated from the university. They needed somebody in the cowshed to replace me as the branch coordinator when I became work coordinator, and they set their cap on this young man. At the same time, our school was extremely short of teachers and the school administration decided to request him for the school. First, they had to convince him to work with children rather than with cows, but, once they made it on the individual level, they also won the case and the democratic system determined that he become a teacher.

In spite of the priority often given to the service fields rather than the production branches, we have been able to increase our productivity. This is a result of luck coupled with a lot of brains, initiative, and effort which we have cooperatively invested in these branches. Our wealth comes mainly from our industries but I still have my doubts about the role of factories in a kibbutz. I know the kibbutz cannot make a living from agriculture alone, yet the character of our industrial projects is not suitable to a kibbutz. The metal factory requires extremely difficult physical labor and a great part of the work there is terribly routine. The olive factory is simply boring. We must constantly strive for technological improvements which will increase productivity without enlarging the work teams. We are short of people everywhere.

Would it be possible to solve some of the problems of the work shortage by absorbing new families, especially those in the twenty-five to forty-five year old age bracket which you mentioned as being in need of reinforcement?

There are two problems involved in such a solution. First is the housing problem—we're short of housing, too. We have planned some construction projects to improve the apartments of our members, and we can't afford to invest more in building than we already have. The second problem is selectivity. We would like people of a certain caliber and with those professions we need most. We have an *ulpan* here, for example, and most of its students are Jewish and potential *olim*. The fact is, however, that we lose more people than we gain through the program; it's a negative absorption process: In some cases, the students marry our sons and daughters and then take them away.

Basically we've become a giant kibbutz, and I'm afraid of the outcome of such size. In such a large system, there's much less reciprocal responsibility. People are less acquainted and therefore less concerned with what's happening outside their immediate surroundings. In my field, this is evident in the lack of consideration of one branch towards the other. When I go to a branch looking for a man to fill a missing link in my work puzzle, the response is: "Go get your man from another branch." I have to walk around with a little booklet of information concerning how many workers are placed in each branch, how many of them I have already tapped to fill various jobs, etc. Without this booklet I forget my count, it's too big for one man's mind.

We keep growing slowly by our own internal expansion. Many of our classes have had as many as thirty children and of these about 50 percent decide to remain here. Many marry outsiders, too, thereby increasing our size. It's a big kibbutz and we have to find ways to manage it efficiently.

N O A *(age 28)*

Noa has recently been elected the women's work arranger in Makom. Until now, she has been a metapelet.

I have never held such a crucial position in the kibbutz before. It's a problem in the kibbutz—many people refuse to take public positions and I personally think they shouldn't be forced to do so. Most of the time, their refusal indicates that they aren't suitable for the job. Not everybody can be effective as a work arranger or a school administrator. Yet people are often forced to accept such positions against their wishes. How are they forced? You are approached directly and told that it's necessary that you do it. If you have any conscience at all, you consent. If you don't consent, you feel like a criminal and everyone continually reminds you of your lack of cooperation. You can avoid public positions once or twice, but they will eventually get you and you will have to accept.

In my case, I was elected and I felt that I had little choice but to accept. I had recently voiced my opinion that the women's work arranger must be a woman. This had been the situation for years: Men's work was arranged by a man, and women's work by a woman. It has become, however, increasingly difficult to find *chaverot* to undertake the women's work arrangements. People, including female members, say that women aren't strong enough to handle such a difficult position and that therefore a male team should assume women's work arranging too. I think it's degrading for women to accept such a point of view. Since I expressed my views publicly, I had no choice but to accept the job myself. It was somewhat of a challenge. And, let me tell you—now that I've been at it for about four weeks, I'm more convinced of that than ever. I wouldn't want a man to listen to all the female troubles which come to my attention. Even I am frequently ashamed to listen to all these things, and I would never want to be in a position of sharing these matters with a man. Men here often have very low opinions about the work women do and regard women as trying to take it easy instead of working seriously. What do they understand? Only last month I had three women come to tell me they had to get abortions. Could they have talked about it to a man?

My routine is pretty hectic. I get up very early in the morning, go to my office and find out about all the problems which have cropped up during the night. All through the night people leave notes pertaining to work problems: So-and-so came down with the flu; so-and-so must urgently visit her sick father, etc., etc. Solving these last-minute problems is my first priority in the morning and keeps me busy searching for replacements until about 8:00 A.M. One needs a lot of intuition to find the necessary replacements and there's a lot of legwork involved in the job, too.

When the arrangements for the present day are finally in order, I start on the requirements of the next day. I am informed about every woman who must take a trip somewhere, or is sick, and I find people to replace her. Then I delegate noontime duty at the infants' homes and the night guard duty in all the children's homes. From Tuesday on, I plan the various duties of Saturday, which is our free day. I assign people, by turn, to Saturday duties in the dining hall, children's homes, etc., and I put notices in their mail boxes accordingly. Then I get the surprises: Notes come back with all sorts of stories. If people plan to go on trips or visits on Saturday it's their responsibility to find replacements. But if they're sick, the job is mine again.

These are most of my daily chores. The vast majority of people here have a regular place of work and my most urgent problem is finding replacements for missing workers. But the assignment of regular work appointments is also my responsibility. We have a work committee, in which the work arrangers and the work coordinator—as well as some other functionaries—sit and try to solve the long-range problems. Suppose a new infants' home is to be opened, or a woman who is working as a *metapelet* is pregnant and has to be replaced for her maternity leave. We have to select candidates for these jobs, then find out if they're willing to assume the responsibilities. Mostly, these candidates have other jobs and must be replaced there—it engenders a whole chain of events. If somebody doesn't agree to accept the new position, we invite them to our committee for a hearing, and often we have to pressure a person to agree. We also meet with the various heads of branches to understand their needs. It's a big jigsaw puzzle and we're always short of workers.

The term of my office is one year. I alternate with my partner for the job on a monthly basis; so actually I spend only six months doing this work. The idea is that the pressure is too great to continue in this position for more than four weeks at a time. In my off-month, I serve as a replacement wherever I'm needed in the kibbutz.

I have found arranging work a very difficult job. It includes an incredible amount of pressure which is terribly oppressive. I feel it when I take care of my daughters, when I read them a story at night. Often, my head is elsewhere, trying to solve the many problems of work arrangement. My work keeps me busy daily until about 7:30 at night, so my husband has to cooperate in taking care of our daughters every afternoon. To be able to do this job, one's mate has to be very helpful and tolerant throughout the whole period. His help is not just technical; to be able to say, "It's so difficult," already represents a certain amount of support. I don't know how I could stand the pressure without his help.

So far I have avoided getting into fights with people—it's not my style, I'm not aggressive. I listen to people and try to use my brains instead of putting pressure on them. I think that a person doing this job should take some sort of human-relations workshop beforehand, to learn how to listen and when to react. Listening is a major component in this job. People have so many problems! It's almost like becoming a social worker. People tell you about their health or marital problems; they're not ashamed of anything. It often embarrasses me to know so much about women in the community. I'd rather not know what they tell me; I'm personally not particularly interested in the intimate details of their lives.

What I encounter more frequently than anything else is human weakness. The problem is how not to lose the proper perspective, how not to draw the conclusion that nobody works or is willing to work. Because most all the people you see, are "problem" people, you might begin to feel you live in a big cuckoo's nest, and that's not an accurate picture, of course. Often, I get the impression that everybody lives under a terrible amount of pressure here, and that actually I'm the least pressured person around; as much as I try to ask for help nicely and wisely, I often get a straight no for an answer.

Naturally it upsets me. During the first week especially, I was awfully depressed by this. I felt as if I were surrounded by mental cases. I wondered how the system kept working at all and I expected it all to collapse any minute. Well, you see everything from a very abnormal point of view, and you want to adapt to the situation. I'm very careful about not wording my reactions in strong language, about not saying what's on my mind. I also try to be really tolerant, not just to make a show of it. I don't want to be a preacher nor become an angry prophet who stands up on high and tells people below how they ought to behave. But I have done so sometimes—I'm only human.

When I took the job I expected it to be terrible. I didn't foresee the possibility of turning it into a learning experience. Now I think I am learning something, and in the future I might even be thankful for the lesson, though right now I'm largely aware of the difficulties. It's not physically difficult and all the problems are somehow finally solved. Yet frequently you face such tough situations and you're all alone and have no one to consult: It's very lonely. I haven't had a female partner so far, and the one I'm getting now is less experienced than I am. Also, I feel critical of our male work coordinator who is not sympathetic towards women's problems. So I have started talking to myself. . . [*laughs*]. But somehow I'm coping with the job and I try to maintain my good spirits.

E V A (*age 53*)

I have heard much about the cultural life of the kibbutz. I had the opportunity to participate in several cultural events and I found out that it was primarily the responsibility of the cultural committee to undertake the organization of all cultural activities. Eva has been the coordinator of this committee three times and I asked her to describe its activities.

At present I'm a student. The Holocaust disrupted my education; I didn't even manage to complete high school in Vienna. Now, after about forty years, I'm back at school studying the Bible and literature. The funny thing is that, although I have not had any formal higher education, during most of my life in the kibbutz I taught and was the coordinator of our culture committee. That's besides raising four children and—recently—grandchildren as well.

The cultural committee is one of the things which has occupied most of my time recently. Running the committee is a full-time job in our kibbutz, though it's difficult to describe what exactly takes up all one's time. In one sentence, I'd say that the coordinator of the cultural committee—with the aid of the members of the committee, of course—has to create something out of nothing. You begin by thinking about what programs to initiate—something new, something original—in the tradition of quality this kibbutz has established. Then you have to do a lot of legwork in solving all the practical problems concerned in a production. There's a saying in the kibbutz that the coordinator of the cultural committee is the one who turns off the lights when the show is over. And that indeed is true.

There are many traditional events which the cultural committee sponsors; for example, our Friday night gathering. Every Friday, an hour after dinner, the adults gather in the dining hall for a cultural event. It could be a concert, a show, or a lecture given by either local performers or guests. The various kibbutz movements have newsletters with descriptions of events organized in different kibbutzim. Even with the shared information, it's essentially the responsibility of the local coordinator to initiate and organize the Friday gathering. Over the years, it's become more difficult to think of interesting ideas for Friday night events, especially since the kibbutz has grown so large and heterogeneous in terms of age and interests. We have found, for example, that local talent or programs attract a larger percentage of the population than "imported" artists or lecturers. (This, of course, is of financial importance as well, since we don't have to pay our own members, and our yearly budget must be spent carefully.) The arrangement for the routine Friday night program is the biggest single task of the cultural coordinator. I'd say it takes about one-third to half of my time.

Another routine duty involves the holidays, which are all celebrated with great pageantry in our kibbutz. Since this involves too much work and responsibility for a single group to undertake, we decided fifteen years ago to divide the various holiday responsibilities among special teams (e.g., the Passover team, the New Year's team, etc.). Each team prepares the main evening festivities of a certain holiday for several consecutive years, gaining expertise and experience in the particular traditions of the holiday. The various committees are supervised by the overall holiday committee, which is separate from the cultural committee. The celebration of the lesser holidays, as well as second or third evenings of the major ones, are organized by the cultural committee, too.

With these two responsibilities, I'd include our Friday night reception before the Sabbath dinner. Again, this is something which is presently run by a separate team, but it all began with the committee during my last term. Three years ago, when I had again accepted the coordination of our cultural committee, I had one dream which I wanted to realize and that was to initiate some Shabbat celebration in our community. In fact, thirty-four years ago, when I joined this kibbutz, I wrote an item for our newsletter entitled "Why Don't We Have a Shabbat Reception in the Kibbutz?" As a teacher, I began organizing receptions in the school, years ago, but we felt like orphans, celebrating without the participation of the adult community. The adults, however, vehemently objected to the whole idea. Why that was so, in a community which cared so much about Jewish values, is indeed not easy to understand. First of all, it had to do with material difficulties. People are used to coming to eat whenever it pleases them. But in order to have a short ritual—lighting the candles, saying the *kiddush*,* reading a poem or a paragraph from the Bible—the whole community must come together at a predetermined time. People said that they wanted to maintain their freedom. . . . Furthermore, we have a

*Traditional blessing of the wine at the beginning of the Shabbat dinner.

self-service system for our meals, and a formal Shabbat dinner requires table service, which is an extra burden for the kitchen and dining hall staff and requires special shifts of duty. But I don't know if the technical difficulties, which are indeed all surmountable, were the main objection to a custom which I wanted so much to observe. To make a long story short, two years ago I managed to win the vote, and since then the Friday festive dinner is accompanied by a short ceremony performed by a different family every week. As a compromise, however, Friday dinners are served in two shifts (we can't accommodate the whole population in our dining hall anyway); the first one at seven o'clock, with the table service and the Shabbat reception, and the second from eight o'clock on with self-service and no rituals. So everybody can have his or her choice. After we initiated this tradition, we appointed another team which took over the routine responsibility, but if anything goes wrong, the cultural committee is ultimately in charge.

Our committee is also in charge of the various study activities within the kibbutz and we are involved in discovering and encouraging local talent. The administration of all these activities is a full-time job for the coordinator of the committee.

Looking back upon my life here, I feel satisfied. I think the kibbutz is the only system in which a woman can realize her potential as both a mother and a professional, and make some sort of public contribution as well. I know some mothers-of-four in town who have pursued careers, but I think it's more difficult for them than for me. I'm among those women of the kibbutz who never complained about or seriously criticized our common lodging arrangement. I found it good for my children and liberal enough for my tastes. We have never been too strict here; we aren't extremists. If a child wanted to spend the night at his parents' room it wasn't a problem for anyone. I suffered from our poverty, from the material conditions, but not from the collective system itself. I remember the deprivations: longing for a chocolate bar, which was such a great luxury; wearing my one and only maternity dress for four months until I gave birth; when something spilled on it I would miss my dinner out of shame. I lived in a tent for almost five years, then raised my four children in a tiny hut without running water. Yet these hardships have not touched me in any deeper sense; I felt I was developing myself. I have always found something important and meaningful to do and I think there are many such areas in our life, even today, despite our affluence.

The Kibbutz
in Support of
the Individual

In our conversations, Makom's members often criticized the present administration for leaning too much towards the individual and his or her specific needs rather than emphasizing communal aims. The conflict of priorities is not simply a matter of ideological debate but of real consequence in allocating resources and manpower to the various community goals.

While "reciprocal responsibility" is frequently mentioned as a primary value of the kibbutz, stories about the old days of the kibbutz indicate that in the early stages of Makom's development the rules and aims of the collective assumed priority over the needs of the individual members. Thus, it often was the case that a member was forced by a group decision to act contrary to his own wishes. The enforced discipline was rather strict; people who chose to live within the kibbutz had to conform to the rules or decisions of the collective, denying themselves many private needs. If some of the past episodes in this area seem today cruel and difficult to accept, some of the lack of sensitivity towards human weakness and desires may be attributed to the youth and limited experience of the founding members. Another factor contributing to the self-denial of kibbutz members was the lack of funds available for personal needs. In many of the personal accounts of older members (Rachel, Zvi, Chana, Na'ama, and Shimon), regret is expressed regarding the early insensitivity of the kibbutz towards children, newcomers, and people with special talents or needs. Yet, in part, such strictness was integral to the values of the kibbutz, which were religiously observed in the early years.

Today, the harsh discipline of the past has given way to profound sensitivity towards the individual in need. Rather than trying to realize the ideal of equality in a technical sense, by institutions such as the former storehouse A, equality is understood as providing each individual with his or her special needs. Makom's members are proud of this aspect of their communal life and consider their kibbutz to be a complete welfare system, without any of the stigmatization that usually accompanies welfare. Many members and ex-members of Makom consider its health services to be superb and its support system for lonely people and aging members or members' parents incomparable to that of any other society.

In reality, however, it is impossible to meet all of the needs of all individuals. Among the members whose stories appear in the following chapter, some still express disappointment at the way in which the kibbutz responds to their specific needs.

The following chapter is divided into three sections according to sub-groups whose needs the kibbutz attempts to meet. First are newcomers to the kibbutz. Whereas the difficulties of assimilation in the early period were presented in "Absorption," this section describes the present absorption process. As the following cases demonstrate, entering the closed system of the kibbutz remains a problematic step today. For some individuals, the process of absorption is relatively smooth; for others it is rather harsh. Those individuals who actually found the process unbearable have probably already left Makom.

The next section contains four cases pertaining to family life or, rather, to the lack of it. An unmarried adult in the kibbutz may find a certain social framework to replace family life. Indeed, that is how Gila sees her life as a single woman in Makom. Interestingly, though, some of the young women who left Makom to live in town (e.g., Yael) blamed the kibbutz for creating an unbearable situation for singles in which constant, albeit implicit, pressure to marry and have children is applied, while opportunities to meet new people remain scarce. Different kinds of loneliness are those of elderly people whose children have all left the kibbutz, as in Dina's case, or of widows who remain single parents in the kibbutz (Shlomit and Naomi). Some of the individuals in these situations praise the kibbutz for its generous and considerate help (see also Devora as a case of a bereaved parent), while others point to the pain caused by the constant contact with and comparison to happy, normal family units.

Finally, a section is dedicated to the services provided for the sick and aging members of the community, certainly one of the best faces of Makom.

B E N N Y *(age 26)*

I wasn't born here. I'm an "outside child."* I don't know how it happened that I arrived at the kibbutz. I had heard a little about it from a neighbor, and when I was thirteen years old I made up my mind to join too. I didn't belong to a youth movement and I knew next to nothing about the kibbutz's way of life. Just kids' ideas, really. My parents objected at first, but I insisted, refusing to go to school in the city until they finally gave their consent. I managed to convince them and didn't have to run away. I've been here for thirteen years now and they still don't regret it [*smiling*].

I arrived at the kibbutz in 1966 as a member of a class of twenty "outside children." The kibbutz was absorbing children then, both from families of new immigrants and from town. At first we formed a separate eighth-grade class of "outside children." We lived in separate lodgings; we had our own teacher and *metapelet,* and joined the kibbutz children only for work. We socialized mostly among ourselves and had only superficial relationships with other kibbutz members. During that first year several "outside children" left or were expelled, so by the time we reached the ninth grade there were only twelve of us. We then joined the main class of kibbutz children and, from then on, we lived and were educated together. By the way, of all those twenty kids who reached the kibbutz with me, only two are now members of Makom.

The process of absorption of an "outside child" in the kibbutz is highly individual and depends primarily on the nature of the child. I know —although I don't personally remember it—that the kibbutz children are a pretty tight group. I had no problems fitting in: I felt comfortable with the kibbutz children and have always adjusted well, socially and otherwise. Many of my original group, however, left because they didn't blend in. Actually I remember that when I went home for a month during the summer vacation after my first year in the kibbutz, I wasn't especially keen on returning. I did return, though I don't quite remember why. From the second year on, the situation changed dramatically for me, since after my first return I was adopted by a kibbutz family.

My adopted father was our group's counselor. He was a young man then and had a six-year-old son. He told me that he had been asked whether or not he'd be willing to take one of us "outside children," and he agreed, choosing me. Neither of us ever regretted this. I developed a close relationship with my adopted parents; I would visit them frequently, and their presence changed my feelings about the kibbutz. Every day I spent the afternoon in their room, doing my homework. Frequently I dropped in during our morning school break, too, to eat chocolate

*Children who come to the kibbutz without their families.

[*laughs*]. This is something I learned from the kibbutz children—to eat a lot of chocolate. We're sometimes nicknamed "chocolate children."

With my adopted family I really felt at home. Whenever I was depressed they'd comfort me. They helped me in many ways. My adopted father used to work as an agricultural instructor and he had a car at his disposal; on Saturdays we took trips together. If I were ever late coming to their room, they'd come searching for me, asking what had happened. This warm relationship existed with the whole family—the grandparents and my adopted father's sisters; they all adopted me. I think it's due to them that I'm a member of Makom today.

As all "outside children," I got leave once every two months to visit my parents at home. All along, we maintained a good, warm relationship. They saw that I was happy, and this made them happy as well. It wasn't a problem having two sets of home and family. It so happened that both my real and my adopted families came from Hungary and good relationships were formed between them, too.

It was, however, understood between us that the kibbutz was my home. My parents never said: "Come back home, this is quite enough." Although my parents didn't know much about the kibbutz, they had the vague notion that it was good for children, that it provided a good education. I think that this came from the stereotype that the kibbutz was a sanctuary for town children who had problems in school and society. I was never a problem child but my parents figured that it was better for me to be in the kibbutz than on the streets of Tel Aviv.

The years passed and I was drafted into the Army. At that point I was ready to be accepted for membership in the kibbutz. All along I was just a pupil. A pupil here is a very protected being; even at seventeen, one still has a *metapelet,* one needn't worry about anything, even clean clothes are provided every morning. However, I knew many adult members and knew enough about the kibbutz life to choose to live here as an adult. In general, an outsider who wants to be accepted as a member of the kibbutz must spend a year as a candidate, and at the end of a year his membership is voted on by the kibbutz. For kibbutz children and for "outside children," the twelvth grade is considered the year of candidacy. Towards the end of this year, conversations were undertaken between the social committee and ourselves, and at the end of the year, as with adult candidates, a list of our names was announced, to offer the community a chance to raise any objections to our candidacy. Two weeks later our request to be accepted as members was brought to the general assembly, this being the established procedure for the acceptance of new kibbutz members. I was accepted before leaving the kibbutz for my army service.

Recently there has been a tendency among the young people here to postpone the act of formal acceptance of membership until somewhat later. First they go to the Army for three years (two years for girls); they then have to give another year of service and then they may take a year's leave of absence to work in town, to go abroad, whatever. Today, at the end of high school, students don't want to commit themselves. Although the act of being accepted is by no means a legal contract, and people who leave the kibbutz today are no longer regarded as traitors, as they once were, people take their decision, their signing for membership, seriously and want to be sure of what they're doing.

In my time, only seven years ago, it was highly unusual to take a year's leave of absence and my class applied *en bloc* for membership when we graduated from school. For me, it was a significant personal achievement to be accepted. It expressed my choice and my good feelings about the kibbutz form of life. My parents were happy with it as well.

R U T H *(age 40)*

Ruth is very German-looking, yet she speaks fluent Hebrew with very little trace of a foreign accent.

I was born in Germany in 1938 and arrived in Israel in 1961. I wasn't Jewish. My father was killed in World War II and I, as a child, read everything I could about the war and the Holocaust. I lived in a small town and hardly knew any Jews at all, but at fourteen I decided that when I grew up I'd live in Israel and convert to Judaism.

I felt appalled by Germany; I had to leave. It was too crowded and I didn't see any meaning to my life there. All the eating and drinking, the alcoholics in the street. . . . I wanted a completely different way of life. I also felt somehow as if I belonged to the Jewish nation and that I was obliged to contribute to this nation with all my might.

I worked as a journalist for a while and saved enough money to travel to Israel. There was an Israeli whom I had met in Germany before my immigration, a physician from Afula, and I sought some help from him in the beginning. This resulted in our marriage and our having two children, a boy and a girl.

I was received in the country with mixed feelings. A German woman coming, just when the Eichmann trial was taking place: What does she really want? I didn't speak Hebrew and I remember once walking in town and speaking German to somebody when I was rudely attacked by a young man, who screamed at me: "What are you doing here? How dare you come here? We don't want to have anything to do with you Germans!" I was shocked, and, as a result, never opened my mouth in public until I mastered enough vocabulary to speak in Hebrew. I could have told this man that I belonged to the new generation in Germany. I could have told him about my motives for joining the Jewish people but, in fact, I could see *his* point all too well.

I started studying the Jewish religion, preparing for the conversion, which required some time and wasn't at all easy. I was sent back to study and prepare more, again and again, but at last I made it. My studies have interested me a great deal. I used to visit religious homes and kibbutzim to see how Jewish holidays are celebrated, and I was deeply moved by these experiences. I have never seriously considered the possibility of living in Israel as a Christian. I see conversion as the only alternative if one wants to live permanently in this country. I have met several Christians who live here and either they're missionaries for their faith, which I resent, or they are completely confused as to their identity. I wanted my children—good, healthy children whom I am returning to the Jewish nation—to grow up with a well-defined identity as Israeli-Jews.

Well, several years later I divorced my first husband. Since our town was not too far from here, I knew Makom and some of its members and decided to move to the kibbutz with my children. This was about nine years ago. In Makom I met a widower, many years older than myself, and we were married. We had five wonderful years together, the best in my life, until he died suddenly, four years ago, exactly seven weeks after our only son was born.

Now I live here as a widow with my three children. I work as a *metapelet* in the high school, a job that I like very much.

Entering the kibbutz was a complicated process, even though the man I loved stood at my side to instruct me in all the intricacies of this society. From the outside, a kibbutz seems a wonderful place and quite easy to understand. Yet I have discovered that for someone from elsewhere, entering the kibbutz society is a very difficult thing. The kibbutz is an extremely complicated, closed, and snobbish society. The people are indeed wonderful individuals, but there aren't any greater snobs anywhere than kibbutzniks. This is something I realized from the start. Kibbutzniks would say hello to you when your paths crossed, but they wouldn't make any further contact or show the least interest in your activities. A new person could sit alone at a table in the dining hall, staring right into members' faces, but no one would join him or her; they're very occupied with their own unfinished business, perhaps, and they tend to join those people with whom they already have something in common. But beyond all these reasons, I think they're afraid, afraid of strangers and of what's outside their immediate environment. Yet they project such a sense of superiority that it's almost impossible to approach them. I believe that this superiority has been implanted in the youngsters by their parents, the founders of the kibbutz. As a person who has lived in many different places, I find that this superiority has, indeed, some objective basis. You find here a much greater proportion of individuals with unusual talents and sensitivities than anywhere else. The mere fact that adults don't have to worry about and struggle for the material aspects of life, like food, clothing, and housing, liberates these people to develop in various "higher" ways. One aspect of these unusual conditions is, however, a lack of involvement in the lives of others.

I have to mention two experiences, which I value greatly and which show that the picture isn't one-sided. First, when our little son was born (this was five years after I had joined the kibbutz, and I wasn't such a stranger anymore), I felt immense participation in our happiness. People came and visited a lot, it was wonderful. For the first time I experienced a sincere sense of sharing and caring in the community. The second experience was seven weeks later, when my husband died, and again people were indeed fantastic. I was completely heartbroken. I didn't want to recover; I wanted to die. For weeks I was completely overwhelmed with grief and throughout this long period I was never left alone. People understood my condition and provided me with constant care and support. I discovered that I had many friends when I really needed them most, and this experience has almost reversed my former opinions about the kibbutz society. Maybe this is the sense or the rhythm of the kibbutz way of life. In daily routine events everybody is very much involved in himself or herself, or with his or her own close family. But when disaster befalls someone, they come to that person's aid more than any other community would do.

I have not experienced widowhood outside the kibbutz, but I think it's probably easier here than elsewhere. My children are well taken care of and economically we have no worries whatsoever. We have a socially supportive system, with holidays, celebrations and cultural activities organized by the kibbutz. Although I'm frequently extremely sad on these occasions, I know it's good for the children to sit together with all the families, in the presence of the whole community, so that they know we are not alone. The kibbutz has also tried to provide me with a new mate, you know. . . . We have here a sort of a matchmaker who has approached me several times with various ideas [*laughs*]. I refuse even to listen. I'm just forty and have a long life before me, but I feel that being married twice is more than enough.

You told me that your older children are fourteen and sixteen now. Did they ask you about your past and the unusual step you took in coming here?

Yes, each one went through a period of being immensely occupied with my past and origin. My daughter when she was eight or nine, and my son when he was somewhat older. Of course they knew even earlier that all my family lived in Germany and they met their German grandmother when she visited. When my daughter started to ask me questions, I told her everything frankly, although I gave her the story of the Holocaust gradually, in ways which I thought were appropriate for her age. She asked me to repeat my account again and again until she felt she knew it well enough and her interest was satisfied. My son went through a similar process; when he felt his curiosity was satisfied he dropped the whole thing. I told them quite a lot about the Holocaust but not all the horrible details which I discovered in my youth. I don't think they should grow up with the same sense of guilt and obligation which characterized my youth. After all, they are Israeli and Jewish. My guilt feelings have also abated since I've been here. I feel I have returned three people to the Jewish race.

J O A N *(age 32)*

Joan is an English teacher. She came to the kibbutz six years ago.

Well, as people have probably already told you, it isn't easy to be a kibbutznik. Had it been easier, there would be more than 3 percent of the Israeli population in kibbutzim, don't you think?

I was born in New York and grew up in an entirely different atmosphere. As a child, my parents always stressed how important it was that I learn and achieve, that I become "somebody." They provided me with the best conditions; I had a desk with just the "right" kind of drawers, I had a lamp which was carefully chosen. They used to close my door and say: "Now it's time for your studies." They checked my school work and showed great interest in my progress. As a result, I graduated from high school with good grades, got accepted at Berkeley and finished M.A.'s in two areas, English and social work.

When I graduated, I returned to New York and lived in my own apartment, near my parents. I was fed up with the counterculture and searched for my roots in Judaism and my family. Though still young, I obtained a good position as a social worker. I was my own boss, had my own secretary, and felt satisfied with my personal development.

As long as I was concerned with the development of my career, I hadn't given any thought to marriage or to children. I took care of myself first of all. I see the profound difference between my development and that of kibbutz women of my age. They take their high-school studies very lightly and then enter the Army. While in the Army, or even before, they feel they must find a mate—they must catch a good husband before it's too late. Then they immediately have three or four children in a row, and never have a moment for themselves. When they reach thirty, about my age, they suddenly discover a great void inside them; they realize that they have no profession, no education, no interests. Perhaps it isn't too late at thirty to develop one's personality, I'm not sure. I was never afraid that I wouldn't "catch" a husband, even after age twenty-five. This is something I try to pass on to my girl students in high school and they seem to be listening. On the other hand they keep reminding me that in the kibbutz it's different, that the choice of men is limited and they have to hurry up in the mating game. Maybe they are right.

I met my husband at a party in New York and found out that he was from Makom; he was a man who had traveled a lot, searching for his place in life. We got married and decided to return to the kibbutz and we've been here since 1972. My absorption here is quite a story. . . . When I arrived I didn't speak any Hebrew and I went through a terribly difficult time. My husband returned to his old group of friends, none of whom spoke any English. I used to sit in their company and go through the agony of feeling a complete stranger. Furthermore, I felt a lot of envy directed towards me and my husband. The women envied me for "catching" him and were testing me to see whether I deserved him. The men envied him for his trips and adventures before he married and also for finding an "American millionairess" for a wife. . . . In Israel, every American is a "millionaire," and the fact that I'm far from rich had no effect on the image. Perhaps I misunderstood a lot, but that was what I felt at the time.

I was tremendously driven to master the language as quickly as possible. I felt I had to understand. At first I went to the local *ulpan* but it was too slow for me so I dropped out; instead, I went to work in the nursery school and started picking up words from the children.

In addition, I had a private tutor and I learned quite a bit on my own. During the summer, however, I went to an *ulpan* in town and that's where I made most of my progress. It was an excellent course, with first-rate teachers, students of my level, and a competitive atmosphere; that's the best way for me to learn fast. It gave me a good foundation and I have advanced a great deal by myself since then. Presently, I speak with complete ease; as you see, I read and write freely and I'm even teaching history in Hebrew and can correct my pupils' mistakes. Well, that says something about *their* level as well as mine, but we'll come to that later.

(By the way, about my experience that the best learning occurred in a competitive atmosphere—I know this is contrary to the kibbutz ideology about studying and teaching. I do feel that I deviate from the common ideology in this sense and I'm aware that I create competition among my students as well, even unintentionally. But I truly don't care; as long as they learn, I think any method is justified.)

Formally, I was well accepted in the kibbutz: I was a member's wife and my handwriting didn't have to be submitted to a graphologist. But excepting that formality. . . . As I said, I was given work in the nursery school in order to learn Hebrew, which was indeed a good idea for that purpose. The work itself gave me a bad shock. Here I was, an academic professional, reduced to the status of a *metapelet*'s helper in a nursery school. I was given instructions to carry out simple manual tasks and I couldn't even follow the instructions. I, who used to have both a cleaning woman *and* a secretary back home, was given a strange rubber broom and a bucket of water, and was told to wash the floors. What is a stone floor anyway? Who ever heard of such a thing and how was I supposed to clean it with water? I had never seen any such thing done before, yet here everyone behaved as if it were the most natural thing, and I was supposed to know how or else I was probably an idiot. . . . Nobody bothered to explain anything, and, even if they did feel like explaining, I wouldn't have been able to follow their instructions with my poor thousand-word vocabulary. How does one wash the basin—what sort of detergent should be used and how am I to know which bottle is for what purpose? Nobody explained anything, yet I was expected to know everything right away, as if the whole world used exactly these kibbutz methods and nothing else [*laughs*].

I imagine the methods I used were quite clumsy and the other workers kept staring at me and talking about my great skills. . . . They used to leave little written notes for me, in Hebrew of course: "do the beds," "sweep the floors," as if unaware that I couldn't read yet. I felt horrible. I hated getting instructions—I had never been used to it—and I felt completely discouraged in my position.

I, for my part, also behaved stupidly, although I didn't know any better. For example, I understood that my working shift ended at 1:30 P.M., so at that hour, on the dot, I'd leave whatever I was in the midst of doing and rush to my room. I didn't know then that here one never works by the clock, that I was supposed to finish certain tasks and not disappear like that. I imagine how the other people in my team gossiped about me. . . . Perhaps they really didn't, but that's how I feel.

Besides all the difficulties of adjustment, I was pregnant at the time and felt miserable. Every evening I used to cry bitterly in our room. My husband was very understanding and supportive. He used to tell me: "Listen, if it's that bad, let's go elsewhere. We're just experimenting. When you have had enough of it, we'll leave." This made it much easier for me. I felt I didn't *have* to adjust, and this made the pressure bearable. Finally, knowing that I didn't have to adjust, I did eventually adjust.

Well, I coped somehow with the first few months and I felt better once I could speak Hebrew freely and understand conversation. I became an English teacher in my second year and this certainly was an improvement over my first job. But I had another crisis when my first daughter was born and we arrived together at the infants' home. Again, there was the same difficulty of understanding what was required of me, facing the assumption that every method used in the kibbutz is well known and certainly the best. I couldn't figure out what my responsibility was and what was the *metapelet*'s. Where should I put the soiled diapers or my daughter's bottle? How should I put a diaper on her? I didn't know these things and nobody bothered to teach me. I had the impression that the whole kibbutz was standing there, staring at me. How funny and awkward I was—I used safety pins to diaper my baby, for example. *They* had another method: you turned the baby right and left, and there he was, nicely bundled without any pins. But I never had a baby brother here, nor worked with infants during my high-school days, so how was I supposed to know? Just as during my first weeks in the nursery school, I felt utterly dumb—never before had it happened to me. . . . But as much as I suffered then, I believe it's a healthy experience for everyone, to feel dumb once in one's lifetime. I know how it feels not to understand. I will never forget this feeling—how I couldn't figure out what a kibbutz was, what they were talking about in their strange language, and how was I going to become a good mother! This was my transition from America to the kibbutz.

My daughter was a very difficult baby. She screamed a lot and I lived under the impression that the whole kibbutz was watching to see how I coped. The competition between the mothers in the infants' home was overwhelming. They were constantly comparing: whose baby was the most calm, whose gained more weight, ate better, sat up first, was the most friendly. It made me terribly tense.

My work as a teacher has enabled me to experience what is going on in our school, and to meet with the parents of my students. The immense difference between the atmosphere in my home as a child and the kind of atmosphere characteristic of my students' homes has been one of my dramatic discoveries. They're simply not encouraged to study, to achieve —it's amazing! The first question parents ask me when they come for a conference is: "How is my child doing socially, is he [or she] popular and active?" That's their first and greatest concern. Only afterwards do they ask how they are doing in their studies, and it's obvious that the parents invest very little time or effort in this area at all. If I tell one of them, "Your child doesn't read Hebrew fluently. Would you work with him daily and help him?" the reaction is, "That's your business, not mine." Parents prefer to keep their contacts with their children as smooth and as happy as possible; so why introduce the tension of school work and achievements into the family room? I have endless confrontations with parents on this issue.

Parents here are too permissive; they throw all the academic responsibility on the teachers and often refuse to participate in any way. Children follow this example and often refuse to make an effort themselves. The whole atmosphere suppresses any signs of ambition or competition. No wonder the educational results are so poor. I worry about it because I have two daughters growing up in this system and, despite all my personal influence, I am afraid that they will turn out like the rest of the kibbutz children. I firmly believe that we are wrong in our educational approach: Children need a fairly strict framework; they must face challenging demands. Otherwise they grow wild or, at best, become mediocre people. People may tell you there's a great drive to study at a later stage of life, that we have so many university students, etc. I think it is exaggerated. The older generation studies more and more whilst the majority of the young ones, who grow up here, are pretty ignorant and don't even mind.

Some of these problems would be solved if our children would study at the regional school, removed from their home environment. Personally, I am very pleased with the local school system; only here could I develop with such independence, put my own curriculum into operation, and teach English to all grades, thus being able to follow the results of my program. It's very challenging, and I know that I am responsible for the results. For the children, as well, there's the advantage of small classes, frequently subdivided into study groups of four or five children, which would be impossible in a larger school. Often I can even do individual work with a child within the classroom.

As you see, I take my work very seriously. It is my number one priority and it determines, to a large extent, my satisfaction with life in general. I hate to be interrupted in my work. Here, however, nobody takes their work seriously, especially women. Women seem to be searching for an opportunity to get out of their tedious places of work. Whenever I'm out of school in the morning, running to visit my young daughter at the nursery school, I see so many people walking around idly, as if on vacation. They go to shop in the supermarket, to have their hair done, to buy a dress, to collect the laundry—as if they didn't have any work. It indeed aggravates me that the shoemaker, beautician, and laundry are open only in the morning: How can I manage to take advantage of these services when I'm supposed to be in school? My husband works closer to the center and he does most of the errands, leaving the garage for a moment, but he hates the interruption as much as I do. At least the supermarket is open twice a week in the afternoon and that's when I can do my shopping.

I'm a person who tries to live by rules. On the other hand, I realize that people all around me are breaking the rules. You have to put your child to bed at 8:00 P.M., but, if there's a good television program in the evening, parents come at 9:00 or later, waking up the other children who are already asleep. I wouldn't do that. I'm strict, for better or worse. I feel it's better for me as a teacher to be strict, and following the rules serves as a good model for my students. But personally it's probably detrimental, since it puts me under a lot of pressure, and even if I consider myself a person who obeys all the rules, the kibbutz never thinks so. People will always find a flaw in your behavior; nobody can stay clear of the constant judgment and surveillance going on within the kibbutz.

With all my criticism of the kibbutz, I enjoy life here, mainly because I find my work so satisfying. My husband and I have very similar views concerning the kibbutz. Both of us live here without ideological convictions. It's accepted between us that I will agree to leave if he has a problem and that he will follow me if I am discontent, so there is an alternative. Right now we both live here because we lead a good life, we are satisfied in our professional fields and can develop our personal interests. My husband works in the garage here. He has built his own motorcycle and he's very happy with his work. The only thing I really miss of the life I might have had in the States is friendship. It's a weird thing about the kibbutz—something I have only discovered gradually—that kibbutz members don't develop intimate relationships among themselves. In the States I had very close women friends. We could talk about anything and our relationships meant a great deal to us. Here I don't find this at all. One is close to one's family, but other relationships are very superficial.

I myself am suited for that kind of relationship, and I have found it even here. But, significantly, it is with another new immigrant, a Swedish woman. My friendship with her is so important that it has changed my whole perspective on my life in the kibbutz, and I know it's had the same effect on her. I feel, however, that the kibbutz is somehow working against such a relationship; real friendship is uncommon. Unintentionally the kibbutz stands in our way, although it's difficult to pinpoint how. The kibbutz is a network in which everybody comes under scrutiny, while to develop closeness one needs a bit of privacy, of secrecy, an atmosphere of romance. It's the same with a love affair. I don't want to sit in the dining hall and hear gossip about my closest friend; I want to have my own private image of her. This is a situation which is quite difficult to maintain. In my case, I change the subject whenever someone tries to intrude upon our friendship.

I have found that my adolescent students don't form intimate friendships either. I believe it is the result of the tendency of kibbutz children to conform, not to deviate from the group in any way, not to enter into confrontations with anyone.

When a couple is formed, one must partially reject others, and this is a highly unpopular thing to do. Friendship is the outcome of an attraction of two personalities, whereas kibbutz-born children try to suppress their individual personalities and just follow the herd. In addition, there's the constant exposure which undermines any romance. When everybody knows everyone else so closely for so long, no romantic love can develop. The constant gossip and criticism can destroy every relationship, and if one has a secret—which is a rare event—they know they can't trust anyone to keep it. For all these reasons you get the absurd situation that while these children live together constantly and are brought up with a social orientation as the focus of their education, they actually become more withdrawn and unwilling to form intimate relationships than people brought up in the privacy of their home and family.

I find it's almost impossible to penetrate the social network of the second and third kibbutz generations. Frankly, I find many of these individuals rather mediocre and uninteresting. The older generation has, however, a totally different character. Although they are much older than I, I am very attracted to them. Frequently I take a place in the dining hall among these elderly men and women, and I listen to their wonderful conversations about ideas, art, books, the landscape, or Judaism; they never engage in dull gossip. But they were brought up in other homes and other times.

B A R U C H (age 70)

In my conversation with Baruch I asked him to focus on his status as a "parent of a member" in the kibbutz.

I was born in 1909 in Galicia, a time and a place haunted by anti-Semitism. In my youth, I was determined to leave that place and immigrate to Palestine. I even prepared myself by learning a useful trade, carpentry, yet, as I couldn't get a certificate and didn't know of any possible way to reach the country, I immigrated to Argentina in 1928 instead, with the hope of somehow reaching Palestine from there. However, it took me thirty-nine years before my dream finally materialized.

In Argentina I worked at my trade, got married, and had two children. I gave them a good Jewish-Zionist education, so that years later they made *aliya* independently of us. My daughter immigrated in 1961; she went to an *ulpan* in Makom, married a kibbutz son and stayed here. My son left Argentina several years later and now lives in Jerusalem with his family. In 1967 we, too, sold our home and boarded a boat for Israel. We boarded just as the Six Day War broke out and we didn't know what to expect when we arrived. But this time I refused to postpone our immigration any longer; I told my friends: "Whatever happens, we'll be together with the whole Jewish people and with our children, too." The war, however, was a victory, and we came directly from the boat to Makom.

I was fifty-eight when we arrived. It's not an age to become a kibbutz member, but we were gladly accepted in the kibbutz with the status of parents. While still in Argentina, I corresponded with the secretary of the kibbutz who said the kibbutz would be happy to receive us, especially as we both had such needed professions—I as a carpenter and my wife as a seamstress. And indeed, for the last twelve years, we have both been working in our former occupations and are both very satisfied with our work. I sympathize often with others in their seventies who don't have a trade and must work on the line in our olive factory in their old age. It's better than not working at all, but I don't envy them in the least.

Some parents who have the means bring their property or savings to the kibbutz when they come to live there in their old age. We, however, were poor. [*Laughs.*] We brought a library of about five hundred books, mostly in Yiddish. I brought the tools of my craft, and with my money I bought an air-conditioner, a T.V. set, and a refrigerator which I use in my room. I hated to come to the kibbutz and say: "I need this and this." We received a small apartment at first and we put these things in our room, including a bookcase that we had ordered for our books. All the rest of the furniture and equipment we received from the kibbutz. Pretty soon after our arrival air-conditioners were installed in all the rooms of people of our age, both members and parents, and T.V. sets were given to everyone. So there was nothing outstanding or unequal about our belongings. Moreover, a year after our arrival, the T.V. set broke down. I called in the technician who took away the old one and gave us a new one instead, and I wasn't asked to pay for it or anything like that. A few years ago, it was our turn to get a new two-room apartment and we moved in. The bedroom furniture was added by the kibbutz just as for everybody else. From the beginning, we got the same annual budget as everyone else. I was never made to feel like a second-class citizen here and we both return our share to the community by working as we do.

Parents don't vote in the assembly, as the rule goes. But nobody even told me about it and sometimes in the assembly meetings I also get a voting ticket and could vote if I wanted to. I attend the assembly meetings regularly because I find it interesting, more so than many members. I don't do guard duty in the kibbutz, neither at the gate nor elsewhere. I don't know if that's the rule. I never saw other parents on guard duty either, although members of our age do walk around with rifles from time to time. Anyway, I was never a soldier so, if they want me to be a guard, they'll have to teach me how to use a gun first . . . [laughing heartily].

Finally, there are the special mobilizations, when people are called to work in a specific branch during its seasonal rush. I don't know if this obligation applies to me, as a parent, but if it were night work I'd certainly participate. As things are, however, our mobilizations are for work on Saturday, and I, as an observant Jew, have never worked on Shabbat, and here too I stick to this rule. I'm not an extremely orthodox person, but this is the only sore point in my life in this kibbutz. I'd really like the kibbutz to observe more Jewish traditions than it does.

In Argentina I used to attend the synagogue on Saturday and holidays. We lived within walking distance from the synagogue, because I wouldn't drive on the Sabbath. Here, however, there's no synagogue whatsoever, and at the beginning it seemed as if nobody was concerned about this. It's a secular kibbutz, I know, yet I believe that we're all Jewish and we can't break so completely from our past tradition. I believe it would add greatly to the spiritual life of the kibbutz if we had a prayer center; people would come in to reflect and our children would know what a synagogue is. I don't understand how Jews can be so forgetful of our roots and heritage.

Before our first High Holy Day season, I spoke to my son-in-law's father about the lack of religious observance at Makom. Through his contacts with the neighboring religious kibbutzim, he arranged to have me invited to spend the holiday in a kibbutz with a traditional ceremony. This has become my custom over the years. On Yom Kippur eve, my son-in-law drives me to a nearby kibbutz, where I stay with a family with whom I have come to have a friendly relationship; there I participate in the prayer services and when the holiday is over my son-in-law picks me up and takes me back to Makom again.

We usually celebrate the New Year with our son in Jerusalem, where plenty of synagogues are available nearby. I go to religious kibbutzim periodically, on different holidays, so I have solved my personal problem, yet I'm still puzzled by the fact that I'm the only person who is seriously concerned by this situation. People who are about my age have been out of the habit of attending religious services for so many years that they are probably not going to change again, and the young ones have never known otherwise.

I have a dream, however, of doing something for the kibbutz in this area. I spoke to several people who are also interested in opening a little synagogue here, but they wanted me to be their spokesman. But as I'm not even a member, I can't assume this role. I told them that we should speak to the secretary together, but one of them declined, saying: "They'd say I've become unhinged in my old age, that I've become a penitent." We haven't gone to the secretary yet, but I sense a change in the atmosphere. Other kibbutzim, mostly from the Ichud, have opened synagogues recently. The Histadrut has special funds to help finance such building efforts, so it's not a question of money. We even have a Torah here, stuck into some closet in the library. I know that several people here share my longing and my dream, and I know it would enrich our life in this kibbutz in many ways. Yet I wouldn't want to start a synagogue if it would just be a lonely, deserted place which nobody would enter. . . .

This, then, is my only criticism of the kibbutz. Just the other week some of my young acquaintances said to me: "Don't worry, Baruch. We'll yet have a synagogue here, don't despair. If the oldsters won't build one, we will." I pray to God that this will take place yet in my lifetime.

The "Non-Family" Unit

D I N A *(age 65)*

Dina, a small woman with pale eyes, works five hours a day, supervising the babies' kitchen; in her free time, she cultivates her garden with immense dedication.

I was born in Jerusalem where my family had lived for six generations. I was one of eight children and in Jerusalem I went to primary school and joined the Scouts. Later, I went to study in an agricultural school. I loved farming, especially working with cows, and I decided to join a kibbutz and do this work. But it wasn't easy. Most kibbutzim didn't have any work for their own people and what work they had was more frequently in the cities than farming their own land.

This was the situation in Makom in 1933 or 1934 when I joined the settlement at the Fountain. The situation was terribly depressing but gradually improved and I adjusted to my new life. Six months after my arrival, some *hachshara* friends also joined us, and as a group we felt better. We planted a vegetable garden and slowly more people came to work in the settlement.

I myself worked in the cowshed for fifteen years. As we bought more cows the job became quite demanding, with very long hours occupied by the morning and evening milkings. We did everything manually, of course, both milking and transporting food. When my second child was born, I felt this work was too much for me. I was always busy in the afternoons and evenings when the children needed me, and their father, who was then the kibbutz cashier, was frequently away in the city, so I left my job and started working in the children's homes. It wasn't much easier in the homes, with the conditions we had then, but the hours were much more convenient for tending my family. Today, *chaverot* who work in the children's homes have relatively less work and less responsibility. But I'm not too well informed about what's going on in the children's homes nowadays, since I no longer have children or grandchildren in the kibbutz. I have four grown-up children and they all left the kibbutz; it is very sad.

My firstborn son was the first to move out. It was in the 1950s, I don't remember exactly the year. He's forty-one now; at the time he was twenty or so. It was a period of many reprisals against the terrorists and he wanted to join the standing Army, but the kibbutz didn't approve. I think he was the first man to ask for that kind of outside work. I remember a very loud and stormy assembly meeting, where all our generals, the heroes of the Palmach and the War of Independence, were against his request. Actually, several of their own sons did the same thing later and remained respectable members of this community. . . .

Anyway, his request was denied and he left the kibbutz. It was terribly important for him to remain in the Army. He was in a select unit of paratroopers that participated in many daring missions. His former commander is today the chief of staff of the Army; at the time, he came in person to persuade me that our son had to stay in the Army. He has participated in so many battles and wars, that it has been a constant nightmare for me. Wherever I have worked I have always run to hear the news broadcasts. I could smell out which news items would be the kind of things in which he participated. As he advanced in rank, he was also sent abroad and he managed to see the whole world. He has had a satisfactory life with the Army, but he has recently begun feeling he's had enough and he's about to start on a new career.

My second son lives in the United States. . . . It's a different story from his older brother's. You see, all my kids were highly independent and very individualistic people; each one had his own special thing. The second one never wanted to study. When he said he was going to leave the kibbutz I went through a difficult crisis since I believed that the kibbutz was the only place in which he could manage at all. But it turned out that the kid was pretty smart and he knew his way about. He became a truck driver, made money quickly, and went to the States to see the big world. Once he was there he started to study, went into the film industry, married an American Jewish woman, and stayed there. Right now he's a building contractor in New York and continues to produce films as well. He and his family plan to return to Israel, they really do—but certainly not to the kibbutz.

My daughter is a sort of glamorous type. She's pretty—all my children are; you wouldn't believe it seeing the way I look [*laughing*]. Anyway, she felt she wouldn't be able to spend her entire life working in the kitchen or in the children's homes. She left and studied movement and dancing and she has a good profession, teaching modern dance. She's married to a professor, twenty years her senior; they have two daughters, and they're all very happy. She also traveled widely: her husband worked for the U.N. and they've toured the whole world . . .

Now, my youngest son is studying in Canada. How did he get there? Well, he met a tourist, a young Canadian woman whose sister lives here, and fell in love. She was a student, about to finish law school, when they met three years ago. He decided to go to Canada with her, but before they left he told her, us, and everybody else that they were going just for the year, so that she could finish her studies. That's what he said. In the meantime, however, he started to study too. He's getting a degree in science and discovering ambitions of which we were never aware. In two years he's going to finish and definitely return to Israel. But again, he won't return to the kibbutz, because his wife doesn't want to live in a kibbutz, she won't even try. He is the one whose leaving is the most painful to me, because he is such a dedicated kibbutznik and he loves Makom. He'd gladly return and be a teacher here, if it wasn't for her refusal.

So, these are the stories of my four children. All of them left the kibbutz and two of them are presently living abroad. I really don't know why; somehow, they were drawn outside to the big world. Perhaps they were too individualistic to conform to kibbutz living, I don't know. But my youngest son could have certainly lived here with us, he really wanted to.

There are several more families like ours, with parents living here alone, all their children having left. Some of these youngsters have, however, left to join other kibbutzim and that's easier for their parents, somehow. There's more give-and-take between parents whose children are in other kibbutzim than in our situation. Actually, however, I'm not so disturbed by the situation. My grandchildren all love to come and visit with us; they come frequently. My eldest granddaughter wants to come live with us and study in school here, but she's too young at the moment. I have a big apartment, two and a half rooms, and I can put them all up, although they usually don't visit here all together. My husband used to have a car for his work and it was quite easy for us to visit our children, too; lately the car is no longer at our disposal, however.

When my children and grandchildren come to visit, they're welcomed by the kibbutz. I never sensed the least bit of reticency towards visitors, at least not directed towards my family. Maybe it's because they are personally so likeable. During the Jubilee celebrations, we brought our guests on the second evening and went alone to the first evening. This was all right with me, really, and for the children as well; they'd never want to come if they felt unwelcome. And although our children are away, we always have good company; we know many young families, mostly classmates of our children, so we don't feel lonely.

We are not young anymore. Last year my husband had a heart attack and since then he has not been very well. That's why we recently received this apartment. It is situated in a very central spot, just a one-minute walk from both the dining hall and the infirmary. It became vacant several months ago, and many people wanted to move here, but the committee for the elderly, together with our doctor, finally decided we should get it. It has helped us enormously. Before, we used to live at a distance from the center, and we had to climb the hill to come to the dining hall. My husband used to stand alongside the road and wait for someone who might happen to pass with a car and give him a lift. At noontime, I would bring lunch to the office where he works, and carrying a tray with a warm meal on it wasn't easy. Often, I forgot some of the courses, and, as I have a leg problem, it was very difficult to shuttle back and forth. With the new apartment, I feel as if we have both started to live again, especially my husband. He can walk to work and to meals, he can again attend the assembly meetings—it really saved us. Furthermore, our new apartment is quite spacious and I organized it in such a manner that I have enough room for any of my children and grandchildren when they come to visit.

I have never felt criticized for the fact that none of my children stayed in the kibbutz. The opposite is true; I feel people sympathize with me for my lot. It is indeed painful, particularly in the evenings; one walks outside and everywhere one sees grandmothers with children. And on Friday nights and holidays, the big families gathering around the tables in the dining hall. . . . So I feel it. . . . In town one doesn't experience this contrast so vividly since many older parents are left alone. But cities have their own disadvantages and I don't think it is generally easier for parents in the city than parents in the kibbutz when their children are away from them. The thing which hurts me most is my youngest son—we really hoped he'd stay near us. But it didn't work out. I tell myself, though, that everyone has the right to choose where and how they want to live, and, as long as they're all happy and in good health, I've nothing to complain about.

G I L A   *(age 54)*

I was born in 1924 in Molad. As a youngster I volunteered for the British Army and I served as a military driver for three and a half years. There were several Jewish women on the job, driving light trucks on the roads of Egypt and the Sinai Desert. It was considered very adventurous work. Even at the kibbutz, there was strong opposition to our volunteering, because there was fear that, as young women, we'd be considered as cheap feminine companions for the British soldiers. . . . This was far from the truth, though, and we became a tight group of Israeli women drivers, barely mingling with anyone.

Well, in 1946 I returned to the kibbutz and after a short while I got married. It wasn't a good marriage; I didn't love the man, but I felt that this was what the kibbutz expected of me. . . . When the War of Independence broke out, I volunteered for the Army again, and as an experienced driver I was very welcome. I drove in very dangerous situations, under fire, day and night, transporting soldiers, ammunition, whatever. By that time I had gotten a divorce from my husband and was involved in a deep loving relationship with a Palmach commander whom I had known for a long time, years before I got married. He was killed, however, in an attempt to break through to besieged Jerusalem. . . . Thirty-five young men were killed in that fatal attempt; it was a famous heroic mission. . . . I continued my military work, driving endlessly. What else could I do?

When the war was over, I returned to Molad. I was quite unhappy there—I had always disliked the place, for it was very difficult for me personally. I had personal problems with my mother and with the whole society. So when the division occurred in 1952, and my brother and his family decided to move to Makom, as well as the majority of my age group, I decided to join them and I came over, too. For ten years, I worked in the chicken coop, then I moved to the olive plant, and presently I'm the kibbutz telephone operator.

I have never formed another relationship since 1948, and I have always lived alone here. I am very close to my brother's family. I have always spent a lot of my free time with them and I consider my brother's children almost as my own. For the last couple of years my sister-in-law, Ora, was very sick and she died recently of cancer. She was an exceptional woman. . . . So, I try to help my brother's family as much as I can. I also have friends here and I don't feel too lonely.

I think that the kibbutz is a pretty good place for single people like myself. I hate cities—the dirt, the pollution, the bustling crowds; I couldn't live in a city. In the kibbutz I feel calm. I don't have to worry about my income, about making ends meet. I have a girlfriend in Tel

Aviv, also single, whom I have known since the time we served in the Army together. She's always in a panic because of financial problems, "finishing the month" somehow. And what if she gets sick? Who will take care of her?

Look, to be single is not great anywhere, but I think it's easier in the kibbutz. I don't have to worry about walking alone outside here, whatever the hour of night, whereas in the city it's completely different. I don't mind going alone to parties or other events in the kibbutz, while for a single woman in town it is always a problem. Growing old alone here is much less threatening. I know that no matter what happens to me—sickness, accidents—I'll be completely taken care of by the kibbutz. I don't think that in town I'd have had a better chance to meet another man and remarry. Here, too, there were several attempts. I simply didn't want anyone after what happened to me during the war.

There's just one thing I sometimes regret, and that's not having a child of my own. Nowadays it's quite common for a single woman to bear a child, and the kibbutz is supportive, not in the least bit critical of this phenomenon. Children of single mothers are raised as the other children are. Just a few months ago, a child was born to a single woman and people came to celebrate with her and make a toast, just as if they were a traditional family.

Well, this is something I didn't dare in my youth, probably because I myself was such a problem child and suffered a great deal because of this. My mother was deserted by my father during her pregnancy. He was a Communist, and he returned to Russia and has never contacted us. As a child, until I was twelve, my mother refused to tell me anything about my father; she said he had died but wouldn't add any details. I didn't believe her and was haunted by various fantasies about him. The children tortured me with questions and insinuations—they probably had heard something of the unhappy affair from their parents. I was extremely miserable as a child. It was my mother's fault—she didn't know how to face me honestly and to reveal the past, nor did any of my relatives or teachers. My mother later married another man and gave birth to my brother, who is eight years younger than I am. He was the first relative I really cared for, actually the only one. When I was twelve, I confronted my mother and demanded to know about my father. That's when she told me. . . . So, I think this experience prevented me from having a child of my own years ago, and now I regret it.

If I were younger today, I'd certainly act otherwise, because the kibbutz of today is much less conservative. Also, Makom is much more liberal than Molad had ever been and couldn't react to a fatherless child in the manner that I remember from my childhood.

All this is in the past now. I live my life and try to be a contributing member of this society which has given me so much. I never retreat into my room in self-pity. That's not part of my character.

. . .

In the following two interviews, two Yom Kippur War widows, Shlomit and Naomi, present their stories. As in many of the other interviews, our conversations dealt with life histories and present situations. In the following account, however, I have concentrated mostly on the aspects which are relevant to widowhood and rehabilitation within the kibbutz.

S H L O M I T *(age 32)*

Shlomit is a pretty young woman, who greeted me with a newborn daughter in her arms. Our conversation took place in her pleasant garden.

I was born here and have spent all my life here, except for military service, of course. I never thought of leaving the kibbutz, for it's always been the most natural choice for me to live here, as my brother and sister do. I feel secure here, in an environment which I know very well, in which I'm acquainted with the people and know how I am expected to behave. It's my home. I feel socially protected in the kibbutz. I know that if I face any kind of hardship, the kibbutz, both the community and the individual members, will always stand by my side and provide all possible help.

I heard that your first husband was killed in the Yom Kippur War and now you're remarried and have a child. People say that you've rehabilitated yourself. Would you care to talk about it?

Well, certainly. I dislike the words "husband" and "wife," you know. I'd rather say "my man," or better still, his name. You mentioned my rehabilitation. It works on two different levels. The first is the contribution of the kibbutz: how the kibbutz helps a member in case of disaster —not just death—and how it helped me, personally, when my man was killed. The second level is my own contribution, my own personal motivation to overcome my grief; in my case, I was extremely interested in rehabilitating myself.

I don't think that my rehabilitation is signified only by the fact that I have remarried. The question is much deeper: To what extent does a person wish to go on living after a disaster, or does he or she prefer to remain in the past, in the sorrow, never to emerge again? It's a matter of one's character, and I have the kind of character which helped me emerge from all this. In addition, I was aided by the fact that my mother is a war widow too, and had been widowed for many years when my husband died. I had her image constantly in front of me. My father was killed in the Sinai Campaign of 1956 and she remained alone in the kibbutz with four young children. At that time there was much less awareness in our society of the difficulties faced by a bereaved person. She received only minimal support, if any, and she had to cope with her problems alone. She clung to her past and to this very day she hasn't entirely chosen to overcome her sorrow. She makes it very difficult to help her as well. She was forty-one years old when she was widowed and she never tried, or perhaps had the chance, to form a new relationship. Maybe she thought that it wouldn't be good for us, her children; or perhaps she's simply the type for whom forming a new relationship is quite difficult. Anyway, my mother is extremely bitter and nervous and dependent on us. I sometimes think that this is due to her difficult life, that she was alone with four children and had nobody to help her or to listen to her all those years. Perhaps she had some of these traits before her loss, I really don't know. Anyway, I had in her a negative model: I knew what I didn't want to become. It's strange, but I think that it was extremely valuable.

I was married to my first man, Amnon, for seven years and we had one child, a boy, who was four years old when the war broke out. At that time, there were suddenly many widows, as many kibbutz members were killed then. The whole kibbutz was in a state of terrible shock, everybody seemed awfully depressed, so I didn't feel isolated in my pain. The way the community rallied to help the families, parents, and widows was really outstanding. They also tried to help those bereaved parents who lived outside the kibbutz, such as Amnon's parents. Groups were organized for parents and for widows where we met several times and discussed our problems. Actually, many of our early sessions dealt with material problems, but the main thing was the feeling that we could meet, talk, and find a channel for our needs. There was a special committee to which we could turn with any of our problems, and it gave me the feeling that people really cared.

Let me give you an example. We all thought that it was important for the widows to be able to travel and move around freely, to visit with family and friends and not to always have to ask for somebody's help in getting transportation. We were therefore offered driving lessons and easy access to cars for personal use. I had obtained a drivers license before Amnon was killed, but I wasn't used to driving at all. Since I was in the middle of my studies at the Teachers' Seminary, I received a private car and I used to drive every day to school in Haifa and back, so that I could be with my son in the afternoons. I was strongly motivated to continue my studies, to be among people, not to bury myself with Amnon. As a result, I graduated from school as scheduled. I used the car for many other purposes as well— I visited Amnon's parents a lot, since we felt very close at the time. The car gave me a sense of independence, something I urgently needed since Amnon wasn't there to give me support. I didn't let myself sink into a condition of self-pity, weakness, and helplessness. Several other widows also used the driving lessons and the cars to their benefit, but none, I think, to the extent that I did. One widow was killed in a car accident exactly on the first anniversary of her husband's death. It was an awful tragedy, and many of my friends stopped driving after that.

Another way the kibbutz helped, in addition to the group meetings and the transportation, was in publishing very fine memorial booklets. They did a wonderful job, really capturing Amnon's spirit in this booklet, and I know that it was done with the greatest love and dedication. The kibbutz took care of organizing all the memorial ceremonies and they also provided help for the children, if we felt it was needed. A little later, the widows and bereaved parents received permission to take trips abroad, using money which was donated by the defense ministry. The kibbutz tried to make us feel better, to compensate us in every possible way. I really think they did all they could.

I remember, however, one difficulty which the kibbutz didn't seem to be able to solve. Right after Amnon was killed, I wanted very much to have a telephone of my own. I needed to talk to Amnon's parents frequently, especially when I was depressed, and I hated to conduct these conversations from the public telephones. Although the defense ministry offered to install phones in our rooms, the kibbutz saw it as a serious breach of the principle of equality and we didn't get them. Actually, I didn't openly demand it, because I myself felt it was an unfair request.

Today, however, five years after the war, I hear that the widows who remained alone are going to get private phones, as are some of the bereaved parents whose other children live outside the kibbutz. I myself am pretty ambivalent towards the issue now, because there are many people in need, old lonely people, widows, and widowers—how are we going to determine fairly whose need is greatest?

Amnon's parents have other complaints against the kibbutz, although I don't know how justified they are. They say that because this is a big kibbutz, people are distant and don't show a spontaneous interest in what they're feeling and doing. Amnon was very popular, and he had many good friends here, among children, adults, and old people alike, so his parents expected that the reactions of the community would express total empathy with their grief. And there was a great deal of participation; I felt it was touching and certainly appropriate, but they were disappointed, as if it weren't enough. I don't know if any community can show complete identification with a bereaved family. Disaster has this property, I have noticed, of closing some people up. Every family is engulfed in its own tragedy. We see it in the memorial services—each family standing alone over its own grave.

I met my new man here in the kibbutz. He was born here, and after his military service he went abroad and lived in the States for several years. I hardly knew him as a child because he's several years younger than I am and as children we weren't together. This is probably the reason we were able to fall in love when he returned to the kibbutz two years ago. Usually, people who know each other from childhood on, like classmates, don't become attracted to each other romantically later in life. He's a carpenter in the kibbutz now. We got married about a year ago and now we have this girl. My son loves him too, so we are a whole family once again.

N A O M I (age 38)

Naomi is a large sturdy woman with kind eyes. Talking about many delicate topics, she was very open and honest, unafraid to express her point of view.

Recently I assumed the role of secretary of services which is a full-time job in the secretariat. I stepped in after Rachel had left and moved to Ginat. I wasn't particularly enthusiastic about it, but I was elected and I figured "better now than later." I might as well pay off some of my obligations.

When I was young, I worked on a ship; I traveled a lot and saw the world. That's where I met my husband; he was a captain on one of the lines, and a former kibbutznik. He was a Holocaust survivor, with no family of his own. I come from a big family; my parents were still alive when my husband and I met, and together with all my four brothers and sisters they lived in Makom. When we got married I convinced my husband to join the kibbutz. He adjusted very well and towards the end he was one of the central figures in our metal factory. He was happy here.

He was killed in the early stages of the Yom Kippur War. Our eldest son was seven and a half years old at the time and the girls were four and two years old. [*Naomi is silent for a while.*] It was horrible to lose him. All those first years after the war were horrible. I have always felt that to be a widow in the kibbutz must be the worst fate. I used to see a woman, a rabbi's wife, who visited many widows in towns, villages, and kibbutzim after the war and I asked her once: "You know so many widows—am I right in my impression that being a widow and raising children alone in the kibbutz is the hardest situation?" She thought for a while, then agreed with my observation.

The thing which makes being a widow so difficult here is the fact that such a large proportion of our life is communal. Everyone observes you and knows everything about you. I accompany my children every evening, each one to his or her children's home, and I'm observed by all the other parents. Every evening I see other children accompanied by their fathers, who sit with them and tell them bedtime stories, and I'm alone. Many fathers bring their children on scooters and my daughter used to say: "Mommy, why don't you get a scooter and take me on it?" The pressure of having to put all three of my little children to sleep, each one in his own dorm, all alone, was hardly bearable. At every party or holiday, every birthday at the nursery school, I always felt different, odd among all the happy families. And it can't be avoided. In town I'd probably not go; I'd be able to lead my life in the way most appropriate for me. Here I decided to attend all the celebrations in which my children participate, but I skip all other events I would have to attend alone. For example, I do attend the Friday night festive dinner with my children, but I don't go to the cultural event later in the evening which is intended for adults only. Whenever I did attend, I was always late because I first had to take care of three children and because entering the hall alone made me feel uneasy and embarrassed, looking for an empty seat and asking myself with whom I should sit. It was terribly unpleasant, so I stopped going. I don't go to trips, shows, or movies either because it's so depressing to return to my room alone and not to have someone with whom to share my experience.

Don't your friends and relatives encourage you to join in the social activities? Don't they come pick you up on their way to various events?

Look, I don't ask anyone what to do and I know what's best for me. The time I love most is Friday night. The children come to the room after dinner, we all watch T.V. and read the papers, and they stay overnight, so I don't feel lonely and don't have to pretend in front of anyone.

Right after the war I joined a widows' group run by a psychologist in Haifa. The group consisted of kibbutz women coming from different kibbutzim. I didn't feel I was getting anything out of it, but I felt it was my duty towards the others to continue participating. Some of the young women were in a terrible mental state—they were helpless and didn't know how to relate to their children. In comparison to them, I felt so strong and in control that I continued coming only to serve as a model and to contribute to the group.

One of the major problems discussed was what to tell the children about their father and the circumstances of his death, whether to take them to visit his grave, etc. My approach, which came completely naturally to me, was to share everything with my children and to let them choose which rituals to attend, even though they were rather young. To the other widows it seemed rather amazing that I could do this spontaneously, and the psychotherapist used my behavior as a model all the time. I didn't hide anything from my children. I answered all their questions truthfully and I found that it did them good.

The funeral took place a year after the war. In our kibbutz it was indeed a tragic event—eleven men were buried at the same time. My son wanted to come to the funeral and so I took him with me. The little one didn't understand anyway, but with my middle daughter I made a mistake. She was in a nursery class with another boy whose father had fallen, and the other family had decided to keep their little boy away from the funeral. The teacher thought it best for my daughter not to participate either, although my daughter herself said she wanted to come. In order not to embarrass the other boy and his family, I made an agreement with the teacher that she would decide at the last moment according to my daughter's wishes. In order to remove all the little children from the scene of this huge funeral, a picnic lunch was planned so they would all be away, including my daughter who seemed to have forgotten about the whole event. However, two years later, when my father died, she said: "I want to attend Grandfather's funeral, not like Father's funeral when I wanted to go to see how he was buried and you didn't let me go." For me, this was a terrible blow. I told myself: "There you are, Naomi. You didn't follow your own intuition; you let others determine things for you, and that's the outcome." I'm amazed that she remembered the whole thing, being so young. They do remember a lot. Only my youngest daughter has no memories of her father, although she keeps telling stories about him—stories she heard from us.

To return to my feelings about the kibbutz, it's obvious that a woman might feel more protected economically in the kibbutz. But the Ministry of Defense takes very good care of widows in town, too, and these widows have the further advantage of freedom to form their own style of life. I, for example, couldn't even get a telephone of my own in the kibbutz even though I wanted it desperately and was willing to pay for it out of my annual budget. People here thought that we, the kibbutz widows, didn't deserve private phones. Everybody had his own opinion and felt entitled to meddle in our private lives. I can't tell you how many tears I shed because of this issue, firstly because I felt the need of a private phone and, secondly, because I was deeply insulted by the attitude of the kibbutz.

All in all, I don't think that I got much help from the kibbutz—not when I really was in need. Nobody ever came to ask me if I needed anything, and I didn't demand any special privileges for myself. I did feel, however, that if I asked a favor, the kibbutz would help. But when I finally did ask for a telephone, something which might be considered exceptional, I was rejected. Yes, it *was* an exceptional request, but isn't my whole *life* exceptional, too? People interpreted my request as if I were looking for some sort of material gain from my situation—and a lot of people made sure that I knew what they thought. Equality! What is equality, since my whole life is not equal to theirs? When Amos came to talk me out of my request, I had a very honest conversation with him about equality and other matters. Did anybody count the number of films, shows, trips, or concerts I attend in the kibbutz? Since I didn't use those services which the kibbutz offers, why couldn't I use a different service which I requested? One can't expect equality to be one-sided. This fight over the telephone was an extremely long and painful process for me; I can't even enjoy the fact that I "won" and will soon get a telephone. The whole story left me feeling very bitter towards the kibbutz.

In spite of these hard feelings, I have never seriously considered leaving the kibbutz. What do I have outside the kibbutz, anyway? My husband had no family, and all my family is here. Starting to build a new life all over again is too great a task at my age and in my position. . . . Furthermore, you must understand that talking to you right now has encouraged many thoughts to surface which I usually don't feel in such an intense fashion. If I were always so preoccupied with my problems, I wouldn't be able to function at all, neither as a mother nor in my job. One cannot allow oneself to be immersed so completely in negativity.

It's strange. People in the kibbutz, including bereaved families, have usually pointed to the immense help that the kibbutz provided for them during times of personal crisis. . . .

I don't know. . . . Maybe I'm being unfair; I hardly remember anything from the period immediately following the news that my husband had been killed. I remember that I received a T.V. set very quickly, although it wasn't my turn to get one. . . . I remember that a lot of people kept away from me just after the disaster, as if shunning my company. They probably didn't know how to show their concern, and I had to approach them to start conversation.

We sat some sort of *"shiva"** after his death. Most of the families followed this tradition, but it is a matter of choice. The kibbutz doesn't have fixed customs in such matters. Anyway, it's accepted that members of bereaved families don't go back to work for seven days or so. You sit at home and friends come and visit you, especially in the evenings. But during the war so many things happened at once that it was difficult to sit passively in my room. I think that I returned to work after three days of mourning. I felt better working.

There is one person whom I fondly remember from those first days. It is Chana, who was then the social secretary. She was really very good. She visited me several times and showed interest in what I felt and thought; she was really there to listen to me. She also gathered us together, all the widows, and encouraged us to talk to one another. She was, however, an exception. Others, outside my own family, didn't show any special interest in our grief.

Well, I'm somewhat better now. I have a boyfriend, a divorcé, who lives in town. We may decide to try living together here, but I still have problems with my children, who don't want to accept a new man in my life. But the kibbutz would be happy to see me remarried. They tried to introduce me to several men, and, now that they know I have a boyfriend, they often stop to ask me: "Well, then, when will we hear some good news from you?"

Health Services and the Elderly

D E V O R A *(age 58)*

Though her husband was among my first acquaintances, I didn't meet Devora until quite late in the process of collecting the data for the book. On my first Saturday spent in Makom, a bald, suntanned man of about sixty was assigned as my archaeological

---

*Literally, "seven"; the traditional Jewish custom is to sit in mourning for seven days after the death of a member of the family.

guide in the area. Under his supervision, we visited two sites which he was digging with the help of the local schoolchildren. At the first site, he had discovered an old winepress, and at the second, which was just in the process of being uncovered, some old buildings had already been exposed. "I'm trying to prove that this area has always been inhabited by Jews, thereby affirming our natural right over this land. I think that I have sufficient evidence already," he added, and brought me several pieces of evidence that he had gathered so far. The amazing fact, however, was that all this serious work was being done after work-hours, as a hobby. In the daytime he is an accountant.

Six months later I met his wife, Devora, in my room.

The health committee assumes responsibility for all medical problems in the kibbutz, including preventive medicine and the maintenance of a high standard of public health. Let me begin by telling you that I believe that the kibbutz today is one of the places which offers the best available medical treatment and health conditions for its members. We conduct many of our activities with the insurance provided by the nationwide Socialized Medical Association, of which we are all members, but we invest much more money than we obtain through our insurance. We have a medical doctor and a dentist living and working here, as well as a large team of nurses, a physiotherapist, and a social worker; with the help of the regional hospital, of course, we can meet all of the medical needs of the community.

The activities of the health committee include the organization of a number of medical branches: our local medical and dental clinics, the local pharmacy, the sick rooms, occupational therapy and physiotherapy, the ambulance and first-aid services, cosmetic treatment (although only part of the activities of this area are under our supervision) and our special dietary kitchen. In the work team at the clinic we have a school nurse and a special nurse who organizes a "healthy-baby clinic," which takes care of our infants' immunizations, medical follow-ups, etc.

The health committee doesn't interfere in the daily activities of these different branches, but oversees the more basic issues and serves as mediator between the various health branches and other kibbutz institutions, as well as between the individual and whichever branch is pertinent to his needs. These are our major responsibilities, in my opinion. In addition, we take care of the problems involved in hospitalization of kibbutz members outside the kibbutz. If a hospitalized member needs around-the-clock supervision, we arrange for this care; we also provide transportation and arrange visits to every hospitalized member. Furthermore, we're the office which handles any specific requests concerning medical problems, either the purchase of specific equipment or consultations with specialists.

One of our concerns, which is usually eclipsed by more pressing needs, is the maintenance of public health. We have various undertakings which involve specific target populations for preventive medicine. For example, there have recently been several cases of measles in adults, and we wrote an article about it in our local newsletter, suggesting that all young women get vaccinations against measles, which is hazardous during pregnancy. Or, we encourage women to come annually for gynecological checkups and preventive examinations for breast cancer. We have found that even if we send a personal note to an individual, inviting her to come to the clinic at a certain date, women tend to disregard the whole matter, so presently our policy is to remind the public of the situation, but leave it up to the individual to come and get a checkup. However, we actually do follow-ups and keep records of women who have come for checkups, and after a certain length of time we personally invite those who don't show up at their own initiative.

This is just an example of our work. Another area with which we have recently been concerned is coronary disease. We had several cases of severe heart attacks, some fatal, so we suggested sending all men beyond a certain age to the heart institute at the hospital for specific examinations for early signs of coronary disease. Our local doctor has, however, vetoed this idea since he felt it would create unnecessary anxiety in the community. Moreover, he felt that he himself has fairly close and regular contact with potential heart patients. Our doctor has been living here for thirteen years and, although he's not a member, he is better acquainted and more involved with the kibbutz than many members. We respect his opinions and would not introduce a medical project to which he is opposed.

There's one medical branch which does initiate and organize regular visits by the whole population—that's the dental clinic. Every member, child or adult, is invited to the clinic once a year for a cleaning and checkup. This way, the dental team can control the situation more effectively as well as allocate their time in a fairer way. People do, of course, come at their own initiative as well. There's one full-time dentist, with two assistants (kibbutz members) who work for him, and they are always extremely busy.

Then we have the issue of allocating budgets for people to see private doctors. People get their initial treatment from our doctor, who can refer them to specialists at the regional hospital. These expenses are covered by our insurance. However, with the general rise in our standard of living, we are receiving more requests from members who wish to consult with private doctors in town. Usually a specialist was recommended to them, and they want to get his opinion about their symptoms. This happens quite frequently; just the other day, I had two cases which were brought to my attention—a man who had an orthopedic problem and a woman who couldn't become pregnant despite previous medical treatment. We have approved both their requests to see another specialist, privately. There's just one condition which we demand very strictly, namely, that our local doctor should be apprised of these private consultations and be informed of the developments. Sometimes he objects to a decision to involve another doctor and tries to dissuade the patient. But if the patient insists, he doesn't persist or interfere. We have a very good and open relationship with him and we don't do anything behind his back.

Some of the requests for private treatment concern psychiatric or psychological consultation. This isn't normally covered by the insurance. The kibbutz is very aware of psychological problems, both in children and in adults, so many members make use of some sort of psychological treatment or another. I guess that the kibbutz system holds the record for the whole of Israeli society in using psychological services. This was once another big item in our medical budget, but it has decreased a great deal since the employment of our own social worker, who manages to take care of the vast majority of our psychological problems.

Recently we have had a wave of requests for plastic surgery. This is the latest trend. Two young members wanted their noses fixed, and then another person made a similar request, and an older lady wanted a face-lift. . . . These procedures are sometimes approved by the insurance, if the requests are accompanied by psychiatric recommendations. But if the insurance rejects the application, then it reverts to our hands. Cosmetic surgery is a terribly expensive procedure that includes private hospitalization, but if it's of profound importance to the applicant. . . . What can we do? After many deliberations, we considered our budget and arrived at the decision that we can approve three plastic-surgery operations a year, and we try to stay within this limit.

You see, we have here a population of twelve hundred individuals, and of course some use more medical services than others. Our computations take this into account, and the average expense per person is about $100 per year. I brought our next year's budget for you to see. Our largest expenses are for dental treatment, about 38 percent of the total budget; that's because insurance doesn't cover dental treatment. The second largest item (19 percent), which again isn't covered by insurance, is for eyeglasses, and the third item is for visiting hospitalized members. All our expenses for private physicians, which include psychological counseling, amount to 8 percent of the general health budget—so after all the arguments and conflicts, it doesn't amount to much.

Actually, I'm also a social worker. In the Yom Kippur War I lost one of my three sons. It was a very difficult time. My two elder sons left the kibbutz years ago; they are both high officers in the Army, and their military careers didn't agree with the kibbutz way of life. This third son was my youngest. He had just returned from the Army after his regular service, and he was the least militarily oriented of them all . . . so he was killed in the war. . . .

Well, while I was recovering, the kibbutz suggested that I go out a bit for a change of air, and just at that time a course for training kibbutz social workers was opened in the kibbutz Higher Education Center, so I joined this program. I studied there for two and a half years and I am now qualified to be a social worker in a kibbutz. In the meantime, however, since there hasn't been an available position, I have been working for the last two years in a nursing home for elderly people in town, not far from here. I have been doing three days of work a week in this nursing home and three days at home, as coordinator of the health committee. What I would rather do next year, if it will be possible, is to resign my work with the health committee—after all, I have been doing it for a very long time —and divide my work week between working as a social worker in one of the nearby kibbutzim—and going back to the lab at the olive factory. This would be a good combination, and I won't have to be out of the kibbutz all week.

I'm pleased with my life in the kibbutz. I have never lived elsewhere in Israel, so I can't compare my life with other life-styles, but I know that my husband would never have considered living elsewhere. I'm bitter towards the kibbutz on one point. I believe that my sons left the kibbutz —especially the second one, who is a pilot—because the kibbutz wasn't flexible enough to allow them to continue their military careers and simultaneously remain kibbutz members. They left in the 1960s. After the Yom Kippur War there was a change of attitude towards Army careers. I felt very frustrated at the time, because I couldn't change the kibbutz decision concerning my second son, and later, after they had both left, I couldn't help them financially in settling down in town. I know that parents who live in town and have worked hard all their lives like we have, could have had decent savings to help their children in buying an apartment or in making their first steps in town. We, however, were helpless in this sense, and I felt it was basically unfair.

On the other hand, years later when our youngest son fell in the war, I felt so supported, protected, and encouraged by the kibbutz community that I can't even express my gratitude. This help has canceled out my former criticism of the kibbutz.

D A L I A *(age 50)*

Dalia is a self-assured, slim, and elegant woman, who doesn't look at all like a typical grandmother.

When I was about forty years old, after filling many roles in Makom, I decided that I wanted to make a fresh start while I was still young enough to do so. Therefore, I requested permission to go and study social work in a special program preparing social workers for kibbutzim. At first, my request was rejected. Our school demanded that I return to my former position as a teacher, and said that the community wasn't prepared for the idea of a social worker in a kibbutz. I didn't relent, however, and I made the rounds among the central kibbutz members, trying to gain their support. Not knowing too much about social work myself, I convinced several people that as a social worker I'd probably return to our school and help to solve some of its problems. (I really believed I'd go in that direction, then.) Anyway, at the second vote, several months later, my program was approved and I went to study at the beginning of 1971.

The course was pretty interesting and its greatest obstacle was myself. The shift I was required to make in my personality, from being an authoritative, managerial person to an accepting and understanding one, never judging others by my own scale of values, was not an easy one for me.

I studied and did some supervised field work for two and a half years, then returned to the kibbutz and started looking for a job. With the experience I had gained, I realized that a kibbutz social worker should never work in her own kibbutz. Why not? Because if you have to work with a couple who have serious marital problems about which you know the most intimate details, it can be very embarrassing to meet them later at a party, or at the children's home where you both put your children to sleep. I don't want to remind them of their troubles whenever they see me in the kibbutz, and I don't want to be a person one has to avoid, either. Furthermore, in my own kibbutz, where people have known me for so long, they may be unable to see me suddenly as a professional who might be able to help them. Their reaction may be: "Who is *she* to advise us— she herself is such-and-such in her private life." So, maintaining a certain distance from your public by working in another kibbutz is beneficial to the social worker herself, her work, and the society in which she's functioning. She may use her expertise for other purposes in her home, as I do with my activities for the elderly, but I'll tell you about that later.

To go back to the early 1970s, when we, the graduates of the first course, were looking for jobs in kibbutzim, we were faced with unwillingness on the part of the kibbutz to accept our role as being at all useful. We met with secretaries of various kibbutzim, visited in clubs and assemblies, and presented ourselves as people who had been trained to deal with both universal human problems as well as with problems specific to the kibbutz system, to which we all belonged. The main objections were questions such as: Why do we need a social worker in our just and equal society? Have we failed in our own principle of reciprocal aid to the extent that we need to rely on professionals? Our answers pointed to the hard times the kibbutz had been obliged to live through, the early material difficulties that prevented the young communities from paying more attention to their individual members. How many individuals were worn down in the long struggle for survival, how many suicides and breakdowns occurred in the early stages, how many people left the kibbutz in despair because they felt rejected, their personal needs unsatisfied? Naturally, just to mention these unpleasant aspects of the kibbutz produced a sense of failure and guilt in the older generations, the founders of the kibbutz. Yet we persisted in presenting our point of view, arguing that human problems were universal and the kibbutz society isn't exempt from them either. A retarded child, an unhappy marriage, death in the family—these universal experiences are common both to Makom and to a remote African village, and the social worker is trained to help people cope with such events, wherever they are.

Well, gradually the kibbutzim got used to this idea and most of them have introduced social workers into their communities. I myself am working in two kibbutzim, so presently I'm away from home five days a week. In return, Makom has another social worker who comes from another kibbutz to work here.

My work is carried out on many levels, focusing partly on the individual and partly on the total community, its institutions, procedures, and rules. Social functionaries of the kibbutz consult with me and refer members to me for treatment and many people approach me of their own accord. If I suggest, for example, that the kibbutz is not paying enough attention to the difficulties its youngsters experience when returning from military service, we can work out a program to improve this area. Or, I noticed that in one of "my" kibbutzim the procedure had been to discuss individual members' requests within various committees and institutions without inviting the person in question to participate or even listen in on these discussions. Since I believe that this is an unhealthy situation, I spoke about it to the key people and I managed to implement the desired change. Another community program with which I am involved is our "singles" project, which is a series of meetings and activities that I have planned with several neighboring kibbutzim to gather single people of various ages into groups in order to provide them with social opportunities and to use the meetings to work on the improvement of their self-image and communication skills.

Besides these kinds of community projects, I dedicate a great deal of time to individual counseling. I find that the kibbutz, besides not preventing universal human problems, has created some problems quite specific to it. For example, if someone is a scapegoat in a kibbutz and she changes her behavior after intensive, supervised effort, it's still impossible to change the kibbutz's attitude towards her. People acquire certain labels pretty early in their lives and these social labels are terribly resistant to change. The kibbutz society was once revolutionary, but today I find it to be ultra-conservative. It's immensely difficult to make any changes in it. On the other hand, this woman can't change her social reference group easily, either. I suggested that she leave the kibbutz, but she's a divorced woman and a mother of two, and doesn't have the resources necessary to start a new life elsewhere. In town, she would be able to enter a different society with greater ease, I believe, but here she's doomed to live within the same framework forever, and that "framework" is stubbornly resistant to changing its attitudes towards such an individual. This is a typical kibbutz situation.

My greatest contribution to the community of Makom, however—one in which I also make use of my professional training—is in my involvement with our senior members. We were among the first kibbutzim to organize activities in this area, and as such we currently serve as a model for other kibbutzim.

I initiated my activities with older members while still a student in social work; the secretariat offered it to me as a challenge and a problem that was bothering the community at large. Our community was growing older: The first generation had passed the age of sixty and many parents of members had joined us. We assumed that those "sixty-plussers" were, by now, quite tired. For fifty years they had struggled with economic, social, and family problems, carrying a heavy burden and great responsibility. What were their present needs? We decided to start very modestly, and passed around a questionnaire, trying to identify some simple needs which we could use as a starting point for our activities. At that time we didn't even appoint a formal committee for the problems of senior members, which would have been the usual kibbutz procedure, because we didn't know if these people were willing to be defined as a sub-group in need of special attention at all.

We have initiated many different activities to assist single or childless senior members. We tried to have families "adopt" these people, a standard procedure regarding "outside children" and volunteers, but it didn't work out too well. Then we had a better idea. Our different nursery-school classes would adopt elderly people who had no grandchildren here. Think of the state of mind of one old lady hearing her neighbor complaining that she had five Hannukah parties to attend, in every grandchild's class, and how could she manage them all . . . while the listener herself had no grandchildren at all! Every nursery and kindergarten class adopted such people—they were invited to the children's parties and they took the children to visit their places of work, etc. This has been working for several years now and it's really nice.

We have also started a tradition of organizing collective birthday parties for the sixty- and seventy-year-olds, gathering all those who reached that age in a given year to celebrate the fact. In this way we wanted to avoid the situation where one member has a big family with whom to celebrate, while another member may have just a spouse or no one at all. We get the families to help us in the preparations, of course, but we include people without families in all the activities, with "surrogate" families to hand them the presents and "adopted" grandchildren to make their invitations, etc. This is done in collaboration with our cultural committee and it's becoming one of the cherished traditions of this kibbutz. We have also organized several trips for elderly people, suitable to their age and health, the climax of these being a recent visit to Jerusalem which included a meeting with the President. While all these activities were going on, we conducted another survey throughout the whole community, regarding specialized care for the elderly. We found that people want to build a health-care center within the kibbutz, with facilities for people who can't live alone anymore. We don't want to send anyone out of the kibbutz, nor to put people away in a distant corner here. We estimate our social resources to be such that it would be possible to carry out such a project. We have already trained three women to take care of the elderly and we have drawn up detailed plans, which other kibbutzim have already adopted, for the proposed center. We, however, have not yet started carrying out these plans because of financial concerns. I hope this will be one of the high-priority projects in our next five-year development plan.

Finally, I would like to add our "Monday Club" to the list of our activities in the social-concern area. We thought it would be good to organize a meeting place for our senior members, but we didn't want to label anybody as "senior." We gave it a lot of consideration, the result being one of the best institutions we have in this kibbutz. By not labeling it as a "senior-members club," we let people decide for themselves if they want to join. Some join at fifty and others don't come although they are past seventy. It's simply an open-club meeting which takes place every Monday at 5:00 P.M. (In the evening people have many activities: T.V. programs, study groups and hobby groups. In the morning, people are occupied with work, so the afternoons are the most difficult hours for lonely people.) After we launched the club, it was taken over by the club members themselves and is currently based almost completely on their own contributions. Members gather for refreshments and informal conversations, or they prepare their own program such as the presentation of a book review or a poetry reading, and quite frequently they have one of the members telling his or her life story. There were some meetings in which Holocaust experiences were shared, or when people discussed how their families were exterminated by the Nazis. I always hear very good things about the social atmosphere of the club and its significance for people who attend it regularly. For some people, it has provided a real change in their lives and I'm very proud to have helped in its initiation.

The most recent project which I undertook in this area was a survey regarding retirement procedures in the kibbutz. We have a certain process of gradually reducing work hours as an individual ages (beginning at fifty for females and fifty-five for males) and according to the health of the individual. It has always been considered one of the advantages of kibbutz life that people can continue working as they grow older, and that it is the responsibility of the kibbutz to find suitable jobs for them, whatever their physical limitations. Members of the kibbutz don't have to live through the trauma of being thrown out of their work. As the coordinator of our committee, however, I have recently received five applications for complete retirement. People argued that after so many years of work they were entitled to total freedom, to dedicate their time to their hobbies, or to visit their children who live outside, etc. One of the people who applied is an artist who wants to dedicate all of her time to her art. Our social secretary was somewhat alarmed by this new trend, since work is one of the sacred values in the kibbutz, but I have encouraged him to face the phenomenon and, first of all, to collect data about the preferences of our entire senior group. I haven't completed the analysis of the data yet, but I have the impression that the choice of full retirement is rather unusual in our community.

So you see, I'm deeply involved in my activities in this area, and it gives me satisfaction to know that I am contributing to *my* kibbutz, not simply to the others where I work.

I know that I have come a long way since I joined the kibbutz, unwillingly, almost twenty-nine years ago. I'm satisfied with my life here, both personally and professionally. I guess this is due to my personal resources, to my ability to cope. It's true, I have achieved my own goals within the system, but I have always been a contributing member of the system and have fulfilled my various functions with love and dedication. It's also true that there are more men than women who feel this kind of satisfaction with their lives here. Women are often bitter and frustrated, in spite of the fact that the kibbutz offers them many opportunities for personal development, if they only knew what they really wanted. I don't think that the kibbutz can be blamed for this situation. If women wanted to change their lot—if they knew what they wanted—they'd surely get it. They seem to want so little though—they want to have a nice family, apartment, and good looks. And I ask myself: Is this enough? Indeed, the family has become much more important in our lives, and it takes much more of the women's energies than their work. Women invest very little in their jobs or branches and they don't show any ambition to advance in position or responsibility.

I believe that husbands have very much to do with this phenomenon. In order for a woman to be able to succeed in her work, she needs the full cooperation of her husband who must become a real partner in their life together. Kibbutz husbands are frequently like Arab *effendis*—they don't do anything around the house, and they take only minimal care of the children. With our bigger apartments and large families, there are many daily routine chores, all of which are considered the wife's sole responsibility. It's not enough that the kibbutz provides its members with kitchen and laundry services and the common-lodging arrangement for children; there are still many household responsibilities, and I believe they should be equally shared between husband and wife. As long as men don't change in that respect, women will remain unachieving and bitter.

I'm lucky. My husband is a different type. When I return home tired, he prepares our meals. He cleans our apartment as often as I do, and, above all, he's always there to listen to me after my long days outside the kibbutz. I don't have a formula for such a match, but it has certainly worked out well for me.

M I C H A E L *(age 62)*

Michael came to pick me up from my room at 6:00 A.M. and together we walked to the kibbutz cemetery. I had been told that he was half blind, yet he walked freely, pointing out different trees, and seemed completely at ease in his surroundings. We walked past an old water tower, which used to be outside the kibbutz and now marks the beginning of a new neighborhood. He showed me the fields and a new garden he was planting.

"For years I was the gardener of the kibbutz," Michael told me as we walked. "We have always paid a lot of attention to our courtyards and common grounds, and have kept all of them cultivated. Years ago, when we moved here, people said that nothing would grow in this soil. We tried everything, hoping that something would succeed and, lo and behold, almost everything did!" He proudly pointed to the big trees and the exquisite flower beds. "Even a Himalayan cedar has taken root in our grounds."

"Twenty five years ago," he continued, "I started the project of affixing signs on all the plants, printing their Hebrew names for all of us to learn. People asked: 'Is it really so? Does every little flower and plant have a Hebrew name?' Just recently our children renovated this project as a present to the kibbutz for its fiftieth birthday."

Finally we arrived at a stately tree-lined boulevard with signs pointing to the graveyard and, after some distance, a massive metal gate.

In 1972 I had an accident, following which I partially lost my eyesight. I was told I'd have to limit my work to only easy jobs. After I returned from the hospital, I tried several office jobs, but after years of working outdoors I simply couldn't adjust to this type of work. So I decided I'd take a small area and cultivate it as a park, and it occurred to me to focus on our graveyard, which was rather neglected at that time. There were just four rows of trees and the gravestones. So I took it upon myself, and started this job single-handedly. At the beginning I was very careful of my health and did just a little; presently, I am working seven hours a day, cultivating an area of about twenty *dunams,* which is a lot for one gardener whatever his age or health. I get great satisfaction from my work.

When I started, I had to decide what the character of our graveyard should be: Should it be a spot of mourning and communion, or a place where people walk in freely because it's pleasant and not forbidding? I visited various graveyards and talked to people, and decided that our graveyard should be a place that expressed homage to our dead, yet in a manner that our children would also be willing to visit without fear or dread. I decided that a pretty garden with flowers would create the right atmosphere, and I believe I have succeeded: Children come here often, with or without their teachers, and even volunteers like to take a walk in the graveyard.

Sometimes little children approach me and ask: "Show me where my grandfather's place is." They feel a sense of attachment to the spot. Other children or family members often come to water the flowers on the graves of their dear ones—the place is never left empty for long. Since I have planted so many different flowers here, each season has its own particular attraction, and many simply come to admire the view; in the winter, the whole area is covered with thousands of cyclamens. Every visitor who comes to the kibbutz is usually shown this spot. It's not just pretty and peaceful here, but it teaches something about the history of the kibbutz.

Right at the entrance you see our memorial monument. It's made simply of four basalt boulders which were dug out of the hills. You see two inscriptions on it: one commemorating the victims of the Holocaust, the other in memory of our soldiers who fell in the different wars. At the top of the hill are the oldest graves, and as you go down the slope they get more and more recent. Some of our dead from the very beginning of the kibbutz are still buried at the Fountain, near our old camp.

Here, among the oldest graves, you see two of our members who were killed by Arabs in the riots of the 1930s, and several graves with the inscription "took his own life." Yes, those are the early suicides—several more are down at the Fountain. We don't try to hide these deaths; they are part of our early history and its hardships, our price for building this kibbutz. Here are some of the dead of the various wars, and down there, the terrible line of eleven tombstones, our Yom Kippur War dead. I put a plant and an empty black clay flowerpot on every grave, for the families to bring fresh flowers whenever they visit. Otherwise I keep away from the graves and tend to the surrounding flora.

I myself do not deal with the burials or the ceremonies involved. We have a special committee which takes care of that, and it's changed every year. We're a big kibbutz now and have about six to eight burials a year. Burials in the kibbutz don't exactly follow Jewish rules; we have developed a tradition of our own. People come, friends read poetry or a chapter from the Bible, a eulogy is sometimes recited. When the family specifically asks for it, a religious ritual is organized, or a family member may say the Kaddish. But I'll tell you, frankly, in most cases the person reading the prayer doesn't understand it anyway, it's just a disgrace.

Individualists

A S H E R (age 69)

Everybody told me I have to interview Asher, because he is "something else." He was busy, however, restoring an old mosaic floor of a synagogue on the grounds of another kibbutz. On my walks in the kibbutz, I noticed his house, somewhat removed from the other houses and easy to recognize because of his mosaic decorations. Finally, during one of my last visits, we met to talk. He showed up in my room in shorts and sandals although it was raining outside. "That's what I always wear. Didn't anyone tell you?"

"No," I answered, "but I was told it would be interesting to talk to you."

"Thank you," he said, "I'm always willing to meet young women. I guess people say it would be interesting to talk to me because, in a way, I'm a moshavnik* *who lives in the kibbutz. My way of joining the kibbutz was pretty unusual, and the way I have been living here is quite unusual, too."*

I asked him to tell me about it.

I'm the eldest Yekke here. I came in 1931, from Germany—as my accent surely indicates. My father owned a bottle factory, which employed about one hundred workers, and at the age of sixteen I was sent to Nuremberg, the big city, to learn about industry and business administration, so that I'd be able to take my place as my father's heir in the factory. The way to learn, then, was by becoming an apprentice, so I became a clerk in a big factory in Nuremberg. When I went to the city, I was completely ignorant of modern political trends. In my hometown I had never heard a word ending with "ism"—idealism, communism, socialism—all these concepts were completely new for me. Zionism was even more remote, and I never heard it mentioned until I was nineteen.

During my stay in Nuremberg, I felt, however, several new thoughts forming within me. Firstly, I felt more drawn to the workers than to their employers, and soon enough I wrote to my father: "When I come back to our town, I'm willing to become a worker in your factory, but I don't want to run the place."

One who lives in a moshava, *an noncommunal agricultural settlement.

A second development concerned my return to nature. As I was being prepared by the family to enter "high society," I was sent to dancing school. Intuitively, I felt the decadence of this kind of society and I felt revolted by this experience. Instead of improving my dancing and polishing my manners, I was drawn to nature, to the woods, to the unspoiled landscapes. I remember I wrote a letter to our town's rabbi and I asked him—if I feel closer to God when I drive my car out to the forest on Shabbat than when I attend, well dressed and groomed, the artificial services in a synagogue, which should I do? And, I must give him due credit for his liberal response—he said he approved of my driving in the woods. Indeed, I used to do this; I worked all week in the factory, and on Saturday I walked in the woods, in the mountains. I wanted to become a farmer. I dreamed of a life with people who shared my beliefs.

The third idea which concerned me then is more complicated to explain today. It was about Judaism. When I was very young, I felt I was a German patriot. I knew I was Jewish; I had read about Moses and considered him to be a great politician, and the Jews of the past, a great nation. But, as a nation, I saw Judaism as a phenomenon of the past; I searched continuously for a contemporary Jewish identity that would be based on nationalism, not on religion.

Well, I grappled with all these problems all by myself. I didn't know other people were struggling with similar dilemmas, nor did I read the writings of philosophers which were very relevant to my search. I was ignorant of the ideological and political movements which had answers to my quest; it's hard to believe how culturally isolated I had grown in my parents' milieu.

At the age of nineteen my direction was determined by a chance meeting with a young man who came from a Jewish Polish family. I remember the time he told me: "You know, right now there is a Zionist Congress in Basel." And I asked, innocently, what he was talking about. He said: "The Zionist Congress is for the Jews like the Reichstag for the Germans." He told me about Zionism, about agriculture in Palestine, about the kibbutz. I felt that this was exactly what I had been searching for. The following morning I went to the Zionist Association in Nuremberg and asked to join a *hachshara* group.

This step started a long struggle with my family, who couldn't understand and certainly could not identify with my choice. Everybody who knew me or my family said: "Well, he's such a wealthy boy that he can allow himself to play with such romantic ideas." The family doctor, also a Jew, who was consulted by my distressed mother, said I was an adolescent going through Werther Leiden*.... That was the atmosphere in my environment. I felt completely alienated from them, but I didn't dare to

---

*Romantic melancholy and disgust of life, an allusion to the romantic desperation of the hero in Goethe's *The Sorrows of Young Werther*.

break my ties with my family, and for a year and a half I maintained my job at the factory in Nuremberg, yet always nourishing my dream of another sort of existence.

After a year and a half, I heard that a group of *chalutzim* was coming to live in town, to work in the factories during the winter since they were out of work on the farms. I was so excited that for two days and nights I waited for them at the train station, finally falling asleep just as they arrived. Later I managed to meet them. (Some of them later came to Makom.) Immediately I felt attracted to them, and I thought to myself: Why am I postponing my final step so much? Why am I struggling so hard with myself? So I took all my savings, left my private apartment and the factory, and joined the group. They were living as a commune in an old wooden hut and I was accepted as a member. This seriously deepened my conflict with my family. An uncle claimed that we were "criminal Communists," and when my mother came to talk me out of my plans, we quarreled so badly that finally she said: "Don't come back home unless you've changed your ways." In the meantime my group went elsewhere, and I ran away to Berlin, following them.

In Berlin I asked to go and work for a farmer—not in a commune of pioneers—as I felt that learning agriculture really well was more important than talking out ideas. . . . People in the Zionist office said that I was a lost cause, that I'd probably become a good farmer, but never immigrate to Palestine. Just the same, they arranged for me to work in a farm. Again I was alone. One day a Zionist functionary of some kind came to visit me and asked me: "Why are you working today?" and I asked him, "Why not?" to which he answered that it was Passover. . . . I was cut off from all that, you see. But I learned a lot about farming.

But in spite of all the predictions that I wouldn't go, in 1931 I arrived in Palestine, with a good background in farming, and very little interest in ideology . . . [*laughs*]. By the way, I was also reconciled with my family before I left Germany. My father gave me the money for the trip and I arrived on a tourist visa.

When I came to the country, I was sent to another kibbutz, older than Makom, in the center of the country. I stayed there for three weeks. At the same time, the group at the Fountain, who considered themselves intellectuals, decided that the German pioneers, with their broad education and cultural background, were more suitable to them. We moved there and I was immediately sent to Jerusalem on a construction job for three months, during which time I was away from the Valley and the kibbutz. During that time, the various kibbutzim couldn't decide who would go where. A lady came and asked me:

"Can you draw?"

I said, "No."

"Can you write stories?"

"No."

"Are you a musician?"

"No."

"Have you ever been to a museum?" [*Laughs.*]

The Makom group was dying for intellectuals. . . . I failed to meet their criteria, but I liked my short encounter with the group and their location and I stood firmly on my ground. I said I had come from Bavaria, from a mountain land, and after three weeks in the plains (in that first kibbutz) I knew I couldn't live there. Thus, I finally became a member of Makom—in a pretty unusual way.

Now that I look back on my life here—forty-seven years is not a short while—I see that I really found the way to realize my dreams: to live by my three principles—being a worker not an employer, cultivating the land, and making my Jewish roots into a national identity. Indeed, lately I visited Germany and met a non-Jewish woman who used to be my friend before I emigrated. We sat in a coffee shop together and she said: "We all forgot everything, all the dreams of our youth. You are the only one who has lived up to your dreams." I feel very strongly about that, since in my case it isn't the actualization of what I was *educated* to become, but of what I personally discovered to be important.

I'm somewhat exceptional among the members of this kibbutz. During the division, for example, almost thirty years ago, when hot arguments were going on about ideology and politics, I was somewhat of an outsider. I kept saying: "The important thing is to feel at home in a place, not the ideology. If people don't feel at home here, let them go." They asked me: "Whom are you for—Mapai or Mapam?" I said: "I'm for this kibbutz. I'm a *mishkist.*" I was considered crazy. Everybody thought otherwise; in school, for example, there was someone teaching political science at that time, but no teacher specializing in agriculture. I don't believe much in education, but once, many years ago, I wanted to prove my point about the need for agricultural studies, so I went to the school and asked the kids two questions: Why did the division take place, and why do we plow the fields every year? I predicted that they would know the answer for the first question but not for the second. . . . To my amazement I found out they were ignorant in both areas to the same degree. . . .

In this sense I was always an outsider; I saw our main role in working and cultivating the land, not in politics. I didn't want any part in the leadership of this kibbutz, either. I have no ambition for such things. When the Hagana activities were going on here, I was never interested in becoming a general. But ask people how many caches I dug with my own hands. . . . I always dealt with the practical side of things. For twenty years I was on the burial committee of the kibbutz; digging graves, rather than dealing with the social or ritual aspects of death, was my responsibility.

I have always managed to live alone, without roommates or neighbors. When I came here, in 1931, there were only a few huts. In 1937 I built my own hut from scratch, with my own hands. I put it somewhat outside the camp. The house I live in now, which is still private and removed from the rest, was one of our military posts once, which I reconstructed by myself. I said to my wife: "If I want to see people—I know where to find them. But I need the space to be without people as well." Furthermore, I never attend the general assembly meetings anymore. How many years can one attend every Saturday night without uttering a word? My area is agriculture, I've grown olive trees for forty-three years, and I'm the person who established our olive-conserving project many years ago—first for our own use, then for the neighboring villages. I left the project, however, when it became industrialized. I'm for agriculture, not industry, as our main line of work. This is a struggle which I lost, obviously. Many years ago, I occasionally had something to say to the assembly. But since young people run all the branches now, old guys like myself have to be content with listening to their plans and reports and I have lost my interest. I'm not bitter about it, I believe it's a normal development, and I personally have found my satisfaction in my mosaic work.

I'm sixty-nine years old, but I've remained childish in many ways, I guess. I still feel ideology isn't worth a dime, and if our youth is staying here, it's not due to our good education, but because they love the place, it's their home. Moreover, I see how the second generation has introduced changes in the kibbutz, how they've adapted it to their preferred way of life—and I find this to be a normal process as well. They're more interested in comfort and privacy, they may even start family sleeping arrangements for their children. Our young generation is actually approaching what has always been my point of view: They stay away from politics. They don't understand—and therefore are willing to forgive—the political splits and arguments of the past. The kibbutz lost much of its national role with the establishment of the State; it isn't as central as it used to be thirty or fifty years ago. So, if it becomes just a pleasant life-style, it will survive; otherwise, who knows. . . .

The only fault I find with our current way of life is the terrible wastefulness I see everywhere. It's a result of the lack of personal responsibility for our expenses. Take electricity, for example; people keep it on for nothing. Or the way they treat cars, as if they don't really belong to them. Or the food waste, and the kind of food people give to dogs here!

Equality today is not what it used to be. Years ago people really didn't have any private money or income of any sort. I had a rich aunt who visited me in 1935 and gave me a present of one and a half pounds to buy some candy for my wife. I took the money and bought thirty meters of rubber water hose which I urgently needed for our olive plant—and I was reprimanded for it, because I didn't give the money to the cashier! In 1941, my brother, who lived in town, volunteered for the British Army. He had a radio and he gave it to me to keep during his absence. As a kibbutznik I felt it was against all my principles, however, to put the radio in my room. So you know what I did? There lived with us here a hired worker, who was our expert in the textile factory. I asked him to put the radio in his room, and all I permitted myself was to visit him and listen to a good concert from time to time.

Today everybody has a radio and T.V. in their rooms—equipment that the kibbutz provides. And if someone installs a stereo of his own in his room, nobody raises a single question about it. It might have been bought from his budget savings, of course, and, as long as people don't feel envious of each other, there is no danger of developing social stratification within the kibbutz, and there's no threat to the kibbutz's existence.

There have been changes in many other areas of our life. One that I can think of is in our attitudes towards Jewish traditions. We still bury people our own way, and no one forces us to do it in a "Jewish way." But people care much more about the Jewish religion today. Some people are even talking about building a synagogue. We had a completely different approach in the past. Take weddings, for example. Just recently a friend's son got married here; the bride wore a white dress, a gold ring, of course, and about three hundred guests came from all over the country to participate in the ceremony which was conducted by a rabbi here. During the celebration, I reminded the mother of the groom, now a widow, about our own common weddings years and years ago [laughs]. I had been living with my wife for twelve years, and our friends—whose son was getting married—had been living in a family tent for six years, when, for various reasons, we decided to have an official wedding. We borrowed rings for the ceremony, and after work we took a horse cart and went to a rabbi in a neighboring village who performed the ritual on the spot. No special clothes, no party—it was just nothing. I had to have a marriage certificate in order to adopt a child—and I don't even know why my friends wanted the rabbi's approval just then. Often it was during the woman's pregnancy that the couple decided to get "properly" married, and if the woman was in an advanced stage of her pregnancy and was embarrassed about going to the rabbi—another *chavera* volunteered to take her place!. . . . Times have changed.

All in all, I see many more positive than negative aspects in our life. There are so many advantages here! I'll mention just two: It's the best place to grow old in, and nowhere is there such good medical care as we get here, from birth until death. If someone needs treatment, he can go to the best specialist, the best hospital. There is no limit to the support given in such cases. I know this from our experience when my wife had difficulties becoming pregnant.

Although many people admit that we in the kibbutz have the best kind of life, it's undeniable that it hasn't become a common choice in Israel or in other parts of the world. I remember in 1948, when poor, disadvantaged new immigrants lived in temporary camps around here and many of them worked here every day, we tried to persuade them to join the kibbutz as members, but we failed completely. They didn't feel attracted to our way of life, in spite of all the immediate economic benefits they could get from such a decision. The kibbutz, somehow, doesn't suit the natural tendencies of the majority of people. It therefore has no real value as a practical socialist solution to the misery of the world. As one socialist thinker told me years ago in Berlin: "You're going to the kibbutz —that's very well for you, personally. But do you think that a drop of pure water can sterilize the huge wound of mankind? A kibbutz is nothing but another monastery." Only years later did I realize how right he was.

Recently I have become an artist and the Israeli Archaeological Society has given me restoration jobs. It's really strange! I, who couldn't draw the simplest face, can create lively pictures in mosaic. . . . It's a beautiful occupation, but I don't have enough time for all I want to do. As a man my age, I'm required to work only two days in my branch, which is still the olive-growing trade. I work more than that, however, because I feel responsible for my trees. Only in the winter, when it's raining hard, do I allow myself to calmly work on my hobby. I know, however, that even if I occupied myself solely with my mosaic work, nobody would object. I search for colorful rocks all over the country, and I personally break them into tiny pieces. I enjoy my work and, surprisingly, I get positive reactions from others, too. I pity all artists, you know, all those poor souls who run after exhibitions and have to sell themselves to the public. Often they create for the public, according to the style in fashion, and hardly ever do what their inner selves dictate. Here again I thank the kibbutz for my different lot.

S H U L A M I T   I L A N   *(age 63)*

Shulamit and David Ilan live in a secluded spot in the kibbutz. Two palm trees grow at the entrance to their house. She says they grew there wild. The shadow of the dense trees adds to the darkness in the room; the windows are ornamented with colored-paper cutouts, blocking the daylight and creating a twilight atmosphere. The room itself is crowded with books, pictures, and photographs, two of which stand out immediately: a picture of a bearded old man, probably her father; and, on the opposite wall, a big picture of her son who was killed in the Yom Kippur War. A peculiar homemade violin hangs near the young man's portrait.

Shulamit herself is dark haired. She is wearing a long dark gown and talks softly, smoking incessantly. She seems to be absorbed in her inner world of memories, mourning and literary inspiration.

People say that she lives a closed life, remote from the public eye. She does not participate in assembly meetings or vote on any issue in the kibbutz. She has never belonged to any committee as far as anyone can recall. Someone remembers that many years ago, perhaps twenty-five years ago, she, as a teacher, had a severe conflict with the school authorities, and as a result declared that she would no longer be a member of the kibbutz but would live there privately with her family. It is not clear whether such an event really occurred. In spite of her seclusion, she is highly respected within the community. She wrote many of the texts of the Jubilee celebrations and published a collection of anecdotes about the early days of the kibbutz. She also writes many of the memorial booklets for deceased members.

At first, Shulamit refused to be interviewed. "I myself am a writer," she said, "and my thoughts are the material I myself use for my writings." But after some unrecorded conversations she consented and gave me the long and moving interview upon which the following picture is based.

For years and years I have been a teacher of the humanities. For thirty out of my forty years in the kibbutz I worked in the school. During the remaining time I studied Bible at the university, worked for a couple of years as an editor, and now I spend most of my time writing.

Actually, I always wrote, but mostly for myself. After my son was killed, however, five years ago, I felt the need to find a new meaning for my life and I started on a project of my own. For years I have been aware of the provinciality of the Israeli culture. It's all imported from the States, completely denying our own rich sources and roots. It's a despicable culture. I decided that, for the few remaining years of my life, I'd dedicate my time entirely to bringing our heritage, our old legends and historical tales, to the general public, especially to children of all ages.

You see, I myself grew up in this tradition. I was born in Jerusalem in an Orthodox home. My father was a rabbi who also had an extensive secular education. Although he died when I was only four, my mother educated me in his footsteps. These old Jewish stories were, therefore, the stuff of my imagination throughout my childhood. I have the sources here in my room, and the earliest tales I heard and learned come back to me very easily. By now, I have published more than twenty books for children, all containing retold Jewish legends. There's a book about witches and demons, about animals, about certain periods in our history, about God and His miracles—there is no end to the wealth of material in our tradition. My goal is to make very young children, preschoolers, aware of and acquainted with the heroes of our history, our scholars, our myths. This should replace the imported fairy tales or cartoons which have dominated our children's literature until recently.

It's not enough to teach our children about the State of Israel and the history of the kibbutz. An Israeli child should be aware of the fact that he's carrying the burden of the long history of the Jewish people, with its martyrs and miracles, with the Ten Commandments and the seven Noachide Laws which are the foundations of the whole world's ethics and religion. He should realize this and be proud of it. Children who receive a religious education are aware of this heritage, but other children sadly enough are not. That's what I aim to achieve through my books, although I'm not a religious person in my daily life.

But in fact, Makom was never too remote from the Jewish tradition. This was due to individuals, not to our ideology. Somehow, we have always respected Judaism, the holidays, etc. But not enough—there's much more to do.

So now I'm a full-time writer. I work for many hours, late into the night. All my income goes to the kibbutz, of course. Sometimes I don't feel like writing and then I look for another use for my time. I was Ora's personal nurse for nine months during her severe illness before she died. I washed her and fed her—everything. Nobody appointed me to do the job; I wanted to do it, because of her. I've done this work with other sick people, too. Or, for example, last year the *metapelet* of one of my grandchildren had to be replaced, so I took that job temporarily.

Nobody tells me what to do. Since my books make good money, it's completely understood that I occupy myself in this manner. But that's certainly not the main point. I know that if I so chose I could write all day even if nothing I wrote were published at all. Our kibbutz is very liberal in this area.

There was never a stage when I formally requested to dedicate all my working day to writing; it just happened this way, without a request, an argument, or a formal decision. I don't know if other artists, writers, or painters are in the same situation; I have never asked them.

You see, although I have lived all my life in a kibbutz, I have always managed to do what I wanted as an individual, a woman, a mother—anything. [*This is said as a statement of fact, with the same somewhat bitter expression that accompanies all Shulamit's utterances. There is no trace of pride or satisfaction in this account.*]

My biography is atypical. It wouldn't fit any of the common beliefs about the kibbutz life. Generally speaking, the kibbutz was established by men for men's sake, and women have always played a secondary role, whether strictly as men's servants or as housewives in the most conservative manner. The *chavera* in the kibbutz continues to serve her husband and children without much interest in her work or investment in her own needs. It's partly her fault and partly the result of the general structure. Take the children's common housing, for example. It seems like a possible solution to the mother's responsibility, a means to liberate women. But in fact, all the women work in the common education system, the only difference being that they work with strangers' children and not their own. I raised your kid and you raised my kid, and we were both bitter and unsatisfied, because I believe, and rightly so, that even the worst mother is the best possible person to care for her own children. This is so obvious! I think that the real reasons for the development of the common sleeping arrangement were physical and economical and not ideological. People used to live in tents, leaking huts, or even outside under the trees, so it made sense to concentrate all the children in the only liveable building.

Yet I think that it's up to a woman to overcome these conditions. I fought for my wishes, while most women don't. While raising three little children, I went to college and got my degree. All my life, I worked all night, working like a lunatic, because it was of utmost importance for me not to harm my children and husband. I did all that was required of me as a mother, a wife, even a housewife, perhaps, and when all was done I sat at my desk all night. When I was a teacher, I always continued studying. I used to go to bed at 2:00 A.M. and get up at 5:30, because I was never willing to neglect my own development.

Actually, I don't think the common sleeping arrangement is helpful to women at all, and I have personally fought against it with all my might. I wanted my children near me, I wanted to take care of them. Once, the issue came to a vote and we had a majority for the decision to switch to private lodging, namely, in the parents' room; but it never materialized. First of all because it was right before the division. The political debate somehow paralleled our educational debate and it threw people into more and more extreme positions. It seemed as if the Mapainiks were for private lodging while the Mapamniks, the "real" kibbutzniks, were for common lodging. I was never occupied with politics, but through my husband I was identified as a Mapamnik, and it was clear that I belonged to the majority which was to stay here. It so happened, however, that the people who left for Adama were those who had supported private lodging, and the people who came from Molad were very much against it. So we lost our case.

My own children have, however, grown up mainly in our room, even when we had only one room and no conditions for such an arrangement. Each of my children went through long periods, indeed years, in which they preferred to sleep with us. I always accepted their wish and we managed. It pleased me when they chose to sleep here, and today they have a similar approach towards this question with their own children. Even when two or three of them slept with us regularly, by and large on the floor, we found it a positive experience, enriching us all. My husband felt the same way as I did. For long periods he was away in the Palmach, or came in very late at night, and the children would sleep here with me, and I'd sit at my desk until daybreak, working.

I believe it aggravated some people in the kibbutz, but I never tried to find out what their reactions were, and they never criticized me directly as far as I remember. The children adjusted very well to this arrangement; they didn't suffer in their own class because of this practice, and they knew we always welcomed them. They didn't feel forced to accept a framework which didn't always suit their needs. The only consequence was that our room never became a social club. People didn't drop in in the evening to drink coffee and chat, and we didn't go to others to gossip; we didn't have any sort of social life. This was probably due to our personalities as well. It doesn't matter.

I spend more time in the room than outside with people. I have most of my meals at home. Lunch is the only meal I eat regularly in the dining hall. I feel as if I were working in an establishment where a warm meal is served at noon—as if I, too, were just eating at work. The kibbutz as a collective, its aims and problems have never interested me. I live in the kibbutz because of my husband, who clearly preferred this way of life. If I'd married someone else, I'd probably be living in the city. I am, by nature, non-materialistic and anti-bourgeois, but I wouldn't have selected the kibbutz of my own free will. David and I loved each other when we were very young. I was thirteen and he was sixteen when our bond was formed. He was a born leader. I followed him and I accepted the ideological importance of the kibbutz. In reality, however, the daily life of the kibbutz is something I deeply resent. This togetherness, the constant friction with people—I hate it. I love my friends but I don't like this constant togetherness. Social life is revolting to me. So I managed to lead my private life within the kibbutz, and I feel I have contributed to the kibbutz in my own way, both in teaching and in writing. I was never elected to any function, nor forced to fulfill any role against my wishes. I don't know how people claim they were forced to do this or that; I was never pressured or forced.

My children have been aware of my attitude; I didn't conceal anything from them. They were exposed to my views and to those of others, and they developed their own values. Somehow, four out of the five have become dedicated kibbutzniks, each one with his or her unique outlook on their lives. Yesha, who was killed, was even more of an individualist than I have ever been. Yet he felt the kibbutz was the only place on earth worth living in. . . . My youngest son absorbed my individualism in his own way and he left the kibbutz. He resents discipline. Furthermore, he had already grown up in the free Valley, in a fairly rich kibbutz, and didn't experience the immense role of the kibbutz in building the country. To tell you frankly, his leaving the kibbutz was a disaster for me, a terrible loss. Not because of the distance, or the fact that I see him less; he lives in Tel Aviv now. I'd simply feel better if he were living in another kibbutz. So you see, I'm aware of a gap between what I say and what I must be feeling. I'm very ambivalent. I'd like to have all my children and grandchildren living in the kibbutz out of their own free choice and happy—not like me.

O F E R *(age 38)*

I was born and raised in another kibbutz, but I married a daughter of Makom and came to live here five years ago. I felt that Makom offered me a better chance to pursue my field, which is electronic devices. I have my own lab, not far from the dining hall, and I work there completely alone. Most of my day is spent thinking. I don't mind being alone all day; I need the time.

Years ago, when I realized what sort of person I was, I decided that my top priority is my work. Since I have been able to do my work here, that is enough to make me happy. Actually, I'm happy about many things in this kibbutz, but my work is the most important factor. It isn't easy to arrive at the position where you can sit all day and think, especially in a kibbutz. . . .

When I came here five years ago, I insisted that I wanted to work in electronics, so I was sent to a nearby town to work in a lab. I commuted to work every day and my salary was paid to the kibbutz. Although this job was roughly in my area, I wasn't completely independent and my salary was pretty low. This made me feel—or perhaps I got the message from other people here—that while most adults in the kibbutz were engaged in serious, productive work, economically supporting all of us, I was just fooling around like a child. Obviously, I didn't want to engage in games all my life. I pressed for a higher salary at the lab, and after two years of work I was fired.

My next position was working in the dining hall, which I did for another two years. This was, for me, like being sent to Siberia; it was a horrible time. But nobody made me work there for so long. I made my decision that I'd work as a moron in the dining hall until I would be able to progress to full-time work on my electronics project. For a while I didn't believe I'd ever reach that point; time seemed to stretch interminably; but I knew the end would come.

Throughout that period, I toiled in the dining hall all day, then I went to my room and worked on my independent projects, trying out various devices for irrigation methods, agricultural machines, whatever. I was searching for an invention that would make people believe in me, or rather, that would be economically feasible and that people would be willing to invest money in. In that case, I knew I'd be free to leave the dining hall.

This was an extremely difficult period. I worked in my improvised lab in my room every night until midnight, trying also to find enough time for my two children, whose education I viewed as one of my primary concerns. I had no financial aid whatsoever for my experiments; I worked almost without tools, which is like walking in total darkness. But I didn't ask for any help or instruments then. . . . During that stage, I frequently thought that I might have fared better had I lived in town; I could probably have gotten a job in a big industrial company on a research and development project. If I'd had my whole day for my project I'd probably have reached the right track sooner than I did here. But since I was living here, in a kibbutz, I preferred to continue my work in the dining hall rather than being sidetracked into teaching science or making T.V. repairs, which people thought would have been more appropriate for my background. In the dining hall, I was sure I wouldn't be tempted to deviate from my path by any immediate distractions. Sometimes, while sweeping the floors, I could even continue to develop my projects in my head.

Finally, after two or three years of nightly trial and error, I did get on the right track. The thing I invented has to do with the operation of cotton-picking machines; it's an electronic device which detects blockages in the machines. When I started to develop it, it seemed to be of some promise, and I built a model and tested it in our cotton fields as well as in another kibbutz. The development was slow and gradual, and I worked on it for two years, every season, until the cotton harvest was over. When I had four instruments which worked pretty well, I got myself out of the dining hall and dedicated all my time to further research and development. At that stage it seemed that the invention might have commercial value and I went into large-scale production. I had most of the work done in town, but I carried out some of the complicated aspects myself, and thus we produced forty instruments for sale. We sold about thirty-five of them at very good prices. The whole idea is that this is a device which costs almost nothing to make, but, as the buyers are big field-owners, they're willing to pay anything if a small addition to their millions of dollars of cotton-picking machines will save them a lot of trouble throughout the season.

We made about 350,000 IL* during the last season and plan to make about 2,000,000 IL next season, covering all potential buyers in the country. I knew I had no competition for my invention. I had the advantage of being able to try everything out immediately in our local cotton fields, and I had a good knowledge of and contact with the Israeli market, as our kibbutz services almost all Israeli cotton-picking machines.

Naturally I was very pleased. In addition to the satisfaction I derived from the invention itself, I enjoyed the contacts with the factories and buyers, the relief from my solitude in the lab offered by the real world. Our plan was to supply the entire Israeli market within two or three years, then start exporting and make a quick profit for the kibbutz. Actually, though, during the last season, with about thirty machines working, we have discovered several difficulties which must be corrected. It is just a tiny problem that I know how to solve. Although I had to recall most of the instruments for repairs, the buyers didn't ask for their money back because they realize the potential of these devices and trust that we can overcome the difficulty. Now I'm full of work and, of course, our large-scale project will be delayed for another year until we can further test the instruments in the coming season.

In the meantime, I am working on other inventions and am very content. It was interesting to observe how the attitude of the kibbutz

*In 1979, about $18,000.

towards me has been going through ups and downs following my success and, later, the recall of the device [*laughs*]. At the beginning, when I worked in the lab in town, I was considered a dilettante. Then, when I worked in the dining hall, opinion fell even further. I was a moron who couldn't work in any better place, and probably somewhat crazy, too, with my imagined inventions. I may be exaggerating a bit, but I really felt that this was my image at the time. Later, when my inventions started to improve our irrigation system, people said, "Maybe he will amount to something after all," but I was still considered a grown-up playing games since I wasn't earning any money for the kibbutz. After that, when the blockage detector began to sell, the opinions about me peaked. "He's a gifted young man," they said. "He's going to bring in a great profit." People smiled at me often and expressed encouragement and congratulations. Finally, when the functional problem was discovered, I noticed some decline. People nodded their heads saying, "Well, he might be gifted, but he still has to prove it."

Although the correlation between the amount of money I have been making and the evaluation I have received might sound ridiculous, I basically think it's pretty logical. A person must bring some good to the community, and money is perhaps the simplest measure of his worth. This is a working society, a productive society, and it sounds fair and proper to me to measure each individual by his contribution. If this weren't under control, society couldn't survive. It's true that a big community like ours can allow itself to maintain several good-for-nothings, eternal loafers, in its midst, but I certainly didn't wish to belong to that category [*laughs*]. We even have a term for people of this kind. In kibbutz jargon one says they "carry a yellow ticket." I don't know how this term was derived; it was here before I arrived. A yellow ticket is "given" to a person of whom the society has despaired. It means nobody will put any more pressure on them, nobody will demand that they work or conform; they're crazy and should be left alone to do whatever they want.

I see this term as representing the antithesis of the extreme discipline which is employed in this kibbutz. I find our discipline stricter than that of any other kibbutz, and I know other kibbutzim quite well. The society makes very heavy demands of its members and they internalize these demands. It is so rare for a person to break away from this discipline, this control, that this individual is given a yellow ticket and left completely alone. This is a technique adopted by the society in order not to reject people. Thus, the "deviants" remain inside, but with a terrible stigma attached to them . . . [*pondering*]. Right now I don't know of anyone who carries a yellow ticket. It's a possibility, though, or perhaps a threat used so that people will comply.

People have had different attitudes towards my work, though. Several people, some of them in central positions, say that in a big community like ours, which is so productive, space must be made for two individuals who might develop inventions with low probability for very high profit. The two individuals are myself and another young man who is trying to develop a new branch for raising lobsters. We're both using our brains for something that might be highly profitable, but uncertain at the moment. All in all, as far as I know there are very few members in the whole kibbutz movement who have such a position, namely, that their whole day of work is dedicated to development.

I have been an individualist ever since I can remember. I have always been occupied with abstract thoughts and loved to discover things on my own rather than memorize what my teachers presented. I didn't like school, but I could tolerate it and, surprisingly, I was fairly popular and active in the children's society. I don't think anybody noticed I was an individualist. I had enough time to do what I liked. School didn't excite me or inspire me to excell, since a kibbutz school is usually not achievement oriented. But at least it didn't impede my development. Instead of wasting my energy on getting high grades and caring about my image, I continued to occupy myself with my own interests, and this way I really learned a lot in the deep sense of the word. I think that the kibbutz education does reinforce mediocrity. When someone is just a bit above average, he's pushed down towards the mean. But if someone has real talent, is very high above the norm, this pressure can't harm him, he'll rise up anyway. This was the case with me, and that's what I have noticed recently with my own son here. I don't worry about the effects of the common education on my son. He has, anyway, an ideal private tutor.

In my adolescence I was attracted to philosophy, sociology and psychology, and thought that these would be my areas of interest. I took some college courses in sociology, though, and I felt rather disappointed. I couldn't see any direction within the field. At about that time, I learned that my former kibbutz wouldn't support my studies in the humanities or social sciences unless I wanted to become a teacher. So I decided to apply for something more practical, electrical engineering. I didn't care what I studied; I looked upon all studies as intermediate stages until I'd be able to sit all day and think. Electronics, however, caught my imagination and I don't regret it. It's comfortable to have a concrete product as the result of your thought process. This way, you can be sure your work isn't wasted and you aren't dependent on the approval of others.

I see myself as an involved member of the community. I care about it—it's my place, my home. Yet, above all else, I need time for my work, so I try to eliminate from my life other activities, including public functions here. It's not just egoism. I simply believe that, through my work, I contribute to this kibbutz to the best of my abilities. If I have to drive nails into a board, my power using the hammer is about the same as that of anyone else, but if I employ my brain I believe I can contribute more.

In principle, I do participate in the general assembly meetings. Why "in principle?" I mean that I want to go and consider it of utmost importance; in fact, every Saturday evening I am in conflict with myself, since I would like to participate in the decision making. Yet, in actuality, I hate to waste the time away from my projects, so I usually stay at home and work. This might change in the future. I see myself as a person who might be elected to some public role and then I won't have any excuse. I'm a member of this society and would have to conform.

Makom is the kind of society where people really feel that they're a part of the community, or that the kibbutz is a part of them, and they're willing to contribute in many different ways. This is something special about our kibbutz. In my old kibbutz, I had a completely different impression—that people just live there together, and that their main concern is how to *take* from the kibbutz, what they can *get,* rather than what they can *give.* I think this aspect is complementary to the strict discipline that I mentioned before. One side of the coin is the discipline, while the other side is the profound identification that the members feel with their kibbutz. There is no alienation here—I'm the commune and the commune is me. This sentiment expresses me personally as well, you know. I have long realized that my strong drive to succeed in my work is not merely personal ambition, so that I may say "I did it." Rather, I have the need to belong to the group of people who contribute to the big community of Makom.

There is, of course, a negative side to the phenomenon of discipline and identification. If one doesn't identify, for some reason or other, then the discipline may be experienced as very harsh, rigid, and even cruel. I felt on the verge of this experience for a while at the beginning, and I sympathize with anyone who feels that way.

I believe that there's more than a grain of truth in the general opinion of people here, that this kibbutz is better than many others, in their pride in their home. But this pride often borders on something that I call "victimization." The strong discipline and identification find their expression in the individual sacrifice of one's self for the common goals. It's very clear here and I see it as a mechanism behind the behavior of many people. Nobody forces them to, nobody sacrifices them—they themselves *want* to feel sacrificed by the group, the kibbutz, for the common goals. It reminds me of the pioneers of former times. As a consequence, the same "victims" have a strong need to have a great tombstone erected, a monument, memorializing their deeds. They are compulsively collecting all documents, taking pictures, making films. They aspire to have a complete record, where everything will be saved forever. I see it as a flaw in their personality, they're somehow twisted; or, rather, it isn't these individuals who are twisted but our communal kibbutz personality.

I think this trend is much more apparent in the first generation, but it still exists in the second generation as well. For example, some people still live here in this climate, without air conditioning, a fact which I see as completely unjustified economically. Even the older members got their air conditioners just a short while ago. I believe that this delay was motivated by the need to keep on feeling bad, to keep the standard of living harsh, to satisfy the "victimization" even though it was totally unwarranted! It's funny, I can laugh at the trend but I think it's a profound aspect of our life here.

Not too long ago I saw a plan for the building which would house the kibbutz Archives. It reminded me of a mausoleum, built partially underground as a cave. I think it's sick to build such a monument so that all the evidence of the hardships that the founders underwent will survive forever, while living people are still living in miserable rooms without air conditioning.

I believe I am among the few people who perceive this undercurrent. This is due to the fact that I come from a different, more normal background. My former kibbutz was so normal that people have always seen it as on the verge of collapsing, and they didn't identify with it but thought of how to exploit it for their own good [*laughs*]. My mother still lives in that kibbutz and when she visits me here she says that everyone here seems to grow old before their time. They're very grave in their appearance, their faces are wrinkled, many are lame or hunched up, she says. They work too hard and are their own victims, is what I say.

N I M A (age 33)

Stepping into my room, Nima has the immediate air of someone "different." I smell some perfume; her clothes are well chosen, and her face is delicately made up. As she speaks, she is often cynical yet not bitter, frequently smiling at her own responses to my questions.

I was born here in 1945 to Shlomo (p. 23), whom you recently met. I went through the normal process of growing up here, but what I have recently become is quite unusual. It is unusual because I'm a mother of two *and* I finished my undergraduate studies as a journalist. The newspaper I work for, which is the weekly magazine of the Kibbutz Hameuchad Movement, is actually a worthless paper, but I enjoy my job there. You see, I wrote a book of short stories for adults after I finished my bachelor's degree, and then I couldn't find my place here, among the cooking pans and the diapers. So finally, a year ago, I found my place working on a newspaper in Tel Aviv, and from then on I've worked half a week in Tel Aviv, interviewing and writing, and the remaining three days I'm here, doing all sorts of odd jobs, mostly in the kitchen, sometimes with children, on the condition that I never have to work with infants. I found a wonderful balance in my current way of life that I wish every kibbutznik could experience: three days inside, three days outside the kibbutz. Actually, however, I see this as partly irresponsible on my part. Since I'm away for half the week, I'm always a guest, somehow, and I rarely assume any responsibility here. I have to ask somebody else what to do in the kitchen or in the children's home. But here I'm willing to do the kind of jobs I don't really like, so that I may spend the rest of the week in the city, doing what I really wish to be doing.

Suppose you could move out of here completely?

I couldn't do that; my children are here and my husband would never agree to leave. So we worked out an arrangement: For the two nights that I'm away, he's in charge of the children, and it works out beautifully. Presently, I don't see how I could work full-time within the kibbutz and find satisfaction. This is one of the problems of women in the kibbutz, and I believe it is the most serious problem in our life here.

A few years ago, I worked on the local paper and my major aim was to raise women's consciousness about our unfortunate position in the kibbutz. Women are so helpless and frustrated here that they can hardly see their situation with the proper perspective anymore. The situation is explained by the fact that everyone wants to have many children here. It is a norm that started with the first generation, in spite of the extreme poverty of that time. Women breed babies and then, of course, they have to take care of them; it's a cycle that traps them all. Yet, when they're offered an escape, a workshop or a day of studies, they refuse, convincing themselves that they can't leave their children. Furthermore, the infants' homes, where so many women are occupied, increase the feeling of loneliness; I think it's a terrible mistake to close in one woman with four helpless babies for the day! Other kibbutz movements have different arrangements; six or eight babies with two *metaplot* is a substantial improvement. I felt utter despair when I was left alone with four babies like that! I simply couldn't stand it.

I believe in privacy in one's life and that's what I like about the large size of our kibbutz—it allows more opportunity for privacy. My children spend much of their time in our room and my son, who is six years old, also sleeps there practically every night. Although it is preferred that children sleep in the children's dorms, and in spite of the fact that it disturbs the teachers when children are brought in at all hours to their morning classes, I believe the majority of young children sleep quite frequently in their parents' rooms. Especially on weekends. But even then you find a few miserable souls who are put to sleep in the children's homes. For such children's parents this whole system was invented, so that they can get rid of their children whenever it suits them. . . . This is very exceptional though.

We're now living in a period of intense family life, the holy family in every room. Again it's probably a reaction to our parents' way of life, going from one extreme to the other. Our parents had no sense of family life, especially our fathers. Who among us saw their fathers at all during childhood? One was on a mission abroad, one in the police, one in the Palmach, and one in prison. . . . For months, even years, they were missing. So the present trend—to stand all day and admire your children, to keep them very closely under one's wings—is a reaction to that deprivation. We have not yet found the middle ground, our children will have to integrate those extremes, perhaps. I see the same trend in many areas, such as in our attitudes towards material goods and possessions; our parents had nothing and needed even less, while we are putting all our energy into Italian tiles in the bathroom and homemade cakes. I hope our children will find the happy medium.

In spite of all my criticism, with my present working arrangement I'm rather pleased with my life here, with the exception of the women's problems I mentioned before. Maybe this is because I chose my life; I wrote a book which is now in its third printing, I have the kind of work I love, I travel a lot, and I meet interesting people. Because of all this my conscience bothers me when I look at the majority of our *chaverot* here. Some women sometimes give me the feeling that they are, perhaps, jealous of me. . . . Like one friend who reacts to almost anything I say with the comment, "Well, you. You're different. You have established your individual life-style and you're not like the rest of us."

I don't know why it's like that. Staying in the room, cleaning, and cooking are all that my women friends are doing. The kibbutz is full of classes, activities, and various opportunities for all kinds of personal development. If you don't feel like studying English you can take sewing or ceramics classes. We're two hundred women here and I hear that only five registered for the sewing course. I myself go to two gym classes a week and there are never more than eight women in a class, although everybody knows how important it is for a woman to keep her body fit.

I don't know why it is like this. Children can't be the whole story. . . . In fact, the kibbutz was created to allow people more freedom to deal with matters of the mind and spirit, since they're not individually responsible for their own livelihood and they don't have to take care of all the money matters like people elsewhere. Yet, somehow, it worked out better for men than for women.

When I was working on our local paper I once interviewed a volunteer who worked here, and it turned out he was a psychologist by profession, although I hadn't been aware of it at the time. As we talked about his impressions of the kibbutz, he made one extremely poignant observation: Women in this kibbutz have an extinct look. Even young women who should be attractive and reflect sexual or personal interest in their surroundings seemed to him somewhat dead or extinguished. They remind him, he said, of women in the small towns or suburbs of the U.S., as if they withered before their time.

His statements sounded very true to me and I published them. The reactions to this interview kept me busy for the next couple of months; some people agreed and some vehemently disagreed, but it stirred a little storm. There are two reactions which I still remember, both by fifty-year-old women, a teacher and a social worker. [*Nima is referring to Dalia and Eva.*] They fully agreed with the volunteer's observation but they themselves felt different, and believed that every woman in the kibbutz could find her way to change her lot. Both of them were dedicated to their professions and lived actively in three spheres—their professional careers; their turns in various duties, e.g. the kitchen and other public work; and in addition, their families, of course. Both were satisfied with their life here. But they are certainly just a tiny minority. A year ago, I joined one of these women in an attempt to organize a women's group. Our idea was that it isn't enough to blame the men for the situation, nor is it helpful at all—it's time we see how we can help ourselves. But all our efforts ended in failure. Young women didn't show up at all and of the elderly ones who came to the first meeting only half returned the next week, and none came to the third meeting. . . . It seems as if they aren't aware of any problem at all—or, maybe I'm making a big problem out of nothing. Yet, it isn't completely accidental, I believe, that such a high proportion of the families who decide to leave the kibbutz do so because the *wives* are unhappy and couldn't—or wouldn't—adjust to this form of life. This is the case in the vast majority of families or couples leaving the kibbutz. It's most difficult for women who come from outside the kibbutz and marry a kibbutz man; they frequently end up by taking the men out with them.

These are the problems of my generation and of our time, though. Our parents seem to me like a completely different sort of people, another race. Frequently I envision them as giants who will soon be gone, while we are dwarfs by comparison. All the things that they underwent and accomplished, I couldn't even cope with. They had fantastic will power for which I admire them, and to this very day they haven't slowed down. My father, for example, still carries a tremendous load, although he's almost seventy. He alone has contributed to so many fields—to education, to the study of geography of the country, to the studies of the Bible, and the tradition of the holidays; I think ten men of my generation couldn't accomplish what he did all by himself. The only thing I'm puzzled about is how it happened that such a generation of revolutionaries bred here a fortress of mediocrity! But my father—and his friends—don't see it my way, of course. Milk and honey is all he sees—as if there's no crack in the building he built during his lifetime. There are weaknesses that he notices, I'm certain, but the sum total is undoubtedly positive and unique in his eyes. I, however, detect mistakes. One of them, perhaps the central one, is the total lack of selection in who could or couldn't join the kibbutz during its early days. Had our parents established some selection process, according to individual morality and education, this place might have indeed become a haven worth living in. They didn't do this though, and I really don't know how they could have been selective. Nowadays many kibbutzim use a graphologist for selection of new members—he must be a millionaire by now, this graphologist.

A few weeks after our conversation, Nima mailed me her book and in its stories I thought I discovered a real artist. "What are you writing now?" I asked upon our next meeting in the kitchen.

"Oh, everybody asks me that question, certain that I'm quietly cooking a second surprise. But I'm not, that is, nothing except my journalistic work—which certainly isn't literature. My fountain has dried up," she says, smiling sadly. "Or perhaps it needs a richer life to renew it. Here, my life turns round and round in the same circle."

Those
Who Left

INTRODUCTION

Many people have left the kibbutz in its fifty years of existence. Most significant are, of course, the cases of those who were deeply involved in the life of the kibbutz, either born in it or founders, and who made the decision to leave for a radically different life-style, urban life.

It wasn't too difficult to trace "defectors" of such a big and well-known kibbutz. The kibbutz itself was very open about this phenomenon, and supplied me with names and addresses of sons and daughters who presently live in town. The fact that the kibbutz authorities were not at all secretive or defensive about this can be taken for an additional manifestation of its security and success. Recent statistics have shown that more than a third of the offspring of the kibbutz have left it, and this is a relatively low ratio in comparison with other, less successful kibbutzim.

I contacted only people who were living in Jerusalem while I carried out my studies, and all those I contacted consented to be interviewed. I openly disclosed my purpose: to discuss the reasons people left Makom and to discuss the kibbutz from the perspective of outsiders. Twelve interviews were conducted, five of which will be presented in the following section.

Although this is hardly a representative sample, there were several ideas common to all the stories. Most outstanding was the predominance of family reasons for leaving the kibbutz: Three couples left because one spouse felt unhappy in the kibbutz; parents said they left because they were severely critical of the communal education; offspring said they left because they couldn't live so close to their parents; and single women said they left because they found it difficult to live alone within the kibbutz and looked for an opportunity of meeting a husband in town.

Other reasons for departure were mentioned less frequently: the search for an independent life, the need to fulfill ideals which were incompatible with the present kibbutz life, and the conflict between following a chosen career or course of study and membership in the kibbutz.

Several people spoke longingly about the economic and social security which the kibbutz offers its members, and often mentioned that the kibbutz members themselves were rather ungrateful of that. "Had I remained in the kibbutz," said a forty-five-year-old woman who had been an "outside child" in the kibbutz, "I'd probably have eight rather than four children. I adore children, but the cost of living in town has prevented me from having more." Others talked about the freedom of kibbutz members from daily financial concerns, yet mentioned that this can lead to irresponsible wastefulness. "I have seen people leaving the heat or the air conditioner on for hours, while they were out, not to mention electric lights indoors and outdoors. If they only knew what I pay in my tiny apartment for electricity—they have no idea!"

People who have lived outside the kibbutz for several years spoke of it as a greenhouse, isolated from Israeli society at large and from its problems. People who presently live in town consider themselves more mature and realistic, more able to cope with a great variety of problems, and in general more independent.

With all their criticism, only very rarely was there any bitterness or resentment expressed towards the kibbutz. The opposite was much more frequently true: People who left Makom spoke of it with longing, remembering its help to people in need, its internal cultural life, its holidays and feasts, and its landscape. Few of them saw, however, a realistic possibility of returning.

R E U V E N *(age 69)* and Z I P O R A *(age 65)*

I met this elderly couple in their apartment in Jerusalem. They were baby-sitting for their grandson in a room lined with books, and answered my questions eagerly, Zipora frequently correcting or embellishing Reuven's more subdued account.

REUVEN—I'm among the founders. I belonged to the old *chug* which we started in Tel Aviv High School, together with Yehuda, Oded, and the others.

ZIPORA—There were many people who left the kibbutz earlier than we did. Actually, in the 1930s many of the kibbutzim suffered from unstable populations, and Makom was stronger than most in this respect, because it did have a cohesive social core throughout the years. Still, people were coming and going for many reasons. It wasn't that noticeable because many of our own members were working and living outside the kibbutz since work in the Valley was so difficult to find.

Some people left because of the difficult material conditions or because they couldn't endure the hard work; others left for social reasons, especially after the wave of suicides, because the atmosphere in the kibbutz was very oppressive and demanded great personal strength. It's not surprising that, with the sharp transition people made in joining the kibbutz and with the constant friction between people living together twenty-four hours a day, individual crises were prevalent. Furthermore, every individual crisis was seen by the whole community as an acute breakdown in the society, in the same manner in which a family participates in each of its members' misfortunes so intensely. This was an important reason for leaving.

REUVEN—Some people had joined the kibbutz as an interesting adventure, for a year or so. They saw their stay in the kibbutz as something which would enhance their self-image, since the kibbutz was, at that time, considered the highest realization of Israeli society. Joining a kibbutz was a prestigious step to take in one's life, but when it was actually weighed against the daily hardships many decided to leave. They could still boast of being an ex-kibbutznik, and this was a feather in their caps. Some left because they were single and couldn't find a mate inside the community; this has always been a major reason for leaving the kibbutz.

ZIPORA—I believe that many people left the kibbutz in those early days because the kibbutz was so extreme. When you want to cure a sick organism, you must use extreme measures. The kibbutz was characterized as a revolutionary movement in its early days, and its radicalness was felt in many areas of our life. The early approach towards child education was perhaps the area in which this radical stance was most apparent, and parents of young children often got into severe conflicts with the kibbutz on that issue; these conflicts led many to finally leaving the kibbutz. (I believe that a statistical survey would still find this as the No. 1 reason for leaving the kibbutz.)

I worked in education, myself, and recall several extreme instances. For example, when a child was sick, he was isolated from everyone; even the child's mother wasn't allowed to visit the quarantined child for days, even weeks, sometimes. How can you accept such a rule? Well, of course there was a real fear of contagion, but there were also those strict principles that the *metapelet*, not the mother, was responsible for the child, and that mothers, carrying on around severely sick children, were nothing but nuisances for the professional nurse. From the *metapelet*'s point of view, however, taking such a responsibility was a terrible burden—she was in constant stress. I remember the nights I spent on night duty, watching over those sick children, with my hand on the gun, fearful—I was just nineteen then—that something might happen to the children under my care. It isn't at all like taking care of your own children. Or, I recall a terrible heat wave, and some infants dying in the neighboring kibbutz; I, in charge of our sick children, almost collapsed under the burden of my responsibility.

The extreme nature of the kibbutz was manifested in the constant pressure exerted on individuals. Everything was voted on or discussed in the general assembly, every private request or deviation from the norm. Often those assembly meetings were terribly cruel, and people were hurt by the public decisions, which were sometimes unfair and almost always insulting. Obliging an individual member to do something against his or her will was fairly common. The group could elect a person to be secretary, work coordinator or store-keeper even if it was really against that person's desire. Then, if this person failed in carrying out the assigned role, he'd come under sharp criticism, that devastating criticism for which the young kibbutz was so famous. The personal crisis that ensued for that person, who hadn't wanted the role in the first place, was inevitable.

Everybody was constantly under extreme criticism. If the food was bad, it was the fault of the cook; if our crops failed, the fault of the farmers. When the children I took care of were spoiled, or tired, or got an infection—God forbid—it was the fault of the *metapelet,* me. People always found somebody to blame, and, once they did, they made his life utterly miserable. I guess this was because everybody was so young. People have to grow up a bit in order to be more considerate.

REUVEN—Another common phenomenon, related to what Zipora has just mentioned, was jealousy among people: not for romantic reasons, but because of status in the group. People were jealous of those who were popular or had central positions in the kibbutz. When the children told Zipora, "We love you, why don't you come to take care of us on Saturday, too?" the other *metapelet* couldn't accept it. She was so jealous, she almost stopped talking to her. And when something small like that happened, it immediately became common knowledge through the channels of gossip, which were terribly active all of the time. People had no privacy whatsoever.

In this small community, people were constantly comparing their lots. One thought that he was working harder than the other, so he felt exploited and angry. One worked hard till nightfall, while the other worked at his hobby all afternoon, yet both ate the same food—so it was unfair. Everybody was on the alert to maintain a strict equality, and often it made normal life quite impossible. All this was intensified by the fact that one couldn't "go home" to relax but had to be constantly with the same people, day and night.

ZIPORA—I remember that for a long time I used to work as a night watch at the children's quarters. I worked at night and slept during the day. It was very difficult work, yet I never complained. One morning, a woman saw me going to bed, and commented: "Look at Zipora, she has a free day again." Or another said: "Where are you hiding all the time? Have you been on a trip somewhere?" I think this is an example of the jealousy Reuven mentioned. I was young, pretty, and in good health, and this was cause enough for some people to resent me.

I think that all these negative phenomena have vanished from the kibbutz over the years; they were simply growing pains. That's the way I see it now. But these were the main reasons which drove people away from the kibbutz in the early, pre-State days.

We ourselves have a completely different story to tell. We were very popular members, we loved the place and were loved by the others. We saw many, many positive aspects in the kibbutz—and still do. Our story of leaving the kibbutz is pretty uncommon; let Reuven tell you about it.

REUVEN—The way I see it, I didn't ever make the choice to leave. I was, rather, mobilized out of the kibbutz. I returned from my first mission to Europe in 1932, and in 1933 I was called by the Hagana for a mission abroad once again. I knew many languages, I passed easily for a student; so, in 1933 the Hagana registered me as a student in Trieste, and under this cover, I was responsible for buying arms and ammunition for the Hagana. From then on, I was their man, a sort of traveling agent. I went back and forth all the time. Whenever I returned home for a while, the Hagana would send its delegates to the kibbutz, to talk the kibbutz into allowing me to go off again. The kibbutz understood the importance of my missions and gave its consent every time. I never went without the permission and blessing of the kibbutz. I wouldn't say that I went against my will, even though I had to leave Zipora and our three children behind. That was the atmosphere of the era, and I knew I was participating in the most important Jewish enterprise of all times. Moreover, I felt that in my work outside the kibbutz I was contributing much more than by being a simple laborer in the kibbutz. (I was never a great physical worker—I never even had a branch which I considered "my own.") Towards the end of the period of the struggle against the British, I was in charge of the underground Hagana broadcasting station, and this job had indeed filled me with enthusiasm.

During that period, while I was mostly away from the kibbutz, the kibbutz underwent a severe political crisis which, several years later, led to its well-known division. Makom vehemently objected to the partition of the country between the Jews and the Arabs, and I was very much for it. After Mapai divided, two distinct camps were formed within the kibbutz, and friendship wasn't friendship anymore. I belonged to the Mapai group, which was a minority in Makom. Those developments somewhat cooled my deep attachment to the place.

When the State was established in 1948, I knew that war was forthcoming and that it would be a long struggle. I didn't want to leave Zipora with our three little children alone in the kibbutz, yet I couldn't leave my post with the Hagana, so I asked the kibbutz to move my family to an apartment in Tel Aviv which was owned by the Hagana. The kibbutz consented to this move with complete understanding. For the first two years of our lives in Tel Aviv, we were kibbutz members on leave. When Zipora left, the kibbutz provided us with some basic furniture, and, during the War of Independence and the food shortage following it, we often received gifts of food, potatoes and other local products from the kibbutz. We, for our part, put up any kibbutz member who had to stay overnight in the city.

After two years, however, we had to return to the kibbutz or give up our membership—because leave is given for a maximum of two years, and rightly so. We couldn't return at that time, though, we were beyond the point of no return. With the establishment of the Israeli government, I received an important appointment in the diplomatic service, and pretty soon I was sent abroad as an ambassador. So, de facto, we left the kibbutz, although we never made the formal step.

ZIPORA—There's something else we should mention. By that time, the kibbutz had gone through the division, and, had we returned, we would have had to go to Adama, which for us wasn't at all an attractive idea. I still feel deeply attached to Makom, to its people and landscape, and moving to Adama seemed like an absurd step to me. So we followed the route of Reuven's career instead.

You see, some people did retain their kibbutz membership together with their government positions in town. But Reuven and I didn't see it as a sensible solution for us.

I want to add something. We have lived in many countries, and have met with thousands of people, yet I find that some of the advantages of the kibbutz society are not to be found anywhere else. One thing I still miss is the way we used to celebrate the holidays in Makom. It was so rich and thoughtful, every detail was worked out with maximal care. More important, however, is the principle of reciprocal aid. When a disaster strikes a family, there isn't a better place to be than in the kibbutz. If a child loses his father, he still lives more or less in the same framework and can function normally, so to speak. If a mother of young children is sick in the hospital, where else would her family be cared for so completely? The whole approach towards the elderly, including members' parents who hadn't even lived in the kibbutz before, is something extraordinary. It is a welfare system without any sort of disrespect to the recipient, and I find it admirable. Children always received the best we could offer in the kibbutz, both materially and emotionally—all kibbutzim are known for their outstanding attention towards their children. I remember my feeling of shock when we moved to Tel Aviv and I saw children selling newspapers in the street, or a child of eight working in the grocery store, lifting a heavy case of bottles. This kind of child abuse could never have happened to children in a kibbutz. Last but not least, the people who remained at Makom are wonderful, outstanding people. I don't think you could find such a group of people anywhere else. So, naturally, these things are much more significant than the petty jealousies and frictions which we mentioned before. Were we younger and healthier, we would visit much more often than we do now.

D A N (age 33)

I met Dan at the television studio, where he works on animation films.

I left Makom five years ago. It seems like an awfully long time ago. I didn't actually live much in the kibbutz after I finished high school. First I went to the Army, then I had a car accident and spent about a year in the hospital, and when I recovered I went to study at the art academy for four years. Throughout this period I was living outside the kibbutz and spent only my vacations there, periods never longer than three months or so.

After my graduation I married my wife, whom I had met in town, and we lived in the kibbutz for two years. But again I wasn't living continuously at the kibbutz, since I worked three days a week as an illustrator in a publishing house in Tel Aviv. During that time, I spent every weekend, at least, in the kibbutz with my wife and son, who lived there permanently.

Well, on the surface, I have a very clear and simple reason for leaving the kibbutz after the two years we lived there, a "wife" reason. My wife couldn't adjust. This is pretty common, as stories about leaving the kibbutz go. But I'll tell you right away that I don't attribute the whole weight of my decision to my wife, and I don't know whether I'd have chosen to live my life in Makom even if I had been married to someone else. At the time, however, this made my decision much easier for me since I saw that my wife couldn't take that kind of life any longer.

We were both very satisfied with our occupations. I had the best job I could dream of, and my income went to the kibbutz, which was fine with me. My wife founded an occupational-therapy clinic in the kibbutz, and she too was successful and pleased with her work. Her problems focused around our son's education. She had many conflicts with the *metapelet* and with the other mothers of our son's group of infants. It was partly bad luck in the formation of the group, but, anyway, there was a severe conflict, following which I announced that we would leave the kibbutz. We left almost immediately after the conflict. We had a place to go, as my wife had had an apartment in town since before we married, and I got a job with the T.V. network right away. Economically we had no problems, which is relatively rare for people leaving a kibbutz. We settled in town, had two more children, and only now, five years later, is my wife planning to return to work on a part-time basis. Our life in the city is happy and content. We visit the kibbutz, where my parents and sister still live, frequently and without any hard feelings; yet we have never considered giving kibbutz life another try.

This is the superficial version of the story; it certainly has many additional levels, although it's not easy to organize them well.

Being born and raised in the kibbutz is not something that can be shaken off that easily. Just the other day, a friend entered my studio and found me talking to a woman, whom I didn't introduce. "That's Dan the kibbutznik," he said after a few moments. "You don't have any manners." Well, the kibbutz is certainly an important part of my life, and I love the place dearly to this very day. It's hard for me, even with these five years' worth of perspective, to analyze objectively its advantages and disadvantages.

The thing which stands out above everything else is that in town we are so much freer of the various pressures that we felt in the kibbutz. Let me start with a very prosaic example: It's indeed very comfortable to walk into the dining hall at midday and eat a good meal that you didn't have to prepare yourself. Yet the other side of this coin is having to do a shift of duty in the dining hall every third Saturday—which was something I deeply resented. I couldn't adjust to the fact that my only day free from work was not really free; a duty shift every third Saturday was a burden for me. That's in addition to all the other assignments which were often scheduled for this "free" day. If at least I could have done my own work for these extra hours, I would have been able to accept it. But working in the dining hall or picking olives made me feel as if I was serving others, and I didn't like it at all.

It may sound petty, of course, but this is just an example of the domination of the system over the individual. It's a framework which can survive only by compulsory rules that apply to every member. Furthermore, the accumulated effect of such everyday occurrences is what determines one's general feelings towards a place or a society. I don't think I could live for long within a compulsory system, where a committee of strangers decided for me when I could go abroad, or when I could go to school. I was able to study so soon after my return to the kibbutz because of my accident and the fact that my studies were partly covered by the insurance. Otherwise I would probably have had to wait several years for my turn.

As for the communal education, which was our main objection to the kibbutz way of life, we certainly prefer determining for ourselves our childrens' environment and direction. On the other hand, there are many things which I remember from my childhood that I would like my children to experience as well: the large open spaces, the landscape, living with nature and the extensive holiday celebrations, which we cannot organize in our small urban family.

I have pleasant memories of my childhood. I was the class artist right from the start, and was always active in decorating and illustrating; these things gave me a certain status as a child. On the other hand, I have always been an individualist, and individualists find it very hard to adjust to a compulsory framework. It's difficult to pinpoint, but I frequently felt an external pressure to be more active socially, or, rather, to be active in a different manner, since I was active in my own way. I stubbornly resisted these pressures, however, and in a way the kibbutz even reinforced my sense of individuality.

Being an adult artist in a kibbutz is quite a peculiar position, too. There used to be times in the kibbutz when people were ashamed to walk around in clean clothes (a "Saturday outfit") during the week. Even today, some of the older members will choose blue fatigues, preferably a bit soiled, to wear while walking around the kibbutz on weekdays, even though they work in an office somewhere and haven't been in the fields or factories for a long time. I was the kind of worker who walked around all week in "Saturday clothes," and I know this was looked down upon by some, although I didn't care about their reaction. In other words, my work wasn't considered "productive," in the "real" sense, and this attitude still exists, even though it's an anachronism. Reality has proven that hard physical labor is not a "must" anymore, so it is archaic to retain physical labor as a central value in the kibbutz. People who work in industry sit in air-conditioned offices, listening to music, while they perform their routine jobs. They make the most money for the kibbutz, yet it's the handful of people who still cultivate the fields who consider themselves the elite, the "real" kibbutzniks.

Living outside the kibbutz, I see several drawbacks in the kibbutz way of life which I don't know if I would have realized from within. The first generation of Makom was composed of a very high level of people, both the Israelis and the new immigrants whom they absorbed. They had wide political and cultural horizons, and were deeply involved in what was happening outside the kibbutz. Their children, however, the second generation, have grown up to be very narrow people. There are exceptions, of course, but on the average they're pretty mediocre people. They read very little (check in the library and you'll find proof of my observation); they have few interests besides their family, apartment, and some local gossip. Just listen to their conversations in the dining hall. . . . I don't know what went wrong with the education with which the first generation provided us. Perhaps their mistake was in being too permissive, in not demanding enough, in discouraging any signs of individual competition among the children—all the things which had been so central in their own education, whether in Europe or in the elite high schools of Palestine of those times. Anyway, the second-generation sons and daughters have turned out to be pretty superficial. I don't mind the fact that they're more materialistically oriented, because their parents' asceticism wasn't to my liking, either. It's a question of proportion and whether other human, social, or spiritual interests beyond basic material needs exist in one's life.

On the other hand, I feel a great deal of respect for those members who do have wider horizons, who are more talented and ambitious, whether of the first generation or the second, and have decided to remain in the kibbutz. I know that they could succeed elsewhere and become important people, but somewhere along the line they decided that contributing to the commune is more important than enhancing themselves. This is something I admire in these people, because I'm different—I have put my individual ambitions before the welfare of my society. Maybe they themselves don't see it this way, but, when I think of two of them—the present two young secretaries of the kibbutz—and know that they both had personal doubts yet decided to stay, I can't help seeing the idealism in their choice, which I admire.

There is, however, a price to be paid for their choice, which I also can't help but see. Looking deep into their eyes . . . those older people who are, deep down, great intellectuals, who could have become great professors, or physicians, or whatever, I detect a bitterness, a sense of failure, in the most personal sense. They have sacrificed a lot, if now, in their old age, you find them sorting olives instead of lecturing to students. Somewhere, deep down, they know it, and I, deep down, feel sorry for them. Of course they won't admit so late in their lives that they may have made a mistake—it's too tragic to admit—yet sometimes I sense this regret . . . as my eyes meet theirs. My father is one of those individuals, although when I'm talking to him he only says how completely satisfied he feels in the kibbutz, and how every form of life has its price and drawbacks, etc. But, in fact, people of extremely high potential often carry out the simplest jobs in the kibbutz, jobs which are held in town by the lowest level of people—so how can their intellectual drives and talents be fulfilled? How can they be really satisfied with that sort of existence?

But mine is a liberal point of view. Every individual has the right to live according to his or her choice, and all the different ways are equally good. No form of life can be considered false. Actually, this is a value which I acquired from my kibbutz education. It used to be otherwise, once, when people who left the kibbutz were considered traitors—but not anymore. I think this is one expression of the kibbutz's strength at present; only in its strength could it have become so open and liberal. And that's why I don't see the kibbutz as declining towards extinction. As long as people live there out of their love for the place, because it's good for them and allows them to fulfill themselves, there's no threat to the existence of the kibbutz. Naturally, it will change, as it has already changed in the past fifty years, but I support the changes which I can detect at present: the growing openness and liberality; the greater acceptance of the needs of the individual; the diminishing rigidity of the external, compulsory, framework. There are some principles which must, of course, be guarded for Makom to remain a kibbutz, but it's not easy for me to formulate them right now. One is equality—not in the absolute, simple, sense, but at a deeper level. Also, the communal education, the economic cooperation, and the reciprocal social responsibility. I don't consider them to be vanishing, although their external symbols or manifestations may change.

YAEL (age 29)

I can describe very clearly the moment I decided to leave the kibbutz, about three and a half years ago. It was during an assembly meeting in which my study program was being voted on. I saw many hands raised against my program—hands of people much older or younger than I, people who hardly knew me enough to greet me on the street. Yet they had the right to vote on my future, the right to get up and declare that I hadn't proved myself as yet. . . . It was then that I decided to leave.

I had taken a year of leave, in order to study theater. The next year, the program was extended to a second year of creative drama, and I wanted to continue with it. That's when the kibbutz voted on my request. I offered to teach drama and organize adult theatrical activities after I completed my studies. People said, however, that I should show my achievements first, then go and study. Yet how could I start when I lacked any experience, training, and, therefore, confidence?

Suddenly I asked myself, "Why should I accept these people's decision on the direction of my life? Why should I agree to work in a place I don't like, under circumstances which I don't care for, instead of doing my own thing?" And I left. I didn't do it in order to see the world or to breathe some fresh air. I didn't do it wholeheartedly either, since I'm deeply attached to the kibbutz, to my friends and family there, and I still consider it my home. At that moment, however, I urgently wanted to go on with my studies, and my step seemed like the most logical choice.

Beneath this on-the-spot decision was, however, a more basic problem—the problem of a single woman in the kibbutz. I was over twenty-five years old when I left the kibbutz and my situation was uncomfortable. Almost all of my classmates were already married—all of the boys and a great majority of the girls. The atmosphere was that of a mad race to join the "young couples club" and I felt excluded. In the dining hall or at parties, I began to feel like an outsider. As people left to go home after an evening together, suddenly everybody paired up into couples, while I remained terribly alone.

A single person in a kibbutz is a lonely island. It's a very strange and subtle situation, produced by the atmosphere of the kibbutz. In exactly the same situations in town, I felt otherwise: I was alone, but not miserably lonely. On the surface, people denied the problem. They'd say: "Why do you feel that way? What does it matter if you're single? Nobody's putting any pressure on you." But it's something in the air, an implicit message. Only my parents asked me openly: "Why don't you get married, too?" Others never did. Yet, when all my classmates had their first babies, and all they would talk about was diapers, baby food, or their new apartments, I suddenly felt as if I were from another planet. Or, on Saturday mornings, while I used to sleep till midday, as we all used to do during high school and the Army, and get up refreshed and looking for company, I found all the new parents pushing their prams back from their morning stroll, hurrying to an early lunch and a nap. It made me feel abnormal, a misfit, and I kept asking myself: Isn't it bad enough that I want someone to love like everybody else? Why do I have to suffer, on top of that, the stares, the questions, the implicit social message? In town, I live in an apartment house. I don't know most of my neighbors. I don't form any judgments about them, nor do they about me. We all live in our different circles without this constant friction and comparison. And, when I finally found an interesting study program and wanted to get out of this tense environment, the kibbutz decided that I'd better wait a couple of years and prove my abilities first. . . .

You see, a big kibbutz like Makom can provide many social and vocational opportunities for its members, *if* they find their place within the society. But, if they don't, it can be like a prison, being in constant contact with individuals you don't really care about, or with people with whom you haven't even chosen to be. I prefer to be alone rather than in continuous contact with people who aren't really my friends.

When I left the kibbutz I felt an immediate improvement in my mood. I found the study program very interesting, I met many new acquaintances (theater people, whom I find fascinating) with whom *I* chose to be friendly, and I could choose to be alone as well. Not being confined to a relatively small community has proved to be of great importance to me. In my four years outside, I have had seven different jobs, from working as a cleaning woman to being a secretary, a youth leader, and a drama teacher (my current occupation). I didn't reject any offer. I have also moved four times already, each move, each new neighborhood, giving me an immense sense of freedom. I discovered in myself resources which I wasn't aware of before—a thirst for learning is one of them. I had been a mediocre student in the kibbutz, but now I am working on my matriculation examinations and have started towards my B.A. in an American program which is based mostly on independent study. I have even joined a philosophy society, in which we read and discuss various philosophical works. The change is probably due to being ten years older, but studying is completely different when it's voluntary. The main thing is that, although I'm still not married, I don't feel lonely at all.

Now that I have put this distance between me and the kibbutz, I can see its many advantages, which I hadn't understood before. First of all, I have discovered that I'm a rural person. I like spending some time in the big city, but I want to live where I'm in touch with the land, where birds, not the sound of traffic, wake me up in the morning. It's not just poetry; I really know that this is an important part of me. Also I hate taking care of financial matters and appreciate the fact that the kibbutz does this for its members. I hate taking care of bills, taxes, rent; I often forget about them and become quite confused.

Furthermore, I long for the local cultural life of Makom. It's admirable that such a society can be almost self-sufficient in the cultural sense, involve so many members, with a great variety of needs and interests, in different study programs, arts and crafts activities, sports, and hobbies. It's wonderful that people enrich each other's lives.

Another thing that I miss terribly are the holidays and the long evenings of singing together. This is the true, authentic atmosphere of Eretz Yisrael, and it can't be found anywhere but in kibbutzim. Last year, for example, when the Passover ceremony of Makom was over, the whole audience sat and sang together into the night—all the good old songs we grew up with—and everybody knew them by heart, word for word. Here in town I have never experienced this. When people speak about having a party, they have only one idea in mind: putting loud rock music on the record player, dancing, and flirting all night. I do enjoy this kind of party from time to time, but I miss the other kind, our kibbutz parties, very much. Last summer I took a group of high-school kids on a hike; we made a bonfire like we used to do in the kibbutz, and we sat around it singing. I discovered, however, that these kids hardly knew any songs except the American ones, or the cheap advertisements we hear on the radio all the time. It was disgusting, and as I saw what was happening I pitied these city kids and thought of my own wonderful childhood. It's the same feeling I get when I happen to join a group of people who talk for hours about the rising prices of dresses, cars, and apartments—there's nothing more boring for me than those conversations, and often I just get up and leave.

An ex-kibbutznik is easily identified in town. Even abroad, people have often recognized me as such. I think we acquire, in the kibbutz, a certain directness of manner, of getting right to the point. We're willing to do any kind of work, we're not choosy. We're not spoiled and can cope with a lot of physical difficulties. We can live on very little, actually. I think we're simply better than many people I have met in town [laughing].

Living in the city has demonstrated to me how much more pure our life is in the kibbutz. The kibbutz is just a small fragment, it's only 4 percent of the total Israeli population. It can be thought of as a model society that realizes all the social values to which we aspire, and in that sense it's of central significance for the whole population. I wish, however, that the kibbutz would be more than an isolated island of all the possible good. It should find ways to contribute more to the total society and not be content with the sole aim of developing itself as a paradise on earth for the select few. I'm working now with disadvantaged children, and I know how much kibbutzniks could contribute, if we only found the appropriate channels.

Life in the city has given me a lot of stimulation for my own personal development, and I'm not sure that I'd have been able to grow in the same manner had I stayed in the kibbutz. But now that I feel the way I do, I'm ready and willing to return to the kibbutz any day, if only I could find a man who will be willing to go and live there with me. Not to any kibbutz, but back home to Makom. I have met enough ex-kibbutzniks in town to appreciate my kibbutz for what it's worth, but I don't feel I could return alone and go back to the lonely life which I led before. I know that in my profession and with my experience I will be able to contribute to the kibbutz in the area of theater, with both children and adults. I have my own internal world now and am not afraid of losing it by being caught up in the mediocrity of everyday life. I know that I would be an active member, professionally and emotionally involved. But the basic condition I need is having my own home and family to return to at night, when my workday is over. Otherwise I can't return to the kibbutz.

L I M O R *(age 29)*

I met Limor at an old, isolated house in Jerusalem, where she runs a half-day private nursery school for a small group of two-, three-, and four-year-olds. She used to have an apartment, but has recently moved to the school since she could no longer afford the rent. The shelves of her room (the children's playroom during the day) are packed with books in Hebrew and English on psychology and education, mingled with toys and educational games. A huge, beautiful dog is her company.

Actually, it's been seven years now since I left Makom where I was born twenty-nine years ago. At first, in 1972, I left on leave to go with my parents and the rest of the family to the States, where my father was on a diplomatic mission. I went to the New School in New York and took different classes on the subject of mental health, although I didn't formally complete a degree. After two years my family returned to the kibbutz, whereas I wanted to continue with my studies and my life abroad. Since my two years of leave were over, I informed the secretariat that I was leaving the kibbutz. I didn't know what I wanted to do with my life, except to stay in New York for a while longer; as a kibbutz daughter, I knew the doors would always be wide open for me. My decision was rather superficial, as I actually was quite uncertain at the time.

In 1976 when I returned to Israel, I already knew that I didn't want to return to the kibbutz, although the reasons are very difficult for me to explain. Actually, it seems to me that I have never completely organized my thoughts on this question. I just *felt* that I didn't want to go back to Makom and acted upon my feeling.

One factor is, undoubtedly, my family. Don't get me wrong—my family is okay and my parents are very popular members. As an individual, however, I felt that in the kibbutz I'd always remain "A and B's lovely daughter" and couldn't become a person in my own right. I know that, had I stayed in the kibbutz long enough, I'd probably have eventually received the chance to develop my own direction and personality, but I felt the need for an independent existence right away, and I sensed that this would be much easier to achieve at a distance from my parents.

Another thing I don't like about the kibbutz is the communal education system. I experienced this system both as a child and, later, as a *metapelet* during the two years between my military service and my departure for New York. As a child I felt terribly pressured by my peer group and the constant togetherness. I felt deprived. For me, the children's society was like a closed institution. I couldn't have expressed what it was that I felt then, but that's the essence of my experience. As a *metapelet*, for example, I resented our procedure for bathing the infants. Three of us standing in a line, an efficient machine—one rinsing, one soaping, one drying—that the children passed through, one after another, like a factory, with no personal attention, no warmth. Moving the children back home to sleep would certainly improve the situation, but the daytime experience alone is still bad enough. I think that a child needs a family, parents and siblings, warm and personal attention, the feeling of natural belonging, his or her own private corner—all these things and not the forced framework of our children's homes. I wouldn't want to have my children grow up in such a context by any means. It produces so much pressure and so many demands, whereas children need much more freedom and flexibility, especially sensitive children, as I was. The fact is that I have very few distinct memories from my childhood, so I probably have repressed much of it. The general impression I retain is, however, far from nostalgic.

The same pressure works on adult members as well. The system wears people out, it makes them lifeless and mediocre. I see my former classmates. I love them, but the majority of them have turned out to be very disappointing as adults. They have almost no personality of their own. Perhaps it's not just the constant social pressure to conform, but also a certain poverty of stimulation and the lack of need for individual ambition, which have produced this sort of flat personality among my age group. They live a beautiful life, but it lacks depth, richness, nuances which are very difficult to put into words. They keep talking about the richness of their cultural life. . . . I hesitate to express myself so bluntly, but this "culture" is also flat and mediocre, as compared to what's offered in the city, if you only open your eyes and ears. I recently attended a musical evening at the kibbutz, organized and performed by members only. It's true that it was quite impressive for a population of one thousand, but as far as concerts go . . . I wouldn't call it "culture" or "music" at all.

On the other hand, a visiting musical trio appeared in the kibbutz several months ago, when I happened to be visiting, and it gave an outstanding performance, yet was attended by only a handful of people, and hardly anyone of my generation at all. You can't compare the second generation of the kibbutz to the national average, because, given the huge investment in our education, we should have been way above the average. Yet the outcome of this education, of this environment, is somehow very disappointing. Perhaps you can't have a real cultural impact, based totally on local talent.

Another characteristic result of the kibbutz education is a kind of ingratitude. People don't appreciate what they have, they just take everything for granted. It's infantile and unreal, and a real difference between a kibbutz and a city child. City children witness real-life struggles all around them. They experience wanting things others have yet not being able to get them, and this makes them grow up to enjoy and value what they do have. We never experienced that. In the intellectual sphere it's the same: You are indoctrinated with ready-made solutions to your life dilemmas, and you never have the chance to develop your own solutions, through doubts and trial-and-error processes.

On the other hand, there are positive aspects of the kibbutz life which I haven't found anywhere else. The idea, and practice, of reciprocal help is first and foremost in my mind. It's not just the mere fact that all your needs are provided for, whether you're sick, old, or whatever; it's the true concern for the well-being of every individual member. There's a deep understanding and commitment in this sense, and it touches me deeply. Take, for example, the recent trip to Sinai which was organized for the older people of the kibbutz: How every detail was thoroughly planned! When I heard about the deep concern of these youngsters, who helped the old ladies in walking, climbing, and in so many other ways, I thought that there is no urban society that could compete in this area with the tradition of our kibbutz.

Despite all my present convictions against the kibbutz, I sometimes long for its security. Struggling with financial difficulties, as a single woman in town, has almost exhausted me completely. If I were married, I'd have more support, both financially and psychologically, but so far I haven't found the right man. Living as a single woman in the city can get pretty tiresome. Men try to take advantage of you, walking alone at night is unpleasant, going to the movies or to a party in feminine company is considered strange; these problems are common in town while in the kibbutz I would feel much more at ease socially. I don't feel that married couples in the kibbutz form such a closed society that a single person cannot be well accepted in their company; at least that is how I feel when I visit the kibbutz.

This is interesting. Several women I've spoken with have claimed that they left the kibbutz for just that reason: that being a single adult in the kibbutz is unbearable, and they feel much better, in this sense, in town.

Is that so? My experience is totally different! They often encourage single people to leave the kibbutz—preferably temporarily, of course— because in the city one meets more people, and one's chances of finding a spouse are greater. This is a consideration which I have often heard—

that singles move to the city to try their luck; but not that single people leave of their own accord because they feel uncomfortable in the kibbutz. For me, at least, the opposite is true. Actually, the place where I felt the least amount of pressure to get married was in New York, where I realized that a single woman's independence is highly valued. Israel is still very conservative in this sense, but the kibbutz is no more so than any other environment.

There's another area, though, which has to do with my struggle toward independence, in which I have a complaint about the kibbutz: the financial position of people who have left the kibbutz. On that point I have a very serious grievance against Makom.

When I returned from the States, I had many debts and I turned to the kibbutz for help. The kibbutz has some way of computing what's due to you when you leave, according to the years you have been an adult member of the society. I had four years of membership, two of which were years of leave, and I received the ridiculous sum of 7,000 IL.* It was almost like in the old days, when a kibbutz member who left was considered a traitor, and left only with the shirt on his back.

I had to rent an apartment in Jerusalem, which is terribly expensive. I have had to wander from one to another, and I desperately want a place of my own. Yet buying an apartment is far beyond my means. I think this is terribly unfair; my parents worked in the kibbutz all their lives, so why shouldn't they have a way of helping me, just like urban families can help in such cases? I think that the kibbutz could start a small savings account for every child, and, if they keep adding small amounts of money into that account, then by the time the child is twenty or twenty-five, and if he or she wants to go live elsewhere, it would be possible to start out with a decent sum of money. I figured out the necessary investment for such a program, and it's not that big a sum, at least not for a kibbutz as rich as Makom.

I don't know why it is that as a daughter of a rich kibbutz, who would be provided with all her needs including a decent apartment *inside* the kibbutz, I have to be a poor ex-kibbutznik in town? Is it a method by which the kibbutz keeps its members from leaving? I can hardly believe that this is so, so it's high time the kibbutz reform its rules in this area.

I have collected many stories about this problem. I know of an ex-kibbutznik my age whose grandfather died abroad. She, being the only family member living independently, thought that it was only fair that she should receive his inheritance and buy a small apartment with the money. Her father, however, an Orthodox kibbutznik, decided that the money, like all inherited money coming to kibbutz members, should go to the kibbutz. . . .

Another case is of an older woman who left recently. The kibbutz

*In 1975, about $350.

provided her with a loan which wasn't enough for a quarter of an apartment, but the interest on this loan was as bad as any bank loan she could have obtained privately.

Some people don't take it so bitterly. I know a man who received, upon leaving our kibbutz, his furniture and a pittance which hardly sustained him during his first year at the university in Jerusalem. But he can drive a truck and a tractor, and the next year he got himself an excellent job and he's made a fortune and saved himself from his poverty. Our men are better equipped for making money in town, and indeed this man is proud of himself and isn't bitter toward the kibbutz. He told me that he believed that soon the kibbutz would solve this problem, because it's a source of shame for the kibbutz movements, with all their resources, that their ex-members, their own sons and daughters, should live like paupers in town. It would be more typical of the second generation to solve this problem for their own children, some of whom will start leaving the kibbutz in the near future.

And do you know what aggravates me more than anything? I found out that both the Ministry of Housing and that of Welfare have certain point-indexes that define which citizens are eligible to obtain help in acquiring apartments, and, according to both, we ex-kibbutzniks cannot get any support. We're considered rich kids coming from affluent homes. . . .

You know, when I had to move into this place, which is actually not an apartment but a nursery school, I had this fantasy that someday I'd be rich, and when I would die I would contribute my money to lots of different causes—but that I'd make sure never to include a kibbutz enterprise in my will!

G I L *(age 27)*

I often hear that I'm the kind of a person who wasn't supposed to leave the kibbutz but should have become a central figure in it instead. This gives you the first clue as to why I left. A kibbutz creates expectations for its members, which then become labels that are almost impossible to change. In my case, because I was a very active child socially, or because my parents were so central in the kibbutz society, people thought that they knew me as an adult, that they could foresee what kind of a kibbutz member I would become, even after six years of absence. When I made the unexpected step to leave the kibbutz, they were all so startled! I disappointed them and didn't live up to their expectations. Yet I wanted to live in my own right and not as a preformed label.

I served in the Army for six years, and, towards the end of that period, I really longed to return to the kibbutz. But, when I did return, I felt that I had to test this form of life to see whether I, as an individual, wanted to live this way for the rest of my life. After about six months, I realized that my answer was no, but I made myself stay for a year. I didn't hide my doubts and I left myself open to all kinds of persuasion. At the end of this process, however, many people whose opinions I highly respect told me: "Gil, if that's how you feel, you should indeed leave."

It's difficult to explain the essence of my decision. One may live in a kibbutz because it's an easy, comfortable life, because the communal economy protects people from a lot of problems, or because the communal education reduces people's responsibility as parents. I, however, couldn't have stayed in the kibbutz for those reasons alone. I'm the type of person who must identify completely with the kibbutz, with all its aspects, in order to live in it. There are values which I want my life to reflect and I feel—I'm sad to say—that the kibbutz is, at present, *not* the form of life in which I could realize those values. A *moshava* or a small town where my life wouldn't be so intertwined with and dependent on the lives of others suits me better. The kibbutz, as a commune, was necessary during the critical period of the establishment of the State when volunteers were needed for various national missions. Today those national goals have vanished—partly because they have been realized and partly due to other reasons. The kibbutz has remained more or less an empty shell, the main characteristic of which is its communal economic system. I don't think that the communal economic system is an aim in itself, nor do I find such a system attractive for me personally.

Some people asked: "If that's how you feel, why don't you stay and try to change the system from within?" The truth is, I don't judge my powers to be such that I'd be able to produce the necessary change. I'd be wasting my life tilting at windmills, and I'd rather move, thereby changing my environment rather than trying to change the whole kibbutz system. The present inhabitants of the kibbutz are excellent workers, which is very important, and by living in the Valley they are contributing to the national goal of decentralizing the population. But, apart from that, they aren't serving the State better than people who live in other agricultural settlements, or even in towns, situated far from the population centers.

When I returned to the kibbutz from the Army I wasn't completely aware of these points. I was, at the time, involved in a relationship with a woman who didn't want to join the kibbutz, but this wasn't of central importance for me. I came, and I wanted to live peacefully for awhile. But the society of the kibbutz started making demands right away, with various appointments and roles they wanted me to fill. They thought these would make me more attached to the kibbutz, but in my case the opposite was true. I felt harrassed. I wasn't in the appropriate state of mind for assuming responsibility and authority, yet I was made a member of the committee for higher education, I had to organize the annual picnic, and there were many other roles proffered which I somehow managed to avoid. Again, I saw this as a continuation of my old image, my label as a socially responsible kid, an image that, after all those difficult years of military service, I was tired of and wanted to change.

Gradually, during this year of home-coming, my ideas became clearer to me. I understood that, had I been living in the 1930s, I'd certainly have found my place in the kibbutz. The kibbutz had an important role then in building the State, in forming the Palmach, in organizing the illegal immigration, and I would have certainly been among its activists then. This national role made it worthwhile and necessary to maintain a cooperative system, and the importance of those goals dwarfed all personal problems or ambitions. Presently, however, with the decrease in the importance of these already achieved goals, we have experienced a decline in the cooperative character of the kibbutz and an increase in the attention given to privacy, to the family and to individual needs. This is very natural. Therefore my goal isn't to start a new kibbutz. In fact, most people must be feeling the way I am—you just have to compare the number of *moshavim* with the number of kibbutzim that have been established in the country since 1967 to prove my point. The big, established kibbutzim have enough problems as it is just surviving; it's a bigger challenge to maintain settlements than to organize new ones. We all know that many communes were tried as a way of life in different parts of the world, but the majority of them had a very short life span, because they didn't have external common goals to sustain them. The kibbutz is a very impressive social idea but somehow it's too big for small-scale, normal human beings today. Makom, however, is still much better off than most of the other kibbutzim I know.

When these ideas started crystalizing, I shared them with other members of the kibbutz, with the secretary, with those I cared about and to whom I wanted to express my feelings. I stated right away that my personal choice was to leave at the end of the year, and I was pleased to find how seriously and respectfully the people accepted both my ideas and decision. They were deeply concerned, but not at all judgmental or intrusive. We were all completely open, and that's why I was able to maintain my personal relationships with members of the kibbutz and I still feel completely at ease whenever I'm there.

My mother and brother are living in the kibbutz. My brother has followed the family tradition—he's a teacher. When I talk to him, however, I sense a certain undercurrent of bitterness. I don't think he's completely content with his life there, either. I feel that I have made the proper decision in leaving. Had I waited a few years more, I'd be a head of a family, and then the decision to leave would be much more difficult to make.

Now it's two years since I left. I'm studying agriculture at the university, and when I graduate I intend to join a *moshava* and have my own farm, and hope to combine my farming with some sort of agricultural instruction or research. I could definitely never live in a city.

The mere fact of being able to survive outside the protective shell of the kibbutz doesn't give me any satisfaction. I make enough money to live by working as a night watchman and I don't see paying my own rent and taxes as a great achievement, which is how some people who have never lived outside the kibbutz see it. But, after all, it really is rather trivial: Why should things which even the most simple person in town can manage to do seem like such extraordinary achievements to us?

I believe that I have retained a great deal of my kibbutz education and basic values in my present life: I resent materialism, I have a deep respect for work, I'm deeply attached to the country. All these I acquired in the kibbutz. Paradoxically, I think that the kibbutz educated me towards independence and towards serious consideration of my decisions, and these were the tools I used to break away from the kibbutz. . . . Because I live according to values, I'm often compared to Don Quixote: I don't cheat, I won't use any connections to get ahead, I don't break rules, and I'm proud of it. This is something I have found that I have in common with other ex-kibbutzniks. You might say that I left the kibbutz out of idealism, if you see what I mean.

The Young
Generation

This last section of interviews will present the stories of four of the younger members of the kibbutz; one of them is a daughter, and another a granddaughter, of members whose accounts appear earlier in the book. In fact, however, many individuals of the second generation are presented in the various other sections of the book. To mention just a few, both of the secretaries and the work coordinator, whose profiles appear in "Administration," belong to Makom's second generation, as do Vered and Iris of the Eisman family, Sara and her daughter Anat of the Dor family, four of the people who had left Makom, and others. In trying to characterize the younger members of the kibbutz and their relationship with the first generation, consider this larger group rather than the four people in the following section.

It is not a coincidence that two of the three adult women who appear in this chapter (the fourth still being in high school) work within the educational system. This is the "fate" of almost all young women in the kibbutz, who carry the burden of educating and supplying services to the four hundred or more children of Makom. Although some women adjust and accept this role, many find it an unwanted obligation, as in the cases of Dafna and Efrat, the remaining young women who appear in this section. (Nima, who appears in the section "Individualists" is an example of one who hasn't accepted this "fate.")

The comparison between the founders and early settlers and the people who grew up in the kibbutz is, probably, a central theme of the book. Herein lies, actually, the criterion for the success of Makom as a kibbutz and the basis for predicting its possible future development.

I chose selections from an interview with a first-generation teacher and mother to use as an introduction to and summary of the younger generations of Makom. Her poignant and thoughtful evaluations should provide additional perspective to the picture painted by the members of this group.

"I see a great deal of good in the second generation, in spite of the fact that they don't care for the ideology of the kibbutz as much as we did when we built it. They're not as tense, serious, pedantic, and severe as we have always been. They can adjust easily and that's why it's a pleasure to work with them. Our seriousness is double-edged; on the positive side, it has made us a highly dedicated group; on the negative side, it has produced constant tension and pressure to accompany our perfectionism. We took everything so seriously—every little poem recited in the Shabbat reception was analyzed and deliberated upon—we conducted endless meetings about every small detail. The new generation decides fast, saying: "Who cares?" and lives more comfortably with its decisions.

"Our children think we've retired too soon. They'd like to see us more involved in the practical leadership of the kibbutz. We don't have a conflict between the generations at all, perhaps the opposite is true.

"In the cultural areas we have perhaps arrived at higher standards than our offspring, but I would hate to generalize about this. In terms of our economy, productivity, industry, they're fantastic, outstanding; there's no doubt about it.

"I find that the second generation has more difficulty assuming responsibility. Perhaps this is due to the fact that they try to avoid conflicts with peers; they hate to insist upon their opinion when faced with opposition and this is unavoidable if you're a leader. They're afraid of their friends' criticism, though not of ours, their parents. Perhaps this is because they grew up together—they've become siblings, really. When second-generation secretaries are elected, they try very hard to pull in somebody of our generation to share the responsibility.

"In my youth we were pretty harsh towards each other. We often obliged people to do things against their wishes; we used social power to gain an individual's cooperation. As adults, our children are much more tolerant towards each other. They use persuasion instead of authority. They're willing to meet many more individual needs and wishes, with greater ease. (Naturally, they also have better financial means to do this.)

"We know very little about the third generation as of yet. They're just starting to come back from the Army. As high-school children, I find them more open and willing to talk about their problems and doubts. Their relationship with the adult community is pretty limited. They're not interested—as our children once were—in participating in the adult parties or cultural events. They live pretty much in isolation in their own quarters. Maybe they feel uncomfortable because it's such a big kibbutz now.

"The third generation works less in the kibbutz than their parents did. They also put less effort, perhaps, into their school work. I think that these kids of the third generation will have to face the real challenge of the kibbutz: how to live decently with the luxuries of time and plenitude, how to raise the quality of life now that our mere survival is more or less assured."

These observations will be developed further in the ensuing accounts by four people raised in the kibbutz.

E L I S H E V A *(age 35)*

Elisheva, Na'ama's eldest daughter, is an art teacher. Although she did not mention it in our conversation, I found some of her lovely paintings in the kibbutz's art exhibition, and discovered that it was she who wrote most of the texts and verses for the impressive Jubilee celebration.

My father was among the founders of this kibbutz. Had he lived, he would have been sixty-seven years old now and could have told you as many stories of Makom as one would ever wish to hear. He was killed in an accident in our olive factory about twelve years ago. After his death, a book concerning his activities in the organization of the illegal immigration to the country, his great endeavor, was published. Many letters he wrote to my mother are in this book. . . . He was born in the United States. Although my grandfather died when he was very young, my father managed to receive a strong Zionistic education, and at the age of fourteen he immigrated to Palestine alone. He lived in a dorm of some sort and studied in Herzelia High School in Tel Aviv, and that's where he, Yehuda, and the others organized the first *chug* which later became the core of Makom. My father was less than twenty years old when they went out to start a new kibbutz.

My mother was born in Israel. She joined the kibbutz through the Machanot Haolim Youth Movement. My parents were among the first couples in Makom. My mother used to work in the greenhouse and the kitchen, but then the kibbutz forced her to become a teacher. Yes, it's true, she was really forced, and she never liked her work as a teacher. Presently she is in charge of our school's teaching-aids lab, and she's relatively more satisfied. She's lived here all her life and has a strong sense of identification with the kibbutz.

When I think about my parents and their generation, even realizing that they were partly the products of their era, I still admire them for their great ability to withstand physical and spiritual hardship. They were very strong and resilient people. On the other hand, take me, for example: I reacted so badly to the Yom Kippur War, it's a trauma from which I still suffer. Even now, I knew I'd start crying right away [*crying a bit and then continuing*]. . . . And then I think of the constant difficulties with which my parents and their friends had to live, and I admire them all the more. I believe that people who have to cope with hardships in their childhood later develop both intellectually and physically a kind of resistance and strength. They had faith. It was their good luck to have been born in a generation with faith, unswerving faith that sustained them through all the years of terrible hardships. This faith directed their way of life; they worked unceasingly to realize their Zionist ideals and an independent Jewish State. Furthermore, they had the immense satisfaction of witnessing and sharing in the actualization of their faith, which took place in their own lifetimes, and this added to their strength. Take Makom, for example. How different it is to be born into this reality than to dream it and create it with one's own two hands. This creativity, the development of the idea and then turning the dream into a reality, is really something.

Even today, although they're pretty old, I see in these people greater fortitude in crisis and difficulty than I feel in myself. On the other hand, some of them are tired of giving. They have sacrificed so much throughout their lives that they aren't willing to do so anymore, and would rather sit quietly and collect their due. In others I often sense feelings of disappointment from certain aspects of our life. They say: That's not what I wanted to happen; that kind of reality isn't worth my great personal sacrifice. This is not a common reaction, but I sense it specifically in parents whose children left the kibbutz or in older members who feel that they are being phased out of powerful positions in the kibbutz. Growing old isn't easy, and the young seem to speak a different language, unknown to the old. . . .

I feel, however, that it is harder being born in my time. I regret not having their faith, their well-defined values. It's much more confusing now; I don't seem to be able to find any articles of belief which clearly delineate a certain way of life [*very excited, in tears*]. I know what I object to: the materialistic atmosphere which dominates our life. I know that I have my role in that too, but I hate to think that materialistic motives are the only forces that make the entire kibbutz machine run. It's a direction that our society has absorbed from the external environment, but for such a trend to be so strong it must also have satisfied our own needs. Perhaps it is due to the fact that we experienced such extreme poverty in our early childhood. I remember that austerity very well. We had no sweets and very rarely had any new clothes. There was no heating in the winter, nor air conditioning in the summer; there was deep mud without any pavements, and half an egg a day. Now we have gone over to the other extreme, and I think it's a shame, because spiritually we're poor today. Is it necessary to live in material poverty in order to have the rich spiritual lives our parents had? Or was the rich cultural life the result of the outstanding leadership of the founders? They were a highly select group who had come out of their free choice, aware of the costs of their decision. We, their children, were simply born here, to follow in their footsteps. It's the difference between a select and a non-select generation.

I see several traits characteristic of the second generation, most of them not very heartening [*smiling*]. I refer to those of us who have remained here, because those who have left for the city could perhaps be characterized as *not* having these traits. The second-generation kibbutz personality is noted mainly for its passivity. This is the result of the fact that our way of life doesn't force people to struggle to achieve, because you receive things, or you don't receive them, independently of your personal efforts. Things just flow, as if by themselves, and one isn't encouraged to initiate any effort, to show an alert interest in the surroundings, or to do anything out of the ordinary. This passivity is even stronger in the third generation, my present art students. Our school children, from six to eighteen, don't seem to make any attempt to achieve anything. Whatever comes, comes. They want to see immediate results, and won't invest in something that might fail or that will demand a long, ongoing effort. They're very similar to children raised in rich families in town, children who can buy everything, get anything, and therefore never learn to strive, to try, to fail and then succeed. This is terribly important for me.

Often I long for the idealistic kind of life our parents had, although I'm sure it can't be found nowadays, not even if you go and start a new kibbutz all over again. I feel a sense of loss and emptiness in our worldly way of life, but I know that this vacuum cannot be filled by nostalgia or an attempt to return to the past. Fasting and walking around hungry is, of course, meaningless today. We have to find a way to fill the void with our present values and experiences.

On the other hand, our generation certainly has some advantages, too. We can study if we choose to; such plans don't have to be delayed indefinitely. We have a wider choice of occupations, and have a better chance of finding something we like. We have more free time, and can develop virtually any interest or hobby. We have more freedom in our choice of clothing and furniture, and there's much more diversity and tolerance in our society towards individual needs. All these are a result of our economic prosperity, no doubt, and I appreciate this a lot. But here, again, one finds the effects of excess. It's good to be tolerant but a framework of discipline is still necessary; otherwise some individuals may be hurt by freedoms taken by others. Take our growing network of internal transportation as an example. The kibbutz is quite extensive now, and it's difficult to get around quickly on foot. So people started to build or buy (out of their individual budgets) little motor scooters that they used for transportation on the kibbutz. It was never approved by the kibbutz, but people took advantage of the general permissiveness and now we have these scooters all over the place, making noise and creating pollution, and endangering children who used to walk around with total freedom. I see these scooters as a regression in our quality of life, and they represent, for me, a condition in which the society has lost control over its members. I don't think it could have happened thirty or forty years ago, with the strict discipline of those times.

I was born here, and I have lived here most of my life. I spent several years in another kibbutz, but returned home for I'm very much tied to this landscape and community; I couldn't live elsewhere. I find city life loathsome: I can't see myself dedicating time to financial problems, I hate to shop and cook, and I certainly wouldn't want to be a housewife in town. My family always eats in the dining hall, even though most of the families of our age eat at home every evening, and I bless the kibbutz for liberating me from the kind of work I really don't enjoy. I do enjoy teaching, and despite all my criticism of our kibbutz, I feel that I can express myself more effectively in this type of life. I can shape my life and have an impact on the life of the total community more effectively here than in any other kind of community.

M I C H A L   *(age 32)*

Michal is a young mother of three and a teacher in the kibbutz. Our conversation concentrated on mother-child relationships in Makom.

When a baby is born, he's brought from the hospital to the mother's room, where she can keep her child with her for six weeks. (It wasn't like that when I gave birth to my eldest son; babies were kept in the parents' room for ten days at the most.) During this time, a mother is on maternity leave and doesn't work at all. The infants' home, however, is ready to take care of the infant during the day, whenever the mother so wishes. If a mother has older children to take care of, or she needs some rest, she can put the baby in the infants' home for a couple of hours, or even for most of the day, but she is in charge of feeding and washing the baby. We have very good *metaplot* who are experts in caring for very young infants, and they take care of the babies for the first six months of their lives. But the mothers are ultimately responsible during the early months.

During this early period of motherhood, the young mothers are forced into very close contact with each other. It's not enough that they have to adjust to the professional team which takes care of their babies, but they also must become accustomed to the constant company of each other. They sit together in the crowded infants' rooms, breast-feeding their babies, bathing them, whatever. Naturally, there's a lot of friction; a lot of comparison and criticism is going on under the surface, frequently erupting. If you're lucky, you're in pleasant company. But if not. . . .

According to the established rules, mothers return to their work, on a part-time basis, after six weeks. A young mother often must leave her work during the day to tend to her baby's needs in the infants' home. But in some jobs, it's very hard to get away during the workday. I, as a teacher, for example, was called back to work before even the first six weeks were over. And when I returned to school, I had to get the *metapelet* to replace me during the hours I spent at the infants' home and I had to manage to teach all the required material anyway. Nobody replaced me in terms of my responsibility for my class. For a teacher, it's terribly difficult. I constantly felt that my teaching was suffering, and I was nervous both with my baby and with my class. The situation is different in other jobs. A *metapelet,* for instance, works with a whole team, and when she misses an hour with her group, she has much less to worry about, if anything.

During this six-month period, a group of four infants is formed. Each group of four will live together in a single room and have their own *metapelet* who will watch over them as they grow up. From my point of view, the members of this tightly knit group—an extremely crucial group—are four infants, four mothers, and a *metapelet;* their close contact usually continues for at least three and a half years, until the toddlers move into the nursery. When many babies are born within a short period of time, there can be a certain flexibility in arranging these groups. But that's not always possible. I have always been lucky with my children's partners at the infants' home, but recently I have heard about many severe conflicts within the groups, and their occurrence is to be expected when you realize how much friction exists within such a formation. For example, a mother comes in and sees another baby soiled, wet, or simply crying. Will she take care of the matter or will she simply ignore it and sit with her own child? Parents expect some mutual responsibility, but in reality it doesn't always work out as intended. I am frequently aware of this in the evenings, when I arrive to put my young daughter to bed at the children's home. We're usually late, since she first accompanies me while I put her two older brothers to sleep, each in his home. When we finally arrive at her home, many of the parents have already left, but quite a few of their children are still awake and are often not yet relaxed. I usually try to calm these children down, yet frequently I see a parent approaching a child who isn't his or her own, in an aggressive manner, saying roughly, "Shut up and go to sleep," or something similar. In the majority of cases, these children are simply ignored by other parents, who are there with their children, and this is just as bad. The whole situation is unpleasant.

These moments of leaving your young child after putting him to bed at night are very significant and difficult moments. I believe they're difficult for the mother, even more so than for the child. The child often reacts to the mother's unspoken feelings. If a child senses his mother's worry, nervousness, or lack of confidence, he will tense up and cling to her and prolong the moments of departure. I feel that this situation can be avoided. I sit with my children for half an hour, telling them a story, then I firmly say good night and leave. I think it's very similar to the situation of putting your child to bed in your own apartment. Some parents can't do it, because of their own doubts. I believe this problem can be helped; when I'm in charge of the evening for my class, I try to help the unsure parents separate themselves more smoothly from their children.

I'm aware that I'm speaking very confidently, but I had my rough periods as well. I remember a time when I, too, wanted my children to sleep in my room. I was intolerant of people and resented those hours of sitting with four strangers, reading a story to my child and not having any sense of privacy or intimacy with him. Indeed, I used to take my middle son to sleep in the room with us quite frequently during that period, until he simply refused to do this anymore and clearly preferred to sleep with his friends. He was six when he switched over completely to the children's home. All of our children sleep in our room on Friday nights, though. Most of the other children of the kibbutz also do this, with the exception of the babies. Babies sleep in the infants' homes even on Friday and Saturday, requiring all of the kibbutz women to take turns in overseeing this. I frequently think it must be strange for the infants to be taken care of by complete strangers, although an attempt is made to send people who are at least related in some way to the children. In fact, the same is true of the night guard in the children's homes. It often happens that a child wakes up alarmed from a nightmare or from feeling sick, and finds a complete stranger trying to calm him down. I think this has an effect on our children: Out of sheer necessity they learn to trust more adults than children in town do. But for some children it is certainly a problem, and frequently their attitudes reflect the suspicions or mistrust felt by their mothers.

My daughter is presently in a mood in which she prefers to sleep with me. She would like to do this every night, but I am fairly strict with her. I feel she, as a girl, might become dependent on me and I don't want that to happen. Furthermore, it's a pity to wake her up at 6:30 A.M. in my room, when I have to leave for work, while at her children's home she can sleep till 7:30. Her angelic pleadings make it even more difficult for me to leave her in the evening. She can say so lovingly: "Mommy, please stay with me here," that it breaks my heart to go. I do leave her, however, but I promise to come back and visit her when she is sleeping. Indeed I do so, always leaving a sign of my visit—a flower or a note—which proves to her that I don't simply vanish during the night. It's frequently very difficult for me to leave her, and I do so completely out of logical considerations and against my strongest feelings. A mother must be strong in order not to tie her children to herself. Yet when I sometimes see mothers creeping into bed near their little children, unable to leave them, I understand their feelings very well.

This visit during the night is something done by the majority of parents of young children, who go to see their sleeping children later in the evening, leaving a sign of their visit. Often it's done by grandparents, too. Some of them leave chewing gum or candy at the bed, something I object to and never do.

When a child reaches the age of six months, the mother is supposed to return to full-time employment. However, the great majority of women don't give up their daytime visits, and find all kinds of tricks in order to visit during their working day. Mostly, they start their day an hour earlier by visiting their baby and giving him breakfast and even bathing him before they go to work. Often this loyalty creates a ridiculous situation, with mothers waking their sleeping child, who would rather continue sleeping. Most women give up the 10:00 A.M. feeding, though, which is done by the *metapelet,* and return for lunch around 1:00 P.M. It depends on one's work schedule. Lately, more fathers visit their infants during the morning, too, especially if they work in the factories, which have a break in the morning and are not too far from the homes. When different women arrive to visit at different hours, it decreases the friction within the group of mothers—they simply don't meet each other so frequently. But the whole visiting system is terribly complicated. There is the tension of leaving work and returning on time, and then there is hardly any privacy, especially during winter when you have to stay in the room, and the whole crowd of four infants is creeping all over you. In summer it's easier, for you can find a quiet corner outdoors.

When the child is about a year old, most mothers stop the early morning visit. The child is awakened, washed and fed by the *metapelet,* while the mother visits once during the day, before the child is taken to the room at 4:00 P.M. Handling one- and two-year-olds is very difficult for the *metapelet,* who's left alone with much work and the entire responsibility for four rather helpless children. Many of those *metaplot* are themselves very young and inexperienced. Furthermore, mothers have many expectations from the *metaplot* as they, themselves, withdraw from very active participation in the infants' home, and these expectations frequently lead to disappointment and tension.

As the child grows up and reaches about three and a half years of age, he moves to the nursery school *(gan),* which is a bigger house with several age groups, ranging from three to seven years old. There, they have all sorts of educational activities with a teacher in addition to the *metapelet.* Mothers, however, continue with their visits, at least once during the day, for it's a very strong habit. Some teachers have positive reactions to the visits and are willing to let mothers in at all hours. Others, however, dislike having the mothers disturb the organized teaching activities. They restrict the visiting hours to recesses.

I had some difficulties on this matter with my second son, whose teacher allowed visits only during recesses, which conflicted with my own schedule as a teacher. In addition, I had my baby daughter to visit, and these two constraints put me under a lot of pressure. Finally, I solved the problem by using my school break to visit my daughter, and teaching my sons to come and visit me in my classroom when they had their own recess. They come in at all hours, even while I'm teaching, but I always welcome their visits. Since only a very little of my teaching is direct, and most of the time I am supervising independent work, my children's visits don't cause any disturbance. Moreover, I keep telling the mothers of my pupils to come and visit while lessons are going on, because then they can share in their children's learning activities; during breaks the children prefer to play with their classmates and to be left alone.

I don't know if all this visiting is worth all of the trouble it creates on all sides, but mothers are reluctant to give up this habit. Even in my class, the third grade, many mothers come in daily though their children hardly pay any attention to them during their visits—they simply nag them, I think. Frequently the mothers take the younger sibling with them when they visit the older one. But gradually this habit declines; by the fourth or fifth grade, mothers stop coming, and they don't see their children from the evening till the next afternoon, when they go to their parents' room. This is more or less the schedule during the school-age years. Our adolescents are quite busy in the afternoon, doing homework and working, as well as participating in various social activities, so their actual visits with their parents grow much shorter. Often they run to their families' rooms during recess at 10:00 A.M. They don't meet their parents, who are at work, but they manage to grab some sweets. . . .

I used to be critical of many areas of communal education, but recently I have become more tolerant of this system, as well as of other things which used to aggravate me. Once, I was angry to see how many people avoid accepting any responsibility or public role in the kibbutz. Today, however, I'm not bothered by this. I have realized that some people cannot contribute to the community because they lack inner harmony and confidence. One shouldn't blame them for this. People try to escape from important positions in the kibbutz; people never come and openly declare: "I'd like to take this function. I'm fit for it." Perhaps this is because of the strong criticism one often receives when holding a position here, but generally I attribute this reluctance to lack of ambition, especially in the second generation. We lack the ambition to stand out as individuals; in other words, mediocrity reigns. I believe that this is a result of communal education. We aim for equality, too much equality, and the outcome is the oppression of individuality for the benefit of the group norms. The final result is our character as adults: petty, mediocre people. I try to break this pattern as a teacher, but there isn't much I can do alone. Our parents were different, I think; they were generous people. They did a lot for the public; they stood out. But they, too, rarely admitted that they got any satisfaction out of their activities, which were always presented as obligations from above. Our indifference is also, perhaps, a reaction to their great dedication.

E F R A T *(age 16)*

Efrat is the youngest person I interviewed for the book. A few weeks before, I had approached another girl, S., a year younger than Efrat. I explained that I was mainly interested in getting a description of the life of high-school students in the kibbutz. S. consented to be interviewed, and we set a time for later that afternoon. She showed up with a girlfriend, and the interview was a complete failure—a chain of questions on my side, and giggles or monosyllabic answers on theirs. I tried another time, with a boy, and again failed to establish an atmosphere of easy conversation. At that point I concluded that kibbutz teen-agers were rather difficult to communicate with, at least for strangers.

Only a few days later I was contacted by Efrat. She was conducting an investigation of the early suicides in the kibbutz, for a term paper for school. "Yes," she said, "I picked the topic myself. It interests me a great deal." She had heard that I was a psychologist, and thought I might help her provide an explanation of the phenomenon.

I agreed to meet with her, and later she came to my room. We started to discuss suicides. She attributed the suicides to weakness, and wondered why people weren't willing to speak candidly with her. I explained about crisis, depression, and guilt, while she listened intelligently. She started to talk about that period. "It was difficult, certainly; but it was reassuring to know so clearly what you were striving for. They could build, put down the rules, establish a community. We . . . we were born right into all this, everything is done already, there's nothing we can contribute anymore. All that's required of us is to live here, in the midst of all this plenty.

"Just a few months ago, at the Jubilee, we, the schoolchildren, wanted to give something to the kibbutz, a birthday present. We searched and searched for an idea, but couldn't find anything. Everything we thought of had already been thought of before. It was an unpleasant realization, a very bad feeling. We finally decided to put identifying name tags on all the trees and plants in the kibbutz. It was nice, but it isn't too significant a contribution, and, besides, this too had been done before. . . . We just renovated the old signs and added some new ones. It wasn't much."

Following this conversation I invited Efrat for a taped interview. She couldn't find time, however, for several weeks, since she was busy in camp. When finally we met, her overall mood seemed to be much better, and the criticism I had detected in her during our first conversation was much less apparent.

I'm in the tenth grade. We have a fixed daily schedule. We get up every morning at 6:15, have our first class from 6:30 to 7:15, and then half an hour of work. Each one of us has a certain job, determined by the schedule and changed every two or four weeks. What we primarily do is clean our quarters—the dorms, the classes and the whole house. We used to tend to the garden around our house, too. Later, we go for breakfast in the general dining hall (we take all of our meals there) and have to be back for classes within half an hour. We usually have five more lessons, and, with all the recesses, we finish at 12:30 P.M. and go for lunch. Some days our schedule is a bit different, but that's more or less it.

In the early afternoon, we work for two hours. The boys usually work in the fields or factories, and the girls work either with children, or, rarely, in other services. Most of the girls hate to work with young children, but there isn't much choice. Anyway, it's all over by 4:30 or so, and then we're free. Well, actually, there should be all kinds of social activities in the afternoon, but right now it's rather slow. Some of the social activities come to life during the summer vacation, when we have camps and conventions. Many of my classmates relax in the afternoon, visit their parents, play ball, whatever. I myself am rather busy. I play on our basketball team, which involves a lot of training, and I go twice a week to Beit Shean where I volunteered to work as a youth leader. Some days I don't even reach my parents' room to say hello, I'm so busy and exhausted. I try to read books, too; I love reading and borrow books at the adult library. This is something that, I'm sorry to say, most of my classmates hardly ever do. They usually watch T.V.; they're not interested in reading.

I'm fairly satisfied with our social life here. I personally feel comfortable in it, but I'm aware of our basic problem, which is the fact that we're living pretty much under each other's noses. If you're an open person, and like our intense togetherness, then it's okay; but, if you live on the margin of it all, you end up being rather miserable. I'm thinking of one girl in my class, for example, who's stupid and ugly and nobody likes her. Nobody ever talks to her—she must feel terrible. She's an "outside child," and I don't think that one of our own kibbutz children would ever be put into such a position; there might be someone among us who isn't too attractive or smart, but, since we have grown up together, we accept everyone with his or her particular traits. We have known each other since we were babies, as in a family, and we accept each other completely. There is one girl, for example, who is very shy and withdrawn, but we keep trying to draw her out, we help her a lot. Our attitude towards outside children is quite different, though. We're much more critical, less tolerant. Actually, there are very few outside children who have been absorbed by our class and have remained here, who are well-adjusted. Most of them left, and I believe it's our fault.

What I just called "living under each other's noses" also means that we rarely have time to be alone. I, personally, don't mind this situation; I'm glad I live closely with my friends and don't feel lonely, perhaps because I'm used to this kind of life. I live with two other girls in a room, and, although we have small problems from time to time, we have learned how to solve them. Again, it's something we acquired over the years. I know all the girls of my class quite well, each one with her own little caprices or whims. Right now, there is a plan to reorganize the housing and mix all the upper-level classes, namely, the tenth, eleventh, and twelfth grades. I look forward to this—it will give me a chance to get to know other people and to mingle with new friends. I'm not worried about belonging to the youngest age in this large mixed group. I don't think we will be dismissed by the older kids, and, anyway, we are a very vocal group.

I think that our school is rather poor academically, and personally I'm not satisfied with it. We are forced to learn, while I think that if someone wants to drop out of school, he should be allowed to do so (if he's old enough to make such a decision, say older than fourteen or fifteen).* People who don't want to study should be given work; learning a trade is no less important than a high-school education. The trouble is that our school offers very limited choices. We all study only theoretical subjects, and there's no way to specialize in one area or to concentrate in vocational training. This simply doesn't suit every single student, and, as a result, the class atmosphere is very unpleasant. Our teachers force us to study and we do them a great favor in conforming to their demands. If someone doesn't want to study, he can upset the whole class, and it ends up with all of us joining in his rebellion, because basically nobody wants to study very much. If there's anyone who does want to study, they can't do any serious work under these circumstances anyway. I think that I, personally, could study better if the atmosphere were different, but, given the way it is, I join in the fun.

Kibbutz schools are known to be based on voluntary activity: You're supposed to study for your own good and not for grades or rewards. Actually this is far from the true situation. In our school, teachers use many disciplinary tactics, and I don't think the system would work without them. For example, if I come late to class twice, I'm suspended from school, and must work somewhere for several days instead. Or, if I oversleep, I must go to the teacher's room at 6:00 A.M. and wish him or her good morning. This is the worst punishment, I think, and it's very common. Some teachers are nice, though, and invite you to have a cup of coffee when you "visit" them at such an early hour. . . .

Now, why do I, or why does somebody else, get up late in the first place? It's probably because I find school uninteresting; why leave my comfortable bed? . . . I think I'm old enough to make my own decisions —my punishment would be the fact that I'm not learning, that I will be ignorant. In the same manner, when I get a poor grade, I suffer from my own feeling of shame or disappointment. I'm against a system, such as ours, which tries to *make* me study against my will. This is the atmosphere at school, however, and it is partially a result of a lack of good teachers. Our teachers are worn out by us; they despair of our situation.

Sometimes, however, they do make a special effort. For example, at the beginning of the school year they decided that one day a week would be an "open day." Various unusual alternatives were offered, and we had to choose the subjects that we wanted, three subjects each. What happened, however, was that so many children didn't like *any* of the subjects, that they ruined the whole project. I took a class on the early history of our kibbutz, taught by Yehuda, and that's how I started to study the kibbutz suicides. But the other two subjects which I took didn't excite me, and I attended only because I had to. So, even when our teachers try to satisfy our wishes for a more flexible curriculum, we throw it all back in

*In Israel, education is compulsory only through ninth grade.

their faces. It's part of the whole atmosphere, as if the kibbutz owes us everything. We never show any gratitude for things we receive. We're indifferent to all this plenty; we even express contempt for the further attempts to give us things and opportunities.

I feel quite guilty because of this ingratitude. I believe we weren't educated properly, to become so spoiled. We weren't educated to appreciate all the wonderful things with which we're provided. We take it all for granted.

I do remember one exciting experience that happened recently, and it involved contributing, instead of always receiving. A few months ago, during the Jubilee celebrations, we organized a "Veterans Day" for the elderly members, the founders of the kibbutz. It wasn't the children's idea, it came from above, but we participated in its organization. We went around to the rooms of the founders with roses and invitations for a trip to Jerusalem, including a visit at the President's house. On the day of the trip we organized a surprise welcome party for them and a festive meal which we served in the dining hall. They were very moved by the reception and it made us all feel very good.

It's so rare, though, to feel good and worthwhile here. Much more common is the feeling of being exploited by the kibbutz. Whenever there's an urgent job to carry out in the field or factory and there aren't enough people, the school is mobilized to take care of the job. Some people say that's why they keep the local school here. This happens quite often, and it makes us feel as if the school were the scapegoat of the whole community. I don't share this view, but many children feel this way about the frequent mobilizations.

Do you ever think about your future?

Sure. First of all, I often think about the future of this kibbutz. It's grown too large, and I don't think it can continue like this. People don't know each other anymore, and this will surely lead to some sort of crisis and change. Maybe a lot of people will leave and it will regain its small size, I don't know. I personally know all the young people, but we have many old people here and I know just a few by name. Just today I saw an announcement that someone had died, and I don't even know who it was. It isn't a kibbutz anymore—because knowing each other is a necessary condition for mutual respect and for equality.

Furthermore, this place is so big and well established that young people rarely have any chance of being noticed or of changing anything. That's why I think that when I grow up I'd like to go to another kibbutz, a young kibbutz, and I think that several of my classmates will do the same. We're afraid of the kind of jobs or social positions we will get here after returning from the Army, and we think that a young kibbutz can offer us much more. At least I know I won't have to go and work with children right away, because a young kibbutz doesn't yet have many infants. I don't know if this is what my friends also plan to do. Some think of city life, and many refuse to think about the future at all. They say that first they want to return from their three years of military service, and then they will plan their future.

I went to a young kibbutz as a volunteer during my vacation and I enjoyed being in a much smaller place. On the other hand, after being there, I could better appreciate the fine things we do have here in Makom. For example, our work ethics are much better here. People take their work very seriously here, they care about it, and don't fool around. There, I found that people came late and left early and didn't make any serious effort. Imagine, they take an hour-long break for breakfast! Who needs so much time? Here, I walk from school to the dining hall, eat and go back, all in twenty-five or thirty minutes—that's plenty of time.

Among my future plans is also the idea of further studies, although I haven't yet decided on a specific direction. If I were in town, I'd probably continue my studies right after the Army, but here I'll have to postpone them awhile. Also, it upsets me that kibbutz "public opinion" will determine whether I'm entitled to higher education or not, or when I can study. It's true that almost everyone may study if he wants to, but the kibbutz's approval is still required. I can tell you a story about a young woman who wanted to go to art school and the kibbutz approved of her plan for the coming year. In the meantime, however, she worked in one of our nurseries and some parents found fault with her work. They said she was irresponsible or something, and demanded that the kibbutz cancel her study program. The whole issue was brought up in the general assembly meeting, before the whole kibbutz, and the decision did indeed, go against her. Naturally, she was terribly hurt and insulted. Now I hear that they have reconsidered the whole matter, and decided she can go to art school; but now she refuses their help and is talking of leaving the kibbutz altogether. This is an extreme case, but things such as this do happen.

I often think about all the good things I'd want to find in my future, young kibbutz, but perhaps it's all a dream. Ginat, for example, is a young kibbutz and it has many problems. Most of them are probably due to the fact that the settlers are city children and don't know much about kibbutz life. It would be better to join a new kibbutz established by kibbutz children—this could turn out to be the optimum combination.

D A F N A *(age 20)*

Dafna is a good representative of the third generation. She is the daughter of one of the first children born in Makom, and granddaughter of one of the founders, Shalom (p. 60).

I returned from the Army a few months ago and requested work in the olive factory; this is the best strategy to avoid being placed in the childrens' homes. I operate a machine all day, and I'm grateful for the job; it has a well-defined beginning and end, and my head remains clear for whatever I want to do after a day's work. Both my parents work at the food factory. My mother is the general secretary and my father is supervisor there, but I have no contact with them during the day.

Returning to the kibbutz from the Army is somewhat disconcerting, but it's even more difficult to make the decision whether or not to return to the kibbutz after military service. This is particularly true for girls, since a girl knows that she has two main alternatives: either to go immediately into child care or to study to become a teacher. I was certain I didn't want either of these choices, and this realization was pretty frightening. Once I arrived here, though, the fear turned into a reality and became easier to cope with. I arrived at the solution of volunteering for the olive factory, and I devised a five-year program for myself, in which this year of factory work is just the first step. I'm certainly not starting the famous seventy-year kibbutz career of being a *metapelet,* getting married, raising my own children, etc.

The second stage of this five-year program involves either working in a community center in Beit Shean or coordinating the volunteer groups active in the North. I have had firm offers in both areas, each for a period of two years, at least. Then, I'll go and study at the university, probably following a year of vacation, in which I'd like to live in the city and travel abroad. The two job offers both involve "outside work," which must get the kibbutz approval. I would have to live outside the kibbutz most of the time, and certainly spend most of my days outside; this doesn't mean leaving the kibbutz, though. Both jobs involve work with underprivileged populations, an area which I find not only appealing personally but also the greatest challenge of modern Israeli society. This, however, is my own opinion, which is somewhat contrary to the kibbutz list of priorities. Therefore, I expect I'll encounter some objections to my plans and will have to put up a fight here.

This is something else I realized during my military service: The kibbutz, as a movement, has an ideological frame of reference that defines certain priorities, which, in turn, dictate certain activities for individuals, whether they personally accept this viewpoint or not. At the moment, the kibbutz has given highest priority to new settlements in the Golan Heights and the Jordan Rift. If I go to the secretary and tell him that I want to go and work for two years with the underprivileged in town, his reaction will be: "If you're that kind of person, why don't you go work in our youth movement in town, in order to prepare the next group to settle in Ginat?" That's the kibbutz priority right now, and they don't understand how it's possible for an individual to feel otherwise. We all have to fit into one framework, so to speak. . . . But I've given it much consideration, and have arrived at the conclusion that everyone lives within a certain framework anyway, and the only difference is that it's a more pronounced phenomenon in the kibbutz.

I recall another realization I had while in the Army. I was invited to the home of a girlfriend and we took the bus together to her town, a suburb of Tel Aviv. As we got off the bus, I commented: "How nice it is to have such a short drive to your home!" And she answered: "This isn't my home yet, wait till we get there." And, indeed, we walked for another forty minutes. Her home was a tiny apartment in a big building, and only when she opened the locked door was she "home." Suddenly I realized how different my situation is. I have a long bus ride to the kibbutz, but then, the moment I get off the bus at the main road and step onto the local road leading into the kibbutz, I'm "home." The road, the trees, all the houses, all the paths are my home. I realized how extensive and solid my home is, which gives me tremendous backing and a profound sense of security. . . . To this day, however, I have not decided whether or not I want that security, because my attempt to cope independently with life is still no less important to me. I have never tried to live on my own. In the Army I met many different people, but the military system provided everything and there was no need to cope with things alone. The same was true during my "third year of service"* which I did before joining the Army. I lived in an immigrants' town, in a commune with other kibbutz children, and we were well taken care of by the kibbutz. That year was extremely important for me. I discovered the other Israel, a country of poverty and hardship, and I learned to love people who were different from me in many ways. Before, I used to just label all these people "underprivileged" or "Orientals"; after this year I found out that they were, above all, people like me. It was often a frustrating encounter; the residents of the town frequently said to us: "You, the kibbutz children, you're used to milk and honey. What do you know about our problems?" We didn't know how to react, but we stayed, and gradually contacts were established and some trust was built between us. I worked with children, tutoring them and working in the local community center. Each of us found some area to work in and help as best we could. This experience gave me my present direction, and I'd like to continue with this kind of work, even if the kibbutz raises objections. If my plan is not approved, I'll have to leave Makom. My work will require me to organize my life in a different way.

Right now I have a strong need to be alone, to think about all these issues. I have noticed that many of my age group have similar tendencies. We work and go home to our rooms and like to spend several evenings a week alone. For most of us it's the first time we have had a private room and the opportunity for a quiet evening. Two of my girlfriends have started to study for their matriculation exams (something they didn't

---

*All kibbutz children give an extra year of voluntary service to the country, in addition to the two to three years of military service required by law.

want to do in high school, three years ago), so they keep pretty much to themselves. As a group, I'd say we're not very cohesive. When we do meet, we keep elaborating on our common problems, which all concern the future. We talk about ourselves vis-à-vis the kibbutz and the former generations; we are becoming increasingly aware of how different we are from them.

You see, we're the third generation of the kibbutz, a rather special group. I feel that this fact alone is enough to put us under great pressure, with so many obligations and expectations to fulfill. I'm the daughter of a woman who belongs to the first group of children born here. Often I've heard her and her friends discuss my own age group, saying that we didn't turn out right. My parents' generation has repeatedly confronted us, saying: "You are a confused generation, a generation of questioners. You don't know what you want. We were different, and we don't know why you grew up that way. You should have been different—the perfect kibbutzniks who follow all the rules." It's an ongoing confrontation, and indeed we are different from the second generation, in many ways.

It's true; we think, we doubt, and we ponder a lot, and I see this as perfectly legitimate. Our parents didn't have so many reasons to doubt the kibbutz—it was quite new then, and the ideological aspects were still very prominent. Today the kibbutz is a middle-class, established settlement. We're all exposed to the media and through them we're aware of the wide world; our parents at our age had little knowledge of what was going on outside the kibbutz. Their only chance to see life outside was in the Army, and this, too, is a very limited experience.

Perhaps they have forgotten, and they too had their doubts. Or, perhaps, they'd rather not think of that period in their lives, before they settled down. In fact, two of my mother's brothers left the kibbutz in their youth, so it's not us who invented this phenomenon. Generally, however, I think they were educated somewhat differently from us. The entire social structure was more rigid—the school, the rules, the regulations. . . . Our parents' parents, the founders, maintained very close contact with the educational institutions and in that way reinforced the strength of the socialization system. We, however, feel that our school, although right here, is completely alienated from the community. Most of the parents are uninvolved and uninterested in their children's school activities, and then they're surprised to discover suddenly—and too late—that their son won't fulfill their expectations since he actually terminated his studies in the seventh grade. . . . The result of this alienation is that the kibbutz ideology is transferred to us in much more diluted form; my mother, for example, is much more conservative in kibbutz matters, while I'm rather permissive. Actually, my grandparents are even more conservative than my mother, so there's a trend towards gradual decline. On the other hand, since we're the third generation, a very select group, I feel we're being observed all the time by the older generations who are asking:

"What will be the face of this new youth? What is the future of the kibbutz?" This is rather demanding. It is almost impossible *not* to disappoint all these expectations.

One can't avoid thinking of very basic problems, though, when the past is taken in perspective. Is the kibbutz a vanishing fairy tale or a well-tested way of life that can withstand the shocks and changes of the future? Comparing my grandfather's, my mother's, and my own viewpoints, I ask myself whether or not the kibbutz has indeed maintained its past image, whether it is today what it used to be forty years ago. And where is it going to be in forty years' time? If there is a trend towards gradual decline in the ethics of the kibbutz, in its commitment to basic principles and values, if we're going to become more and more permissive, where is this development going to lead us? What do we maintain, even today, of the kibbutz's original form? Is it still truly a kibbutz or should we rename our form of life? It might be that fifty years from now the kibbutz form of life will be totally erased—the buildings and gardens would be here of course, but people might be living in them in a private manner or a *moshav* system, perhaps. We can't foresee the future, but it's certain that the kibbutz is undergoing profound changes. For better or worse—we don't know yet.

Actually, I often feel that the present path the kibbutz has taken is the best one for me, for my needs. Today we have greater flexibility. Even if it were possible, I wouldn't want us to push the kibbutz back to its past, stricter form; I'd feel very frustrated by such a system. On the other hand, were it to become even more permissive than it is now, it would risk ceasing to be a kibbutz. I can think of several recent incidents which make our life look more like anarchy than a kibbutz, although "anarchy" might be too strong a term. There is an atmosphere that finds its expression in a popular saying we have here: "Fight for it and you're bound to get it. Whatever you strive for, you'll finally get." As an example, take the case of a member who installed a color T.V. in his room—God knows where he got it from. . . . Or a young woman who insists that she won't do a third year of service after returning from the Army, because she simply doesn't feel like it. "Nobody can tell me what to do," she says. It's so absurd! No one from my parents' generation could ever have come out with such a statement. He would have been tossed out immediately [*laughing*].

It reminds me of last Friday. We worked late at the olive factory, and one of the workers had a scooter, so I said to him, "Because we worked so late, you have to give me a ride all the way up to my room."

And he answered: "Why, just because of you, I'll have to drive on the sidewalk!"

This was so typical, because he belongs to the second generation of children born and raised in the kibbutz, people who follow all the rules, people who'd never drive a scooter on the sidewalk [*laughing*]. I'm sure that, had he been five or ten years younger, the issue of driving on the footpath would never have even been mentioned. My parents' generation are the last people to stick to the rules. For them, the kibbutz was something still in the process of formation and actualization, so to speak—whereas for us, it's something which has already arrived. It's completely self-supportive, it makes a lot of money and will probably make even more. From a personal point of view, this means that the kibbutz can provide its individual members with complete security, with full satisfaction of all their needs. This is what I mean about my feeling of having such a strong home.

Is it helping me grow, though?

Part 4

MAKOM –
WHERE TO?

Fifty years after its establishment, Makom is a large collective with a substantial standard of living. Socially and culturally, the kibbutz is evidently at a crossroad, facing the future with hope as well as trepidation. However, Makom's members have always been its own most critical judges, and what they may consider crucial developments may ultimately be nothing other than components of a normal changing process.

As an outside observer listening to members' accounts, and sensitive to their insinuations, it was not difficult to detect basic themes which focus on the dilemmas and concerns of Makom vis-à-vis its future. One central issue is the size of the kibbutz and the various social, cultural, and economic problems resulting from its growth. The size of Makom represents a potential threat to the principle of equality, to the discipline, control, and tight organization integral to the original idea of a kibbutz, as well as to the high quality of the membership, which characterizes the kibbutz. Another source of concern is the new generation, its hidden face and the promise it may hold for the future. This concern borders on a related issue, the evaluation of the kibbutz's educational system and its results. On another level, the conflict between ideals and affluence is something that the kibbutz members often viewed as a major challenge for the future; this dilemma is closely associated to problems of ecology and the quality of life. Finally, Makom's inhabitants seem to be aware of their present isolation within the larger Israeli society and are weighing the advantages and disadvantages of this position.

In addition to these major concerns, which are clearly interrelated, there were others dilemmas which hold implications for the future of the kibbutz: the role and position of women in the kibbutz community, relationships among the individual members, patterns of responsibility in the sharing or delegation of authority. These dilemmas and the developments arising from them were often articulated by some of Makom's most thoughtful members.

Starting from a group of seventeen members, and thriving now with a population of twelve hundred, the question is whether the kibbutz can maintain its original principles at its present size. Besides the obvious technical and organizational problems (cooking for a thousand people, taking care of four hundred children, etc.) it becomes more and more difficult to know or control all its members. People no longer know each other intimately; many contacts are strictly formal or of a highly superficial nature. Deviations from the norm and social marginality are more likely to develop in such a large, impersonal community. Breaches of the basic principle of equality can pass unnoticed; people may withdraw from communal activity and avoid responsibility or involvement in social interactions. As it becomes difficult to gather the whole community for an assembly, some system of delegation of authority, signifying a change in the direct democratic process, seems almost inevitable. From a cultural point of view, interests, tastes, and levels of education have diversified, so that engaging the whole adult community in any sort of cultural activity or event is an almost unmanageable task. Following the last High Holy Day season, for example, many people felt deeply disappointed by their inability to plan or enjoy a common celebration in a satisfactory manner, a situation possible in the past. Subgroups seem to develop, and the family unit, the most natural subdivision, assumes an increasingly important place in the life of the kibbutz. Two major subgroups are the native kibbutzniks and the members absorbed from outside. While the first group grew up in the kibbutz and takes for granted many aspects of its life, the second group brings with it a completely different perspective on kibbutz society. Both groups are less involved with the ideology of the kibbutz than with its mundane problems. The original zeal of devotion to principles and values seems to be undergoing a process of diffusion and decline in response to the growing size of the kibbutz.

Restricting the size of the kibbutz is a delicate issue. Historically, this was one of the debates engaged in by the various kibbutz movements, with Kibbutz Hameuchad, Makom's movement, standing for the large, nonselective kibbutz. Although Makom presently does not absorb any new candidates from the outside unless special conditions exist (a spouse or relative of members, people in specific much-needed professions, Ulpan students who want to join), members are often critical of the past nonselective policy which allowed the kibbutz to reach its present size. Because of the large families, an important source of the population growth is the absorption of second- and third-generation members. Traditionally, the kibbutz has always viewed the departure of its own sons and daughters as a loss. Although this attitude has been relaxed today, parents still wish to have their children settle with them and continue their creation. The successful absorption of offspring is a major source of pride for the elder members. In fact, the kibbutz is perhaps the only form of rural settlement which produces sources of livelihood for all its offspring. Yet, if all Makom's children decided to stay, the kibbutz would grow still further, compounding all the existent problems of size.

Will Makom need, therefore, to take deliberate steps to control its size? How large can a kibbutz community successfully grow? What are the social changes which might result from this growth? While the answers to these questions remain dependent on future developments, it is important to note that several members approved of the large kibbutz and pointed to its advantages. The current size allows more personal freedom, for the pressures of the collective become more diffused in the daily lives of individual members. Socially, the diversity may allow greater choice in interpersonal relationships, based on similarity of interests and attraction between people. Finally, a larger number of workers ensures a stronger economic structure, based on self-sufficiency rather than necessitating the use of hired hands. A large work force enables the kibbutz to free more individuals for study programs or various socio-political missions outside the kibbutz. This, however, appears a vicious circle for, as the community grows, it requires more workers in its service and educational fields, so the economic system does not seem to profit from the larger size of the kibbutz.

These dilemmas are clearly related to the issue of the kibbutz as an affluent society. The initial concept of a kibbutz stressed a simple, modest, close-to-nature life-style, a society of farmers living off their own produce. Although a rich community may technically be able to realize the ideals of equality and cooperation, in Makom, whose history tells of many poverty-stricken years, wealth still poses a problem. Some members did claim that equality, roughly based on the same annual budget for every individual, is actually greater today than in former days; yet others mentioned trips abroad or modern kitchens as possible breaches of this first principle of the kibbutz. All state with pride that the present economic affluence enables the community to meet the different needs of individual members in the areas of education, health, and psychological welfare, thus adding more profound and significant dimensions to the concept of equality.

Besides the problem of sharing equitably, Makom's members are concerned with becoming a materialistic (their term) or bourgeois (my term) society. According to them, it is not fitting that people who put into practice the idea of the kibbutz should dedicate so much of their time and resources to the mere material aspects of life; they have become a society of consumers. Bigger apartments, a better swimming pool or gym seem somewhat inappropriate as aims. The community cultural center is just a blueprint as yet, while new buildings for factories and private apartments are given high priority. Almost as in town, cars park in the kibbutz, scooters ride the paths, and a constant fight goes on between the ecology-minded members and those who put their own comfort above everything; it is not clear which side will gain the upper hand. This growing involvement with individual comfort and the material aspects of life is accompanied by a decline of cultural and political interests, even a sort of cynicism regarding the ideological basis of kibbutz life. Can a kibbutz become an economically affluent cooperative while its other values gradually become only chapters in its past?

Factories and stores, today a very common feature of the kibbutz, were once alien to it. The factory is fertile ground for social stratification —a boss, an employer, or an administrator versus the blue-collar worker.

In the kibbutz factories, everybody comes to work in blue fatigues and the administrative positions are rotated. Yet, in complex technological projects, talents do determine one's position, and, although everybody makes the same salary, some may feel superior to others. Kibbutz members are the first to be aware of these problems and try to cope with them in such a manner that the principles of the kibbutz *and* economic considerations are both realized. Still, they often seem unable to completely adjust to the vast industrial projects in their midst.

The oft-argued issue of hired work is closely associated with the dangers of economically based stratification. The finite number of workers provided in a closed society such as a kibbutz poses a constant problem for new initiative in the economic sphere. It is tempting to use the talents of the kibbutz members to plan and direct different enterprises, while hiring lower-level, salaried people from outside to serve as blue-collar workers. Although Makom has so far managed to keep hired labor to a minimum, it is a continuous struggle to prevent any future breach of this crucial value. Clearly, Makom's founders have always considered this a major threat to the future of the kibbutz.

A recent example of the conflict of interests between economy and ideology is seen in the recent controversy over the kibbutz's use of German reparation monies. In the 1950s, when the money was initially received, it was used, at the direction of the members, for the general kibbutz budget, for encouraging in particular its economic development and a higher standard of living. This was considered just a temporary arrangement, but in the critical period of the early 1950s it was undoubtedly one of the major factors in the transition from a spartan economy to financial security. Yet, today people are asking the simple, disarming question: Aren't we rich enough? Hasn't the time arrived to stop the economic spiral? Consequently, several of the central members of the kibbutz suggested discontinuing the use of incoming German funds for the general budget, and directing these monies solely toward cultural activities which focus on perpetuating the memory of the Holocaust. Another senior member, seconding this proposal, attributed the measure's opposition to adults who still retain vivid memories of the cruel poverty and deprivation that characterized Makom's early development. This memory may indeed be the motivation behind Makom's constant striving for greater economic security, as well as the "materialism" which —as the kibbutz members observe—presently dominates the community.

Another concern shared by all three generations of Makom is the enigma of the third generation, which holds the key to the future of the kibbutz. In studying the kibbutz, I more often met with older members, either founders or early settlers in Makom. They were generally more available, more talkative, and more willing to share their fascinating life stories. Second-generation members, now about forty years old, carry the burden of the administrative and economic responsibilities in the kibbutz; busy during the day and tired at night, they tended to be more closed and uncommunicative. I did manage to interview many of them, but frequently their stories were shallow in comparison with those of their parents. By and large, the third generation was the least accessible. Still children, students, or soldiers, many on leave and on missions outside the kibbutz, they were generally undecided about their future in Makom. As a result, it was hardest for me to form an impression of the young generation. Actually, it seems that their parents and grandparents have the same difficulty in understanding their offspring; they share my questions of what the third generation is really like, what is necessary to assure their absorption in the society, and what Makom will become when left in their hands.

Focusing on these aspects, the stereotype of each generation in the kibbutz emerges. When compared with other modern societies, the harmony between the three generations of Makom is outstanding; the term "generation gap" is irrelevant here. It is generally agreed that the old were better than the young; the young continuously seek their company and advice. Clearly, the first generation, the generation of the founders, is presently viewed as towering over all others. They were the giants; they conceived of a dream and had the extraordinary powers necessary to implement its realization. They had consummate strength in the face of suffering and deprivation, supreme devotion to their ideology. Such individuals are not to be found anymore. Even when criticized for their present fatigue and reluctance to take responsibility in public matters, it is evident that the senior citizens of Makom are highly respected by all.

The second generation receives the credit for the present prosperity of the kibbutz, which is, as demonstrated earlier, a mixed blessing. This is also the generation that currently runs the kibbutz and assumes its central responsibilities. Being the generation between children and the elderly, they have both ends of the age continuum to take care of and support. Considered effective administrators and responsible workers, the second generation is also much criticized, they themselves being their major critics. In many ways, they seem burdened with the fate common to children of outstanding parents; they have a sense of inferiority vis-à-vis the "giants," an acute awareness of many demands and expectations, and of being constantly judged, appraised, and criticized for their achievements.

While their parents were the dreamers, their stories clearly reveal that the second generation contributed to the realization of the dream. Yet many of them consider themselves to be flat and mediocre in comparison to their parents and they accept their parents' reproaches about their ignorance of, and lack of concern for, the underlying ideology of the kibbutz. For them, Makom is primarily a home and an extended family. They are involved in the practical problems of maintaining this large community and providing the best for their own families, rather than with the ideological and political issues which constituted the fulcrum of their parents' lives.

The third generation is an enigma, clouded with apprehension. They are the future. People frequently employ traditional rules of thumb to try to explain the nature of this impenetrable young generation, saying that, if the first generation was dedicated to ideology and the second to practical issues, the third will probably return to ideology. Or that, if the first generation was poverty-stricken and the second went to the opposite extreme of striving for the comfortable life, the third generation might find the proper middle way. So far, there is very little evidence to reinforce either view. The youngsters of the third generation seem to keep a certain distance from the adult community. From what they reveal about themselves, they are clearly aware of the society's expectations of them, the great interest they excite. They are searching for their own way, they are raising questions, and are not in a hurry to settle down. Several of them say that they are afraid that their parents and grandparents did not leave much for them to accomplish. At last year's Yom Kippur in Makom, a day used for moral reflection, one of these third-generation youngsters stated his position clearly: "If the first generation was the dream and the second its realization, we feel that what we are expected to do, what remains for us, is to live with this realized dream. Well, I think that this is a very frustrating proposition. I am not willing to live in a society that closes before me the gate of the dreams. We need more dreams and ideals before us—and, in the condition the State is in, there are plenty of dreams all over, a lot of challenges to meet. The trouble is, however, that the kibbutz is satisfied with its own green lawns. It has become a comfortable home, nothing else. All the potential we offer seems to be wasted in the contemporary kibbutz. We have lost the spirit that used to accompany daily life in the kibbutz. There must be a change—and it is my generation's task to produce it." What change, and whether it will indeed take place, is another of the mysteries of the future.

The older members of the kibbutz frequently use the puzzle posed by the third generation and the demonstrated characteristics of the second generation as criteria by which to judge the educational system at Makom. Education in the kibbutz is a fundamental concern, since it plays a central part in determining the kibbutz's future. The challenges and aims established by the kibbutz educational system are broader and more ambitious than those of most educational institutions elsewhere. Communal lodging and communal education, stressing a noncompetitive atmosphere and the importance of social skills, are among the most outstanding innovations of the kibbutz. Teachers and *metaplot,* grandparents and parents search for clues concerning the results of their educational system, but the educational problems are different for each age group and cannot be generalized.

The notion of common lodging is something that the adult population, especially mothers of young children, treats with ambivalence. The growing tendency to let children sleep overnight in their parents' room may indicate a trend towards a permanent arrangement of familial lodging, a modification which many kibbutzim have already established. Criticism of the communal lodging system was often voiced by women who resented the fact that such a vast majority of them had to work in child care despite other interests or work preferences. They blamed the system —originally created to establish equality between the sexes and to liberate women from household chores—with enslaving them nevertheless to service in child care, working with "strangers' children" instead of their own.

Many questions are directed at the local school as well. While the teaching teams are not always as highly trained or specialized as those in comparable urban schools, they certainly work with immense dedication. But in spite of tremendous input, there is a sense of disappointment in the intellectual caliber of the products of the educational system. Adults consider the youngsters unfocused, not highly motivated towards learning and achievement. The children themselves are highly critical of their school, and some hold negative attitudes towards the communal lodging system as well. Again and again, people examine and question the value of the local comprehensive school, and suggest the use of a regional school for educating the higher grades. It is certainly an immense burden and challenge to educate all children through the high-school grades here in the kibbutz; in the future Makom may follow the vast majority of the kibbutzim and try the regional alternative to the local comprehensive school.

In personal and social realms, the educational system is more difficult to assess. Makom's educators nevertheless seem somewhat dissatisfied with their results. They often describe their students as spoiled, unwilling to exert themselves in their studies or work, and lacking initiative. Adults who belong to the second generation, some of them teachers or *metaplot,* frequently cited mediocrity as the general product of the communal educational system. In their view, this is the result of a permissive education which does not make any challenging demands, thus extinguishing personal ambition and inhibiting the individual desire to excel. Children learn that conformity and loyalty to the norms of the group are the preferred values; they become primarily concerned with criticism from their peers. This may also explain the tendency of adults raised in the system to refrain from public roles and to avoid the formation of any deep, intimate friendships within the kibbutz. There is certainly a quest on the parts of parents and educators alike for a solution that would combine the benefits of a competitive school and a conservative family life with the advantages of the innovative educational system created by the kibbutz.

Significantly, concern over child-rearing and educational aspects of the system was more frequently expressed by women than men. Many mothers experience dissatisfaction with the communal living arrangements for their children, and second- or third-generation women often retain unpleasant memories from their own childhood in the children's homes. Most common, however, are women's complaints about their predetermined fate to work for twenty years of their prime adulthood in child care or early education. Thus, there seems to be a strong correlation between women's status in the kibbutz and the communal education system.

Most people agree that women in the kibbutz are often "second-class citizens." They are indeed concentrated in the less prestigious service and child-care occupations; they refrain from public activity and the assumption of central responsibilities in the administration of the kibbutz, and are often resentful of their lot. The fact that the majority of the second-generation women of the kibbutz tend to withdraw into their home and family may be taken as a contradiction to the declared ideology of equality of the sexes, an ideal which seemed to exist for the first generation. In fact, however, once children were born into the young kibbutz, it became solely the women's responsibility to care for them, and this fact immediately prevented them from holding other positions in the community. The ideal of equality was never realized by placing men in the nursery schools. . . . On the other hand, Makom was always noted for its large families, and the greater number of children, considered a blessing, created a growing need for nursemaids and teachers. Thus, although there are exceptions, it seems that the high rate of reproduction in the kibbutz traps women into occupations that many dislike. Paradoxically, however, bearing children is perhaps the only productive "work" available to women of the kibbutz.

Whereas second-generation women are for the most part accepting of their feminine role, the seeds of change may be detected in the young women of the third generation. While the second generation wanted to fulfill themselves as mothers—perhaps in rebellion against their more liberated mothers—the third-generation daughters rebel in turn against their own mothers' lives by choosing more independent paths in their personal lives. They declare that they will postpone becoming permanently attached, try to study or travel first and develop their own characters before having children of their own. It is too early to examine the sincerity of these declarations, but they bear promises of change in the status of women in the kibbutz of the future.

Finally, an area of constant concern and debate is the relationship between the kibbutz and its external context. It is true that Makom has accomplished much as a self-contained universe, yet what is its impact on the world beyond? What does it do for its neighboring kibbutz, which is slowly declining towards disintegration? What is its contribution to Beit

Shean, with its social and economic hardship? How does it fulfill its promise to help the fledgling Ginat? These questions become even more damning when they move out of the local sphere, and are applied to an inquiry into Makom's contribution to the State; its share in national leadership, whether in the political, economic, or military arena; its cultural impact; its role in any activities and events which take place outside the courtyard of the kibbutz. Whereas in the past Makom actively participated in historic events of the State, it is presently somewhat apathetic and alienated from the problems of the larger society. Makom's members are almost ignorant of the severe economic struggle of the country. In a period of political confrontation,* the kibbutz seems to be withdrawing into itself. Even in the local sphere, faced with its commitments to Beit Shean and Ginat, Makom is unable to gather the support of enough members to fulfill its expectations of itself. As one member wrote in the newsletter, "Statistically we, the whole kibbutz movement, are but 3 percent of the Israeli population. If we continue as we are, we will be worth no more than 3 percent. We used to be much weightier in terms of our impact, voluntary support, productivity. And now?"

In order to "weigh" more, Makom has to place ideology above material goals; it must spawn and reinforce new generations of dreamers and leaders; it must find ways to function as more than a rich collective. This is clearly its challenge for the future.

As an outsider, my impression of Makom and its people was in many ways more positive than its own. I found the members to be severe judges, applying constant criticism towards their own community and deeds. Yet, in an attempt to depict Makom from the perspective of its own inhabitants, it is appropriate to end with the words of one of its members.

The following is an open letter written by Amos, the social secretary, to Gideon, who was elected as his replacement:

To Gideon as he begins his new role:

The transition from a society of dreamers to a society of "home" is inevitable, and it cannot occur without pain. The relinquishing of faith as our prime motivation comes about too quickly for the dreamers to organize themselves against it. Despondency is the price of this relinquishment, for this loss is not erased by splendidly green lawns. From here grow the questions of destiny. When the basis of partnership is not faith but the satisfaction of material needs, there is then no social method to preserve equality among men. The "yours" mediates between consumers, while ideas are the mediators between true partners. Mutual trust,

---

*While this study was being conducted, Israel was governed by the Likud Party, which is considered right-wing, as opposed to the socialist Labor Party.

the measure of our strength, signifies the potential of our future existence.

The dilemma which the kibbutz faces is the result of a basic paradox. A society that derives its strength from an idea is obliged to bend its individuals to the fulfillment of that idea. At the same time, the kibbutz must retain a certain measure of humaneness, for only with the recognition of the value of human life can the kibbutz exist. The ability to live in harmony with this contradiction necessitates a personal level of awareness unequaled in any society. Hence, the constant tension which must accompany those who believe that there can exist a society in which the ideal of the equality of man is not merely a cliché. This tension results from the compromise made between two powerful demands: the liberation of the individual from the primordial struggle for survival versus the adherence of the individual to societal demands.

Where do we stand?

Something that is hard to measure—maybe it's the smile that is saved just for public ceremonies, maybe the abundance of bitter expressions, maybe it's the recoiling from the stranger who comes to us, maybe the reluctance to bear another burden, maybe the coarseness of the personal touch, maybe the heaviness that characterizes the bearing of the yoke—something that is hard to measure is flashing red, cautioning us.

Is it possible for the message to reach us? Is it possible for this organism to muster its will to survive? Is it possible to respond to the demands transmitted by the signals?

We have found an organization's answers to peripheral questions, and we have returned to the starting point: the question of man. In our innocence, we thought that this, too, had an answer in method, organization, and initiative. It may be that we are standing before the question of questions: can the individual, in his personal responsibility—for there is no other— subjugate himself to the greater considerations upon which depends, for better and for worse, the existence of communal society?

If we can answer this question, there is no worldly difficulty which cannot be overcome.

Amos

Glossary

Achdut Haavoda. Union of work. Center-left party, now part of the Labor Party.

Aliya (pl. *aliyot*). Literally, "ascent"; immigration to Israel; also, a wave of immigration.

Beit Shean. New immigrant development town near the Jordanian border, not far from Makom.

Ben-Gurion (B.G.). First prime minister and head of Mapai Party.

Bnei-Moshe. A secret Zionist association functioning in Poland and Israel at the end of the nineteenth century.

Chalutz. Pioneer.

Chaver (masc. pl. *chaverim*, fem. *chavera*, fem. pl. *chaverot*). Literally, "friend" or "comrade"; a member (esp. of a kibbutz).

Chever Hakvutzot. Former name of the present Ichud Movement.

Chug. Literally, "circle"; a group of people with a common interest.

Gan. Kindergarten or nursery.

Ganenet. Kindergarten or nursery teacher.

Garin. Literally, "kernel"; a group of people brought together for the purpose of settlement.

Ha'apala. Literally, "ascent"; the illegal immigration to Mandate Palestine.

Hachshara. Preparation period (esp. preparation for an agricultural settlement).

Hagana. Literally, "defense"; the Jewish defense organization in Mandate Palestine.

Histadrut. National organization of workers' unions.

Ichud Hakvutzot Vehakibbutzim. Kibbutz movement (founded 1951) that broke off from the Kibbutz Hameuchad, closely aligned with Mapai.

Kibbutz Haartzi. Left-wing kibbutz movement, closely aligned with Mapam.

Kibbutz Hameuchad. Center kibbutz movement that tended left after the division from the Ichud.

Kiddush. Traditional blessing of the wine, at the beginning of the Shabbat dinner.

Likud. The right-of-center political party in power in 1980.

Machanot Haolim. Youth movement aligned with Mapai.

Mapai. The Israel Workers' Party, for years the largest and most powerful party in Israel. It was headed by David Ben-Gurion until 1963.

Mapam. The United Workers' Party, a left-wing socialist party.

Metapelet (pl. *metaplot*). Person in charge of caring for a group of children.

Meuchad. See *Kibbutz Hameuchad.*

Mishkist. Nickname for a kibbutznik who is a good worker but uninterested in ideology.

Mitzva. A religious commandment.

Moshava (pl. *moshavot*). Non-communal agricultural settlement.

Nachal. The part-military part-agricultural branch of the Israeli Army, which is organized to help settle the border areas.

Olim. Immigrants.

Oriental Jews. Jews from North Africa and Arab countries, as opposed to Jews from Europe and the Americas (Ashkenazees).

Palmach. The military branch of the Hagana.

Sabra. Literally, "cactus fruit"; nickname for native Israelis.

Shomer Hatzair. Left-wing youth movement aligned with the Kibbutz Haartzi.

Third-year service. A year of voluntary national service (like the Peace Corps), done before or after the two to three years of obligatory military service.

Ulpan. An intensive Hebrew course, usually in a live-in setup, as in the kibbutz.

Yekke. Nickname for German Jews.

Yeshiva. A traditional religious institute of learning.

Zahal. Israeli Defense Force (IDF), the Israeli Army, which took over from the Hagana with the establishment of the State in 1948.

ABOUT THE AUTHOR

Amia Lieblich

is a professor of psychology at the Hebrew University in Jerusalem. She also does clinical work, primarily as a group therapist working with students. Dr. Lieblich has published numerous articles in academic psychology journals and her first book, *Tin Soldiers on Jerusalem Beach,* appeared with Pantheon in 1978. She lives in Jerusalem with her husband and three children.